Gangs
in the
Caribbean

Gangs
in the
Caribbean
Responses of
State and Society

EDITED BY
ANTHONY HARRIOTT
AND **CHARLES M. KATZ**

THE UNIVERSITY OF THE WEST INDIES PRESS
Jamaica • Barbados • Trinidad and Tobago
UWI PRESS

The University of the West Indies Press
7A Gibraltar Hall Road, Mona
Kingston 7, Jamaica
www.uwipress.com

© 2015 by Anthony Harriott and Charles M. Katz

All rights reserved. Published 2015

A catalogue record of this book is available from the National Library of Jamaica.

978-976-640-507-6 (print)
978-976-640-519-9 (Kindle)
978-976-640-530-4 (ePub)

Cover photograph: Pashley Street, Success, Laventille, Trinidad, 2008. From the series
Caribbean Gangs, by Alex Smailes, alexsmailes.com.
Cover design by Robert Harris
Typesetting by The Beget, India
Printed in the United States of America

Contents

Illustrations

Figures

Tables

Acknowledgements

This book is made possible by the collaborative effort of its authors and all who provided invaluable support of various sorts to them. As editors of the volume, we wish to thank the authors for the effort that they put into their work and for their patience – especially those who had to endure our critical comments and repeated prodding for new drafts. We hope that the product was worth the effort.

In 2012, the Inter-University Consortium for the Study of Caribbean Gang Violence was formed with the purpose of conducting a programme of research on the gang problem in the region and to use this basic research for problem-solving. The participating universities are American University, Arizona State University, Sam Houston State University and the University of the West Indies via its Institute of Criminal Justice and Security. The consortium brings together a pool of experts on gangs and organized crime and a programme of coordinated action that promises advances in this field of research. This book is perhaps our most important project thus far. We thank our universities for their support of the consortium.

Earlier drafts of this book were written with a knowing disregard for the publishing guidelines of the University of the West Indies Press. We owe a special debt of gratitude to Cher Stuewe-Portnoff for her meticulous work in detecting our errors and formatting the manuscript in a manner that was acceptable to the Press. Without her effort this book would not have seen the light of day. We also thank the editorial staff of the University of the West Indies Press for their effort. The authors of each chapter have benefited from the support and generosity of different institutions and individuals. These debts are acknowledged in the text.

An Introduction to the Gang Problem in the Caribbean

CHARLES M. KATZ

Not until the past decade have policymakers, public criminal justice officials and researchers begun to take seriously the existence of Caribbean gangs and gang-related problems. For example, not until the 1990s in Jamaica (Moncrieffe 1998), the mid-2000s in Trinidad and Tobago (Katz and Choate 2006) and 2008 in Antigua and Barbuda (Katz 2008) did those in authority take steps toward resolving these issues. Other island nations are just beginning to publicly acknowledge their gang problems and to explore possible responses (UNDP 2012), for – due primarily to media coverage – few of them can any longer overlook the fact that numerous local crimes are being perpetuated by gangs and that a growing proportion of homicides are being committed by gang members. Today, for instance, about three-quarters (74 per cent) of homicides in St Kitts and Nevis, half (52 per cent) of homicides in Jamaica and a third (35 per cent) of homicides in Trinidad and Tobago are officially recognized as gang related (Hill 2012).

Such startling numbers have captured the attention of Caribbean nation states and international development organizations that are considering the options for responding to the region's different gangs, individual gang members and overall gang violence. Appropriately, their discussions are encompassing systemic social issues, such as unemployment, concentrated disadvantage, poor education and family problems, in an effort to isolate the conditions that are conducive to gang formation as well as the factors that motivate gang joining and lead to gang violence (UNDP 2012; Katz and Fox 2010; Katz, Maguire and Choate 2011). The discussions are beginning to yield thoughtful long-term strategic plans, but these will take years to implement, if not generations. Meanwhile, there remains an urgent need for more immediate action to mitigate gang violence in the short term. Relatively little useful research and planning have occurred on that level to date (Maguire 2012).

Attacking the short-term problems associated with gangs is a daunting prospect. To be effective, such an effort must begin with a systematic and region-specific understanding of gangs, gang members and gang problems, a step that few policymakers and researchers have attempted to take. Caribbean police organizations historically have not had the capacity to systematically collect and analyse gang intelligence, and relatively few scholars have approached the issues with research methods well-grounded in the social sciences. (For exceptions, see Harriott 2008, 2009; Katz and Fox 2010.)

This book is intended to provide the kind of sound research that will stimulate data-driven discussions among criminologists and policymakers. Our intent is to use this opportunity to help shape the public dialogue in the Caribbean and to guide it in a constructive direction, given the relatively recent incitation of the problem. Public dialogue based on shared myths and perceptions that are grounded in fear and anecdotal evidence rarely lead to effective solutions to complex problems. Only through accurately diagnosed problems can we hope to design prevention, intervention and suppression strategies that will, in fact, work to address violence in Caribbean communities.

The book is broken into two sections. Section 1 focuses on the scope and nature of the Caribbean gang problem. It not only provides a cutting-edge description of the extent of the Caribbean's gang problem but it also details differences between organized crime groups and street gangs, and how these differences impact the types of problems that communities face. Section 2 focuses on policies and programmes designed to respond to Caribbean gangs. It stresses the unique challenges in developing effective strategies and the promising strategies that have yielded positive results so far.

The purpose of this introduction is to set the stage for the following chapters by reviewing the current body of literature on gangs and the response to gangs in the Caribbean. We start by defining street gangs. This is followed by a cross-national approach to examining the scope and nature of the problem(s), the causes of street gangs and gang membership, and the current responses to street gangs throughout the region. The introduction concludes with a broad overview of the book's content.

Defining Street Gangs

The tendency in previous manuscripts on Caribbean gangs, crews and organized crime groups has been to discuss them, regardless of type, as fundamentally alike. However, despite inherent commonalities, they differ in significant ways, and their distinctive problems require distinctive responses. Thus, differentiating between crews, street gangs and organized crime is critical in order to accurately and effectively diagnose and respond to problems associated with each group. Without question, organized crime produces enormous consequences for nations and deserves much attention. Derivative policies and action plans simply redirected toward delinquent youth in general and gangs in particular, however, are not only misguided, but also they are often poorly conceived and implemented, thus putting youth at risk.

We rely on the definition of a street gang as "any durable street-oriented youth group whose involvement in illegal activity is part of their group identity" (van Gemert 2005, 148). "Durability" means that a group has existed for more than a few months and continues to exist regardless of membership turnover. "Street-oriented" means that the members spend substantial time away from home or school, that is, on the streets and in parks and other public places. "Youth" refers to individuals who, on average, are in their teens or early twenties. "Illegal activity" is a level above disorderly conduct or being a public nuisance; it refers to criminal actions. "Identity" in this context means not one's self-identity but a sense of the group's characteristics apart from those of individual members (van Gemert 2005, 148).

Organized crime, on the other hand, is characterized by "enterprise activity, the use of violence (actual and/or threatened) and corruption as typical means, and exploitable relationships with the upper-world" (Harriott 2011, 6). Enterprise activity involves the provision of illegal goods or services; traditional examples have included drug, gun and human trafficking, as well as extortion. Organizational sophistication, generally in either corporate or relational form, is another feature of organized crime groups, a feature rarely or only loosely shared by street gangs. The corporate model is structured with a formal hierarchy and clear lines of authority while the relational model relies on personal and social networks such as those that often exist in a community or particular area (Harriott 2008, 31–32).

Consequently, street gangs differ from organized crime groups in several ways. Gangs typically lack organization and have a limited centralized leadership. Their members are more likely to be motivated by issues of status, while organized crime groups are often economically motivated. Street gang members are most likely to be operating on the ground, involved in neighbourhood-level drug sales, while organized crime groups manage the wider distribution and trafficking of drugs. Understanding these and other differences has practical implications for developing effective strategies for responding both to gangs and organized crime.

Few studies have examined the differences between types of criminal groups in the Caribbean. One of the few is the work of Horace Levy (2012) in his examination of youth violence and organized crime in Jamaica. Levy points out that in Jamaica there is no "standardised and widely accepted usage of the terms corner crew, gang and criminal gang" (p. 18). He then sets out to define the differences between these types of groups. On the one hand, he defines the term "criminal gang" much the same way we define organized crime groups above – as a group, not necessarily tied to any community, which engages in serious forms of criminal activity, often transnational in nature, that results in economic gain (pp. 15–23). On the other hand, Levy uses the term "defence crew" to describe what we define above as a street gang. Defence crews (or street gangs), he writes, are defenders of the community who use guns to protect their communities against violence from rival groups from other communities. He explains that they fight for turf, respect and street justice, and that their members develop a common sense of identity through belonging to their group and community.[1] His discussion of the differences between what we call organized crime and street gangs is an important first step in the Caribbean toward differentiating the features of these two types of groups. Further work in this area is needed not only to help develop a common terminology but also to understand the structural, functional and behavioural characteristics that differentiate them.

Scope and Nature of the Problem

The United States and, more recently, Europe have conducted considerable research on street gangs. Caribbean scholars, though, report that citizen insecurity in general and the gang problem in particular have received little public attention until lately, so it is not surprising that systematic research into Caribbean street gangs is lacking. What little we have learned about the prevalence of the problem, characteristics of street gangs and their members, and gang behaviour comes primarily from the two largest Caribbean nations: Jamaica, and Trinidad and Tobago.

Prevalence of the Problem

Street gangs are active in much of the Caribbean region, according to multiple data sources, although the magnitude of the problem varies substantially across nations. Of several methods available for understanding the street gang problem, researchers most often collect and analyse official police data and self-report data. Official police data capture information from those who come into contact with the police; this information tends to come from older and more criminally involved individuals (Katz, Webb and Schaefer 2001; Katz 2003).

In 2010, the Jamaican police identified 268 gangs and approximately 3,900 gang members (Hall 2010). In Trinidad and Tobago, police have identified 95 gangs and approximately 1,269 gang members (Katz and Choate 2006). Antigua and Barbuda law enforcement officials have reported 15 gangs and estimated between 264 and 570 gang members (Katz 2008). Barbados reported 150 gangs and 4,000 gang members[2] (although those figures are possibly inflated). Police estimates of the street gang problem in Guyana, Suriname, St Lucia and a number of other Caribbean nations have been unavailable, suggesting that those policymakers perhaps have not fully examined the extent of their problems.

Self-report data is possibly the more common source of information for examining the prevalence of gang-related phenomena. Self-report data has, in fact, proven to be a robust, valid and reliable method for collecting information from gang members by both researchers (Esbensen et al. 2001; Katz et al. 1997; Webb, Katz and Decker 2006) and the police (Katz and Webb 2003; Katz 1997; Webb and Katz 2003). Several researchers have used this method to collect data on the prevalence of gang involvement in Caribbean nations. This body of work, however, has largely been limited to cross-sectional studies examining school youth. As seen in table 1 below, while Fox and Gordon-Strachan (2007) reported relatively low rates (5.5 per cent) of Jamaican school youth reporting to have ever been in a gang, others have reported that 11 per cent or more of school-attending youth have ever been in a gang (Ohene, Ireland and Blum 2005; Katz and Fox 2010). Other sampling strategies relying on community-based

Table I.1. Proportion self-reporting gang association in prior cross-sectional research

Source	Location data collected	Sample	Cases (number)	Gang definition	Gang-involved (%)
Ohene, Ireland and Blum (2005)	Antigua, Bahamas, Barbados, BVI, Dominica, Grenada, Guyana, Jamaica, St Lucia	School-attending youth	15,695	Ever	17–24 (males) 11–16 (females)
Wilks et al. (2007)	Jamaica	Community-based (ages 15–19 years old)	1,315	Current Ever	1.9 6.4
Fox and Gordon-Strachan (2007)	Jamaica	School-attending youth	2,985	Ever	5.5
Wortley (2010)	Jamaica	General population (age 16+ years old)	3,056	Former	0.5
Katz and Fox (2010)	Trinidad	School-attending youth	2,206	Associate Former Current	7.7 6.8 6.2
Katz, Maguire & Choate (2011)	Trinidad	Adult arrestees, recently booked	412	Current	5.1

Source: Appears in a previous version of this chapter: "Reducing the Contribution of Street Gangs and Organized Crime to Violence", in *Caribbean Human Development Report 2012: Human Development and the Shift to Better Citizen Security*, 65–90 (New York: United Nations Development Programme).

samples, the general population, and recently booked adult arrestees have yielded divergent results as well (Wilks et al. 2007; Wortley 2010; Katz, Maguire and Choate 2011) which suggests that the Caribbean has a long way to go toward understanding the prevalence of the gang problem.

Gender and Age Composition of Caribbean Street Gangs

Not a great deal is known yet about the socio-demographic characteristics of Caribbean street gang members. The early evidence from Jamaica and Trinidad and Tobago indicates that among school-aged youth, males compose the majority of street gang members, although female members are prevalent as well. Katz, Choate and Fox (2010), for example, have reported that among a national sample of Trinidadian youth in urban schools more than 40 per cent of self-reported gang members were female; earlier, Meeks (2009) also reported a strong presence of females in Jamaican street gangs.

Data from the police also have suggested that gang membership is predominately male. A survey of police experts from the Trinidad and Tobago Police Service (Katz and Choate 2006) and a later study comprised of police experts in Antigua and Barbuda (Katz 2008) found no female-dominated gangs in those countries. Considered together, these findings might suggest that Caribbean females are involved in street gangs but are not frequently coming to the attention of the police. Regardless, their numbers suggest a need to understand the impact that females have on Caribbean gang structure, culture and criminality, and the role they fill in the gangs.

This same body of research suggests that individuals join street gangs at a young age. Trinidad and Tobago school youth who self-reported gang membership claimed that, on average, they first became involved at twelve years of age (Katz and Choate 2006); surveys of Antigua and Barbuda school officials indicated that most gang members were between the ages of twelve to fifteen years (Katz 2008). From these preliminary findings, we could speculate that the regional street gang problem begins largely with young and possibly marginalized males.

Organizational Characteristics of the Caribbean Street Gang

The available research indicates that the organizational characteristics of Caribbean street gangs vary by nation. Data collected from law enforcement officers in Antigua and Barbuda, and Trinidad and Tobago, showed that street gangs typically had a group name, referred to themselves as a gang or crew, spent considerable time in public places and claimed turf. In Trinidad and Tobago, police gang experts claimed that most street gangs did not have symbols such as clothing, ways of speaking or signs (Katz and Choate 2006), but in Antigua and Barbuda, police gang experts reported that most street gangs did make use of such symbols (Katz 2008). The Royal Barbados Police Force suggested that street gangs in that country used symbols and initiation rituals.[3]

In Trinidad and Tobago, self-report data from self-identified school-aged gang members found that although most gang members stated that their gang held regular meetings (56 per cent) and had rules (52 per cent), fewer than half stated that their gang had a leader (45 per cent) or insignia (45 per cent) (Pyrooz et al. 2011), exhibiting relatively low levels of organization. Pyrooz et al. reported that gang organizational structure was positively related to delinquency – that the more structurally organized the gang, the more the members self-reported delinquency.

In Jamaica, street gangs appear to be more organized. According to Leslie (2010), gangs operated with a hierarchy and division of labour, typically having an all-powerful leader and an upper echelon, middle echelon and "workers" at the bottom. Jamaican gangs have been characterized by several different typologies that could be placed along a continuum with smaller, loosely organized gangs on one end and larger, highly organized gangs on the other. These characterizations are largely influenced by what academics and practitioners know about street gangs and organized crime groups and are then generalized to other criminal groups such as crews. With that said, most of the discussion about gang organizational structure in Jamaica has been focused on *dons*, the leaders of organized crime groups. Of the 268 gangs in Jamaica (Hall 2010), Harriott reported that about twenty of them were organized crime groups who were led by a don. Dons are typically male and historically have had broad and sweeping control over Jamaica's garrison communities. Initially dons served members of parliament who used them as intermediaries to give out government contracts to their constituents and to facilitate their re-election (Harriott 2003).

Over time, however, dons became less reliant on members of parliament and exerted their own control through finances acquired from drug trafficking (Harriott 2003; Levy 2012). They provided food, education, electricity, water and housing for the most needy. Additionally, because of the weak formal social control mechanisms in place within garrisons – that is, no police protection and lack of justice in the courts – dons stepped into the void to exercise their own form of "jungle justice" whereby they implemented swift and harsh punishments to those who violated social norms (such as having committed robbery, rape) (Levy 2012, 22). (Harriott thoroughly addresses the gap in our understanding of dons and their relationship with the community in chapters 1, 7 and 8.)

Street Gang Violence

Perhaps the most publicly visible consequences of street gangs are crime and violence. Available data suggest substantial variability in the degree to which countries are affected by these consequences. In Antigua and Barbuda, for example, 2006–7 homicide data showed only one of twenty-nine homicides reported in that country to be gang related (Katz 2008). Meanwhile, in St Lucia, gang homicides appeared to be increasing, contributing to an increasing proportion of that nation's homicides, yet no effort has been made to systematically examine the issue. Periodically in Barbados and Guyana there are news reports of gang homicides, but again, while the problem does not appear prevalent in these countries, its extent has not been systematically examined.

In Jamaica and Trinidad and Tobago, not only has the proportion of gang-related homicides increased, but also the number of gang-related homicides almost doubled in each country from 2006 through 2009. In Jamaica in 2006, of 1,303 homicides, a third (32.5 per cent) were classified as gang homicides; by 2009, the number had risen to 1,680 homicides and almost half (48.1 per cent) were gang related. In Trinidad and Tobago in 2006, of 371 homicides, more than a quarter (26.4 per cent) were classified by police as gang related; by 2009, the number of homicides had increased to 506 of which more than a third (34.8 per cent) were gang related.

As concerning as they are, the figures above still might have under-reported the actual extent of the problem, according to prior reports. Several researchers in recent decades have pointed out the limitations of gang homicide data and the under-classification of homicides that are gang related (Maxson and Klein 1990; Katz 2003). Katz and Maguire (2006) conducted one such study in Trinidad and Tobago to examine the nature of one of the worst homicide problem areas in the nation, that of the Besson Street Station District. They determined that although police had classified about 25 per cent of the district's homicides as gang related, a more accurate estimate was at least 62.5 per cent according to interviews and document reviews. This suggests that the gang homicide problem throughout the Caribbean could well be more serious than official police statistics and news reports might reveal.

During this period, the Republic of Trinidad and Tobago's Ministry of National Security funded a study to diagnose the street gang problem (see chapter 6). The study, conducted in Trinidad and Tobago, examined official data, self-report data from school youth and self-report data from arrestees. All three data sources yielded similar outcomes, producing perhaps the best understanding we have to date of how street gangs pose a threat to the Caribbean. The official data found that when compared with non-gang members, gang members were twice as likely to have been arrested for property crime; three times more likely to have been arrested for a violent, gun or drug offence; and five times more likely to have been arrested for drug sales (Katz and Choate 2006). Self-report data from school-aged youth determined that compared with non-gang members, gang members were about eleven times more likely to be involved in drug sales, seven times more likely to be involved in violence, five times more likely to be involved in property crime and three times more likely to have been arrested (Katz, Choate and Fox 2010). Similar numbers were reported by adult arrestees (Katz, Maguire and Choate 2011), with the additional findings that many gang members possessed a firearm (52.6 per cent) and carried it for self-protection and defence (Wells, Katz and Kim 2010).

Causes of Street Gangs

Why do Caribbean youth become involved in street gangs? To answer that question, we need both to identify the causes and correlates of street gangs in the Caribbean and to examine the conditions that sustain them. Below, we review Caribbean social-structural conditions that give rise to these phenomena – issues such as community cohesion, social cohesion and informal social control – and their relationship to the concentration of street gangs. Next, we discuss the risk and protective factors associated with street gang membership.

Community-Level Factors

Community and social cohesion create an environment that fosters and enables shared goals and collective action. *Collective efficacy*, a term coined by Sampson, Raudenbush and Earls (1997), encompasses the willingness and ability of community members to develop and achieve shared goals. It includes cooperative efforts to define, monitor and condemn undesirable behaviours that occur within a community. In the absence of such social ties and relationships, communities are unlikely to exercise informal social control over their neighbourhoods. With the diminished capacity for control comes the risk of higher levels of crime and delinquency (Katz and Schnebly 2011). Prior research has found that factors such as community cohesion, social cohesion and informal social control are related to gang formation and other group-based criminal activity.

Where there is a lack of social and community cohesion with formal and informal social controls, a void exists that can readily be filled by street gangs. As well as posing risks, these groups fulfil some social purposes; they can become empowered by and engrained in the fabric of daily life of certain local communities. Indeed, in Jamaica, traditional formal and informal social controls and social and community cohesion have deteriorated to such an extent that some now rely on dons and street gangs to maintain a certain level of local order and services. (Harriott discusses this in more depth in chapters 7 and 8.)

Several years ago, Mogensen (2005) reported that in Jamaica citizens no longer believed that the police could effectively address crime and that, instead, they were seeking justice from local dons through "kangaroo courts". Leslie (2010, 22) further notes that dons controlled criminal activity, enforcing discipline (often with beatings or executions) that to a certain extent was commensurate with the offence.[4] Dons could, when they wished, also provide housing, food, medical assistance, policing services and even early childhood education for citizens who were loyal to them (Harriott 2008; Leslie 2010). They also controlled opportunities for political advancement for loyalists with political aspirations (Harriott 2009). Harriott (2008) noted that as a result of controlling the goods and services that could make life better for many, leaders of street gangs became the role models and mentors in some communities, thus perpetuating a community culture that came to value criminal organizations and their role in the community.

Although there have been very few studies examining the relationship between the presence of gangs and gang members and community levels of homicide, Katz and Fox (2010) reported a strong relationship after controlling for social-structural factors. The authors collected police data on the number of gangs and gang members in each police station district and linked that data with homicide and census data. They reported that for every one additional gang member in a community, the number of homicides increased by 0.4 per cent.

Likewise, for every additional gang in a community, the number of homicides increased by 10 per cent. Substantially more research is needed in the Caribbean to understand community-level factors and their relationship to crime and gang-related phenomena.

Individual-Level Factors

The risk factor paradigm is another approach to explaining and understanding delinquent and criminal groups. In this context, *risk factors* are the characteristics or symptoms that increase the odds that an individual will become involved in problem behaviours. Conversely, *protective factors* are characteristics or symptoms that decrease those odds (Blum et al. 2003). The risk and protective model has been used extensively in the field of public health (for example, factors such as tobacco use, lack of exercise and family history increase the risk of heart disease and protective factors such as exercise and proper diet decrease that risk [Hawkins et al. 1999]), particularly as a basis for public policy for addressing cancer, mental health and other diseases. More recently, that model has been applied toward understanding the issue of gang joining.

Almost no research has yet been done on the risk and protective factors associated with street gang membership. Prior research in the United States and Europe, however, leads us to consider the relationship of gang membership to predisposing factors such as neighbourhood social disorganization, local levels of crime and drug use, lack of attachment to school and poor school performance, unemployment, poor family management, attachment to anti-social peers, and a history of delinquency and drug use. Katz and Fox (2010) examined school youth in Trinidad and Tobago and found several factors associated with gang involvement: (1) parental attitudes favouring antisocial behaviour, (2) residency in a neighbourhood with a high risk for mobility, (3) wide access to handguns, (4) early-age antisocial behaviour, (5) intent to use drugs, (6) antisocial peers and (7) peers who used drugs. Interestingly, they found that, for the most part, school-related risk factors were not significantly associated with gang involvement. Subsequent analysis using the same data, however, suggested that the Caribbean community might consider developing a unique set of items to measure risk and protective factors among Caribbean youth rather than relying on those developed in the United States, because there might be issues related to the construct and concurrent validity of measures created in the United States and then wholly imported for use in the Caribbean (Maguire, Wells and Katz 2011).

Responding to Street Gangs

Responses to street gangs can be varied and multidimensional. Domestic responses can fall into five broad strategies: suppression; provision of academic, economic and social opportunities; social intervention; community mobilization; and organizational change and development. For this chapter, I discuss those responses that have been or could be implemented in the Caribbean to address street gangs under three strategic categories: legislation, suppression and prevention/intervention. Together, these could offer an integrated, balanced, locally appropriate and highly effective response to street gangs.

Legislative Strategies

The process of drafting legislation for addressing the Caribbean gang problem would involve offering a public forum in which to uncover the scope and nature of the gang problem and to define its terms. Thoughtful, well-articulated legislation would provide consistent law enforcement guidelines and national standards for documenting gangs and gang membership. The process could bring citizens into the discussion and, for individuals accused of gang crime, it would establish legal processes and rights under the law, such as the rights to review one's own records and to appeal court decisions.

Trinidad and Tobago, and St Kitts and Nevis each have enacted gang legislation (Hill 2012) that criminalizes being a gang member, recruiting individuals into a gang and preventing individuals from leaving a gang. In Trinidad, the law's definition of gang membership is vague at best, stating that "any evidence reasonably tending to show or demonstrate the existence of, or membership in, a gang shall be admissible in any action or proceedings brought under this act" (First Session Tenth Parliament, Republic of Trinidad and Tobago, Act No. 10 of 2011, 6).[5]

Likewise, the legislation gives sweeping powers to the police while providing few checks or balances for individual rights. For example, it allows police without a warrant to enter and search any place they reasonably believe to be harbouring a gang member. They are further allowed to arrest and detain for seventy-two hours, without warrant, any individual they believe to be a gang member. The punishments for gang-related offences are harsh. A first-offence conviction would result in a ten-year sentence; a second would yield a twenty-five-year sentence. Anyone found to be aiding a gang member also could be imprisoned for as many as twenty-five years.

A legislative response to gang problems could be a step in the right direction, but in Trinidad and St Kitts, the laws as written contain a number of deficits that may actually exacerbate the situation or even create new problems. These laws were created without sufficient attention to procedural or distributive justice. They do not sufficiently guide and limit (with quality control reviews) police and court discretion in designating any group as a gang or any individual as a gang member. The legislation could therefore fall short of fulfilling its purpose – that is, to suppress gangs, gang membership and illegal gang activity. As it is, many Caribbean nations have quite low clearance and detection rates for gang-related crime. In a study conducted by Katz and Maguire (2006), for example, fifty-three gang homicides occurred in one Trinidadian community, but only three suspects were arrested and none were convicted. Even if the proposed legislation were to result in a modest increase in arrests, it could thwart the conversion of arrests to convictions. Conviction sentences are severe enough that gang members would have even stronger motivation to threaten potential witnesses to dissuade them from offering damaging testimony.

If prior research is a guide, such legislation could have effects that are completely contrary to the ones desired. In El Salvador, for example, the "Mano Dura", or "iron fist", policy criminalized gang membership and, as a consequence, youth who were even remotely associated with a gang were arrested and incarcerated, and then were discriminated against upon their return to the community after serving prison time. The policy was found to have the unintended effect of increasing gang cohesion and the proliferation of gangs (USAID 2006). Similarly, Klein (1995) noted that in Los Angeles, California, gang sweeps by the police were an ineffective means of generating gang arrests. Klein claimed that such tactics may actually have had a negative impact on the community's gang problem because the majority of those who were arrested were immediately released without charges being filed. This, he argued, may have strengthened gang cohesiveness and reduced any possible deterrent impact on gang members. A similar result might be found in Trinidad where in the year following the enactment of anti-gang legislation, 449 people were arrested for gang-related offences. Most of these individuals were never charged by prosecutors, however, and none were convicted (Julien 2012). Such findings not only illustrate the ineffectiveness of such strategies but most likely send a strong message to gang members that they are invulnerable, which in turn reduces the public's confidence in the justice system. The potential certainly exists for legislation to be structured in a way that creates an effective foundation for responding to the gang problem in the Caribbean, but thus far this potential remains unrealized, and these early efforts may even be making the problem worse.

Suppression Strategies

Few of the Caribbean nations (other than Jamaica and Trinidad and Tobago) are operating in accord with an organized strategy for responding to gangs and gang members, who are disproportionately involved in crime. Instead, they are currently responding primarily with suppression strategies. These are almost always reactive in nature, using criminal law to control or isolate behaviour. Typical suppression strategies include arrest, prosecution, intermediate sanctions and imprisonment. Caribbean law enforcement officials employ these tactics as they react incident-by-incident to crimes perpetuated by gangs. Among the problems that inhibit progress is the fact that the majority of law enforcement officials still lack the intelligence systems that are essential for identifying gang members and the groups who are most involved in violence.

In Jamaica in 2004, Operation Kingfish was launched in an effort to restore community confidence and reduce fear of crime, by targeting gang leaders and drug dons and breaking up organized crime groups. This task force reportedly made a major dent in crime, arresting some of Jamaica's "most wanted" and dismantling at least two gangs while disrupting six others (Sinclair 2010). Later, the Jamaica Constabulary Force implemented an anti-gang strategy aimed at further disrupting gang activity. Its objectives were to (1) increase the effort in street and public spaces; (2) set and meet a deadline for identifying, profiling and disrupting or dismantling gangs; and (3) open a Proceeds of Crime Act (POCA) file, a precursor to stripping criminals of profits from criminal acts, on each arrestee charged with a serious gang- or drug-related crime. According to an article in the online edition of the 8 April *Jamaica Observer* (2011), security officials believed that these actions had reduced killings by 44 per cent in the first quarter of 2011. Trinidad and Tobago also was one of the first Caribbean nations to establish a specialized unit with trained personnel to respond to gangs. Its Gang/Repeat Offender (Gang/ROP) Task Force was established in May 2006, staffed with about forty specially trained and coached sworn officers (recorded by Katz 2008, internal memo). The unit was responsible for apprehending wanted persons, collecting and disseminating gang intelligence to units across the police service, and conducting random patrols in areas with gang problems.

The initial police responses to street gangs in both Jamaica and Trinidad and Tobago have been limited and subject to significant setbacks, but this slow start is not inconsistent with the early experience of developed nations (Katz and Webb 2006). First, although policing policies defining gang phenomena are being developed, those policies are not yet well known in police services, and when they are present they rarely are followed by the police. Gang "intelligence" remains unreliable; officers are continuing to document persons in accord with their own individual ideas, beliefs and biases rather than consistently documenting individuals in accord with standardized behavioural criteria.

Second, several specialized police units dedicated to responding to gangs have been suspected of serious misconduct and human rights violations. In Trinidad, to cite one example, the Repeat Offender Programme Task Force was disbanded after repeated allegations implicated its members in kidnappings and extra-judicial killings, tipping off criminals to raids, arranging for illegal extra security for certain nightclubs and running ghost gangs to fraudulently acquire public money (Simon 2010a, 2010b). Similarly, the Jamaica Constabulary Force has been accused of (extrajudicial) killing of up to forty-four civilians while cracking down on gangs and pursuing Christopher Coke, a powerful gang leader, in the gang-controlled garrison Tivoli Gardens (Office of the Public Defender 2013).

Third, though few evaluations of the Caribbean police response to gangs have been conducted, those few have shown their suppression efforts to be largely ineffective. In Trinidad and Tobago, for instance, the Gang/ROP Task Force made 495 arrests from May 2006 through August 2007, but the majority of those arrested were released or transferred; only 110 (22.2 per cent) were charged. The capacity of police agencies to adequately collect, maintain and disseminate intelligence – the core function of the Repeat Offender Programme Task Force – proved to be disorganized and unreliable (recorded by Katz 2008, internal memo). Some new research conducted in Jamaica suggests that recent suppression strategies have been implemented without sufficient regard for human rights (Levy 2012), but if they were to be implemented properly under the rule of law, these gang suppression strategies might yield effective and powerful results (see chapter 7).

Across the board, early efforts to suppress street gangs have been weak and ineffective or, worse, corrupt. Suppression tactics in the Caribbean are too often part of the problem rather than an appropriate solution. In addition, there remains the need not only to address immediate problems (for example, to arrest individuals for criminal activity) but also to reduce the role of suppression as a response to gangs. Instead, the goal should be to deter youth and adults from organizing or joining gangs in the first place and to deter members from engaging in future crime. For that, the opportunity lies in intervention and prevention strategies.

Intervention and Prevention Strategies

Well-conceived and well-implemented suppression tactics can be an effective supplement to other elements of a strategic response to gangs and gang crime. At best, however, suppression addresses only part of the problem. Intervention and prevention strategies take the longer view, aiming to weaken or eliminate the attraction of forming or joining a gang in the first place. They seek to provide timely skills and opportunities that susceptible youth need to realize their goals in other more productive and rewarding ways. So far, Caribbean governments have seemed reluctant to adopt such intervention and prevention strategies.

Caribbean nations could tap into their community cohesiveness to mobilize regional coalitions of schools, churches, public health services and criminal justice agencies. Such coalitions with a focused aim could prove to be powerful agents, collaborating to develop, coordinate and deliver locally specific responses to street gangs. To date, some Caribbean coalitions have been formed for broader purposes, but thus far they have not focused on "big pay-off" issues such as those surrounding gangs. Much opportunity lies in coalitional responses to gang problems.

One example of such a strategy can be found in Jamaica's Peace Management Initiative (PMI). In 2008, the PMI brokered a peace agreement between gang leaders in one community where an already high level of gang violence was rising. As part of the peace agreement, gang members were no longer to carry or use guns, and community leaders were to discourage violence and encourage members to tolerate political diversity. Additionally, the PMI established a peace council that was responsible for monitoring the terms of the agreement. The agreement was signed by gang leaders, members of civil society and political leaders. The peace agreement was largely credited with decreasing violence in the community. Levy (2012) illustrates its success by noting that in the year prior to the agreement there were more than sixty-five homicides in Greater Brown's Town, a collection of communities in East Kingston, while for each of the five years following the agreement, there was an annual average of only eight homicides (p. 33). While this example illustrates the potential promise of such strategies, more rigorous research and evaluation is needed to understand their impact.

Another productive strategy for Caribbean nations could be to identify and address the "root causes" of street gangs and gang crime which can differ across regions. We can assume that if they do not have reasonable access to legitimate opportunities to accomplish their aims otherwise, a significant number of individuals in a given locale will be more apt to engage with criminal groups to achieve their goals and obtain resources. Root cause strategies focus on improving academic, economic and social opportunities for disadvantaged youth emphasizing educational success, job training and placement, and problem-solving skills.

Social intervention strategies are another intriguing option. Here, the specific aim is to reduce the likelihood of violent outbreaks in communities. It requires that trained outreach workers be available to provide time-sensitive guidance and services that can defuse escalating emotional situations – crisis intervention, temporary shelter or counselling, for example – following a violent incident. Outreach workers can be skilled at inter-gang mediation, group counselling and conflict resolution at points of crisis, all tactics that have proven themselves effective in preventing violent incidents (Burch and Chemers 1997; Spergel 2007; Spergel and Grossman 1997; Spergel, Wa and Sosa 2006).

Some Caribbean countries have begun to implement social intervention strategies through the importation of the Chicago CeaseFire programme (also known as Cure Violence). The Chicago CeaseFire programme, a popular strategy for addressing gun violence, has been implemented in several American cities as well as in locations throughout the world including Iraq, England, South Africa and Colombia.[6] CeaseFire is based on the idea that not everyone in a community engages in violence and so intervention should be focused on those select few who are the most at risk for "being shot or being a shooter" in the near future. The programme attempts to change norms about violence among targeted individuals and neighbourhoods by altering how they perceive the short- and long-term prospects of violence (Skogan et al. 2008). The Chicago CeaseFire model includes core strategies that are intended to have an impact on the decision making of those who are involved in shootings, to reduce the risk that they will engage in violence and to change the attitudinal norms toward violence within the community. In March 2013, the Inter-American Development Bank (IDB) announced its plans to fund the implementation of CeaseFire over a three-year period in East Port of Spain, Trinidad. The Chicago CeaseFire programme has indicated that it also has a partnership with Jamaica.[7]

An initial evaluation in Chicago found the programme promising (Skogan et al. 2008), but there have been only a few formal evaluations of the effectiveness of CeaseFire. Outside of Chicago, for example, only four sites (Newark,

Baltimore, Pittsburgh and Phoenix) have been formally evaluated. In Newark, the evaluation suggested no programme effect (Boyle et al. 2010); in Baltimore, the evaluation suggested that the programme had reduced homicides (Webster et al. 2012); in Pittsburgh (Wilson and Chermak 2011) and in Phoenix (Fox et al. 2013), evaluations suggested that their programme had resulted in increased violence in the communities where it was implemented. Together, these findings suggest that the Chicago CeaseFire programme has the potential to result in adverse effects, which in turn suggests that rigorous monitoring and evaluation should be conducted alongside implementation so that in the event of adverse effects programmers and policymakers will be alerted.

Last, Caribbean youth are in need of primary prevention programming in their communities – programming that can redirect their life trajectories toward accessible, appealing and productive futures, away from gang joining and engagement in gang activities. Primary prevention programming offers services to a community's families and youth, or even to the entire community, often in the most high-risk neighbourhoods. Service providers may include schools, non-governmental organizations, government agencies and faith-based organizations, among others. The applicable theory, proven in other con-texts, holds that while most community members share values and aspirations for themselves and their children, even with effort and dedication some will face more obstacles to achieving their goals than others. Whether those obstacles are societal or personal in nature, effective prevention efforts can inoculate youth against problem behaviour. At this time, Caribbean youth have access to few or none of the kind of formal intervention and prevention services that might dissuade them from becoming involved in street gangs in the first place.

Recent evidence from the revised Gang Resistance Education and Training (GREAT) programme suggests that students who have received programme delivery have lower odds of gang joining. The programme is designed to achieve three primary goals: (1) teach youths to avoid gang membership; (2) prevent violence and criminal activity; and (3) help youths to develop positive relation-ships with law enforcement.[8] The curriculum, delivered in about thirteen one-hour lessons taught by a trained professional, teaches life skills such as conflict resolution, responsibility, appreciating cultural diversity and goal-setting. It emphasizes important information such as the effect of crime on its victims and how to meet basic social needs without gang joining. Recent analysis indicates that those youth who had participated in the programme, compared with those who had not, were more positive about the police, less positive about gangs, less likely to join a gang, less likely to self-report crime and more able to resist peer pressure (Esbensen et al. 2011; Esbensen et al. 2012). Based on these findings and the magnitude of the growing gang problem in the Caribbean, implementation of the GREAT programme might be beneficial.

This Book

This book is partially an outcome of a meeting held by the Inter-University Consortium for the Study of Caribbean Gang Violence. Arizona State University, the University of the West Indies, American University and Sam Houston State University established the consortium in 2010 for the purpose of conducting rigorous research toward understanding the root causes of gang formation violence in the Caribbean. The consortium holds periodic symposiums to disseminate research findings concerning gang-related problems in the Caribbean. The first symposium was held in 2012 where a number of those at the forefront of understanding Caribbean gangs presented their work to an audience of academics and US and Caribbean policymakers and diplomats. At the urging of Anthony Harriott (co-editor of and contributor to this book), a number of the presentations were adapted and developed into manuscripts for inclusion in this edited book.

In chapter 1, Harriott outlines the evolution of organized crime in Jamaica and discusses its emergence from street gangs. This chapter relies on his recently conducted research that describes the nature of the problem, the conditions that foster and sustain street gangs and organized crime groups, and the evolution and future of organized crime groups in Jamaica. He pays particular attention to the roles of politics, corruption and the criminal justice system in the rise of organized crime in Jamaica. In a similar vein, in chapter 2, Lillian Bobea examines the scope and nature of criminal groups in the Dominican Republic. She differentiates between street gangs and organized crime groups and discusses their evolution, prevalence, organizational structure and criminal activity. She focuses particularly on the impact of such groups within the social, institutional and political context of the Dominican Republic.

Randy Seepersad, in chapter 3, provides a comprehensive overview of what is currently known about street gangs in Trinidad and Tobago, relying on data from the Ministry of National Security of Trinidad and Tobago and the United Nations Development programme, as well as findings from prior research conducted in Trinidad and Tobago. He reports on the prevalence of the street gang problem, the characteristics of gangs and gang members, the spatial distribution of the gang problem, and the relationship between community levels of crime and the presence of gangs and gang members. Seepersad concludes with a discussion of the impact and consequences of policies and programmes that are being implemented as responses to gangs throughout the nation.

In chapter 4, Christopher A.D. Charles and Basil Wilson discuss the criminal entrepreneurial experiences of a Jamaican posse whose members immigrated to New York City for economic gain. The authors found that although a few posse members successfully accumulated wealth through drug distribution networks, the vast majority became addicted to crack and either were arrested and sentenced to prison or died. Others laundered and invested the money they had made through illicit activity into legitimate enterprises, while some successfully left the posse directly to pursue legitimate opportunities.

In chapter 5, Charles M. Katz and Andrew M. Fox examine whether street gangs in Trinidad are similar to those in the United States. The chapter draws on self-reported data collected from school youth from both nations to understand the prevalence of gang membership; the demographic characteristics associated with gang membership; risk and protective factors associated with gang joining; and similarities and differences in delinquency, drug use and victimization between gang members in Trinidad and the United States. Katz and Edward R. Maguire, in chapter 6, outline the basic steps involved in carrying out a systematic diagnosis of a nation's gang problem. They demonstrate the process by presenting a case study of a project carried out in the Republic of Trinidad and Tobago. The authors maintain that diagnostic processes should involve two steps, one external and one internal – the external diagnostic component focusing on understanding the nature of the gang problem itself, particularly with regard to gang violence, and the internal diagnostic component focusing on understanding the presence and effectiveness of formal and informal social control mechanisms to address the nation's gang problem.

In chapter 7, Harriott discusses the challenges and benefits of gang suppression in a case study of Jamaica's response to Christopher Coke and the Presidential Click in Tivoli Gardens. He provides a detailed analysis of the difficulties associated with gang-control strategies in Jamaican garrison communities as well as their potential for reducing the violence. In the case of Christopher Coke and Tivoli Gardens, Harriott argues that gang suppression activities indeed resulted in human rights violations, but they also resulted in a significant decline in gang violence and associated problems in the three years following implementation. Harriott follows with a discussion in chapter 8 of Jamaica's anti-gang strategy pertaining to the Spanglers – one of Jamaica's oldest gangs – and the community within which the Spanglers exhibited control. Using case study methodology, he focuses on how suppression strategies can be successfully integrated within a larger and more comprehensive response to gangs that incorporates elements of social prevention. He pays particular attention to the importance of neighbourhood collective efficacy and informal social control as a means by which communities can sustain gang-control efforts following successfully implemented suppression programming.

In chapter 9, Maguire and C. Jason Gordon discuss faith-based programming as it was implemented in Gonzales, a distressed community located within Trinidad. They discuss the community's gang problem and the role of the faith community in responding to that problem. The case study is presented through the lens of both a professor (Maguire) and a Catholic priest (Gordon) who reflect on the experiences and outcomes of Father Jason's and others' efforts to empower community members, provide prevention programming to youth, and negotiate and carry out a gang truce.

In the final chapter, Anthony Harriott takes on the challenging task of synthesizing the authors' findings reported throughout this book. He highlights the most important findings and draws upon them to further detail their meaning for the Caribbean region. Harriott outlines a number of issues that should be considered by future academics and lays the foundation for a future research agenda. This concluding chapter, working in concert with those that come before it, serves as a foundation for future Caribbean gang scholars and provides guidance on research methodologies and necessary areas of study.

Acknowledgements

A previous version of this chapter appeared as "Reducing the Contribution of Street Gangs and Organized Crime to Violence", in *Caribbean Human Development Report 2012: Human Development and the Shift to Better Citizen Security*, 65–90 (New York: United Nations Development Programme).

Notes

1. There are many reasons to believe that the terminology and description of the youth groups described by Levy are limited and socially constructed. His typology and discussion, however, are an important initial step for academics, who need to test them and discuss the implications of such labels and definitions.

2. Reported in 2008 by the delegation of Barbados at a special meeting of the Organization of American States, Washington, DC, speaking on their vision and experience regarding the phenomenon of criminal gangs.
3. From unpublished notes taken during remarks made by A. Goodridge, RBPF, to a Parent Teacher Association meeting, 24 March 2010.
4. Leslie's argument that dons dispense punishment that fits the crime should be thoroughly tested and examined by academics as public reports indicate that don-imposed justice is often harsh, excessive and unchecked. Leslie's discussion might reflect an idealized notion of don justice rather than reality.
5. See at http://www.ttparliament.org/legislations/a2011-10.pdf.
6. See http://www.ceasefire.org for more information about the programme.
7. See http://cureviolence.org/news/latin-america-looks-to-cure-violence.
8. For additional information on GREAT and similar programmes, go to the National Institute of Justice website, http://www.crimesolutions.gov/ProgramDetails.aspx?ID=249.

References

Blum, R.W., L. Halcón, T. Beuhring, E. Pate, S. Campell-Forrester, and A. Venema. 2003. "Adolescent Health in the Caribbean: Risk and Protective Factors". *American Journal of Public Health* 93(3): 456–60.

Boyle, D.J., J.L. Lanterman, J.E. Pascarella, and C.C. Cheng. 2010. "The Impact of Newark's Operation Ceasefire on Trauma Center Gunshot Wound Admissions". *Justice Research and Policy* 12(2): 105–23.

Burch, J.H., and B.M. Chemers. 1997. *A Comprehensive Response to America's Youth Gang Problem*. Office of Juvenile Justice and Delinquency Prevention, US Department of Justice, Washington, DC.

Esbensen, F.A., D. Peterson, T.J. Taylor, A. Freng, D.W. Osgood, D.C. Carson, and K.N. Matsuda. 2011. "Evaluation and Evolution of the Gang Resistance Education and Training (GREAT) Program". *Journal of School Violence* 10(1): 53–70.

Esbensen, F.A., D. Peterson, T.J. Taylor, and D.W. Osgood. 2012. "Results from a Multisite Evaluation of the GREAT Program". *Justice Quarterly* 29(1): 125–51.

Esbensen, F.A., L.T. Winfree Jr., N. He, and T.J. Taylor. 2001. "Youth Gangs and Definitional Issues: When is a Gang a Gang, and Why Does it Matter?" *Crime and Delinquency* 47: 105–30.

Fox, A., C.M. Katz, D.E. Choate, E.C. Hedberg. 2013. "Evaluation of the Phoenix TRUCE Project: A Replication of Chicago CeaseFire". Unpublished manuscript.

Fox, K., and G. Gordon-Strachan. 2007. "Jamaican Youth Risk and Resiliency Behaviour Survey 2005: School-Based Survey on Risk and Resiliency Behaviours of 10–15 Year Olds". Manuscript.

Hall, A. 2010. "Gang Buster, Security Minister Vows to Disrupt Criminal Networks". *Gleaner*, 3 January. http://jamaica-gleaner.com/gleaner/20100123/lead/lead1.html.

Harriott, A. 2003. "The Jamaican Crime Problem: New Developments and New Challenges for Public Policy". In *Understanding Crime in Jamaica: New Challenges for Public Policy*, ed. A. Harriott, 1–12. Kingston: University of the West Indies Press.

———. 2008. *Organized Crime and Politics in Jamaica: Breaking the Nexus*. Kingston: University of the West Indies Press.

———. 2009. *Controlling Violent Crime: Models and Policy Options*. Kingston: Grace Kennedy Foundation.

———. The Emergence and Evolution of Organised Crime in Jamaica. Unpublished manuscript, last revised in 2011.

Hawkins, J.D.., R.F. Catalano, R. Kosterman, R. Abbott, and K.G. Hill. 1999. "Preventing Adolescent Health-Risk Behaviours by Strengthening Protection during Childhood". *Archives of Pediatrics and Adolescent Medicine* 153: 226–34.

Hill, S.. 2012. "The Rise of Gang Violence in the Caribbean". Paper presented at the Symposium on Gangs and Gang Violence in the Caribbean, American University, Washington, DC, 17 February 2012.

Julien, J.. 2012. "Anti-gang Legislation Not There to Catch Criminals". *Trinidad Express*, 23 August. http://www.trinidadexpress.com/news/_Anti-Gang_legislation_not_there_to_catch_criminals_-167276215.html.

Katz, C.M. 1997. *Police and Gangs: A Study of a Police Gang Unit*. No. 98-20701 UMI.

———. 2003. "Issues in the Production and Dissemination of Gang Statistics: An Ethnographic Study of a Large Midwestern Police Gang Unit". *Crime and Delinquency* 49(3): 485–516.

———. 2008. *The Scope and Nature of the Gang Problem in Antigua and Barbuda*. Phoenix: Arizona State University.

Katz, C.M., and D. Choate. 2006. "Diagnosing Trinidad and Tobago's Gang Problem". Paper presented at the annual meeting of the American Society of Criminology, Los Angeles, California, November 2006.

Katz, C.M., D. Choate, and A. Fox. 2010. *Understanding and Preventing Gang Membership in Trinidad and Tobago*. Phoenix: Arizona State University.

Katz, C.M., and A. Fox. 2010. "Risk and Protective Factors Associated with Gang Involved Youth in a Caribbean Nation: Analysis of the Trinidad and Tobago Youth Survey". *Pan-American Journal of Public Health/Revista Panamericana de Salud Pública* 27(3): 187–202.

Katz, C.M., and E.R. Maguire. 2006. *Reducing Gang Homicides in the Besson Street Station District*. Phoenix: Arizona State University.

Katz, C.M., E.R. Maguire, and D. Choate. 2011. "A Cross-National Comparison of Gangs in the United States and Trinidad and Tobago". *International Criminal Justice Review* 21(3): 243–62.

Katz, C.M., and S. Schnebly. 2011. "Neighborhood Variation in Gang Member Concentrations". *Crime and Delinquency* 57(3): 377–407.

Katz, C.M., and V.J. Webb. 2003. *Police Response to Gangs: A Multi-Site Study*. Phoenix: National Institute of Justice.

———. 2006. *Policing Gangs in America*. New York: Cambridge University Press.

Katz, C.M., V.J. Webb, P.R. Gartin, and C.E. Marshall. 1997. "The Validity of Self-Reported Marijuana and Cocaine Use". *Journal of Criminal Justice* 25(1): 31–42.

Katz, C.M, V.J. Webb, and D.R. Schaefer. 2001. "An Assessment of the Impact of Quality-of-Life Policing on Crime and Disorder". *Justice Quarterly* 18(4): 825–76.

Klein, M.W. 1995. *The American Street Gang*. New York: Oxford University Press.

Leslie, G. 2010. "Confronting the Don: The Political Economy of Gang Violence in Jamaica". Small Arms Survey, Occasional Paper 26. Geneva, Switzerland: Graduate Institute of International and Development Studies.

Levy, H. 2012. *Youth Violence and Organised Crime in Jamaica: Causes and Counter-Measures*. Kingston: Institute of Criminal Justice and Security, University of the West Indies.

Maguire, E.R. 2012. "Preventing Gang Violence in the Caribbean: Problems and Prospects". Paper presented at the Symposium on Gangs and Gang Violence in the Caribbean, American University, Washington, DC, 17 February 2012.

Maguire, E.R., W. Wells, and C.M. Katz. 2011. "Measuring Community Risk and Protective Factors for Adolescent Problem Behaviors: Evidence from a Developing Nation". *Journal of Research in Crime and Delinquency* 48(4): 594–620.

Maxson, C.L., and M.W. Klein. 1990. "Street Gang Violence: Twice as Great or Half as Great?" In *Gangs in America*, edited by C.R. Huff, 71–100. Newbury Park, CA: Sage.

Meeks, J. 2009. "Caribbean Children's Involvement in Gangs". Paper presented at the Teleconference on Research Activities, University of the West Indies Open Campus, Kingston, 2009.

Mogensen, M. 2005. "Corner and Area Gangs of Inner-City Jamaica". Report for Children in Organised Arms Violence, Kingston.

Moncrieffe, D. 1998. "Gang Study: The Jamaican Crime Scene". Criminal Justice Research Unit, Ministry of National Security and Justice, Kingston.

Office of the Public Defender. 2013. "Interim Report to the Parliament", 29 April. http://www.mattathiasschwartz.com/document-the-public-defenders-interim-report-to-parliament-on-the-tivoli-gardens-incursion/.

Ohene, S., M. Ireland, and R. Blum. 2005. "The Clustering of Risk Behaviors among Caribbean Youth". *Maternal and Child Health Journal* 9(1): 91–100.

Pyrooz, D., A. Fox, C.M. Katz, and S. Decker. 2011. "Gang Organization, Offending and Victimization: A Cross National Analysis". In *Youth Gangs in International Perspective*, edited by F. Esbensen and C. Maxson, 85–105. New York: Springer.

Sampson, R., S. Raudenbush, and F. Earls. 1997. "Neighborhoods and Violent Crime: A Multi-Level Study of Collective Efficacy". *Science* 277: 918–24.

Simon, A. 2010a. "Police, Criminals 'Working Arm-in-Arm'". *Trinidad Express*, 12 September. http://www.trinidadexpress.com/news/police_criminals_working_arm-in-arm_-102713764.html.

———. 2010b. "The 'Killing Squad'". *Trinidad Express*, 12 September. http://www.trinidadexpress.com/news/The_killing_squad_-102713759.html.

Sinclair, G. 2004. "All Out Assault: 'Operation Kingfish' to Target Dons, Gangs". *Gleaner*, 20 October. http://jamaica-gleaner.com/gleaner/20041020/lead/lead1.html.

———. 2010. "'Kingfish' Targets a Dozen Macro Gangs". *Gleaner*, 26 October. http://www.jamaica-gleaner.com/gleaner/20041026/lead/lead1.html.

Skogan, W.G., S.M. Hartnett, N. Bump, and J. Dubois. 2008. *Evaluation of Ceasefire-Chicago*. Washington, DC: US Department of Justice, Office of Justice Programs, National Institute of Justice.

Spergel, I.A. 2007. *Reducing Youth Gang Violence: The Little Village Gang Project in Chicago*. Lanham, MD: AltaMira.

Spergel, I.A., and S.F. Grossman. 1997. "The Little Village Project: A Community Approach to the Gang Problem". *Social Work* 42: 456–70.

Spergel, I.A., K.W. Wa, and R. Sosa. 2006. "The Comprehensive, Community Wide Gang Program Model: Success and Failure". In *Studying Youth Gangs*, edited by J. Short and L. Hughes. 203–24. New York: AltaMira.

UNDP (United Nations Development Programme). 2012. "Caribbean Human Development Report 2012". New York: United Nations Development Programme.

USAID. 2006. "El Salvador Profile". *Central America and Mexico Gang Assessment*, April. Bulletin produced by the USAID Bureau for Latin America and the Caribbean Office of Regional Sustainable Development. http://pdf.usaid.gov/pdf_docs/PNADG834.pdf.

van Gemert, F. 2005. "Youth Groups and Gangs in Amsterdam: A Pretest of the Eurogang Expert Survey". In *European Street Gangs and Troublesome Youth Groups*, edited by S. Decker and F. Weerman, 147–68. New York: AltaMira.

Webb, V.J., and C.M. Katz. 2003. "Policing in an Era of Community Policing". In *Policing Gangs and Youth Violence*, edited by S.H. Decker, 17–52. Belmont, CA: Wadsworth.

Webb, V.J., C.M. Katz, and S.Decker. 2006. "Assessing the Validity of Self-Reports by Gang Members: Results from the Arrestee Drug-Abuse Monitoring Program". *Crime and Delinquency* 52(2): 232–52.

Webster, D.W., J. Whitehill, J. Vernick, and F. Curriero. 2012. "Effects of Baltimore's Safe Streets Program on Gun Violence: A Replication of Chicago's CeaseFire Program". *Journal of Urban Health* 90(1): 27–40.

Wells, W., C.M. Katz, and J. Kim. 2010. "Firearm Possession among Arrestees in Trinidad and Tobago". *Injury Prevention* 16: 337–42.

Wilks, R., N. Younger, S. McFarlane, D. Francis, and J. Van Den Broeck. 2007. "Jamaican Youth Risk and Resiliency Behaviour Survey 2006: Community-Based Survey of Risk and Resiliency Behaviours of 15–19 Year Olds". Kingston: University of the West Indies Press.

Wilson, J.M., and S. Chermak. 2011. "Community-Driven Violence Reduction Programs". *Criminology and Public Policy* 10(4): 993–1027.

Wortley, S. 2010. *The Jamaican National Crime Victimization Survey*. Report prepared for the Ministry of National Security, Jamaica. Toronto: University of Toronto.

1

The Emergence and Evolution of Organized Crime in Jamaica

New Challenges to Law Enforcement
and Society

ANTHONY HARRIOTT

O rganized crime is rightly receiving considerable attention among policy-makers and law enforcement officials. Foreign governments have forcefully brought the problem of organized crime into focus and caught the undivided attention of the Jamaican authorities via requests for the extradition of major drug traffickers, some of whom were named "drug lords" and "King Pins".[1] The international and hemispheric governance structures of the United Nations and the Organization of American States respectively have similarly given considerable attention to the issue of transnational organized crime. This is evident both from the array of international conventions that have been devised to control it and from the cooperative documents which Jamaica has been encouraged to sign.[2] Local business groups have highlighted the negative economic impact of the activities of organized crime networks, particularly extortion and protection rackets, and the influence of organized crime groups on employment practices and the quality of work outputs, especially in construction (*Sunday Gleaner*, 6 June 2010).[3] Tourism industry officials have focused their attention on the damage that has been done to the image of the country by the periodic violent clashes between organized crime groups and security forces, as well as by crime that victimizes foreigners, such as lottery fraud.[4] Whole urban communities experience the consequences of the dominant presence of organized crime groups in these communities. These groups may participate in the political administration of their host communities and help to secure these communities from predatory attacks by other groups. Crime groups may also, as a consequence of their reputation for violence, secure a range of material benefits for the community which its members may enjoy *simply by belonging* to the community. For example, the Jamaica Public Service Company estimates that prior to June 2010, only thirty of the households in the Kingston inner-city community of Tivoli Gardens, less than 1 per cent, actually paid their electricity bills.[5] Organized crime groups ensured that the remaining households retained "free" electricity. The community's reputation for violence and the known capabilities of its don(s) also protect the members of the community beyond its boundaries. Protection is not narrowly bounded by territory; it travels with (collective) reputation and demonstrated capabilities.

Given the present conditions, the people, particularly young adults, therefore seem to have an interest or rational stake in preserving this reputation and capacity for violence. There are, however, trade-offs and negative consequences for their freedom of political association, right to vote and protection under the law. They also risk their lives, the physical safety of their female children and recruitment of their male children. For example, in two major confrontations between Jamaican security forces and the Christopher Coke–led Presidential Click/Shower group, twenty-seven people were killed in 2001, and more than seventy were killed in 2010.[6] Organized crime has its victims and its beneficiaries. Many individuals occupy both roles, and the balance between victim and beneficiary may shift or be made to shift by the actions of the dons, the state and/or the people.

The more powerful countries of North America and Western Europe typically regard themselves both as victims of the trade in illegal commodities and services that are offered by transnational organized crime networks (TOCs) and as the protectors of a globally threatened moral order. While the realities are much more complex, TOCs do present multiple threats to those societies. The threats are financial, including the potential corruption of the international financial system by the transfer of drug profits to home countries. Money laundering is thus a central concern of these countries and responsible international regulatory agencies. The threats also include the actual and potential social harm caused by drug dependence and drug-related crimes. Spill-over violence from conflicts between competing drug-trafficking organizations, as is currently the case with the Mexican–American drug trade, is another serious threat. Furthermore, large Western nations perceive illegal migration to be straining their social services and threatening societal cohesion. Human trafficking, an activity that is associated with organized crime, is regarded as a serious border-breaching threat. Potential alliances between transnational organized crime networks and inter-national terrorist groups pose perhaps the most serious security threat (Shelley and Picarelli 2005; UNODC 2010).[7] Organized crime networks may also seek to profit from armed conflicts – especially internationalized conflicts such as those occurring in Afghanistan and Iraq which are run on large budgets and which offer opportunities to supply goods and services to the parties in conflict and to extort less powerful third-party actors, such as non-governmental organizations that provide assistance to war victims (Green and Ward 2009). These aspects highlight the transnational character of organized crime, the security threats that it may present and the possible implications for the relations between their host countries and the countries to which they supply their goods and services.[8]

It must be expected that affected countries will treat these matters seriously. With globalization and an end to the Cold War, crime is becoming a more cen-tral issue in the relations between countries. In this regard, the insistence of the Jamaican government on procedural rectitude in the extradition of Christo-pher Coke, who has been indicted by American law enforcement authorities on drug- and gun-trafficking charges and who is the reputed leader of one of the main organized crime groups in Kingston, did, for example, considerably strain the relations between the United States and Jamaica (see "Government May Fall", *Daily Observer*, 29 March 2010).[9] Much research on organized crime is therefore focused on the transnational dimensions of this phenomenon.

More recent assessments of the national crime problem have suggested that the organized crime and gang problems are more central to its understanding. Jamaica has experienced very high levels of ordinary criminal violence and extraordinarily high rates of homicide for almost three decades (Harriott 2003). A major contributor to the homicide rate and violent crime more generally is gang activity, including the activities of organized crime networks. According to esti-mates produced by the Jamaica Constabulary Force, perhaps as much as 80 per cent of all homicides that occurred in 2008 were "gang-related".[10] The organized crime groups undoubtedly contribute to this figure both directly and indirectly.

Direct everyday violence by these groups usually arises from internal as well as inter-gang conflicts that are associated with their income-generating activities. The "lotto scam" or advanced-fee fraud, for example, has reportedly accounted for some 150 to 200 murders in the parish of St James (see "Lottery Scam Caus-ing Many of Montego Bay's Murders," *Gleaner*, 3 September 2009). There are also the occasional armed encounters with the police and military. When these occur as battles between the garrison communities and security forces, the loss of life and (depending on the outcomes) the impact on the population's sense of insecurity may be great.

Indirect violence includes modelling the violence-for-profit activities of organized crime, such as the successful extortion rackets. It also includes motivating the violence of young men who wish to gain violent criminal reputations as credentials for getting into these rackets. Organized crime networks may also facilitate the violence of street gangs. For example, gun trafficking for commercial purposes provides common street gangs with greater access to the means of violence.

As is the case in several developed and developing countries where there are high rates of immigration and emigration, in Jamaica there is concern regarding external sources of serious crime problems. The deportees, or forcibly returned emigrants, for example, are often depicted as the embodiment of the international criminal linkages.[11] The growth of international drug and gun markets has been a major facilitator of emerging organized crime networks, but their development is deeply rooted in Jamaica's internal dynamics. In this chapter, the analysis of organized crime is thus more internally directed.

This chapter elaborates aspects of the broad outlines of the evolution of organized crime in Jamaica from recently formed street gangs that cohere around conflicts to maturity as entrepreneurially oriented groups and identifies the factors that account for its consolidation in Jamaican society. The current challenges that organized crime present to society are also discussed. The chapter draws on and extends recent work by the author which emphasizes the facilitating role of corrupt and, at times, violent politics in the rise of organized crime.[12]

The rise of organized crime represents a particularly problematic stage in the long evolution of the crime problem in Jamaica.[13] The evolution of criminal gangs into organized crime networks is a story about shifts in social and political power at the national and community levels. Organized crime groups have been able to exploit these shifts since organized crime itself represents power and has become a significant power holder and actor in the Jamaican polity and society.[14] Some groups have the power to dominate whole communities and many aspects of the lives of the people who reside in them. They invariably do so as personalistic authoritarian systems of local political administration (rule by dons). Understanding the evolution of the organized crime problem involves tracking its accumulation of power, its location in the illegal opportunity structure and how people begin not only to tolerate but also socially facilitate and accept this form of crime and its authoritative (devolved and or direct) insertion into the administration of their communities. Analysing its evolution means understanding organized crime as a product of both elite (principally political elite) and mass, or citizen, facilitation.

Behind the influence and power of organized crime in Jamaican society are changes in the illegal opportunity structures at the global and local levels, particularly chances to participate in international drug markets at the high end of the distribution chain and maintain local demand for protection. Organized crime groups can realize these opportunities due in large measure to (1) a permissive and indeed facilitative politics; (2) social facilitation, that is, a supportive subcultural normative order that is anchored in marginalization and alienation, and (3) weak law enforcement.

The Tivoli Gardens events of 2001 and 2010, a similar battle with the security forces in the community of Canterbury in Montego Bay in 2003, and the occasional "wars" between the main organized crime groups have openly revealed the extensive nature of the organized crime problem that Jamaica faces. These events exposed the breadth of their influence and power; their ability to deliver violence, often with impunity, and to engage in armed confrontations with the security forces; the extent to which they dominate their host communities; and their imbricated connections with the political parties and business and professional upper-world partners. The events that mark the shifts in power and influence of the organized crime groups (attempts by the political administration to shield them from justice and the quantum of funds involved in contracts awarded to them by state agencies) also signify the progressive movement or migration of street criminality from the margins of society into its mainstream. This is the significance of the development of organized crime.

The level of impunity enjoyed by these groups may be taken as evidence of fundamental weaknesses in the criminal justice system and chronic corruption in the society. Some of the leaders of the major organized groups are occasionally arrested, killed or extradited, but these events tend to confirm rather than disprove the point as arrests rarely result in convictions and may precipitate community protests. Killings may reflect the frustrations of the police and lack of confidence in the system, and extraditions are usually the outcomes of the investigative actions and demands of foreign law enforcement rather than proactive efforts by Jamaican officials.

The primary goal of this chapter is to describe the development of organized crime and analyse its meaning for the security of the country. The proffered explanation of this process remains incomplete. It emphasizes, for example, the changes in the illegal opportunity structure to which organized crime responds – including the opportunities created by corrupt politics. However, the problems associated with the conventional opportunity structure (its limitedness and issues of bias and unequal access) precede (in time order and the logic of the causal processes) the growth of this scale of illegal opportunities. While the illegal opportunity structure partly explains not just organized crime but also a broader class of crimes, the main thrust of this analysis is restricted to the more direct and proximate factors and processes that are associated narrowly with the growth of organized crime.

The rest of the chapter is organized as follows. First, the challenges that Jamaica now faces from organized crime are described and contextualized. Secondly, its evolution is tracked, its current character is described and the bases of its resilience are identified.

Character of the Problem

Within Jamaican society and its law enforcement institutions, there is considerable definitional confusion regarding organized crime. Legal definitions tend to emphasize the associational and activity requirements, that is, at least three persons must be involved in a criminal enterprise.[15] This associational characteristic is profoundly consequential as, consistent with the United Nations Convention on Transnational Organized Crime, some jurisdictions define membership in such organizations as a crime. Association is often overemphasized and taken as a sufficient condition for characterizing a group as organized crime. This is a rather dangerous and problematic notion that lends itself to abuses of power and tends to collide with fundamental human rights. Moreover, legal definitions and their focus on association miss much that is conceptually useful and thus lack analytic power. Consequently, and perhaps contrary to the purpose of criminalizing association, the law enforcement and perhaps even security challenges that organized crime presents are minimized.

The conceptual challenge is distinguishing organized crime networks from other less threatening types of criminal groups. A group of pickpockets, for example, would perhaps satisfy the associational requirement, but they could hardly be considered an organized crime network and a major challenge for law enforcement and danger to national security. Organized crime is usually best understood in terms of its activities, which include drug- and gun-trafficking, extortion and protection rackets, construction rackets and money laundering – that is, the trade in illegal commodities and services. In its broadest sense, organized crime is characterized by enterprise activity, the use of violence (actual or threatened) and corruption as typical means, and exploitable relationships with the upper-world. Organization and/or association are merely resulting characteristics of such activities. These are typical features; they are not all regarded as necessary conditions of organized crime groups.

Organized crime networks tend to be dynamic and adaptive. Some enterprise groups may not have the capacity to engage effectively in violence or even to protect themselves. By their activities, however, they create the demand for protection and may be able to outsource this service. Some groups may thus employ violence without permanently retaining gunmen and being attached to territory, which gives their leaders the advantage of being able to present themselves as "businessmen" with no visible attachments to the underworld. These variations and degrees of flexibility may cause some confusion in categorization.

There is a more restrictive definition of organized crime groups, of which the Mafia is the archetype. This is the idea of organized crime networks as violent entrepreneurs. According to the Italian sociologist Diego Gambetta (1993), Mafia is a specific economic enterprise – "an industry that produces and sells private protection". In his book *The Sicilian Mafia: The Business of Private Protection*, Gambetta illustrates this point with an example from the meat markets in Palermo. In the official meat market, taxation is considered high. There is consequently an informal market in meats. This informal market operates in conditions of low trust, and buyers and sellers often look for opportunities to cheat each other. The informal market therefore needs a third party that protects buyers and sellers. Gambetta convincingly argues that the Mafia arose out of this demand for protection. This brand of organized crime may therefore be seen as a special type of enterprise and *as providing a service, which, under certain conditions, people willingly accept.*

This definition provides considerable analytic power but excludes closely related phenomena which may be considered other varieties of organized crime. It may be argued that Gambetta overemphasizes violent entrepreneurship as a defining feature of organized crime and in so doing, equates organized crime with Mafia. Conflating both would, for example, foreclose any consideration for classification as organized crime those networks of criminals who are able to use their bureaucratic and political positional power to engage in large-scale enterprise crimes and who rely more on corruption than violence. If the broader definition is accepted, we may be more open to identifying different types of organized crime and thus regard Gambetta's definition as identifying the violent entrepreneur, or what has become known as Mafia, as a special type of organized crime. Though other types of organized crime groups should be considered and analysed, this chapter focuses primarily on the rise of the violent entrepreneur.

Jamaica is a low-trust society. Interpersonal trust is somewhat low, and trust in government and the main institutions of the state is even lower (Powell 2007, 24–27).[16] There is a large informal economy. For example, there is an open and thriving market in meats that are supplied by illegal abattoirs where stolen cattle are slaughtered. Providing protection for transactions in the informal economy is not, however, how organized crime initially developed in Jamaica since the informal economy was a later development. Rather, organized crime arose from the supplying of international markets with illicit drugs and responding to the demand for violence within the political system. Thus, the demand for violence developed independently of the domestic illegal commodities sector. Both drug-trafficking and political violence co-occurred over an extended period. Crime groups that participated in both kinds of activities were able to trade in drugs as well as protect this activity. Furthermore, both types of activity added new aspects to the illegal opportunity structure. First, selling illicit drugs internationally broadened the scale of material wealth that crime group members could achieve. Second, involvement in politics favourably altered risk-reward ratios by affording crime groups the occasional opportunity to provide political support and cover by using violence and gaining ongoing access to wide networks involving party-affiliated lawyers and police officers, as well as access to civil servants and private contractors who could be exploited. With political sponsorship, considerable wealth could be corruptly extracted from the state at very low risk – especially if the criminally acquired capital from the drug trade was used to establish front firms in construction, trucking and other services that are usually contracted by state agencies. The street gangs that operated in the most contested areas of Kingston were politically mobilized, and in this context they sought to leverage their increased value within the political system to access the resources of the state on a larger scale. The corresponding supply of protection was a response to the demand for violence within the political system; this was extended to the protection of illegal, informal and legitimate businesses sometime later.[17] Historical differences aside, the general point that we may take away from Gambetta is that protection as a violence-related service is at the centre of the criminal enterprise that we call organized crime. This is a definition that highlights its activity and methods. Without discounting these aspects, I also wish to emphasize the relations that make these activities realizable and enduringly successful – at least until now.

If it is accepted that protection is the distinguishing feature of organized crime, then involvement in enterprise crimes such as drug trafficking and trade in other illicit commodities is not sufficient to warrant classifying a group as an organized crime network. Some groups are able to engage in the trade of illicit commodities, such as drugs and guns, and are also able to protect these activities. Other drug-trafficking organizations (DTOs) may seek protection from violent, usually community-based entrepreneurs who are able to provide this service. Some of the Jamaican North Coast DTOs, for example, did not have the capacity to protect their drug-trafficking operations. An outcome of this is that some may have been partially taken over by more powerful organized crime groups. Weak DTOs, or those that are not well protected politically and which do not have a developed infrastructure for the disciplined delivery of violence, are even extorted, meaning, in this case, that they are "taxed" without receiving any protection from the group that levies the "tax". Thus, there is a powerful impetus for DTOs to develop the capacity for violent self-protection. They achieve this through community involvement and the sponsorship of street gangs and/or by corrupting the police force.

An examination of the activities of organized crime networks reveals that much of the high-end or high-yield enterprise crimes are made possible by criminally exploitable relationships that reach beyond the underworld in different directions, but especially to politicians and senior officials in the state agencies which engage in housing and road construction and other activities that may present income-generating and power-enhancing opportunities for crime groups. These relationships enable criminals to defraud the state of billions of dollars. Garnering immunity is also made possible through direct relationships with corrupt police officers, other law enforcement officials and powerful agents within the political system. The garrison as a safe haven is a special expression of this relationship. Organized crime networks are able to reach into the mainstream of society and its centres of power via these relationships. This feature distinguishes organized crime and highlights why it presents a political danger in Jamaica and elsewhere in the region where the state is weak (as in Guyana, and Haiti without the presence of the United Nations).

The rise of organized crime may be considered one of the important developments in the security situation in Jamaica. It presents the greatest challenge since the intense political violence of the 1980s strained the existing political arrangements and tested national commitment to a system of free and fair elections as a method of changing political administrations. It presents a special challenge for law enforcement because its entrepreneurial character tends to stimulate a crime contagion, internationalization, crime innovation, corruption of law enforcement and a generation of considerable violence. The death toll from organized crime activities has certainly been great. It is, for example, estimated that the death toll from a single racket (the "lotto scam") in a single city (Montego Bay) in a single year was approximately two hundred.[18] This death toll was the outcome of the violent settlement of conflicts over the proceeds from these crimes and for the bits of information on prospective victims that are used to gain their confidence and thereby make the racket a success. Therefore, much of the violence was directed at those individuals who were directly involved in the racket. Much of the everyday lethal violence that is generated by the organized crime groupings is self-consuming or directed at other similar groups.

The homicide rate may be expected to increase with successive demonstrations of immunity to law enforcement efforts. The conviction rates for even the most serious violent crimes are low. For murder, it is less than 8 per cent.[19] The high degree of immunity to convictions enjoyed by street gangs and organized crime networks can be explained in part by their mutual code of silence and other aspects of the subculture of violence. However, the power these groups wield in their communities and their influence over political parties and law enforcement also contribute greatly to this outcome. The Christopher Coke extradition case encapsulates this new power reality. In this instance, the power and influence of organized crime were manifested in the delay in approving the extradition order. Apprehending Christopher Coke in his fortified home community of Tivoli Gardens led not only to reputational and economic loss, but also to the loss of lives. This destructiveness serves as a stark expression of the power of organized crime and the intricately woven web of relationships involving dons, politicians, contractors, state bureaucrats, party lawyers, party-affiliated police officers and other mediating agents who may be called the crime-politics nexus.

Conditions that Sustain Organized Crime

The conditions that gave rise to organized crime may be somewhat different from the conditions that are sustaining it. It is a fallacy to think that organized crime networks will be "dismantled" and dissipated if the concrete conditions that gave rise to their existence are minimized or removed (unless these conditions remain unchanged). For example, the demand for a particular illicit good, such as ganja and for a particular service such as politically directed violence may have been originating stimuli. As the demand for these specific goods and services softened, the more capable organized crime groupings shifted to other illicit goods and services that were in demand (locally and globally). These new opportunities forced the more capable criminal enterprises to make adaptations and to become more complex organizationally. Thus the shift from ganja trafficking to cocaine trafficking would have had this effect on the more successful groups. There is change and continuity. Change is evident in the specific activities such as shifting between drug trafficking, lotto rackets and protection rackets, and continuities are revealed in the forces and conditions that persist such as the broadening illicit opportunity structure. Similarly, the sources and sites of the demand for these services may change but the demand for them persists. For an understanding of its sustaining conditions, we must therefore examine organized crime historically, that is, while it is in motion. The changes that mark its dynamism and adaptability are therefore highlighted (as a method of isolating the factors that sustain its existence).

The most powerful and enduring organized crime groups are territorial and are located in the areas of high spatial concentration of violent crime, that is, they are centrally located in the criminal opportunity structure. This spatial location in the opportunity structure is what sustains them in time. By criminal opportunity structure is meant the set of facilitating (and inhibiting) conditions for crime (Clarke 1995). These facilitating conditions are local and national. Taken together, these conditions include expanding networks of exploitable relationships that extend into the state system at both local government and national state levels as well as related sets of relationships that reduce the impediments to organized crime and provide these groups near immunity from (local) law enforcement.

Some of the markers of the evolution of Jamaican organized crime are (1) changes in its activities (the types of goods and services that it supplies), which may be based on changes in the external and internal demand for illicit goods and services, especially illicit drugs and protection; (2) changes in transnational supply chains and transportation routes; (3) the responses of law enforcement; (4) shifts in the types and character of the main relationships which serve to broaden opportunities for legal and illegal income-generating and income-laundering activity and which enhance or diminish its power; (5) development of the infrastructure that allows it to realize these opportunities, including the infrastructure for the delivery of violence and the use of corruption; and (6) changes in how it is viewed by the communities in which it operates and by the general population, that is, the extent and basis of its acceptance in society and authority in the communities and more generally the degree of social and political facilitation. (The latter has been extensively discussed elsewhere [Harriott 2008b] and is not emphasized here.) The groups that best adapt to these changes in the environment are the ones that endure. Discussion of this issue is largely limited to how it is related to other factors that account for and mark the development of organized crime, such as its infrastructure for the delivery of violence.

Growth and accessibility of major drug markets stimulated and sustained the development of the organized crime groups. During the 1970s and 1980s, Jamaica was a leading exporter of cannabis, and it still exports significant quantities of this drug (Harriott 2008b, 38, table 1.1). Exports peaked in the late 1980s when Jamaican traffickers entered the American retail market on a large scale. During this period, the value of ganja exports may have been as high as US$2 billion (Griffith and Munroe 1997). This was the heyday of the posses. Those who were best positioned to establish cross-border contacts, and who were somewhat organized and most audacious, became the pioneers in moving up the distribution chain and violently entering the American retail market. For example, in the case of one of the most successful organized crime groups, the founder and future leader was the one who took the risk of boarding a ganja flight to the United States. This gave him and his group direct connections in the American market that were needed to move beyond simply guarding and loading ganja flights and to enter the trafficking enterprise. Other pioneers were fugitives in Jamaica who found ways of fleeing to the Bahamas. From the Bahamas, they discovered ways of moving drugs to the United States. Each group has a different story. What is clear is that drug involvement led to internationalization, greater organizational complexity, intensity of intra-group contact and cohesion, increased use of violence, continuous access to weapons and greater autonomy or independence of the political parties to which many are affiliated. The groups that became more powerful as a result of these processes are better able to survive the pressures from law enforcement.

Politics, a critical facilitator of the rise of organized crime in Jamaica, remains an important factor in sustaining it. Political participation was vital for gang cohesion in the earlier stages of gang development in the 1960s and 1970s and remains an important factor in sustaining it. The party political conflict of the 1970s was internationalized and given added intensity by Cold War geopolitics. Strained relations between the then-Democratic Socialist administration and the American government meant that law enforcement cooperation between the two countries was weakened. As is the case in Venezuela today, this lowered the risks associated with drug entrepreneurship.

Jamaican law enforcement was also weakened by the intense political conflict and polarization in the country at the time. Crime was even more politicized than it was in the 1960s and so, too, was policing criminal activity (Lacy 1977). This had a profoundly corrupting influence on the police force and afforded the emergent DTOs and politically affiliated organized crime networks considerable freedom of action. The police force is now considerably less influenced by this type of political corruption, but organized crime has its independent corruption means of purchasing immunity from law enforcement.

Political conflict had other consequences as well. It turned violent in the middle and late 1970s and stimulated the demand for political-community protection from organized crime groups. The many urban communities that could be identified by their party affiliation, particularly those in the western section of Kingston, suffered considerable destruction of their housing stock, closure of schools and displacement of people. Politicized gang warfare caused much desolation in Kingston and resulted in the creation of an area called "No Man's Land". In this context, the gangs were accepted as community protectors. Since then, the continuing gang wars, the constant threat of ordinary predatory criminality and under-policing explain the sustained demand for community protection and thus remain factors sustaining organized crime.

This relationship with the community provides reinforcement for the activity (the legal and seemingly social, as well as the outwardly directed illegal and predatory) of the organized crime groups, gives them political leverage and immunizes them against law enforcement. This operates on two levels: (1) as social facilitation and (2) as active support via the involvement of ordinary citizens in the protective systems of the criminal groups.[20] Relationships with political parties also sustain them by providing income-earning opportunities through state contracts and, with this, the power and influence to determine which community members are employed on these projects. These relationships also facilitate access to a wide network of people across the country and in state institutions, and contact with other gangs of similar political affiliation.

A progressive privatization of protection has also favoured the rise and maintenance of organized crime, particularly the violent entrepreneurs. The sharp increase in the number of private security firms and the number of their employees, especially in the 1980s, points to the growing privatization of protection. This growth continued prior to the rise of organized crime as a supplier of protection via protection rackets. In its broadest sense, the privatization of protection is also evidenced by the rise of community protectors who provide protection against other gangs and political incursions from external competitors. This was later extended to internal crime control, or crime regulation, such as determining who may be robbed and when and where. Such regulation of crime by the more powerful criminal networks is not evidence of their social character but rather is a logical accompaniment to protection rackets.

A decline in legal suppliers of protection, namely private security firms, adds to the continued demand for protection from organized crime groups. Private security firms have declined from some two hundred employing approximately 20,000 guards in 1987 (Stone 1988, 38) to 170 with 15,778 guards in 2009.[21] During this period (1987 to 2009), there was an inverse relationship between the number of private security guards and the frequency counts for murder. The decline of the former had nothing to do with the changes in the demand for protection. This decline may thus be partly explained by the protracted stagnation in the Jamaican economy and its contraction in periods of international economic and financial crises, conditions which would likely reduce opportunities for private security companies even if violent crime rates and feelings of insecurity continue to increase. Some displacement of these legal providers of protection may also be occurring due to the growth of protection rackets, or the supply of protection by criminal monopolist providers.

Thus, opportunities in the illegal protection business seem to be growing. A brief vignette may sufficiently illustrate this point. In various types of business places, it is not uncommon to see notice boards with cheques that have not been honoured posted on them. This practice may be taken to mean that the owners of these businesses often have no other recourse than public shaming. Clearly, this is evidence of a demand for protection. A group with a widely known reputation for violence could guarantee that all or at least most transactions are honoured. Indeed, there is a general demand for services in the collection of bad debts. In micro-financing, however, bad debts are almost unknown. This is not just attributable to the supposedly greater virtue of the urban poor who are the beneficiaries of these loans. The dons or violent entrepreneurs are supplying transaction-guaranteeing services to some of these loan companies. If the demand for protection is not spontaneously created, the organized crime groupings may always intervene to create it. This may be done by orchestrating robberies and other threatening activities that make protection services perpetually necessary.

This changing and perhaps increasing demand for illicit goods and services, especially protection services, makes organized crime very resilient and *projects it into the mainstream of society*. The collection of bad debts for legitimate firms illustrates this capacity. Protection and extortion rackets provide a steady income stream at low risk. With protection rackets, territory becomes even more important, and larger numbers of individuals are directly involved at the community level. Jobs, such as elaborate information-gathering operations, are selectively offered to unemployed young men. Just being at a location and in a position to hear the everyday conversations of fellow residents may become a job. The resulting efficiency and certainty of punishment in the event of attempted resistance increases the reputation of enforcer groups. These groups thus become more entrenched and more powerful in communities. Much of this increased demand for protection is the outcome of a weakened criminal justice system and ineffective policing.

The Weakness of the Criminal Justice System

Low conviction rates for crimes such as murder, extortion and defrauding the state – crimes that are generally associated with the organized crime networks – reveal the weakness of the criminal justice system. As noted earlier, the conviction rate for murder has been dramatically declining and is estimated to be between 5 and 8 per cent.[22] Arrests for extortion are so few that they are not even reported in the official crime statistics that are submitted by the police.[23] The justice system even experiences great difficulty in convicting powerful violators of the criminal law. Prior to the state of emergency in 2010, some of the leaders of the more powerful organized crime groups operated openly yet were, and still are, not wanted for any crimes in Jamaica.

Extradition may seem to be a solution to the conviction rate problem, but this is a short-term solution for particular cases. As a solution to the general problem of the immunity enjoyed by powerful drug traffickers and leaders of organized crime networks, extradition may do considerable long-term harm to the Jamaican criminal justice system. The recent extradition of Christopher Coke serves as a prime example of this danger. After armed attacks on fourteen police stations, two of which were completely destroyed, two days of open armed battle with the military, which resulted in some seventy-three deaths, including one soldier and several persons injured by gunfire, the man who was primarily responsible for much of this destruction was sent abroad without having to face a single charge in a Jamaican court.[24]

If the further weakening of the system is to be avoided, these extraditions must be properly managed by the Jamaican authorities. With extradition, a strong American system substitutes for a weak Jamaican system. Over time as dependency develops, the strong system is likely to become stronger and the weak system weaker. The Jamaican population then loses even more confidence in its own system as the extradition of the more powerful criminals reinforces the idea that it is exceedingly difficult to convict powerful criminals in the Jamaican courts. There is consequently even less active support for the system from the population. In these conditions, the use of advanced weapons systems and protective gear including face masks only reveals the deep weaknesses of the system. A system that cannot effectively protect the public will be forced to increasingly protect itself and provide even less security service to the population.

The above is a discussion of selected factors that account for the development of organized crime and their interaction as elements of a process. Not yet discussed are other factors that help to sustain organized crime and to further root it in the society. These factors are discussed below as indicators if its maturing and growth processes.

The Maturation of Organized Crime

The explained developmental conditions have nurtured organized crime and increased its political, economic and cultural power.[25] The environment has not remained static and neither has organized crime. Organized crime networks and groups are now more active and powerful, more entrenched and perhaps more tolerated and even supported by the people and some of their political representatives than they have ever been. Organized crime has matured as a phenomenon in Jamaican society.

Some markers of the evolution and maturation of organized crime units include age, adaptability, resilience, product and services specialization, and the development of a supporting infrastructure (the organizational dimension); diversity of the illegal opportunity structure (the activity dimension); penetration of the formal economy and main institutions of the state (the relationships dimension); autonomy, freedom of action, immunity from law enforcement and involvement in the governance of communities (the power dimension); and the prevalence of supporting ideas that seek to justify its activities and celebrate its leaders (the authority/legitimacy dimension). Space does not permit a full discussion of all of these aspects. The order in which they are discussed below is thus slightly different from the order in which they are listed above.

Age and Maturity

Age is usually associated with maturity. Some organized networks have their origins in the 1950s and 1960s, including some that have emerged in Montego

Bay. This should not be taken to mean that in the 1950s and 1960s they existed as organized crime but rather that they have a line of continuity to street gangs that existed in that period. Continuity is manifested in the name and/or location of the groups, in elements of their membership and in family "ownership". An example of this is the Spanglers, a family firm which has its origin as a politically affiliated street gang that emerged in the 1950s (Sives 2010; Harriott 2008b). The rapid growth of urbanization in the 1950s and 1960s swelled the slums of Kingston and Montego Bay. The attempts at industrialization and the high growth rates of the period attracted rural dwellers to the cities, but the cities could not absorb them. As Colin Clarke (2006, 161) notes, in 1960 "one-third of the city's population were living in dilapidated accommodation, the greater proportion in West Kingston". These conditions led to intense political competition to integrate the slums into the polity and to create safe seats. The competition often turned violent. Competitive street politics increased the political value of these gangs. They could help to win and politically monopolize territory.

Some of the more powerful gangs have thus survived amidst a variety of different conditions including periods of intense violent political conflict; periods when the party with which they were affiliated formed the political administration of the country and periods when they were out of power and in opposition; periods of great pressure from law enforcement such as formally issued states of emergency (as in 1966, 1976 and 2010) when there were lengthy special operations and pressures from foreign law enforcement agencies; and long periods of gang warfare. While matured organized crime networks have at times lost their leaders, they have been able to transfer leadership more or less successfully. In some cases, periods of external and internal pressures may have actually increased group cohesion and community support for these groups, especially when law enforcement responses to organized crime violence failed to have bipartisan support. Having survived these moments, some groups have become stronger, more adaptable and more resilient to future pressures.

Adaptability, Resilience and Opportunity Structure

Organized crime groups have exhibited considerable adaptability and resilience (see table 1.1). Generally, adaptability signifies responsiveness to the environment in ways that increase fitness in order to survive and indeed to flourish. Specifically, adaptability involves responding to and creating new illegal and legal opportunities. The survival of organized crime groups is dependent on

Table 1.1. The evolution of organized crime

1950–60s	Ordinary territorial street gangs
1960–70s	Gangs supply political protection and receive patronage as party-affiliated and party-subordinated thugs. The garrison community emerges as a politically protected safe haven for party-affiliated criminals.
1970s	Increase in the number of garrison communities and a deepening of the crime-politics nexus in context of ideological polarization and political violence. The gangs are fully co-opted by the parties.
1970s	Ganja exportation – as drug-trafficking networks. This may have peaked in the 1980s.
1980–90s	Violent penetration of drug retail markets; independent transnational operations
2000	Maturity. Its indicators include: • Differentiation among OC groups more evident (violent entrepreneurs, DTOs and DTO racketeers) • The conduct in formal terms of legitimate business with state agencies and private sector firms • Geographic monopolies as administered territories; a shift in power with greater autonomy of parties, control of an independent infrastructure for violence and the penetration of the state and political system • Growth of criminal firms as monopolies led by "super-dons" that seek to subordinate other groups ("one order"); some become national in their operations and influence • The successful cultivation of social support in their host communities and greater cultural influence as expressed in popular music • Immunity from local law enforcement (untouchable "super dons") • Reverse co-option of elements in the political parties/administration (indicating the shift in power since the 1960s and 1970s when the street gangs were fully co-opted by the parties)

Source: Compiled by the author from information in this chapter.

how the illegal opportunity structure develops and how access to these opportunities is regulated. Participation in corrupt networks which extend into the mainstream of society, including the political parties, the state bureaucracy and the business elites, increases criminally exploitable opportunities and lowers the risk of being detected by law enforcement. Corrupt networks make rackets possible – low-risk construction rackets that exploit state-created opportunities, for example. Low-risk rackets nevertheless provide a bridge to the formal economy. The more mature groups now have several front companies which operate as formal businesses. State control agents may choose or be induced to turn a blind eye to these activities.

Adaptability is also dependent on the degree of flexibility within these criminal organizations. Flexibility aids their ability to avert and manage challenges. For example, allowing senior members greater independence and freedom to establish franchise operations and to operate side rackets may prevent leadership challenges. This flexibility may create its own risks such as a splintering of the group (as opposed to flexible associations), but these are merely tests of the leadership skills of the dons. In order to survive, they must maintain group cohesion and meet community expectations.

The most resilient networks are

- Transnational and engaged in multi-country operations; increased difficulties in one country results in a shift in operations to another. Thus, the suppression of Jamaican organized crime networks in the United States in the 1990s may have resulted in greater activity in Canada and the United Kingdom.
- Those with diverse income streams. Disruptions in their drug-trafficking operation simply motivate the development of more reliable sources of funds at home, such as extortion and protection rackets.
- Those with legitimate businesses that are supported by state contracts.
- Family businesses (reduces the risk of implosion when a leader is removed).
- Those that are territorial and community embedded and responsive to the expectations of the community. They are sustained by a structured support system and/or a more generalized and diffused social facilitation, including a code of silence.[26]
- Politically affiliated and valuable to the parties for maintaining local one-party monopolies at the constituency and national levels.

Specialization and the Development of Infrastructure

Greater product and services specialization among organized crime groups and networks is an indicator of the growth and increasing complexity of the underground sector. This suggests that a broader range of illegal opportunities now exists. The ability to exploit these opportunities requires dedication to the development of the specific competences some of which are not particularly or exclusively criminal craft. Criminal groups and individuals alike try to seize whatever opportunities are presented. Thus, while larger groups have tended to become involved in multiple income-generating activities, individuals have tended to become involved in multiple occupations, or rather hustling. For example, the extortionist also regulates and takes a proportion of the income from robberies and may be involved in drug trafficking and solid waste rackets. However, a tendency toward specialization in a particular enterprise has become more evident. The specialization in "lotto rackets" is one example of this development. This racket requires skills that are akin to those that are required to operate a legitimate call centre.

Although multiple income streams and multiple sites of operation may contribute to resilience, the consolidation of each racket may require specific competences and the construction of supportive networks which are specific to the particular racket. Otherwise, a multiplicity of activities and sites may increase vulnerability to competition and to law enforcement intervention. The drug-trafficking business, for example, requires different competences than those that are needed in extortion, although linkages between rackets such as drug and gun trafficking may be exploited for greater criminal efficiency. Similarly, the protection of an exporting firm may open opportunities to get into the drug trade that did not previously exist.

Specialization may be viewed as a strategy for managing risk, or it may simply have this effect. A group that specializes in extortion and protection may avoid the risk of exposure to international law enforcement that would come from involvement in drug trafficking. In this context, to remain in multiple activities requires even more complex operations and organizations or networks. Some groups now appear to have this capacity. "Shower" is one such transnational network which has at its hub the very hierarchical and highly disciplined Presidential Click. In order to sustain this capacity, they must invest in infrastructure that supports their activity.

The more mature organized crime groups, particularly the territorially based ones, have succeeded in developing elaborate infrastructures for sustaining their operations. Infrastructure implies the means that are available for supporting the activities of organized crime and the systems for delivering these means. As organized crime networks rely mainly on violence and corruption, the infrastructure is designed to support these methods. The infrastructure for violence includes well-positioned and group-controlled armouries, people with the required range of competences for using and moving these weapons, a reliable supply of ammunition which may involve constructing a long supply line from abroad, safe houses in the cities and countryside, and counterintelligence systems that reach into law enforcement and the political decision-making centres.

Increased illegal opportunities and changes in the opportunity structure require varied competences and with this greater specialization. Extortion and protection require a "brand". That brand may be the name of a criminal enterprise that is successful at these rackets or has a reputation for the effective delivery of violence. Thus, for example, as the demand for violence increases, efficiency and effectiveness demand that those who seek to supply violence must seek to develop an infrastructure for the delivery of violence. Protection rackets require an enforcement capability that includes not just operational but also intelligence capability, or a system for gaining speedy access to reliable information on the activities of those who might violate the system of protection. Similarly, if an organized crime network provides protection services (in the broader sense of violence-related services) to the political party with which it is affiliated, such a network must have the capability to intimidate political opponents. If the group is nestled in a garrison, the garrison must be managed and its borders constantly patrolled and defended against incursions by security forces and by political and criminal competitors. These demands spur the development of greater violence-related capabilities. An indicator of the centrality of violence in their businesses and very existence is the level of investments that they make in the development of this infrastructure.

The western section of Kingston has been a high-violence zone for some four decades. The available evidence suggests that over these four decades, there has been a progression in the intensity of this violence and capabilities of the groups that operate in this area. The two major battles between the Shower and security forces in 2001 and 2010 allow for an estimation of the infrastructure of this group. The first was a three-day battle resulting in the deaths of twenty-seven people. The second also lasted for three days and resulted in as many as seventy-three deaths. The Shower group and others have been able to fight extensive positional battles against the police and military. The scale of the confrontations has become progressively greater. In the case of the 2010 events, the available physical evidence and the official reports seem to suggest that there were hundreds of combatants on both sides. Reflecting its greater national reach, in 2010 the Shower mobilized gunmen from several other parishes to fight with it in Tivoli Gardens. The record of deaths in the armed confrontation includes young men from eight parishes; only 32 per cent of those killed were residents of Tivoli Gardens.[27] The increased capability and broader geographic reach was also evident in the assaults on some fourteen police stations in Kingston. The burning of one of these police stations (Hannah Town) appeared to symbolize a weak state on one hand, and, on the other hand, a willingness by the Shower to use their significant capabilities against the state.

The armed confrontations between the Shower and security forces in 2010 revealed that this organized crime group was well armed. Between 23 May 2010 and 8 June 2010, some eighty-seven firearms (forty-five rifles), fourteen thousand bullets and eighty-three explosive devices, including nineteen grenades and thirty-two improvised explosive devices (IEDs), were seized by the security force (see *Sunday Gleaner*, 6 June 2010, A6, and the *Gleaner*, 6 September 2010). Given its organizational level and experience, the group's actual number of weapons and its supporting forces in the neighbouring communities may be taken as a multiple of what was found.

The results of the violence included a death toll of more than seventy civilians including the Shower gunmen.[28] In addition, one soldier was killed in the battle zone, and two police officers were killed in what may have been secondary encounters outside of the battle zone. Several soldiers and six police officers were injured by gunfire. Two of the fourteen police stations which were attacked were fully destroyed. The immediate economic cost of this violence has not yet been accurately estimated but is expected to be higher than the cost of the 2001 events. Moreover, the qualitative damage done to the reputation of the country will add to these costs.

The extensive reach of the Tivoli-based Shower or Presidential Click is not typical. Its record of violent encounters with security forces suggests that its violence-delivery capabilities are superior to those of most criminal groups. However, other groups have been able to wage wars with them, thereby also revealing substantial capabilities to inflict considerable harm and to at least be disruptive.

Exhibiting violence for profit and violence for political power and influence constantly creates enemies. The need for protection against enemies and the desire for extensions of power necessitates that an organized crime group have a standing force of armed persons and a reliable supply of weapons. Furthermore, the group and the communities in which it operates must also receive provisions. This leads to more violence for profit enterprises, such as extortion or rackets, which require protection. These activities stimulate a further demand for and supply of violence. Given this dynamic, the supply of violence does not seem to ever satisfy the demand for it.

For violent entrepreneurs, the increased capability to use violence and to deliver it in multiple locations against powerful enemies, including law enforcement, may be taken as a marker of growth and power. The actual use of violence rather than the use of their reputation for violence may reveal vulnerabilities, however, especially when the use of this violence is unsuccessful. These situations may precipitate a successful turn against organized crime. It is the combining of a reputation for violence with successful implementation methods that is more likely to result in greater coexistence with organized crime, and in this sense that may be taken as an indicator of greater maturity.

There is evidence that professionals are being drawn into organized crime networks. The incorporation of professionals in the infrastructure for violence and corruption is an important marker of a group's maturity. Such a capability not only permits violent resistance to the state but is also able to inflict significant costs in support to any political administration that acts in substantial ways to weaken their power. Development of highly political infrastructures, then, indicates a new relationship for organized crime with politics that ensures greater autonomy for crime groups. To the extent that some groups have developed this kind of infrastructure, politicians will tend to lose any veto power over their decisions to use violence.

Autonomy

As noted above, organized crime networks in Jamaica have had a long and deep relationship with the two political parties that have alternatively formed the government. The garrison communities are an expression of these close ties. In these communities, the affinities between organized crime and political parties are based on mutually supportive criminal and political monopolies. Criminal groups participate in the administration of these communities in association with the political parties. The request by the American authorities for the extradition of Coke brought this relationship between organized crime and the political parties into sharp relief and threw the community of Tivoli Gardens into crisis.

This case has further revealed the magnitude of the power of Coke's Presidential Click and its considerable influence in the decision-making centres of the party and the political administration at the national level. In this regard, it is worthwhile quoting from the United States Department of State's International Narcotics Control Strategy Report (US Dept. of State 2010, 377):

> The GOJ's (Government of Jamaica) unusual handling of the August (2009) request for the extradition of a high profile crime lord with reported ties to the ruling Jamaica Labour Party . . . on alleged drugs and firearms trafficking charges marked a dramatic change in GOJ's previous cooperation on extradition, including a temporary suspension in the processing of all other pending requests and raises questions about the GOJ's commitment to combating transnational crime.

Such is the strength of the relationship between the ruling party and the Presidential Click/Shower group that the administration was prepared to risk a loss of its popular support and a tarnishing of its image and that of the country by behaving in a manner that has left observers to conclude that they had simply put up a political defence of the leader of a violent transnational criminal organization (see *Gleaner* and *Observer* editorials, 2–4 March 2010). Indeed, a concerted effort was made to lobby the American political administration on matters related to the extradition. The American firm Manatt, Phelps and Phillips, which had strong connections with the Democratic Party and the White House, was contracted to assist in quashing or at least delaying the extradition request.[29] Much political capital has been exhausted on this issue.

The veil behind which the political influence and power of the leaders of the major organized crime groups are exercised has slipped. A new reality has been more fully revealed. It is that political parties must take into account, even at great political risk, the independent interests of the major organized crime groups and the "super dons" who lead these groups. It is not just the strength of the crime-politics nexus that is evident but, as importantly, the increased autonomy of these groups and their ability to influence political administrations and agencies of the state. It now seems as if organized crime has co-opted political leadership or has become so powerful that any effort by the political administration to act against organized crime affiliates would be mutually destructive.[30]

The historical trajectory of these criminal networks has been toward greater independence of the parties. Indeed, autonomy is a primary condition for characterizing these groups as organized crime. Without a measure of autonomy, they would simply be ordinary thugs and clients of the political leaders, clients whose interests may be easily sacrificed by the political parties. But the major organized crime groups now have greater autonomy in the context of strong relationships with political parties. These two features, that is, belonging and autonomy, are aspects of a dynamic relationship; they are not mutually exclusive and seem logically contradictory. This suggests that there is a greater interdependence between the two sets of actors rather than a dependent clientelism, as was the case in an earlier period in the relationship. Put another way, greater autonomy has meant greater power and influence for organized crime *within* the parties.

Autonomy is an important indicator of maturity, especially in Jamaica where most of the older and more powerful territorial gangs were and are closely tied to political parties. This process has not been free of tensions and conflicts between the criminal and political elites. In an interview with radio talk-show host Anthony Abrahams, former prime minister and member of parliament for Western Kingston, the territorial base of Coke and the Shower group, Edward Seaga acknowledged this development. He reported:

> I have no control over these fellows, no control whatsoever. That has nothing to do with politics. I have no lack of control in terms of politics in the constituency, but I have no control over these thirteen men who have a pattern of brutality that I will not tolerate, will not accept and will fight against. They have blow(n) off the leg of a young girl . . . , they have killed two sons of one lady within three days, they have killed a seven-year-old, a nine-year-old boy. They sent fifteen-year-old boys with pack guns into the Rema community in order to chastise, in order to mete out what they call justice. . . . I have no control over this thirteen and I don't want to bear any responsibility for them. I don't want them to have any control over the constituency.[31] (*Gleaner*, 29 September 1994)

This was the same Shower group that had violently sought to suppress political dissension and the attempts to switch party loyalties among their former allies in the neighbouring community of Wilton Gardens, and which has continued to be actively involved in electoral campaigns within and far beyond Western Kingston (see "Tivoli Gardens", *Jamaica Observer*, 30 October 2005). The tensions between the leader of the group and the leader of the party did not preclude efforts by the group to discipline others who wished to break with the party.[32] Seaga's lament reflected a new power relationship and the tensions and stresses that were and are associated with negotiating this new relationship, including efforts by the parties to maintain the old party control and command type relationship in a context of the declining material resources available to the state for welfare-type projects and without the disciplinary power that was required to do so. Their political influence within the police force was and is an important element of this disciplinary power, and this has noticeably declined since the early 1990s with the post–Cold War ideological convergence of the two parties and efforts to reform the police force. In this new situation, the Shower group now funded the sports teams and provided a computer centre for the community. This was done prior to the full establishment of the protection rackets. Seaga clearly did not succeed in preventing them "having any control over the constituency" or at least over the community of Tivoli Gardens. A power shift did occur, and they did become more autonomous with greater power in the constituency and, indeed, in the country.

Some of these groups have been able (at various moments) to co-opt the political parties and to use the parties to help in obscuring the character of their criminal racketeering, which is often presented as doing business with the state. Even their violence is at times misrepresented as community defence against political attacks by elements from the opposing party and as legitimate community defence against politically biased "incursions" from security forces. Whenever these criminal groups are able to mobilize political support in these ways, law enforcement efforts are often nullified. The major territorially based and party-affiliated organized crime groups have been fairly successful in neutralizing such efforts (Harriott 2008b). The military-police operation in Tivoli Gardens in 2010 is an exception.

Shower was also able to secure construction contracts from state agencies even when their party formed the opposition. According to the Office of the Contractor General, between 2006 and May 2010, Incomparable Enterprises, a company owned by Coke, received several contracts from five government agencies and entities (including the NWA, NSWMA and UCD) valued at some US$219 million.[33] Incomparable Enterprises and other groups were now able to prepare and present professionally prepared bids for state contracts and to deliver the services (such as road construction, building construction) via front firms that are well known. No effort is made to mask the connections of these firms as this has not proved to be an impediment to securing state contracts.

This increased autonomy has its basis in factors such as the retreat and general weakening of the state, shifts in social power that are grounded in changes in economic and social/occupational structures that have enlarged the potential social support base of these organized crime networks, providing helpful shifts in the illegal opportunity structure. Criminal gangs have travelled a long way from being the recipients of small state contracts which served to tie them closely to the parties to becoming firms that are able to extract hundreds of millions of dollars from the state each year and that have multiple income streams, some of which are independent of the state. Large-scale drug trafficking, transnationalization and the development of successful extortion and protection rackets were major turning points in the maturation of organized crime groups.

There is now a dynamic underground economy with emerging new rackets that expand the range of opportunities. Consequently, dependence on the state has been reduced, and the subordinate relationships with political leaders of a patron-client sort are somewhat altered. Autonomy is underpinned by not just multiple income streams and the development of an independent infrastructure for violence but also by the extent of social support for the dons.

The Prevalence of Supporting Ideas and Legitimacy Claims by Organized Crime

The activities and relationships of the organized crime networks are such that, in the absence of armed clashes with other groups and or law enforcement, their corrupt character is cast in doubt. By its very nature, organized crime is able to mask aspects of its criminality, and some groups are able to present themselves as being, at worst, engaged in some illegalities but simultaneously legitimate. Their visible business activities either are legal or appear to be legal. Their leaders present themselves at news conferences where they co-sign business contracts with ministers of government. They are accepted in the major political parties where some are regarded as important figures and informal leaders. Organized crime is business. It is social power and influence. It is politics. A marker of the maturity of organized crime is a lowering of the visibility of its street crimes while progressively taking on an increasing resemblance to normal business. It engages in business-activity-as-rackets, preferably rackets that are facilitated by the state, such as construction rackets. Several leaders of organized crime groups have now formed registered companies and describe themselves as businessmen. With this development, a greater acceptance of organized crime may be expected. Thus, for example, during the Tivoli events of 2010, women demonstrated their support for the leader of the Shower group by marching with slogans such as "Leave Dudus Alone" and "No Dudus No Jamaica" (see "Diehards Defend Dudus", *Gleaner*, 12 May 2010). This type of supportive activity is not new but has now become a predictable feature of these situations.[34]

This raises the issue of the authority and legitimacy of these groups. The use of the word legitimacy to apply to the illegal may seem contradictory, but legality and conventionality are not necessary conditions for legitimacy. Legitimacy is the approved use of power by appropriate institutions. Appropriateness is a standard that may be met by a justification from necessity. Thus it may be and is argued that in the high violence conditions of urban Jamaica, the ruthless control methods of the dons that are not constrained by the law are situationally necessary and appropriate. Necessity minimizes ethical considerations that are associated with means, resulting in legitimacy.

Some organized crime groups take on proto-state characteristics and the political administration of territory, and as political administrators, they must then seek the approval of the citizens over whom they wish to rule. They must contest for support and claim authority. Authority is the ultimate source of legitimacy. Most dons, such as Claudius Massop, Lester Coke and Christopher Coke, have ruled by what Max Weber (1919) would call charismatic authority. They are said to have displayed qualities of individual leadership that inspire loyalty and confidence. There are several embellished stories and myths of their bravery, wisdom and fairness with members of the group and ruthlessness toward enemies.[35] Thus, even after Coke's extradition, one of his affiliates, Cedric Murray, a reputed leader of the Stone Crusher Group that operates in the city of Montego Bay, noted in his diary, "My don is free. . . . I am loyal to the Coke's family and my gun will always be ready. I may never see my don again for years to come, but he knows I will always be there for him" (see the *Gleaner*, 13 August 2010).[36]

The Jamaican underground is not particularly distinguished by group loyalty. Such privately documented, reflective expression of loyalty and commitment is thus extraordinary and revealing of Coke's authority. This authority was manifested in Coke's routine interactions with the residents of Tivoli Gardens and some of the neighbouring communities. He had "presidential" office hours when he made himself available to receive residents who sought his assistance to solve or resolve a wide range of everyday problems. Unfortunately, when his office was captured by the security forces, a record of the number of visits, the types of requests and their outcomes was not found.[37] An examination of the range of requests for his problem-solving interventions would have revealed the extent of his authority. This practice, however, indicates that there was (and is) a measure of acceptance of his leadership and role in community governance and shows a degree of institutionalization. If the range of his authority is difficult to estimate, so too is its degree. The latter is difficult to estimate as the threat of force was ever-present. There was therefore no opportunity to observe free compliance in the administration of the affairs of the community. Observable were the authority-giving narratives (they provide the justification for the right to be obeyed), the legitimacy-giving results and the conforming and supportive behaviour.

Any attempt to remove their type of leadership must therefore contend with their authority. Thus, during and after the pursuit and arrest of Christopher

Coke, the police launched a campaign to show that he was cowardly and lacked the personal traits and leadership characteristics that it was believed that he had. It was reported that he fled the battle scene after the first shots were fired and was later found disguised as a woman (see the *Daily Observer*, 23 June 2010). That the police found it necessary to do this indicates that they perceived the strength of his authority in the community.

Some dons now enjoy other sources of authority. In some cases, the territorial groups have empowered eminent families with histories of criminal-political-community involvement to take control of their own turf as mini-kingdoms. In some sense, leadership may now be inherited. The Cokes are an example of this; the family has led the Tivoli group for some thirty years, that is, since 1980–81.[38] There have been transitions from Lester Coke, the first member of the family to lead the Tivoli-Shower group, to his eldest son Mark in 1992; then also in 1992, from Mark to his brother Christopher; and possibly now from Christopher to his brother Leighton. Tradition is, however, not an unassailable source of authority, especially when it is not based on a long-established pattern and must contend with ideas that are drawn from the larger, more democratic environment.

Perhaps the most powerfully appealing source of organized crime groups' claim to legitimacy is their provision of services to the communities. These groups often provide welfare support for the poor who reside in their communities (Harriott 2008b). The legitimating power of these efforts lies not so much in their volume and material effects but rather in their symbolism as care for the poor and those persons who are neglected by the state. Its appeal is in its interpretation as an expression of values and as a façade of social rather than anti-social character. Like all political symbolisms, these efforts mobilize the emotions of the people for purposes of shifting or consolidating power. The intensity of these sentiments was, for example, expressed during the attempts to block the extradition of Coke by protestors whose slogans included "Jesus died for us; we will die for Dudus" (Spaulding 2010).

The most valued service appears to be the provision of security. This is understandable as (in the absence of this service) people in this part of the city where there are high levels of violent victimization and weak police protection may be expected to have high levels of anxiety about their safety.[39] This, too, is highly emotive and symbolically loaded. The use of violence in policing the community and in protecting it from external enemies may be illegal, but it is seen as serving socially useful and approved ends. The means are also eventually approved as being situationally appropriate, and the actors gradually gain respect and authority in the community.

Myths about the value expression of these groups mask their predatory character. The Robin Hood myth, for example, masks self-interestedness. Welfare programmes as symbolic expressions of community-interestedness may have some material impact on the lives of people, but they are also tools of control. The myth that organized crime effectively controls crime masks its intent to establish a criminal monopoly. The manipulation of party-political symbols is useful for masking turf control and presenting it as being not just about self-protection, protection rackets and political leverage but about advancing political causes.

This manipulation often succeeds locally because it is linked to the delivery of benefits and, importantly, exploits stable social and political (poor, and People's National Party and Jamaica Labour Party) identities. Such symbols tend to evoke strong emotive reactions due to the reality of inequalities and marginalization and *experientially* conditioned "symbolic predispositions" against such occurrences as injustice and inequality. In other words, it is not simply the exploitation of a mindless and easily manipulated public that secures the authority of organized crime groups. Thus, although incidents of injustice may be fabricated for manipulative purposes, some individuals may believe that crime groups better their communities and, therefore, endow them with authority. To that end, gunmen may be presented as innocent victims who were murdered by a wicked and oppressive rights-violating police officer, because systematic rights violations and abuses do occur and have been occurring for generations. Given imperfect information, one must choose whose stories to believe. According to political psychologists, the manipulation of these symbols involves the technique of "transfer of affect" (for example, see Sears 1993). For example, people have stable responses to "poor", "party" and "community"; thus, when these are conflated and linked with Shower or any other organized crime group or leader, transference of meanings will tend to occur. It is a linkage that relies on consistency; thus, if one strongly supports the JLP, then she should strongly support the Tivoli Gardens–based Shower. (Tivoli Gardens is JLP-affiliated). This may partly explain why many JLP core supporters defended Coke, why the decision to sign the extradition order was so politically problematic for the political administration and why Prime Minister Golding's subsequent signing of the order brought into doubt his party loyalty.[40] One's position on Shower came close to becoming a political identity and loyalty test. A similar pattern may be observed in some corruption cases. Party symbols are always treated as being worthy of emotionally grounded support.

In this context of territorial administration, a supporting set of ideas may develop as a challenge to the dominant ideas that express disapproval of the activities of the organized crime groups. A contest between community and society develops, with the community feeling reinforced in its rightness that the organized crime groups are worthy of their support, particularly when the society is seen as socially unjust.

Supporting ideas often take the form of myths that criminal groups redistribute wealth to the poor. Others are about its *effectiveness* in the delivery of services which ought to be supplied by the state – particularly crime control. While there is partial truth to this myth, the unjustness of the punishments and the torture and murder of alleged rule-breakers are either not acknowledged or are justified as being situationally appropriate.[41] Violent resistance to law enforcement is regarded as being justifiable on the grounds that the state is always the rights-violating aggressor, and the strength of the historical evidence in the affirmative permits every new incident to be fitted into this pattern, regardless of the facts. This is of considerable importance as the justifiable use of violence is a strong test of legitimacy. That violence against law enforcement is considered justifiable demonstrates an even higher standard. If this assessment is correct, then violent encounters may strengthen community cohesion and ties to organized crime groups. There is a *representational*-symbolic aspect to legitimacy as well. The leaders of some of the more entrepreneurial criminal groups are viewed by some as champions of the financial aspirations of the poor who have had the courage and the means to realize the material elements of these aspirations. The success of organized crime networks and their leaders are thus regarded as the successes of the community and as victories over marginalization.

These supporting ideas are able to travel widely via popular music and other art forms. Some groups use their economic power to fund their cultural influence (Howard 2010, 8–15). The Shower and Clansman groups, for example, both invest in recording. Popular music is used to propagate the legitimizing myths. Such power and popular support protect these groups from law enforcement efforts.

Immunity Achieved/Immunity Ended?

Immunity of the criminal elite from law enforcement is usually an expression of the influence and power of organized crime and is thus another useful marker of its maturity. The more powerful Jamaican organized crime networks have achieved immunity from local law enforcement. This must be viewed in the context of a general waiving of negative sanctions, an overload of the criminal justice system and the emergence of a subculture of violence whereby behaviour patterns such as the observance of a code of silence render law enforcement ineffective. The decline in the arrest rates for homicide and other serious crimes, and the low number of arrests and convictions for core organized crime activities such as extortion and protection rackets, are some indicators of this immunity. Even in the recent state of emergency, of one hundred high-value criminal suspects affiliated with major organized crime groups and street gangs, many had clean police records, and only some twenty of them could have been and were charged by the police for the many crimes that they were all suspected of having committed. Thus, it is expected that, at best, 5 per cent faced the prospect of a conviction.[42] This is immunity.

For the "super dons" and the politically protected there is almost complete immunity. Of these, the garrison dons are the best protected. This group adds to their political protection the ability to use their command of the means of violence to discourage police action against them by increasing the risk of high casualties and by extracting a political price for any attempt to make them accountable to the law and to break their power. This approach worked well for the organized crime groups in the 2001 occurrence. Success turns on the ability to mount enough resistance to politicize the encounter with security forces and to exploit the popular distrust of the state and particularly of the police.

The Coke case was a test of a don's degree of immunity. In this case, the political administration was willing to openly resist *external* law enforcement and internal political pressure. If this resistance had succeeded, it would have raised immunity to a new level, that is, as not just immunity against Jamaican justice but also against foreign law enforcement and the justice of the most powerful countries. This would have would have signalled a willingness to bring about a total immunity for politically protected super dons. It would have made them a special class of criminals who would be unconditionally protected by the state.

Future governments will not want to take this risk. Some organized crime groups may make adjustments to their activities. There could be greater specialization with violent entrepreneurs remaining nationally focused, avoiding transnational operations and the drug trade and specializing in violence-related businesses such as protection rackets, including protecting and extorting drug traffickers. If the Jamaican criminal justice system is not strengthened, then these groups could enjoy nearly complete immunity. Alternatively, if this type of group remains in drug trafficking and becomes more independent of the political parties, then there is likely to be greater anti-law-enforcement and anti-state violence. This would result in a more unstable environment, and this instability would stimulate a political tendency that would support appeasing these violent groups; but anti-state violence would also further strain their relations with political parties and make the violent groups more vulnerable to law enforcement intervention.

The Future of Organized Crime: Indicators of Its Further Evolution

A discussion of the evolution of organized crime would not be complete if limited to tracking the pathways from its origins to the present. If, however, in so doing a trajectory is shown and the processes that account for this trajectory are identified, then, all things being equal, we may make informed, if not somewhat speculative, projections about the future. Below are some indicators that should be monitored in order to track the further evolution of organized crime networks. The significance of these indicators is discussed elsewhere (Harriott 2008b).

- Penetration of more sectors of the legitimate economy and increased crime dependency (at the community and national levels)
- Related to this, the deepening and expansion of their relationships as measured by their political influence in local government, their relationships with individual candidates and their influence in the parties, and their relationships with the state agencies
- Strengthening/weakening of the infrastructure for violence
- Extension/contraction of the infrastructure for corruption
- The extent to which it becomes more parasitic and less entrepreneurial or vice versa[43]
- The degree of social facilitation of organized crime in marginalized communities and in the larger society

It is difficult to properly understand the evolution of organized crime without referencing prior efforts to control it and showing how these groups have adapted to those efforts. The further evolution of organized crime in Jamaica is likely to be even more greatly influenced by official responses to it. As has been suggested elsewhere, effective law enforcement responses in the United States and the United Kingdom may have led transnational groups to open new income streams in Jamaica, leading to the growth of protection and extortion rackets. Targeting the leaders of these networks may lead to greater organizational flexibility. Targeting their assets may lead to greater co-mingling and partnerships with legitimate businesses.

The events of May–June 2010 have revealed the advances that may be made by loosening the hold of these groups on their host communities and by exposing and weakening their ties to political parties. An assault on the host communities with a view to breaking the power of these groups may involve military-type operations, but these are essentially law enforcement exercises. As a matter of policy, there should be an abundance of caution in making generalizations from the armed confrontations with the Shower group. Few groups have the capacity to present that level of armed resistance. During the events of 2010, the Shower may have adopted insurgency-type tactics. While this should be recognized and responded to appropriately, it is another step altogether to categorize all armed actions as insurgency and to treat organized crime and ordinary street gangs as if they were parts of an insurgency. This is dangerous. The immediate dangers include derailing the democratization of law enforcement and efforts to reform the JCF (perhaps stimulating the further militarization of law enforcement), and a further deterioration in citizen-state relations if people and communities that are facilitative of organized crime are treated as insurgents and enemies of the state.

If the people are treated as enemies, then criminal groups are likely to be viewed by them as a kind of resistance to injustice. Criminal violence and particularly criminal anti-state violence then becomes politicized. This response could trigger another evolutionary turn. It would further politicize the problem and thereby make its control more difficult. The opposite is required, that is, to depoliticize the problem by highlighting the evident criminal character of the core activities of these groups and their use of politics as a cover for these activities.

Conclusion

Jamaican organized crime has been maturing and penetrating various aspects of everyday life and economy. A mature organized crime is one that does not strangle its host but lives symbiotically with it. The likely result is a corrupt stability with moments of instability. But such a state of corrupt stability is likely to generate political resistance. Thus, for example, an inner city controlled by politically affiliated dons offers a corrupt stability in a context where the state is unable to provide effective protection for the citizens residing in these areas.

However, inevitable abuses that are associated with control by dons are likely at some point to precipitate unrest. Similarly, unfair competition in construction may result in resistance by legitimate contractors.

In the absence of effective democratic solutions or management of the problem, further violence that is directed at the state and its agents may result in increased support for altering the political framework for managing the problem. This may take the form of support for the authoritarian management of the security problem within what is by any definition a stable and electorally competitive democracy. This tendency is usually expressed as support for greater involvement of the military in crime control (UNDP 2012, 157). Alternatively, it may even be manifested as support for regime change. The survey for the Caribbean Human Development Report that was conducted in 2010 found that there was some 23.4 per cent popular support for a resort to a military government as a means of better controlling the Jamaican crime problem (ibid.). These outcomes must be guarded against. With each lost opportunity to effectively respond to the problem of citizens' insecurity, one or both of these responses may gain popular support.

What is perhaps most instructive from this analysis of the evolution of organized crime is the failure to effectively intervene and to better control it at earlier stages of its development when it is more vulnerable to law enforcement. This is the lesson from the past that informs the responses of the present. If present opportunities are lost, then later the country will be confronted with an even more mature organized crime presence – and perhaps a less robust democratic orientation toward its control. Thus far, the responses have been limited and externally induced. With the exception of a few moments, the practice of the state has largely been to offer only symbolic responses, particularly legal symbolisms. It was forced to go beyond this in the Coke extradition case of 2010. This response of 2010 revealed both the constraints on the state as well as the possibilities for overcoming these constraints and making the country safer.

Notes

1. *King Pin* is an official American designation. It is a legal category under the King Pin Act (1999) that allows the American government to freeze the assets of those thus named and to forbid Americans from entering into commercial transactions with them.

2. For example, the United Nations Convention against Transnational Organized Crime (2000), The Inter-American Convention Against Corruption (1996), the

Inter-American Convention on Mutual Legal Assistance in Criminal Matters (1996) and the OAS Convention on Illicit Firearms Trafficking (1997).

3. The impact of organized crime on construction practices would be sadly revealed after an earthquake. Organized crime groups typically force contractors to hire unskilled workers at the pay rate of skilled workers and have them actually do jobs that require skills that they do not possess. The result is faulty construction practices and defective buildings, roadways and other infrastructure. In some cases, quality control professionals feel intimidated and unable to submit honest evaluations of these projects without risking their lives.

4. People are contacted and told that they have won lotteries and that they are required to make various payments in order to claim the much larger sums that they have won.

5. The frequency count was provided by the Jamaica Public Service Company. The percentage of households is the author's estimate.

6. See the Report of the Commission of Inquiry into the Upsurge of Criminal Violence and Other Matters in Urban Communities within the Kingston Metropolitan Region (2001) and the *Sunday Gleaner,* 6 June 2010, respectively, for reports on the two events. The death toll for the 2010 events was reported as seventy-three, but this number includes two constables who were killed outside the zone of operations. The security forces' estimate has been contested by the Office of the Public Defender (2013, 58), which claims that the number of civilians killed during the operation was at least seventy-six.

7. In some conflict settings this type of threat may be considered credible; in others, the consideration of this as a potential threat may be a linkage strategy that is simply aimed at magnifying the dangers that are associated with organized crime.

8. The threat associated with the nexus between organized crime and terrorism has perhaps been magnified. The evidence of linkages between TOCs and international terrorism is at best very thin. The idea of narco-terrorism is the best case for this linkage, and doubt has been cast on this characterization of the relationship between guerrilla groups in Colombia and drug traffickers. Threat magnification by linkages is, however, a good method of political mobilization for increased powers and resources. This remains a very contentious issue.

9. For the position of the Jamaican government, see the statement by Dorothy Lightbourne, minister of justice, which was made in the Senate on 29 October 2009. It suggests that the request was not consistent with the terms of the treaty. Available to this author is an undated print of her speech, which was read in the Senate and therefore recorded in Hansard. The *Commission of Enquiry into the Extradition Request for Christopher Coke* (2010) took the position that much of the evidence that was used in support of the extradition request was illegally acquired and improperly given to American law enforcement, and in breach of Coke's constitutional rights (page 14).

10. The *Economic and Social Survey of Jamaica, 2008* (2009) conducted by the Planning Institute of Jamaica, reports that 45.5 per cent of all homicides were "gang related"; this is the official figure. A high proportion of homicides remain "unknown". I suspect that these were added to those officially categorized as "gang related" in order to arrive at the figure of approximately 80 per cent. It should also be noted that how the police use this term is not clearly defined, and how the incidents are coded by them is not rigorous. All homicides that fit a certain style of killing as well as homicides by individuals who are or are suspected to be gang members may be included in this estimate. Although the approach of the police may be quite reasonable, 80 per cent may be an overestimation.

11. As Headley (2005) has noted, the actuality of this problem is often inflated.

12. These include Harriott (2008b); politics created a demand for street violence and provided illicit economic opportunities in the mainstream of the system.

13. The argument in Harriott (2008b) is revisited. The use of the word evolution should not be taken to mean a uniform trajectory of every gang that inevitably progresses to organized crime. Some groups will emerge as youth gangs and disappear. Others may remain street gangs that are primarily engaged in conflicts with similar others and never become organized crime. Still others will seize opportunities to engage in enterprise crimes and to supply violence-related services.

14. Estimates of the size of the drug trade suggests that organized crime's economic power is not insignificant, but too little is known about this dimension of its power.

15. Many of these instruments take their cue from the definition in the United Nations Convention against Transnational Organized Crime, signed in Palermo, Italy in 2000.

16. Using a different indicator, however, Powell and Lewis (2008, 32) later reported much higher levels of interpersonal trust.

17. The term *protection* is used to mean not just the use of the reputation for violence to guarantee transactions but to guarantee the security of firms against potential predators.

18. The "lotto scam" is a confidence racket that copies the typical Nigerian 419s. Victims are told that they have won a lottery and must transmit processing fees to the organizers of the "scam". This death toll estimate was given by the commissioner of police and repeated by senior superintendent of police Fitz Bailey, head of Organized Crime Investigations (OCID), in his presentation at the seminar on organized crime hosted by the Ministries of National Security and Justice in collaboration with the Delegation of the European Commission to Jamaica, 6–7 October 2009. This estimate of the number of death is inflated. The murder toll for St James, which is at the epicentre of the lotto racket, exceeded two hundred (214) for the first time in 2008. While killings elsewhere may have been attributed to the lotto racket, it is unlikely that the total loss of lives in that year would have been two hundred. I therefore use

the word approximately to accommodate the overestimation by the police officers that are cited and this text as a cautionary note.

19. This is an estimate that is based on official court statistics from the Government of Jamaica. The conviction rate could be as low as 5 per cent.
20. These two aspects have already been discussed elsewhere; see Harriott (2008b).
21. See websites of the Private Security Regulation Authority, Ministry of National Security, Government of Jamaica (http://www.psra.jm) and the OAS Observatory, (http://www.oas.org/dsp/observatorio/database/countriesdetails.aspx?lang=en& country=JAM).
22. This estimate was provided by the Jamaica Constabulary Force. It is not official but is a fairly accurate one. The conviction rate for murder was estimated to be some 20 per cent in the late 1990s (Harriott 2008a, 61).
23. Statistics as reported in *Economic and Social Survey of Jamaica,* 2009 and previous years.
24. These bits of information were provided by the Office of Civil-Military Relations of the Jamaica Defence Force.
25. As Dennis Howard (2010) notes, leaders of organized crime are often celebrated in popular music. Several dons are indeed owners of recording studios and labels.
26. For a discussion of the indicators and impact of the subculture of violence, see Harriott (2008a).
27. Information provided by the Jamaica Constabulary Force.
28. This was the count on 4 June 2010.
29. See United States Department of Justice, 5864-Exhibit-AB-20091112-3, for a letter from Manatt, Phelps and Phillips to Harold Brady, dated 1 October 2009; also a press release from the JLP which was published in the *Gleaner,* 28 April 2010. The prime minister has insisted that this lobbying was aimed at getting the Americans to respect Jamaican law, and there may be some merit in this, but the appearance and effect was of a defence of Coke.
30. After the operation against the Coke group, there were several media reports of how unpopular the prime minister had become in his own constituency of Western Kingston; see the *Gleaner* from 13 May through 17 May 2010.
31. Interview with Anthony Abrahams on the Breakfast Club; I thank Professor Trevor Munroe for bringing this interview to my attention.
32. The gang wars between groups from the two communities occurred at a time when tensions remained between the party and the "group of thirteen".
33. From the response of the contractor general to questions by Nation Wide Radio, 5 June 2010, and sent to the author via personal email correspondence with a senior representative of this radio station on 8 June 2010.
34. As early as 1977, there were similar expressions of approval for Claudius Massop, a predecessor of Coke (Bryan 2009, 158).
35. I have collected a number of these stories as a part of a larger work on violence.

36. The police reported that this diary was found on Murray's body after he was killed in a shoot-out.
37. Shortly after the operation, I asked both the military and the police about this. There may be a video tape of the activities in the Presidential office but this was removed before the office was captured and is likely to have been destroyed.
38. His predecessor died in 1981 but there may have been a transition period beginning in 1980.
39. The service is valued because the people are unable to imagine life without it. The low levels of serious crimes within these communities are attributed to the dons.
40. Talk of his past leadership of the National Democratic Movement recurred as explanation of his compliance with the request for the extradition of Coke.
41. These practices are widely known to those associated with the "jungle justice" of the dons of organized crime. Donald Phipps, the former don of the Mathews Lance group, was convicted for this practice. Some of these practices were further revealed after the rout of the Presidential Click in Tivoli Gardens (Matthews 2010).
42. Personal correspondence with JCF officials and investigators during the 2010 state of emergency.
43. This may depend on the degree of access to international drug markets and other external illegal opportunities.

References

Bryan, P. 2009. *Edward Seaga and the Challenges of Modern Jamaica*. Kingston: University of the West Indies Press.

Clarke, C. 2006. *Kingston, Jamaica: Urban Development and Social Change, 1692–2002*. Kingston: Ian Randle.

Clarke, R. 1995. "Situational Crime Prevention". In *Building a Safer Society: Strategic Approaches to Crime Prevention. Crime and Justice*, edited by M. Tonry and D. Farrington, 19: 91–150. Chicago: University of Chicago Press.

Gambetta, D. 1993. *The Sicilian Mafia: The Business of Private Protection*. Cambridge, MA: Harvard University Press.

Green, P., and T. Ward. 2009. "The Transformation of Violence in Iraq". *British Journal of Criminology* 49(5): 609–27.

Griffith, I.L., and T. Munroe. 1997. "Drugs and Democratic Governance in the Caribbean". In *Democracy and Human Rights in the Caribbean*, edited by I.L. Griffith and B. Sedoc-Dahlberg, 74–94. Boulder: Westview.

Harriott, A. 2003. *Understanding Crime in Jamaica: New Challenges for Public Policy*. Kingston: University of the West Indies Press.

———. 2008a. *Bending the Trend Line: The Challenge of Controlling Violence in Jamaica and the High Violence Societies of the Caribbean*. Kingston: Arawak.

———. 2008b. *Organized Crime and Politics in Jamaica: Breaking the Nexus*. Kingston: Canoe.

Headley, B. (with graduate students M. Gordon and A. McIntosh). 2005. *Deported, Entry and Exit Findings of Jamaicans Returned Home from the US Between 1997 and 2003*, vol. 1. Kingston: Stephenson Litho Press.

Howard, D. 2010. "Political Patronage and Gun Violence in Dancehall". *Jamaica Journal*, 32(3): 8–15.

Lacy, T. 1977. *Violence and Politics in Jamaica 1960–1970*. London: Frank Cass.

Matthews, K. 2010. "Photographs: Shallow Graves, Torture Chamber Found in Tivoli". *Jamaica Observer*, 4 June.

Office of the Public Defender. 2013. "Interim Report to Parliament Concerning Investigations into the Conduct of the Security Forces during the State of Emergency Declared May, 2010 – West Kingston/Tivoli Gardens 'Incursion' – The Killing of Mr Keith Oxford Clarke and Related Matters". 29 April.

Powell, L.A. 2007. *Probing Jamaica's Political Culture*, vol. 1. Kingston: Centre for Leadership and Governance, University of the West Indies.

Powell, L.A., and B. Lewis. 2008. "Political Culture of Democracy in Jamaica, 2008". *The Impact of Governance*. A report of the Americas Barometer project by LAPOP.

Sears, D.O. 1993. "Symbolic Politics: A Socio-Psychological Theory". In *Explorations in Political Psychology*, edited by S. Iyengar and W. McGuire, 113–49. Durham: Duke University Press.

Shelley, L., and J.T. Picarelli. 2005. *Methods and Motives: Exploring Links between Transnational Organized Crime and International Terrorism*. A report for the National Institute of Justice (US), July.

Sives, A. 2010. *Elections Violence and the Democratic Process in Jamaica 1944–2007*. Kingston: Ian Randal.

Spaulding, G. 2010. "The Sacrifice: Souls Lost for the 'Cause'". *Gleaner*, 30 May.

Stone, C. 1988. "Does Jamaica Have the Political Skills for Crisis Management?" *Caribbean Affairs* 1(3): 38.

UNDP (United Nations Development Programme). 2012. *Human Development and the Shift to Better Citizen Security: Caribbean Human Development Report 2012*. New York: UNDP.

UNODC (United Nations Office on Drugs and Crime). 2010. *World Drug Report 2010*. United Nations Publication, Sales No. E.10.XI.13.

US Dept. of State, Bureau for International Narcotics and Law Enforcement Affairs. 2010. *International Narcotics Control Strategy Report 2010*. Drug and Chemical Control, 1: 377. http://www.state.gov/j/inl/rls/nrcrpt/2010/.

Weber, M. 1919. "Politics as a Vocation". In *Max Weber: Essays in Sociology*, edited by H.H. Gerth and C.W. Mills, 77–128. New York: Oxford University Press.

2 | Organized and Disorganized Crime

Gangs, *Naciones* and *Pandillas* in the Dominican Republic

Lilian Bobea

Throughout the Caribbean, escalating violence has been primarily attributed to youth gangs and their street cultures (CARICOM 2010).[1] In the Dominican Republic in particular, gangs known as *pandillas* or *naciones*[2] have been a major subject of political debate and a real public policy conundrum. They are often portrayed as the main promoters of citizen insecurity and thus as a national threat. Yet, while official and media discourse define these groups according to certain stereotypes, we actually know little about them: Why and how have they evolved? What are their goals and *modus operandi*? How are they empowered or disempowered vis-à-vis other community actors and agencies? What impact do their actions have on local institutions?

Specialized literature recognizes a great deal of variation among gangs, *pandillas*, *naciones*, *bacrims*, *barras*, *maras* and other youth groups in Latin America and the Caribbean in terms of their structure and nature (Cruz 2006; Lesley 2010; Moser and Holland 1997; Mogensen 2005; Moncrieffe 1998; Katz, Maguire and Choate 2011), their evolution (Rodgers, Muggah and Stevenson 2009; Arias 2010) and their political influence and power (Arias 2006, 2010; Arias and Goldstein 2010; Harriott 2008; Townsend 2009; National Gang Intelligence Center 2009; UNDP 2012). Van Gemert (2005, 147–48) characterizes *pandillas* and similar organizations as "any durable, street oriented youth group whose involvement in illegal activities is part of their group identity". Contrastingly, organized crime groups are conceived as "more sophisticated organizations in corporate and relational terms, operating within more formal and hierarchical lines of authorities, based on personal and social networks that exist in a community" (Harriott 2008; UNDP 2011; UNDP 2012, 67).

Despite this working distinction, there is a lack of consensus within the academic community on how to conceptualize gangs and, consequently, on how to develop adequate policies to address them. Moreover, the connections between the multiplicity of youth groups in the region's English- and Spanish-speaking countries and organized crime are simply not clear (Hagedorn 2008, 23–24). That nexus provides material for discussion across Latin America and the Caribbean (Rodgers 1999, 2005; Jutersonke, Muggah and Rodgers 2009, 4; Katz, Maguire and Choate 2011).

In this chapter, I examine the connections between organized crime and *pandillas* (street gangs) in the Dominican Republic. My research recognizes that as complex criminality becomes more ubiquitous, it tends to blur the distinctions among the actors involved. As we shall see, young people who join *pandillas* are often motivated by a desire for identity affiliation, territorial control and simple self-preservation. However, *pandillas* have become more and more permeated by entrepreneurial criminality that is transnationally connected and involved in drug trafficking, extortion, money laundering, smuggling and racketeering, all of which result in violent competition among syndicates and between *pandilla* members and security forces. This does not imply that all juvenile gangs are criminal. Indeed, the word "criminal" itself contains a host of contradictory connotations that reflect the tendency to criminalize the daily lives of poor people. Nevertheless, complex criminal agents do intersect with youth gangs since daily life in poor Dominican neighbourhoods presents both sets of actors with opportunities that look plausible and beneficial. Daily life in the *barrios* provides the scenario in which some youth groups evolve to embrace a more criminal and violent profile.

The *barrios* also provide new forms of social and political influence for both youth groups and organized criminals. In those areas where political clientelism has been a longstanding practice, gangs, *pandillas* and *naciones* learn from these practices and become determinant informal political actors in the developing of alternative forms of local governance and representation. In some cases, they either promote or participate in local protest because of self-interest or in support of social demands for public services made to the state and local authorities. More recently, they have also played an instrumental role as intimidators of local electorates in favour of political candidates.

Indeed, that influence is one of the most worrying aspects of the growth of organized criminal activity in the Caribbean. In many Caribbean countries, groups of non-state actors have acquired territorial control and legitimacy in relation to weak or easily permeated governmental institutions. In some nations, this has reached a dangerous level, causing other nations to question the state's effective sovereignty (Arias 2006, 2010; Arias and Goldstein 2010; Adams 2011; Koonings and Kruijt 2004; Griffith 2011).

This chapter concentrates on the construction of alternative social orders in the Dominican Republic's highly conflictive environments. It relies on an emerging subject in the expanding literature on conflicted reconfigured spaces and violent armed actors (Arjona 2008; Koonings and Kruijt 2004; 2007, 7–16; Tilly 1985). I argue that there has been an emergence of what I call "transgressive eco-systems" in which a socio-political order that was once based on confrontation between criminals, the community and the police has evolved toward collusion and eventually coalition among unregulated and opportunistic actors within those population segments of Dominican society. This trajectory contests the idealized notion that follows the Weberian ideal-type of the state's monopoly of legitimate violence, producing instead fragmented sovereignties with gradients of power and control unequally distributed among violent private and public actors, both informal and formal, including rogue police (Staniland 2012; Salcedo-Albaran and Garay Salamanca 2012).

In the process of transforming social orders, trans-generational values, rules and social control practices also change (Bobea 2011). New informal institutions come to establish implicit and explicit rules such as controlling petty crime and score-settling in order to minimize police intervention in the neighbourhoods, prohibiting inquiries about the "disappeared" and punishing betrayal or *choteo*. Despite very different national histories, the conditions I describe are similar to those found by Ana Arjona (2009) in Colombia regarding the ways that new social orders give authority to different actors and submit locals both to violence and co-optation that require either obedience or endorsement.

Given the significant social impact of complex criminality, it is not surprising that to the media and the authorities, gangs often become the epitome of the "violent other" to the point of being considered "a new urban insurgency" (Manwaring 2007; Williams 1998, 2001). However, that discourse obliterates the permeable frontier between criminal and legitimate actors who include professional criminal groups, corrupt bureaucrats and politicians, the police and community organizations, and business owners, as well as many ordinary citizens. The simple dichotomy of "us" versus "them" loses its meaning in the context of the transgressive communities emerging in the Dominican Republic and elsewhere in the Caribbean. This perspective aligns with the 2012 UNDP report which recognizes the growing overlap between street gangs and organized crime groups even as it maintains a distinction between them. Moreover, even when members of *pandillas* and *naciones* do engage in illicit activities the intensity and continuity of their involvement with these groups vary.

This chapter is divided into three sections. In the first part, I briefly survey both the evolution of crime and violence in the Dominican Republic in the last two decades and the emergence of transgressive ecosystems. In the second section, I offer a theoretical framework that permits a greater understanding of the intersection between complex criminality and gang activities, emphasizing the roles of plural violent and illicit agents and the consequences for street gangs or *pandillas,* as well as for the broader national criminogenic spectrum. This section is based on field research that I have been conducting for the last five years in poor neighbourhoods of Santo Domingo and elsewhere. Finally, I examine how recent theoretical approaches that emphasize resilience and adaptive dynamics in poor communities should shape both our thinking about and policies toward criminal violence in the Caribbean.

Crime and Violence in the Dominican Republic

From the transition to democracy in the late 1970s through the democratic consolidation of the 1990s, the Dominican Republic experienced a substantial decline in citizen security as criminal violence increased, first gradually and then sharply. This trend was accentuated early in the 2000s, reaching its peak in 2004. From 2001 to 2004, the homicide rate jumped from 12.5 to 25.2 per 100,000 inhabitants. Despite year-to-year fluctuations thereafter and a decline in violent death rates as a consequence of the execution of a citizen security policy, the Democratic Security Plan 2005–2007, by 2011, the homicide rate was almost the same as it was at the time of its initial spike in 2004 (Procuraduría General de la República Dominicana 2011).

Feelings of insecurity have changed over this period. In 2006, 57.7 per cent of the population surveyed felt insecure, a percentage that declined sharply to

39.5 per cent in 2008 after the Government of the Dominican Republic implemented the above-mentioned citizen security strategy. By 2012, the figure had risen slightly to 43.6 per cent (Espinal, Morgan and Seligson 2012, 105). Feelings of insecurity and fear are more acute among those residing in the metropolitan areas of Santo Domingo and Santiago, further evidence of the generally urban nature of criminality.

Returning to the spike in violent deaths, an obvious question is "what explains the sudden upswing after 2001?" Many commentators attributed the boom in real and perceived crime to the activities of drug traffickers since the Dominican Republic was at the time evolving from an important transshipment point for drugs moving from South and Central America to the United States and Europe into a growing consumer market (Bagley 2012; Bobea 2011). This meant that despite the decreasing prominence of the Caribbean region at the end of the 1990s, after the disarticulation of the Colombian drug cartels and the emergence of Mexican and Central American groups and alternative routes, the Dominican Republic continued to be an important channel for Colombian traffickers. These traffickers were supplied with drug storage, transshipment, internal distribution and money-laundering services. The Dominican criminal diaspora in the eastern United States also contributed to maintaining the country as a key part of the circuit of inflow and outflow of illicit merchandise.

From a long-term perspective, however, we can hypothesize that the surge of criminal violence resulted in part from the pattern of development that had unfolded since the middle of the last century. Government policies during that time had accentuated inequality and social exclusion for most Dominicans – for example, generating jobs in the informal sector for a majority of the urban population. In addition to those long-term trends, four other factors contributed to increasing violence. First was the growing presence of organized crime in the country including drug traffickers and those involved in other illicit transnational activities. Second was the increasing autonomy of state actors, such as members of the police, the military and the judiciary, who became associated with criminal networks through corruption and infiltration. A third factor was the emergence of territorially based gangs with a propensity to become instruments of complex criminality. Finally, in facing organized criminals, corrupt officials and youth gangs – evidences of the convergence of the first three factors – the Dominican government failed until very recently to create a strategic policy of human and citizen security that could effectively curb the internal and external vectors of crime, instead relying on simplistic, outdated and reactive approaches to the crisis.

A Conceptual Framework: Transgressive Ecosystems

In order to understand the processes described, I have coined a term that explains the relationship among state and non-state actors and their socio-political context: "transgressive ecosystems" (TEs). A transgressive ecosystem is a socio-spatial construct based on the different modalities through which organized criminal and opportunistic illicit actors establish symbiotic relations to negotiate control and distribute benefits. The type of criminality that has penetrated these poor neighbourhoods, which embrace and produce transgressive ecosystems as alternative social orders, leads ordinary people to behave in new ways to circumvent, adapt to or resist danger.

The TEs have flourished as a result of the external inputs that informal drug selling and illicit accumulation have offered to *barrio* dwellers as a survival alternative. As the Dominican Republic has become more entrenched into the transnational illicit economy in the last fifteen years, a favourable structure of opportunities has promoted the presence of more organized crime actors, activities and connections. Those conditions have opened niches and opportunities for transnational groups to develop relationships with members of more local parochial national groups. Since the local groups generally lack resources and capital, they are compelled to play an intermediary role and assume the most risky tasks within the criminogenic systems.

Within TEs we identify processes that interconnect licit and illicit, formal and informal institutions, activities and actors, and which often involve instrumental violence. Although most studies of the kinds of territorial and social spaces that I qualify as TEs emphasize violence, it is crucial to acknowledge that through them benefits are also widely distributed. In the process, every actor in the TE develops certain levels of adaptation as well as resilience.[3] In describing a paradigm similar to transgressive ecosystems, scholars of complexity theories (Kenney 2007; Powell 1990; DiMaggio and Powell 1983; March, Sproull and Tamuz 1991) emphasize the connections among actors sharing social systems, learning from those interactions and having an impact throughout those relations on the restructuring of the ecosystems.

In these socio-spatial scenarios, different types of arrangements can develop among local institutions (community organizations, churches and street associations) regarding their accommodation, tolerance or resistance to the role played by gangs and *pandillas*. In one focus group that I facilitated, a community activist gave a concrete example of such an interaction: "When the community plans to put in place some social or cultural activity, we give information about the event to the head of the drug *puntos* that are operated by *pandilleros*. But that doesn't mean that we are asking for their permission, we are just informing them in order to avoid any conflict or violent act on their part." Similarly, the drug dealers who are among the main producers of income in the TEs develop a complex negotiated relationship with the police. In the eyes of residents in the poorer *barrios* of Santo Domingo, the police "tax" the *puntos* where drugs are sold: "Police members take drug dealers' money and merchandise for themselves, then they turn the drugs over to another drug dealer to reap the benefits," said one interviewee (a resident of Capotillo, Santo Domingo). The threat of being arrested, robbed or killed by the police makes drug dealers eager to find a *modus vivendi* with the authorities. "On the other hand," according to another resident (a focus group participant), "there are occasions when the drug dealers cut deals with the police if they need them to arrest or make a rival dealer 'disappear'. Then it is the drug-dealer who owes the police; it is a system where what goes around comes around".

The Reign of the *Tigueres*

> The night that Tito Moya was murdered, I knew that the killers were the same guys that were arrested a few days before by the police. That day I was sitting on my front porch and I saw one of them pushing his pistol into Tito's mouth, who used to live in front of my house. Then, I heard a *cartuchazo* [bang] that sounded like a *tumba-gobierno*. The police post is located near to the place where the killing occurred, they clearly heard the shooting but nothing happened. I looked through my window and just saw the dead Tito sitting there, in his seat, with a hole in his head. (Focus group participant, Gualey, Santo Domingo, 2006)

In the Dominican Republic, the murder of a *tiguere* (TEE-gare-ay) usually does not make the front page of the newspapers despite the fact that these deaths are the most basic manifestation of the escalation of violent criminality and the clearest expression of failed public security policies. The *tiguere* in Dominican slang is an aggressive street-smart young man; perhaps the closest word in English is "hustler". Often pictured as survivors at any price, *tigueres,* in fact, do not usually have long life expectancies.

Residents of the *barrios* who participated in the focus groups of my study identified activities in which those *tigueres* who are *pandilla* members get involved in "the art of making easy money". These activities may include selling drugs, transporting drugs as mules, renting drug-selling *puntos*, engaging in extortion, defending a territory against rival groups and confronting the police. Despite the common misconception of uninvolved people about the "easy process" of selling drugs by gang members, there are few activities as risky and costly as that one. The division of labour in the drug trade exploits to the maximum already existing social inequities, meaning that those with the least power end up doing the most dangerous and least profitable jobs.

In 2005, 46 per cent of all homicides in the Dominican Republic were committed against individuals from eleven to thirty years of age despite the fact that this demographic accounted for only 38 per cent of the total population (World Bank 2007). These young people lost their lives in armed confrontations among *pandillas* or were killed by the police. Likewise, the number of individuals under the age of eighteen who were arrested for homicide grew from two in 1994 to 113 in 2004 (FINJUS and CONAEJ 2006, 2011); 95 per cent were male. The World Bank report showed that from the 1990s to the mid-2000s, homicides here increased by 195 per cent.

Juvenile violence, characterized as "homicides and nonfatal attacks perpetrated by or against persons between the ages of 10 and 29" (World Bank 2007), affects a growing segment of Dominicans from preadolescents to young adults. In barely three years, from 2002 to 2005, youth violent death rates jumped from 10.2 to 26.4 per 100,000 inhabitants (Dominican Republic National Police 2006). Most of these young people lost their lives due to gun violence involving either gangs or the police. Official data show that 71.4 per cent of all juvenile deaths in 2006 involved guns; in 2008, the figure rose to 78 per cent (Brea and Cabral 2010). A national study on risk factors and juvenile violence carried out by Brea and Cabral identified violent death as a preponderant insecurity factor that affects particularly people in the age range of twelve to thirty-five years. The study shows that in 2006, violent deaths for this population represented 63 per cent of all national homicides. By 2008, this figure had escalated to 67 per cent. The study also found that 40 per cent of these deaths were associated with criminal activities such as violent robbery, drug issues, kidnappings and police shootings, with the remainder associated with traffic accidents, suicides and undetermined causes (2010).

Police shootings account for an astonishingly high percentage of these gun deaths; extrajudicial executions and line-of-duty killings made up 16 to 18 per cent of annual killings between 2006 and 2008. Official actors are motivated either by the rational-choice decision to eliminate once and for all the *"tigueraje* in the *barrios*" or by being the protector of criminals, making use of their power to violently regulate contested territories. In other words, corrupt security agents provide impunity to the networks and individuals that they affiliate with in an exchange of benefits and control. Moreover, they also conduct social cleansing through extrajudicial executions of rivals whom they present as alleged criminals. In the broadest sense, the high rate of police killings suggests a state fighting to regain its monopoly over legitimate violence when facing challenges to its authority mounted by non-state actors.

Associative Violence: Contestation vs. Anomie

The development of juvenile *pandillas,* tribes and nations in the Dominican Republic has its own history. During the 1970s, under the authoritarian government of Joaquin Balaguer, youth groups with a political orientation were formed, often camouflaged behind the apolitical exterior of sports and social clubs or student and community organizations. During this period, youth were the key actors fighting for the democratization of the country. Even so, systematic repression exerted by the police, military and paramilitary forces such as the infamous Banda Colorá led to the decline of these juvenile movements (Cassa 1995). More recently, more or less formally organized youth groups have emerged under "liberal" governments but this time for social rather than political reasons. Those groups, against whom social prejudice abounds, have also been the object of brutal official repression since their emergence among young people living in exclusionary conditions.

Until recently, people in the *barrios* used to see the *tigueres* as a sort of anti-hero. The *tigueres* rarely operated within their own *barrios*. Quite the contrary – their *vecindarios* (neighbourhoods) became the territory to be defended from rival groups coming from other places. That shared interest between community residents and emerging youth groups helped to minimize intra-neighbourhood conflicts.

Nevertheless, parallel to the rise in violence and the penetration of organized crime in the Dominican Republic, youth groups evolved toward other activities and different relations with their communities. In the poorest neighbourhoods of Santo Domingo and other urban areas, populated by unemployed, unskilled and stigmatized cohorts of young people, deprivation and lack of opportunity have been important push factors for their embrace of informal and part-time illicit activities. An abundant labour supply in these poor areas becomes a relevant local asset when criminal actors move into these environments. That is how, as recently as 2001, *naciones* abruptly emerged and started mushrooming, proliferating in copycat schemes throughout the most economically deprived neighbourhoods of the two metropolitan areas of the two main cities, Santo Domingo and Santiago. Since their appearance, rising conflict has been constant among the newly formed gangs and between them and the police. At the time, 90 per cent of the people interviewed in the *barrios* confirmed the existence of a variety of street gangs exercising, with different intensities, modalities of violence (Bobea 2005).

Although there are still no reliable statistics about the current number of groups in the country, since they often dissolved as fast as they were constituted, some police assessments suggested that in the last six or seven years they have been concentrated or reduced to about fifty groups with a membership ranging from approximately one hundred up to one thousand.[4] One study on a dozen of these groups in two *barrios* of the capital revealed that most of the young members stay in the group for three-and-a-half years while 19.5 per cent stay for more than five years (Miric 2008). These developments have been both the cause and consequence of the emergence of transgressive ecosystems in many *barrios*. Many of these gangs were, however, dissolved and parts of their leadership destroyed either by inter-gang killings or extrajudicial executions by the police.

Among the structural factors that contributed to their proliferation, the most influential has been the deterioration of the socio-economic conditions of the most vulnerable neighbourhoods where members of *pandillas* grew up. These social conditions left a majority of young people stigmatized and disenfranchised, without basic services, and precariously inserted into volatile labour markets (see table 2.1). A study by Rubio (2006) found that within the Dominican *barrios* the young people who had dropped out or were expelled from school were more likely to get involved in a gang.

In 2002 and 2004, the rate of unemployment among Dominican youth was 23 per cent and 31 per cent respectively, a rise over two years of about 8 per cent (CEPAL 2008). Later, in 2008, the Dominican Central Bank reported that despite the fact that youths aged ten to twenty-four[5] represented 24 per cent of the country's total labour force, they accounted for 43 per cent of the total unemployed population. Among the youth employed, 36 per cent were engaged in self-employment activities – that is, in low-productivity jobs with limited upward mobility and without labour protection (2008).

By 2011, according to the International Labour Organization, 31 per cent of Dominican youth between fifteen and twenty-four years old were unemployed,

Table 2.1. Out-of-school and unemployed youth (2008)

	Ages 15–19	Ages 20–24
Out of school & unemployed	N = 54,667	N = 99,056
Male	42%	37%
Female	58%	63%
Urban	66%	69%
Rural	34%	31%

Source: Central Bank, National Labour Force Survey Database, second semester (2008).

putting the country on the top of the list of Caribbean countries with the highest open unemployment rates. The average for the region that year was 14.6 per cent. This pattern was reinforced by the condition of poverty; by 2010, 39 per cent of Dominican youth aged fifteen to twenty-four years fell into this category (19 per cent of whom were under the official guidelines for poverty) compared with 30 per cent of young poor in the remainder of Latin America and the Caribbean (CEPAL 2013). The situation was further aggravated by the high rate (5.3 per cent) of youth dropping out of formal schooling. Seventy per cent of those who dropped out gave as the reason, "need to work" (PNUD 2008). Moreover, for those who were employed, income was usually very low. This implied that there was no correlation between what they learned in school and the demands of the labour markets.

The Evolution of *Pandillas* and *Naciones*

Pandillas and *naciones* are not new phenomena in the Dominican Republic, but they are no longer what they used to be. In fact, they are constantly changing. More study in this field needs to be done, but the limited work on Dominican *naciones* found these groups initially self-defined as identity and self-protection oriented more than crime inclined. Indeed, their constitutions often forbid criminal activity although even at this early stage of their development individual members strayed from the code (Bobea 2005; Ceballos 2004; Vargas 2008). Some gang members explained to me that in the past when someone from the group was found engaging in criminal activity, it was considered a betrayal of the spirit of the *nacion*. At the time some members described the *nacion* as an alternative project of nationhood. As one former gang member framed it, "I was almost 100 per cent proud to belong because most of the norms, rules and ideals of that *nacion* were about putting an end to political corruption and discrimination" (Bobea 2005). That said, it could also be argued that members of *naciones* explicitly swear allegiance to a criminal entity rather than the sovereign state from which they feel thoroughly disfranchised.

Naciones used to have, and some still have, a hierarchical and centralized structure strictly regulated by a set of rules accepted by their members.[6] Those rules, statutes and laws upheld their commitment to loyalty and unconditional belonging. In some respects they appeared to be more or less democratic within their constituency. For example, the rules of the Latin Kings in the Dominican Republic included a section titled "How Laws Are Made", specifying that "any member of the *nacion* has the right to make a proposal", and explaining in detail how such proposals would be evaluated.[7]

Naciones also shared elements of the conventional culture that they formerly denied. These elements included not only socialization to accept violence but also the authoritarianism, homophobia, sexism and patriarchy that are evident in the hierarchy of these groups which locates the "Inca" or "Supreme One" at the top, commanding loyalties and demanding favours from underlings. They also have served to empower their members, giving them status that they have otherwise been denied. *Naciones* have worked as an integrated system of loyalties and providers of necessary services, especially security, to their members.

Despite the value of trying to distinguish among the different forms of youth organizations, *naciones* are a dynamic and amorphous phenomenon that can thwart categorization, because some members engage in criminal activities, such as murder for hire (*sicariatos*), kidnappings and violent robbery, even if the *nacion* those members belong to does not openly embrace such activities. For pragmatic reasons, we suggest an empirical rather than essentialist definition of criminal gangs, one in which if a significant segment of a group's membership regularly carries out illicit and violent activities or has some connections with organized crime, then the group can be considered as highly transgressive regardless of the declarations of its constitution or by-laws of membership.

Involvement in illicit and violent activities certainly depends on social context as well as on state responses or policy toward those groups. The strong identity politics of the youth groups, their demographic characteristics (between ten and twenty years of age) and their transnational organization from the Caribbean to the United States and Europe make them especially attractive as instruments of illicit trade, even though these same features also make the groups obvious targets for the police. In the low-income settlements of Santo Domingo, where 89 per cent of declared *nacion* members have been recruited, they become a ready-to-use *petite gendarmerie*. As the police told me in confidence, currently there are approximately one hundred such groups, twenty-five of which are the most noteworthy, with five considered security threats.

Broadly speaking, gangs, *pandillas* and *naciones* distinguish themselves from more corporate criminality groups. They are portrayed here as intermediary entities potentially evolving towards more articulated organized violence and crime. These types of gangs are not necessarily territorially based, but the transnational profile of some of them, facilitated by the circular migration of their members and the growing use of the internet, allows them to form branches or chapters in other countries. Despite shared rules and symbolism, they might differ in terms of values and ethics especially regarding the use of violence and intimidation. Their high mobility also facilitates a more heterogeneous vision and doctrine among the different chapters of the group depending on the social, institutional and organizational structure of opportunities they find in the countries where they operate. By these means, they also learn from each other and share information, rules and strategies. In contrast with more local gangs, these trans-local entities usually include members of other nationalities, like Puerto Ricans and Central Americans. However, from my interviews in 2009 with Spanish police officials and gang members established in Spain, it was clear that Dominicans are less inclusive and more reluctant to associate with other Latino groups.

Like youth gangs elsewhere in Latin America and the Caribbean, *pandillas* and *naciones* in the Dominican Republic still encode generational needs for constructing identities, loyalties and alliances in a frantic search for sociospatial belonging. But in the case of the poor young urban Dominicans, *pandilla* members live in communities that have had decades of disconnection from basic economic, social and political institutions. In their daily performance of resistance and adaptation to a hostile environment, *pandillas* and *naciones* often nurture symbols and codes that the general public sees as perversions of normative citizenship. Frequently they create a vicious cycle of self-defeating logic within the *barrios*.

A major shift in gang orientation toward profitability and violent competition has provoked even more substantial changes in their traditional relationship with the communities where they reside and operate. The communities now harbour feelings of mistrust towards the *tigueres* who, years ago, residents used to idealize as protectors of their neighbourhoods. At that time, as protectors, they were unwilling to rob or otherwise injure people who had known them "since they used to run naked and snotty-nosed in the streets".[8] Respondents in my own research, conducted in 2006 in several marginal *barrios* of the National District, found that as many as 65 per cent of the residents thought that gangs and *pandillas* (along with police violence) were a serious problem for their communities. Together they were considered the main factors of insecurity experienced by locals (Bobea 2011). Regionally, the Dominican Republic ranks among the highest in the perception by its citizens of the presence of youth gangs in their neighbourhoods.

Despite that disconnection, only by looking at the level of mistrust those residents express about the police and the justice system can one understand why communities still develop relations of interdependence with *pandilleros*. It is not surprising that the two institutions most inclined to engage in repression and corruption (the police) and clientelism (the major political parties) are among the least-trusted institutions in the country (see table 2.2).

As confidence in public institutions declines, youth groups have been assuming state-like functions such as providing employment and mediation. At the same time, as living conditions in marginalized areas deteriorate

Table 2.2. Confidence in institutions (2012)

Institutions	Level of Confidence (%)
Communications media	72.0
Catholic Church	67.4
Protestant Church	62.1
Armed forces	58.2
Central Electoral Council	52.5
Elections	50.9
President	47.7
Supreme Court of Justice	47.4
Congress	44.6
Justice system	42.7
Police	34.9
Political parties	32.3

Source: Americas Barometer 2012 (http://www.vanderbilt.edu/lapop/dr/ DomRepublic-2012-Report.pdf).

even further, people look to *naciones* and *pandillas* for support to help them to get much-needed resources and services. As documented in the literature, collective action and mutual aid have always been a survival strategy used by slum residents (Jankowski 1991, 201–2).

The Search for Alternative Citizenship

Many young people who eventually joined gangs and *pandillas* found themselves disenfranchised from formal citizenship. They lacked birth certificates, which is an impediment to registering for school and obtaining national identification. Through the *naciones,* marginalized young people are re-assimilated as citizens of an organization that is transnational, violent, youthful and freighted with symbolism. At the level of symbolism, *naciones* reject established norms, but they also act as a channel for negotiation on issues that would otherwise be resolved through violent conflict, whether it was with other groups or with the authorities. As highly structured underground societies based in solid allegiances with their own codes of *omertá, naciones* are marked for attention from the authorities as vehicles for organized crime.

If alienation from the larger society is one reason that young people join gangs, their sense of alienation is only reinforced by gang membership, as described to me by a member of the *Trinitarios.* "People in our community judge us; the police search us because of how we look and dress," he said. "There is prejudice everywhere; they put us in jail without justification. They beat us. Anything that happens in the *barrio* they blame on us and they treat us like shit. They say, 'This one is the next to go' " (Trinitarios member Barrio Guachupita, Santo Domingo, 2006).

Renewed presence of gangs and *pandillas* in the streets of Santo Domingo has reignited debate around a hybridized subject who is seen as both the main producer and receiver of violence. The existence of violent gangs is not particular to the Dominican Republic. Since the 1990s, it has been found that Latin American and Caribbean youth gangs members "are responsible for three to five times the amount of violence and crime than non-gang, at-risk youth" (Cunningham et al. 2008, 109).

In the Dominican social imagination, there is a widespread public perception that *pandillas* and gangs are confined to the poorest urban communities. However, *pandillas* also exist in middle- and upper-class neighbourhoods. In these wealthier areas, *pandilla* members conduct illicit and criminal transactions but are shielded by the corrupt justice system and by the police, who never carry out indiscriminate *redadas* (raids) in well-to-do neighbourhoods and are open to receiving bribes from middle- and upper-class kids seeking to avoid incarceration.[9]

There are factors besides poverty that put young people at risk of joining a gang, including lack of connectivity with adults within their communities, also with influential people outside their communities. Nevertheless, as some scholarly work has pointed out (Venkatesh 2008), economic motives figure prominently among the reasons young people join gangs. Miric (2008) conducted research that examined Dominican street gang members ages fifteen to twenty-four years. The study revealed that 39 per cent of gang members entered into the gang for economic reasons, despite the precarious income produced by risky drug-selling activity (*micromenudeo*). Another 16 per cent declared their main reason for joining a gang to be that they already had problems with the law and the judicial system. Once a young person has been *fichado* by the police – or has a criminal record – it is nearly impossible to get the *carta de buena conducta* that is essential for obtaining a decent job in the public or private sector.

The gang recruitment process depends on the existence of *pandillas* in the *barrio* and the previous experience of members of *pandillas*. Recruiters are motivated to incorporate ten- to twelve-year-old males because they are not subject to incarceration within the Dominican justice system. As I was told by members of La Sangre, or Blood, "La Sangre used to recruit twelve- to thirteen-year-old kids whom they motivated by giving them things, showing off in front of them, inviting them to parties and finally to be part of the *nacion*." According to a former member of the Dominican branch of Blood, at that point they have to make a blood oath, which is considered the ultimate commitment to the gang. New pledges sign a contract in their blood and follow an order from the leader of the gang to prove how much he or she is willing to sacrifice for their new family. As one member explained, "First, [the recruiters] talk to them, they give them money and a pistol, they show them how to steal. After that, the new recruit can talk to the king or the second king." Active and former *pandillas'* members explained, "The only accepted way to leave the *pandilla* is through the affiliation of the deserting member to a protestant church" (interviews with *pandilleros*, Gualey, Santo Domingo, 2006). For the last two decades there has been an impressive upsurge of Evangelicals and Pentecostals churches in the Dominican Republic. This increase has been more noticeable in marginalized urban settlements, where the younger population has become a main target for religious conversion. The paradoxical belief of becoming part of another otherworldly

"Reign" (as evangelism preaches), makes it so that you can only truly leave the gang either being "born-again", or by death.

Pandillas tend to rely on networks of loyalties validated through ritualized patterns that help members consolidate their informal business of *narcomenudeo*. These street groups distribute goods and services and provide protection from other gangs and a sporadic source of income to reaffirm their power among acolytes. In contrast to an earlier period when *naciones* and *pandillas* offered a sense of belonging and self-esteem, today, the most important motivation for joining a gang is the opportunity to get involved in illicit markets. Today, gangs are not necessarily organic and local. Many *pandillas* and *naciones* colonize neighbourhoods by sending emissaries from other places, even from other countries, to form or consolidate a particular chapter. According to members of the Dominican gangs Collares and Forty Two, whom I interviewed in Barcelona in 2009, they were briefly sent back to the Dominican Republic by the Inca, or head of the organization, with the mission to reinforce, dissolve or create a chapter in a particular area of the country. Likewise, when I interviewed a member of the special police unit of the Mossos d'Esquadra, he admitted that they had intercepted phone calls from the leadership of some of the *pandillas* in Barcelona to their chapters in the Dominican Republic where instructions and information were exchanged. Chapters overseas enjoy a certain level of autonomy regarding the kinds of activities in which they are involved, and even the type of relationships and liaisons they can establish with other groups. Both local and transnational scenarios are heavily conditioned by the country context, such as police attitude, the possibility to bear arms and the opportunities for getting involved in illicit or criminal activities. In the case of a newly created entity, it does not initially reflect the micro-social characteristics of the new social and institutional environment. These *pandillas* need to learn how to deal with other young members of unfamiliar social, cultural and ethnic backgrounds upon their arrival and how to forge relationships with enforcement officials in a different system. Some groups (like Dominicans) tend to self-segregate into exclusive pockets that complicate potential negotiations and communication with authorities. On the other hand, when I conducted an interview with one of the members of the Dominican 42, he remarked that the police in Barcelona tended to be more lenient than the Dominican officials, who "could go as far as killing you in cold blood" (inteview with a Dominican 42 member in Barcelona, 2009). As time passes, however, these gangs become more established in the local subculture and become more independent from their matrix organization in the Dominican Republic where the "Crown" (*Corona*) is located. Their growing independence is reflected in promotions and reporting on the type of activities taking place in the new country of residence, without the need to get the approval from the home branch.

Generally speaking, joining a gang can bring members numerous rewards. Besides admiration from their peers and respect from members of the community whom *pandilleros* protect or extort from, gang membership ultimately brings some financial compensation. The economic benefits of joining a gang may be short-lived, however: gang memebers only maximize earning when connected to or acquiring a strong corporative profile that balances the cost-benefit equation. Second, the gang lifestyle involves, by definition, consistent violent exchange between other gangs, and sometimes even internally, and there is a high risk of being killed. One study found that 45 per cent of reported gang killings were between rival groups (Abreu 1998). According to the study, conflicts in the *barrios* occurred between gangs and the police 43 per cent of the time, among rival gangs 34 per cent of the time, and with neighbours 15 per cent of the time. Gang violence basically reproduces existing conditions of social and economic inequality, because the poorest, youngest and lowest-level gang members are the most vulnerable and usually the more exposed. Many of those involved at the bottom are not even drug professionals, but informal or opportunistic participants whose earnings are unstable and emanate from multiple sources. This profile also fits many members of street gangs, who do not consistently participate in illegal activity. While well-protected elite members benefit the most from sophisticated illicit activities, younger, less professional participants end up as the primary victims of the violence generated by competitive, street-level drug markets.

One-Way Ticket: The Transmutation of *Pandillas* into Something Else

The process described here shows how *pandillas* and young transgressive entities have been affected by national and international processes, as well as by social and political contexts. There are criminal gangs that closely model new criminality as trans-local, urban, armed, entrepreneurial, opportunistic and state-tropic. This new criminality is more evident in cases of transnational profile, such as Dominicans Don't Play (DDP) and Los Trinitarios, located in both Spain and the United States and constituted almost exclusively of Dominican nationals.

Nationally, the traditional *pandillas* tend to follow another pattern of merging into criminal constituencies, given the systematic insertion of the Dominican Republic into the international criminal economy. The transformation of Dominican gangs, from a street youth association to a more violent criminal entity, varies among and within gangs. Some branches are more oriented towards violence and drug-trafficking activities through their connections with criminal entities in New York and Madrid. The hybridism and mutation experienced by certain gangs have given police the opportunity to gather social support for their gang-control efforts. As mentioned before, Dominican transgressive groups have been massively subject to lethal coercion from the military and the police.

From a sociological perspective, this new delinquency signals the emergence of a new social structure – not necessarily a social class, but a type of social aggregation whose organizing codes, functional rationality and rules of the game differ from those of other social arrangements. This new social strata also enjoys a more dynamic social mobility, even if frequently cut short by premature death. In other words, we are witnessing a restratification of society by the new violence. New actors start occupying an intermediary position; later on they can socially escalate while maintaining their articulations with the lower strata. As gang members interviewed during my research pointed out, "The *Bichote* does not live here anymore, he move to a more upper scale neighbourhood, but he is present in a daily base to check on his business" (a resident, 2011). Collaterally, for beginners, these intermediate members become models of how far you can get if you work carefully by the rules of the game.

Sometimes, the gang's leadership plays by informal institutional arrangements established by traditional politics, such as clientelism and patronage, in order to gain the favour and protection of actors within their environments. These practices cut across class and social position. It works, politically and economically, at either the upper levels of influence, or more territorially. During electoral times, opportunities to enhance their connection with the influential upper levels increase as gang leaders become instrumental for getting votes. A system of politically administered compensation is expected to pay off their involvement. They become more articulated to the personalized system of local politics.

Conclusion

The ascendance and transformation of gangs, *pandillas* and *naciones* in Dominican communities can only be understood in the context of decreasing state legitimacy and increasing consolidation of complex criminality, as well as the illicit national and transnational economy, as alternative ways of obtaining what the state is unable or unwilling to provide. The conditions founded in marginalized urban areas where the state has been only partially present and has often behaved abusively create opportunities for transgressing actors to gain ground based on their own local ties and relations as a result of being part of those communities.

When I first conducted research in several *barrios* of Santo Domingo in 2005, *pandillas* were exerting a significant coercive control over local institutions. This was made clear by the community leadership who declared their frustration over their inability to confront *pandillas* and gangs, as well as by the limitations that people admitted to having in their freedom to circulate within the *barrio* at certain times or places. These dynamics changed when the government implemented a strategic citizen security policy that brought more police presence to the *barrios*. But without introducing major changes in the social and economic conditions of the population, illicit informal survival alternatives continued to appear that were and are more plausible and appealing to gang members.

In a more recent visit to the *barrios* in 2011, *pandilla* presence had noticeably diminished. Their visibility to the national media had also declined. A possible explanation of this invisibility could either be that the *pandillas* are experiencing a process of adaptation – if not by disintegration, then by diffusion – or that they are transforming themselves into more benefit-seeking criminal groups. On the other hand, my interview with the leader of one of the biggest *naciones* in the country, Amor Dorado, introduced another way out for some of these entities – that of becoming legalized associations (as in Spain, mentioned below), revisiting their role and relationships, not only with their communities, but also with formal political and enforcement structures.

These developments suggest that there has been a gradual evolution of the traditional identity of street gangs. New arrangements were made among gangs, between the police and the gangs, and between gang groups and the community in search of how to serve each sector's interests and needs. This changes the balance of power and the type of social order and governance in these poor settlements. As Leeds (1996, 50) found several years ago, the dysfunctional democracy that unfolds in the local settlements and the selective procedural democracy reinforced by political elites and the upper class put squatter populations in a critical balance of resilience and accommodation to state and non-state violent actors.

This chapter accounts for a complex, interactive and kinetic process remaking social orders in many neighbourhoods of the Dominican Republic based on plural violence and transgressive values in relation to previous social orders. These new social orders operate simultaneously and sometimes symbiotically, meaning they are not exclusive, but complementary.

During the earlier years of their formation, Dominican *naciones* and *pandillas* functioned as integrated, local structures. They were based on community allegiances and the provision of a sense of belonging. Further deterioration of social and economic conditions in these marginal communities made competition for scarce goods, services and political contacts ever more urgent. Violent criminality grew, subsuming pre-existing relationships and institutions and redeploying actors according to a harsh new logic based on benefits and opportunities.

Youth gangs became one of many institutions remade by violent and complex criminality, both formal and informal (Bobea 2012). The longing of poor young Dominicans for membership in a new *nacion* that existed underneath the broken formal one could be interpreted as an act of resilience – if only the gangs had not mimetically reproduced authoritarian, sexist and punitive practices so similar to the ones that defined the nation that had rejected them. Nevertheless, because they challenge the boundaries of the existing social order, *pandillas* and *naciones* can become crucial actors in the transformation of unjust and exclusionary social arrangements. They do not necessarily have to become models of negative adaptation for their communities. In fact, their creation of identity through solidarity and their search for inclusiveness can become an important generational reference for communities to create more autonomous forms of control.

An initiative put into place in Barcelona, Spain, over the last decade is one example of how *pandillas* and *naciones* can be approached without compromising their cultural and identity nature. In Barcelona, the municipal government put together a comprehensive, socio-cultural proposal for reinsertion of Latin American youth gangs who were willing to give up violence. The gangs that cooperated worked with Barcelona's *casas de juventud* to develop music and theatre projects, such as Unidos por el Flow. Another example is Casa Morada in Medellin, Colombia, where young people gather around multiple cultural activities, such as dance, painting, conducting radio programmes, independently of any predetermined agenda. In each case, their own communities recognized that these juvenile groups helped to foster a sense of belonging and ethnic pride. The strategic initiatives of these two local governments, Cataluña and Medellin, reinforced rather than suppressed the rituals, symbols and behaviours that had once stigmatized young people from the Dominican Republic and other parts of Latin America. In the case of Cataluña, even the special unit of Barcelona's Mossos d'Esquadra that works with the gangs seems to understand that the young immigrants are seeking to create a viable, meaningful *nacion*.

Notes

1. Despite incongruities in the data that suggest a de-escalation of violence in the Caribbean between 2007 and 2011, the World Bank reported in 2007 the occurrence of 30 homicides per 100,000 inhabitants, while the most recent UNDP Global Study on Homicide tallied 23 homicides per 100,000 for 16 of 22 countries. The Caribbean and Central America are the only two sub-regions where homicide rates have consistently increased since the mid-1990s (UNDP 2011, 22). The UNDP homicide report places the Caribbean after Africa for death by firearms (68 per cent) for at least 11 of 22 Caribbean countries. The majority of those who die are males between 15 and 24 years old (pp. 40–41).
2. *Naciones*, or nations, has been the term that Dominican *pandillas* use to refer to themselves since their first appearance. Its symbolism was made apparent to me during an interview with a member of the nation Amor Dorado. He expressed the group's desire to create something different than the current Dominican nation, implying that for these social actors, their *naciones* are a kind of reifying version of their idealized one.
3. Both terms come from the expanding literature that transfers the notions of resilience and adaptation from the field of natural sciences. See Adger (2000, 1) and Davis (2012, 32).
4. Interview in 2012 with a police member of the Department of Youth Groups in Conflict with the Law (*Manejo de grupos en conflicto con la Ley*), Dominican National Police.
5. The Dominican Central Bank organized these data for ten- to twenty-four-year-olds, while the International Labour Organization reported similar data for fifteen- to twenty-four-year-olds. The difference in age range makes it difficult to attempt comparisons based on these data.
6. In the words of a former young *nacion* member, "A gang is a group of fifteen to twenty members that don't have control, they all do whatever they want, they are all superior, they're all the boss, they're all bullies, which means they have no direction" (personal interview, 2005).
7. The document containing this unpublished information was made available privately to the author.

8. Interview with a Capotillo resident, 2006.
9. Here, I am only studying *pandillas* in poor neighbourhoods.

References

Abreu, F.A. 1998. "Violencia juvenil en la República Dominicana: actitudes, situaciones y propuestas", *Revista de Estudios Sociales* 31(113): 19–36.

Adams, T. 2011. *Chronic Violence and Its Reproduction: Perverse Trends in Social Relations, Citizenship and Democracy in Latin America*. Washington, DC: Woodrow Wilson International Center for Scholars.

Adger, W.N. 2000. "Social and Ecological Resilience: Are They Related?" *Progress in Human Geography* 24(3): 347–64. http://phg.sagepub.com.

Arias, E.D. 2006. *Drugs and Democracy in Rio de Janeiro: Trafficking, Social Networks and Public Security*. Chapel Hill: University of North Carolina Press.

———. 2010. "Understanding Criminal Networks, Political Order, and Politics in Latin America". In *Ungoverned Spaces, Alternatives to State Authority in an Era of Softened Sovereignty*, edited by A. Clunan and H. Trinkunas, 119–35. Stanford, CA: Stanford University Press.

Arias, E.D., and D.M. Goldstein, eds. 2010. *Violent Democracies in Latin America*. Durham, NC and London: Duke University Press.

Arjona, A. 2008. "Local Orders in Warring Times: Armed Groups' and Civilians' Strategies in Civil War". *Qualitative Methods* (Spring): 15–18.

———. 2009. "One National War, Multiple Local Orders: An Inquiry into the Unit of Analysis of War and Post-War Interventions". In *Law in Peace Negotiations* (FICHL Publication Series), edited by M. Bergsmo and P. Kalmanovitz, 199–242. Torkel Opsahl Academic Epublisher and Peace Research Institute Oslo (PRIO).

Bagley, B. 2012. *Drug Trafficking and Organized Crime in the Americas: Major Trends in the Twenty-First Century*. Washington DC: Woodrow Wilson International Center for Scholars, Latin American Program.

Bobea, L. 2005. "Baseline for the Democratic Security Plan". http://www.seip.gob.do.

———. 2011. *Violencia y seguridad democratica en República Dominicana*. Santo Domingo: FLACSO.

———. 2012. "Organized and Disorganized Crime; *Muertos Legales* and *Ilegales* in the Caribbean". In *Revista: Harvard Review of Latin America*, edited by C.J. Erlick, 56–58. Cambridge, MA: Harvard University, David Rockefeller Center for Latin American Studies. http://revista.drclas.harvard.edu/publications/revistaonline/winter-2012/organized-and-disorganized-crime.

Brea, M., and E. de Cabral. 2010. "Factores de riesgo y violencia juvenil en República Dominicana". In *Revista PsicologiaCientifica.com*. http://www.psicologiacientifica.com/violencia-juvenil-factores-de-riesgo-republica-dominicana.

CARICOM. Implementation Agency for Crime and Security. 2010. "Observations on Youth Violence and Gang-Related Activity in the CARICOM Region".

Cassa, R. 1995. *Los jóvenes dominicanos: Situación y tareas.* Santo Domingo, DR: Grupo de Investigación para la Accion Comunitaria.

Ceballos, R. 2004. *Violencia y comunidad en un mundo globalizado.* Santo Domingo: Ediciones Amigo del Hogar y Centro Cultural Poveda.

CEPAL. 2008. *La República Dominicana en 2030: Hacia una nación cohesionada.*

———. 2013. "Empleo juvenil en America Latina y el Caribe: Desafios para el cambio estructural, para la igualdad y opciones de politicas". http://www.redeamerica.org/Portals/0/Documentos/Foros/V_foro_apertura_hugobeteta.pdf.

Cruz, J.M. 2006. *Maras y Pandillas en Centroamérica: Las respuestas de la sociedad civil organizada,* vol. 4. San Salvador: UCA.

Cunningham, W., L. McGinnis, R.G. Verdu, C. Tesliuc, and D. Verner. 2008. "Youth at Risk in Latin America and the Caribbean: Understanding the Causes, Realizing the Potential". *Directions in Human Development.* Washington, DC: International Bank for Reconstruction and Development/The World Bank.

Davis, D.E. 2012. *Urban Resilience in Situations of Chronic Violence.* Cambridge, MA: USAID/MIT.

DiMaggio, P., and W.W. Powell. 1983. "The Iron Cage Revisited: Institutional Isomorphism and Collective Rationality in Organizational Fields". *American Sociological Review,* 48: 147–60.

Dominican Republic National Police. 2006. Statistics Department, Santo Domingo.

Espinal, R., J. Morgan, and M. Seligson, eds. 2012 *Cultura politica de la democracia en República Dominicana: Hacia la igualdad de oportunidades.* LAPOP/Barometro de las Americas. Nashville, TN: Vanderbilt University.

FINJUS (Fundacion Institucionalidad y Justicia) and CONAEJ (Comision Nacional de Ejecucion Procesal y Penal). 2006, 2011. *Censo Penitenciaro de la República Dominicana.*

Griffith, I.L. 2011. "Drugs and Crime as Problems without Passports in the Caribbean: How Secure is Security, and How Sovereign is Sovereignty?" Paper presented at the thirteenth annual Eric E. Williams Memorial Lecture, Florida International University.

Hagedorn, J.M. 2008. *A World of Gangs, Armed Young Men and Gangsta Culture.* Minneapolis: University of Minnesota Press.

Harriott, A. 2008. *Organized Crime and Politics in Jamaica: Breaking the Nexus.* Kingston: Canoe.

Jankowski, S.M. 1991. *Islands in the Street: Gangs and American Urban Society.* Berkeley, CA: University of California Press.

Jutersonke, O., R. Muggah, and D. Rodgers. 2009. "Gangs, Urban Violence and Security Interventions in Central America". *Security Dialogue* 40(4–5): 373–97.

Katz, C.M., E.R. Maguire, and D. Choate. 2011. "A Cross-National Comparison of Gangs in the United States and Trinidad and Tobago". *International Criminal Justice Review* 21(3): 243–62. doi:10.1177/1057567711417179.

Kenney, M. 2007. *From Pablo to Osama: Trafficking and Terrorist Networks, Government Bureaucracies and Competitive Adaptation.* University Park, PA: Pennsylvania State University Press.

Koonings, K., and D. Kruijt, eds. 2004. *Armed Actors: Organized Violence and State Failure in Latin America.* New York: Zed Books.

Leeds, E. 1996. "Cocaine and Parallel Polities in the Brazilian Urban Periphery: Constraints on Local Level Democratization". *Latin America Research Review* 31 (Fall): 47–83.

Lesley, G. 2010. *Confronting the Don: The Political Economy of Gang Violence in Jamaica.* Geneva: Small Arms Survey.

Manwaring, M. 2007. "A Contemporary Challenge to State Sovereignty: Gangs and Other Illicit Transnational Criminal Organizations (TCOs) in Central America, El Salvador, Mexico, Jamaica and Brazil". Carlisle, PA: Strategic Studies Institute, US Army War College.

March, J.G., L.S. Sproull, and M. Tamuz. 1991. "Learning from Samples of One or Fewer". *Organization Science* 2(1): 1–13. http://dx.doi.org/10.1287/orsc.2.1.1.

Miric, M. 2008. "Evaluación y documentación participativa de las estrategias para el cambio de comportamiento implementadas con jóvenes miembros de organiza-ciones de la calle (naciones, gangas y pandillas juveniles)". *Documento Resumen. ONUSIDA/COPRESIDA. República Dominicana*, mayo.

Mogensen, M. 2005. "Corner and Area Gangs of Inner-City Jamaica". In *Neither War nor Peace: International Comparisons of Children and Youth in Organized Crime Vio-lence*, edited by L. Dowdney, 229–45. Rio de Janeiro: Viva Rio.

Moncrieffe, D. 1998. "Gang Study: The Jamaican Crime Scene". Kingston: Criminal Jus-tice Research Unit, Ministry of National Security and Justice.

Moser, C., and J. Holland. 1997. *Urban Poverty and Violence in Jamaica.* Washington, DC: World Bank.

National Gang Intelligence Center. 2009. *National Gang Threat Assessment.* Online annual reports, 2006, 2007. Procuraduría General de la República Dominicana. http://www .fbi.gov/stats-services/publications/national-gang-threat-assessment-2009-pdf.

PNUD. 2008. *Informe sobre desarrollo humano, República Dominicana: Desarrollo humano, una cuestion de poder.* Santo Domingo, DR: Editora Taller.

Powell, W.W. 1990. "Neither Market nor Hierarchy: Network Forms of Organization". In *Research in Organizational Behaviour* (12), edited by B.M. Straw and L.L. Cummints, 295–336. Greenwich, CT: JAI Press.

Procuraduría General de la República Dominicana. Online annual reports, 2006, 2007, 2011. www.procuraduria.gov.do.

Rodgers, D. 1999. *Youth Gangs and Violence in Latin America and the Caribbean: A Literature Survey.* LCR Sustainable Development Working Paper No. 4. Washington, DC: World Bank.

———. 2005. *Urban Segregation from Below: Drugs, Consumption, and Primitive Accu-mulation in Managua, Nicaragua.* Working Paper No. 71, Working Series No. 1. London: Crisis States Research Centre, Development Studies Institute.

Rodgers, D., R. Muggah, and C. Stevenson. 2009. "Gangs of Central America: Causes, Costs, and Interventions". Geneva: Small Arms Survey, Occasional Paper No. 23. http://www.smallarmssurvey.org/fileadmin/docs/B-Occasional-papers/SAS-OP2 3-Gangs-Central-America.pdf.

Rubio, M. 2006. *Del narcosendero a la pandilla, violencia juvenil en República Domini- cana.* New York: Inter-American Development Bank.

Salcedo-Albaran, E., and L.J.G. Salamanca. 2012. "Understanding Informational Fea- tures of Transnational Criminal Networks: Cases from Mexico and Guatemala". *Small Wars Journal,* 9 April. http://smallwarsjournal.com/jrnl/art/understanding- informational-features-of-transnational-criminal-networks-cases-from-mexico-a.

Staniland, P. 2012. "States, Insurgents, and Wartime Political Orders". *Perspectives on Politics* 10(2): 243–64. doi:http://dx.doi.org/10.1017/S1537592712000655.

Tilly, C. 1985. "War Making and State Making as Organized Crime". In *Bringing the State Back In,* edited by E. Peter, D. Rueschemeyer, and T. Skocpol, 169–91. Cambridge: Cambridge University Press.

Townsend, D. 2009. *No Other Life: Gangs, Guns, and Governance in Trinidad and Tobago.* Geneva: Small Arms Survey.

UNDP (United Nations Development Programme). 2011. *Caribbean Human Devel- opment Report (Human Development and the Shift to Better Citizen Security).* New York: UNDP.

———. 2012. *Caribbean Human Development Report (Human Development and the Shift to Better Citizen Security).* New York: UNDP.

Van Gemert, F. 2005. "Youth Groups and Gangs in Amsterdam: A Pretest of the Euro- gang Expert Survey". In *European Street Gangs and Troublesome Youth Groups,* edited by S.H. Decker and F.M. Weemarn, 147–68. Violence Prevention and Policy Series. New York: AltaMira.

Vargas, T. 2008. *Jovenes, delincuencia y drogas: Estudio cualitativo acerca d la delincuen- cia juvenil en Guaricano.* Santo Domingo: Casa Abierta.

Venkatesh, S. 2008. *Off the Books: The Underground Economy of the Urban Poor.* Cambridge, MA: Harvard University Press.

Williams, P. 1998. "Organizing Transnational Crime: Networks, Markets, and Hierarchies". *Transnational Organized Crime* 4(3–4): 57–87.

———. 2001. "Transnational Criminal Networks". In *Networks and Netwars: The Future of Terror, Crime and Militancy,* edited by J. Arquilla and D. Rondfeldt, 61–97. Santa Monica: RAND Corporation.

World Bank. 2007. *Crime, Violence and Development: Trends, Costs, and Policy Options in the Caribbean.* Washington, DC: United Nations Office on Drugs and Crime and World Bank.

3 | Gangs in Trinidad and Tobago

RANDY SEEPERSAD

We know very little about gangs in Trinidad and Tobago or the extent to which gangs contribute to the republic's crime problem. With the exception of Katz and Fox (2010) and Katz, Maguire and Choate (2011), researchers have failed to examine this issue systematically. The present study examines the nature and extent of the gang problem in Trinidad and Tobago and offers an assessment of the impact of criminal gangs on violent crime, as well as recommendations for addressing the problem.

This study draws from a range of data sources including official crime and gang data, criminal history data, police expert survey data and data gathered from a nationally representative sample of 1,595 adults in Trinidad and Tobago (UNDP 2012).[1] Although there are controversies about the definition of a gang, a distinction must be made between social groupings that refer to themselves as gangs but do not engage in illegal activity and social groupings that do engage in illegal activity. This study is concerned solely with the latter. It adopts the definition of gangs used by Klein, Weerman and Thornberry (2006, 418), who define a gang as "any durable, street oriented youth group whose involvement in illegal activity is part of their group identity". Here, durability refers to the persistence of the group beyond just a few months, and *street-oriented* means that the group spends a substantial amount of time on the streets and in public places. The present study adopts the UNODC and World Bank (2007) definition of *youth* to be persons between fifteen and twenty-four years of age.

Katz and Choate (2010) reported that in 2006, there were approximately ninety-five gangs in Trinidad and Tobago with approximately 1,269 gang members, the majority of whom were concentrated in Port of Spain and the Western and Northern Police Divisions. Katz and Choate further indicated that approximately 83 per cent of gang members were of African descent, 13 per cent of East Indian descent, and 4 per cent of other ethnic backgrounds. All of the gangs in Trinidad and Tobago were male dominated and about 87 per cent were composed of adults. Two-thirds of gangs had between six and fifty members; 95 per cent of gangs were composed of citizens of Trinidad and Tobago. The majority of gangs in Trinidad and Tobago (86 per cent) had a group name; 61 per cent referred to themselves as gangs, 26 per cent as crews, and 4.2 per cent as clips or units. A large proportion (88 per cent) claimed turf, while 75 per cent defended their turf. The vast majority (85 per cent) did not have special symbols or identifying clothing, and, almost without exception, illegal activity was accepted by all gang members. More recent data indicate that as of 2012 there were 102 criminal gangs in Trinidad and Tobago.[2]

Twenty-six per cent of the gangs in Trinidad and Tobago located their dates of origin prior to 2000, while the remainder originated after 2000. Gangs in Trinidad and Tobago typically were smaller than gangs in Latin America and the United States and did not have linkages to gangs in other parts of the region or to gangs in other countries. This contrasted with some of the larger gangs in Latin America, which had connections to other gangs within their regions and in the United States (Wells, Katz and Kim 2010; Katz and Choate 2010).

The Besson Street Gang Intelligence Criminal History Project conducted by Katz and Choate (2010) offers additional insight into the nature and composition of gangs in Trinidad and Tobago. In this project, 368 gang members were interviewed in 2005. The age distribution of the sample gives an indication of the typical age ranges of gang members.[3] The majority of gang members were young adults between the ages of 18 and 45. More specifically, 26.1 per cent were between the ages of 18 and 21, 25.4 per cent were between the ages of 22 and 25, and 33.7 per cent were between the ages of 26 and 35. Only a small proportion (5.3 per cent) of the members in the sample were 17 or younger at the time of interview, whereas 8 per cent were between the ages of 36 and 45, and 1.5 per cent were between the ages of 46 and 55. Of the gang members in the sample gathered at the Besson Street project, 87.5 per cent were of African descent, 0.8 per cent of East Indian descent, and 1.9 per cent of mixed descent, while the ethnicities of 9.5 per cent were unknown. Gang members were almost exclusively male (95.3 per cent).

Gang Involvement in Illegal Activities

Katz and Maguire (2006) examined gang intelligence data from the Besson Street Police Station and found that 51.4 per cent of gang members had been previously arrested, with each member having an average of 2.09 arrests. Compare this with a non-gang sample (n = 878) in which 20.2 per cent had previous arrests, with the mean number of arrests being 0.68. Not surprisingly, arrest data indicated that gang members had committed a larger number of crimes than persons who were not in gangs (see table 3.1). Arrest data in table 3.1 indicate that gang members committed violent offences at approximately three times the rate of persons who were not in gangs (31.5 per cent vs. 10.4 per cent). Almost 26 per cent of gang members were arrested for firearm-related offences compared with 8.7 per cent of non-gang persons. Similarly, 15.2 per cent of gang members were arrested for drug trafficking compared with 3.2 per cent of non-gang members. Similar overrepresentation in criminal offences for gang members exists for property offences, sexual offences and drug use/possession.

Table 3.1. Per cent of gang members and non-gang members previously arrested

	Gang members (N = 368)	Non-gang members (N = 878)
Ever arrested	51.4	20.2
Arrest by crime type		
Violent offences	31.5	10.4
Firearm-related	25.8	8.7
Drug trafficking	15.2	3.2
Drug use/possession	23.4	8.0
Property offences	13.9	7.6
Sexual offences	2.7	1.8
Other	12.5	5.7

Source: Katz and Maguire 2006.

Data on the mean number of arrests also support the argument that gang membership is associated with a disproportionately high crime rate (see table 3.2). The mean number of arrests for gang members for violent crimes was 0.81 compared with 0.33 for non-gang members. When only firearm-related offences are considered, gang members had almost twice the average number of arrests (0.45) compared with non-gang members (0.22). The disparity becomes much larger when considering drug trafficking. Gang members had an arrest rate that was almost five times that of non-gang members (0.24 vs. 0.05). In a similar manner, the arrest rates for gang members exceeded that of non-gang members for drug use/possession and property offences. Only in the case of sexual offences were the arrest rates similar for gang and non-gang members. The above findings are consistent with previous research, which points to an association between gangs, guns, illegal drugs and other illegal activities (Montoute 2010; UNODC and World Bank 2007; Katz and Fox 2010; Wells, Katz and Kim 2010; Katz and Choate 2010).

Trinidad and Tobago Police Service data (TTPS/CAPA) on the spatial distribution of gangs and on the spatial distribution of crime suggest that gang members may be responsible for a significant proportion of violent crimes that occur in Trinidad and Tobago (Maguire 2012). Occurrences of violent crimes tend to be concentrated in the same areas where gangs are located. Data from the Trinidad and Tobago Police Service indicate that the police divisions[4] with

Table 3.2. Mean number of arrests for gang members and non-gang members

	Gang members (N = 368)	Non-gang members (N = 878)
Number of arrests	2.09	.68
Number of arrests by crime type		
Violent offences	.81	.33
Firearm-related	.45	.22
Drug trafficking	.24	.05
Drug use/possession	.32	.12
Property offences	.36	.17
Sexual offences	.03	.03
Other	.20	.16

Source: Katz and Maguire 2006.

the largest number of gangs are the Port of Spain Division, the Western Division and the Northern Division. Other areas with a notable gang presence include the Eastern Division and the North Eastern Division. The number of gangs in each police division is shown in table 3.3.

According to Katz and Choate (2010), the five police station districts[5] with the most gangs are, in order of priority, Besson Street, San Juan, Sangre Grande, St Joseph and Belmont. The five police station districts with the highest number of gang members in order of priority are Besson Street, Belmont, San Juan, Caranage and Sangre Grande (see table 3.4).

The spatial distribution of gangs can be compared with the spatial distribution of crime to assess the extent to which areas with a higher concentration of gangs have higher levels of crime. It should be noted here, however, that data for the spatial distribution of gangs are only available for 2009 and 2012. Table 3.5 provides data on gang-related murders for the period 2001 to 2012, while figures 3.1 and 3.2 indicate the per cent of gangs and the per cent of gang-related murders according to police division for 2009 and 2012, respectively.

Analysis of the data in table 3.5 shows that the spatial distribution of gang-related murders in Trinidad and Tobago bears a striking similarity to the spatial distribution of gangs. For the period 2001 to 2012, a total of 1,244 gang-related murders occurred in Trinidad and Tobago. Of these, 568, or 45.7 per

Table 3.3. Number of gangs in Trinidad and Tobago by police division

Police Division	2009	2012
Port of Spain	16	44
Southern	3	04
Western	12	16
Northern	12	13
Central	2	3
South Western	1	2
Eastern	6	3
North Eastern	5	12
Tobago	3	5
Total	60	102

Source: Katz and Maguire 2006.

Table 3.4. Police station districts with the highest number of gangs and gang members

Police station districts with the highest number of gangs		
	Number of gangs	**Number of gang members**
Besson Street	19	385
San Juan	8	130
Sangre Grande	8	90
St Joseph	7	55
Belmont	6	165
Police station districts with the highest number of gang members		
Besson Street	19	385
Belmont	6	165
San Juan	8	130
Caranage	4	100
Sangre Grande	8	90

Source: Katz and Maguire 2006.

Table 3.5. Gang-related murders by location

Police Division	Number of gang-related murders												Per cent of gangs by location	
	2001	2002	2003	2004	2005	2006	2007	2008	2009	2010	2011	2012	2009	2012
Port of Spain	3	10	28	14	33	37	61	116	87	40	59	80	26.7	43.1
Southern	0	1	2	1	0	0	4	3	1	4	1	2	5.0	3.9
Western	0	0	3	5	27	18	22	47	42	15	13	20	20.0	15.7
Northern	0	1	5	1	9	17	55	44	23	5	10	13	20.0	12.7
Central	0	0	0	0	0	1	3	10	0	0	2	5	3.3	2.9
South Western	0	1	0	0	1	0	1	0	0	0	0	1	1.7	2.0
Eastern	0	0	0	0	1	0	6	6	1	3	0	2	10.0	2.9
North Eastern	0	4	4	11	10	25	53	52	22	8	8	21	8.3	11.8
Tobago	0	0	0	0	0	0	0	0	0	0	0	0	5.0	4.9

Source: Ministry of National Security.

cent, occurred in the Port of Spain Police Division, while 183, or 14.7 per cent, occurred in the Northern Division. In addition, 212, or 17.0 per cent, occurred in the Western Division, while 218, or 17.5 per cent, occurred in the North Eastern Division. These are the same divisions that have a disproportionately large number of gangs.

When gang locations and gang-related murders are restricted to 2009, the spatial distribution of such murders closely resembles the spatial distribution of gangs (see figure 3.1). In 2009, 49.4 per cent of all gang-related murders took place in the Port of Spain Division, which is also the division with the largest proportion of gangs (26.7 per cent). The Western and Northern Police Divisions also had a disproportionately large number of gang-related murders and a correspondingly large number of gangs. In 2009, 20 per cent of all gangs were located in the Western Division. This division accounted for 23.9 per cent of all gang-related murders. The Northern Division accounted for 20 per cent of all gangs, and 13.1 per cent of all gang-related murders. As figure 3.1 also illustrates, police divisions with fewer gangs have fewer gang-related murders.

Data for 2012 also exhibit similar spatial consistency (see figure 3.2). In 2012, the divisions with the largest proportion of gangs (the Port of Spain Division – 43.1 per cent of all gangs, the Western Division – 15.7 per cent, and the Northern Division – 12.7 per cent) are also the divisions with the highest proportion of gang-related murders.

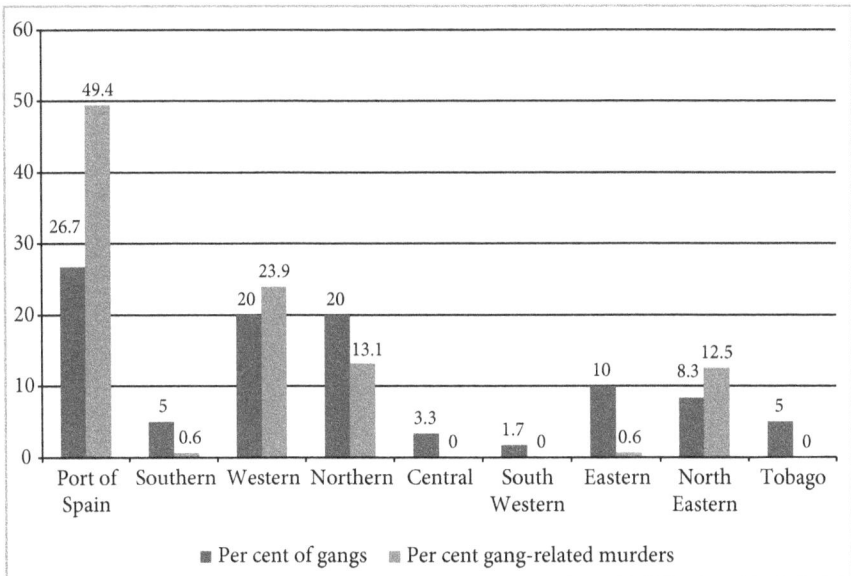

Figure 3.1. Gang locations (2009) and gang-related murders (2009)

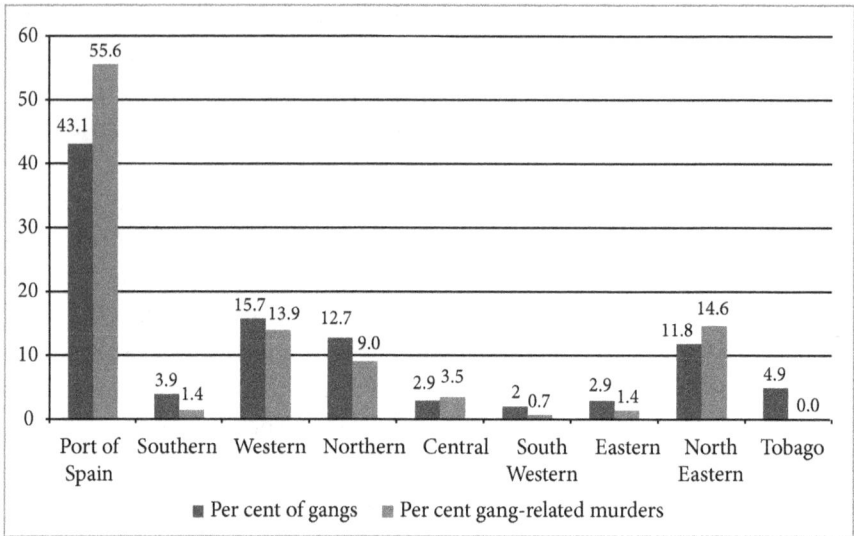

Figure 3.2. Gang locations (2012) and gang-related murders (2012)

Although a close association between gang presence and gang-related murders should be expected, similar spatial patterns are observed for a range of other crimes, even where no distinction is made between crimes committed by gang members and crimes committed by other persons.[6] The spatial distribution of a range of crimes compared with the spatial distribution of gangs supports the possibility that perpetrators may be gang members, even though official records are unable to verify whether or not such crimes were committed by gang members. Table 3.6 indicates the distribution of gangs in Trinidad and Tobago as of 2009, and also the percentage of distribution of various crimes, according to police division, for the period of 2009 to 2010.

In priority order, the spatial distribution of gangs most closely resembles the spatial distribution of murder, woundings and shootings, robbery, narcotic offences and burglary (see figure 3.3). The spatial distribution of gangs is unrelated to the distribution of sexual offences and kidnapping.[7]

Table 3.7 indicates the spatial distribution of gangs in Trinidad and Tobago as of 2012 and also indicates the percentage of distribution of various crimes, according to police division, for 2012.

The spatial distribution of gangs most closely resembles, in priority order, the spatial distribution of murder, woundings and shootings, and robbery (see figure 3.4). The spatial distribution of gangs is unrelated to the distribution of sexual offences, kidnappings, narcotic offences and burglary.

Table 3.6. Spatial distribution of gangs (2009) and the spatial distribution of crime (2009–2010)

Police Division	Per cent of gangs by location	Murder	Woundings/ shootings	Sexual offences	Kidnapping	Robbery	Narcotic offences	Burglary
Port of Spain	26.7	22.5	24.1	6.8	14.2	17.3	13.4	12.2
Southern	5.0	9.7	10.3	14.1	16.4	14.5	14.2	14.2
Western	20.0	14.2	12.5	7.1	6.6	9.2	4.3	9.0
Northern	20.0	21.9	16.8	15.2	15.7	25.0	23.2	19.5
Central	3.3	9.1	11.0	10.6	15.0	14.5	7.0	14.8
South Western	1.7	4.3	6.3	10.2	13.9	4.6	6.1	7.2
Eastern	10.0	5.3	5.3	16.4	8.0	4.9	18.5	6.7
North Eastern	8.3	10.5	11.3	13.2	4.4	8.1	5.2	8.7
Tobago	5.0	2.5	2.4	6.4	5.8	1.9	8.1	7.7

Source: Ministry of National Security.

Note: Crime figures indicate the percentage of crime that occurred in each police division. Data upon which these calculations are based are available from the author upon request.

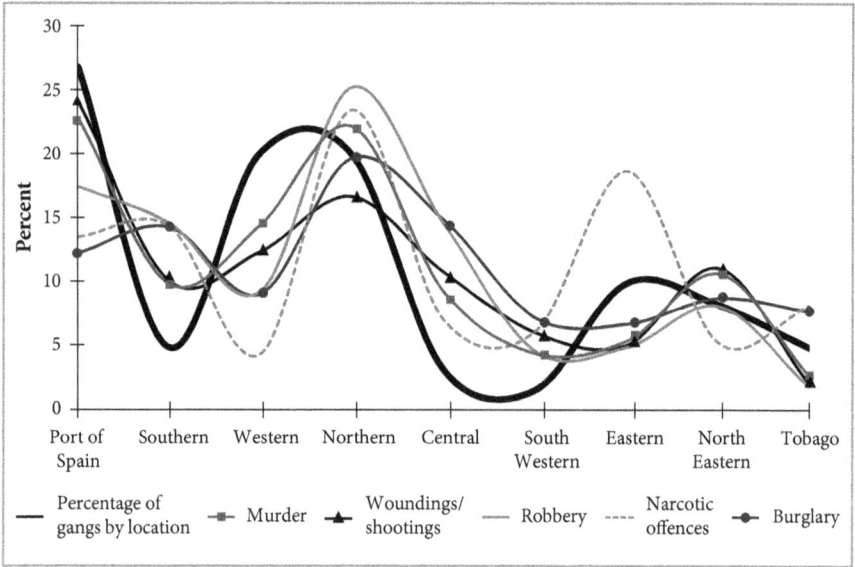

Figure 3.3. The spatial distribution of gangs (2009) and the spatial distribution of crime (2009–2010)

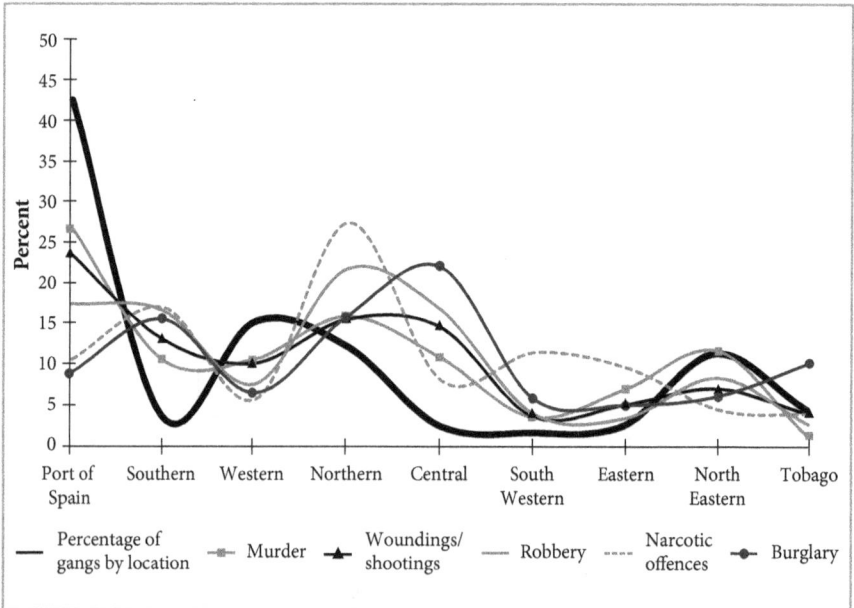

Figure 3.4. The spatial distribution of gangs (2012) and the spatial distribution of crime (2012)

Table 3.7. Spatial distribution of gangs (2012) and the spatial distribution of crime (2012)

Police Division	Per cent of gangs by location	Mur- der	Woundings/ shootings	Sexual offences	Kidnapping	Robbery	Narcotic offences	Burglary
Port of Spain	43.1	27.2	24.0	6.2	5.9	17.6	10.8	9.4
Southern	3.9	10.8	13.5	21.2	17.8	16.8	17.2	16.0
Western	15.7	10.8	10.5	12.0	7.6	7.7	5.9	6.9
Northern	12.7	16.1	15.9	13.3	7.6	21.9	27.7	16.3
Central	2.9	11.1	15.0	10.8	20.5	17.0	8.2	22.5
South Western	2.0	3.7	4.0	7.5	10.8	4.2	11.7	6.3
Eastern	2.9	7.1	5.4	13.5	15.7	3.5	9.8	5.4
North Eastern	11.8	11.9	7.4	9.4	3.8	8.5	4.6	6.5
Tobago	4.9	1.3	4.3	6.0	10.3	2.8	4.1	10.6

Source: Ministry of National Security.

Note: Crime figures indicate the percentage of crime that occurred in each police division.

The data indicate that locations with a higher concentration of gangs have higher crime rates, particularly for murder, shootings and robbery, and, to some extent, for burglary and narcotic offences. In the case of sexual offences, while these may have been committed by gang members, the distribution of such offences was not concentrated only in areas with a high gang presence. Similarly, kidnapping was distributed throughout the country. It may be the case that some kidnappings were committed by gang members who moved to locations outside their areas of residence to commit these crimes.

Although the above data are suggestive of the possibility that gangs are responsible for a disproportionate number of crimes, and that gangs tend to commit crimes within their areas of residence, caution is warranted in drawing these conclusions. Data on the location of gangs were limited to 2009 and 2012. Ideally, the distribution of gangs and the distribution of crime should be mapped on a year-to-year basis, both with and without a lag on crime data. It may also be useful to map the location of gangs, even where such data are restricted to 2009 and 2012, to crime data which precede that period. The spatial distribution of crime in Trinidad and Tobago has exhibited stability over the last ten years, and, to the extent that the spatial distribution of gangs also exhibits stability, it may be reasonable to use data for the period 2001–2012 to examine the relationship between gang location and crime. Given that gangs in Trinidad and Tobago tend to be localized in terms of territory or turf (Katz and Choate 2010), the assumption of stability in the location of gangs is a reasonable one. It should be noted, however, that such analysis will be open to the criticism that the occurrence of the crimes precedes the presence of the gangs in the specified locations, at least based on the time period for which data on gang locations are available.

Another issue that must be considered is that of causal order. The reasoning above implies that gangs influence crime rates in various places, but it may be the case that gangs gravitate to places with high crime rates for various reasons, or it may be that other factors such as the number of illegal opportunities (Cloward and Ohlin 1960) influence both the crime rates and the density of gangs in various places.

Additional evidence that gangs are responsible for a disproportionate number of violent crimes derives from homicide data from the Trinidad and Tobago Police Service (see table 3.8).[8] Fully 29.5 per cent of all murders for the period 2001–2012 are attributed to gangs. Even more troubling is the finding that the proportion of murders being committed by gang members is increasing over time. Whereas the proportion of murders committed by gang members for the period 2001–2003 was 11.3 per cent, the proportion rose dramatically to 36.7 per cent for the period 2007–2012. Gang murders exhibit a consistent increase for the period 2001–2008, with a decrease from 2008 to 2010 and an increase thereafter (see table 3.8). Note that the observed increase in gang-related murders could be due to increasing awareness and emphasis on gangs or to the improved ability to solve murder cases. This argument implies that the proportion of gang-related murders may have been high in the past but is only now coming to light due to greater awareness of gang involvement in violent crime. At the same time, given the limitations in Trinidad and Tobago in assessing whether or not murders are gang-related (King 2012), it is quite possible that official data underestimate the proportion of murders that are committed by gangs.

Some of the most recent data on gangs in Trinidad and Tobago come from a United Nations Development Programme survey of 1,595 adults in Trinidad

Table 3.8. Total murders and gang-related murders (2001–2012)

Year	Total murders	Gang-related	% Gang-related
2001	151	3	2.0
2002	171	17	9.9
2003	229	42	18.3
2004	261	32	12.3
2005	386	81	21.0
2006	371	98	26.4
2007	391	205	52.4
2008	547	278	50.8
2009	506	176	34.8
2010	472	75	15.9
2011	352	93	26.4
2012	379	144	38.0
Total	4,216	1,244	29.5

Source: Ministry of National Security.

and Tobago. Respondents were eighteen years and older, and data were collected in November 2010. It was found that 14.5 per cent of respondents indicated that gang violence occurred in their neighbourhoods in 2009, while 13.9 per cent indicated that there was a criminal gang in their neighbourhoods. Fully 18.4 per cent of respondents indicated that gang violence was a somewhat serious, serious or very serious problem in their neighbourhoods. When the sample was restricted to persons who indicated the presence of a criminal gang in their neighbourhoods, fully 71.7 per cent indicated that gang violence was a somewhat serious, serious or very serious problem in their neighbourhoods. When the entire sample is considered, 12 per cent of the respondents indicated that gangs made their neighbourhoods less safe, while only 0.6 per cent indicated that gangs made their neighbourhoods safer. When the sample was restricted to neighbourhoods with criminal gangs, 82.4 per cent indicated that gangs made their neighbourhoods less safe, while 3.2 per cent indicated that gangs made their neighbourhoods safer. Overall, 15.2 per cent of the sample indicated that their neighbourhoods experienced a small amount of gang violence, while 8.1 per cent lived in neighbourhoods with some gang violence, and 2.3 per cent lived in neighbourhoods with a large amount of gang violence. When the sample was restricted to neighbourhoods with criminal gangs, 34.2 per cent of the sample indicated that their neighbourhoods experienced a small amount of gang violence, while 45.5 per cent indicated that their neighbourhoods had some gang violence, and 14.4 per cent indicated that their neighbourhoods had a large amount of gang violence. Importantly, it was found that 16 per cent of respondents in neighbourhoods with gangs reported some form of criminal victimization, as opposed to 9.6 per cent of respondents in neighbourhoods without gangs. Persons in neighbourhoods with gangs were almost three times as likely to be victims of violent crimes compared with persons in neighbourhoods without gangs (10.1 per cent vs. 3.7 per cent). Where property victimization was concerned, 5.3 per cent of persons in neighbourhoods with gangs reported victimization compared with 4.2 per cent of persons in neighbourhoods without gangs.

Strategies for Addressing the Gang Issue

Interviewing key stakeholders and officials in the Trinidad and Tobago Ministry of National Security, the police service and other bodies, Katz, Choate and Fox (2010) found that "gangs and gang-related violence are at epidemic proportions in Trinidad and Tobago", but that there is "almost no attention to primary gang prevention programming" and there is "strong resistance to its implementation within some Ministries". Suppressive strategies are limited in their effectiveness and must be complemented with preventive mechanisms. A comprehensive policy for dealing with gangs must include primary and secondary prevention strategies, (Brantingham and Faust 1976) and must focus on proximal, as well as distal, risk factors that are at varying levels of analysis, including the individual, peer group, family, community, economy and society. Such a strategy must be based on empirical evidence that indicates which factors are the most important, such that the factors focused upon are the ones that have a demonstrated link with the reduction of gang membership and violence.

Primary prevention refers to those strategies that target the general population and are designed to reduce the likelihood of criminal offending. In the context of the present study, such strategies should focus on reducing the likelihood that persons will join gangs, should place emphasis on neighbourhood and school social life and safety, and should build a sense of community cohesiveness and develop informal systems of social control. As indicated above, preventive strategies must be grounded in research that indicates which factors are most closely related to gang formation and violence. Katz and Fox (2010) identified which risk and protective factors are predictors of gang membership in Trinidad and Tobago. Their sample consisted of 2,206 students with a mean age of fifteen years. The sample was drawn from twenty-two high-risk schools.[9] Almost 60 per cent of the students in the sample were female, while 41 per cent were of African descent, 23 per cent of East Indian descent, and 15 per cent were mixed (one parent of African and the other of East Indian descent). The majority of respondents (79.4 per cent) reported never being in a gang, while 6.2 per cent were current gang members, 6.8 per cent were former gang members and 7.7 per cent were gang associates.

Katz and Fox (2010) assessed the association between thirty risk factors, thirteen protective factors and gang membership. These factors belonged to the peer-individual, family, school and community domains. Risk factors that were important within the peer-individual domain were having antisocial peers, having peers who used illegal drugs and alcohol, early initiation into antisocial behaviour, and the intention to use drugs. Within the community domain, residential mobility and the availability of guns were important predictors. Within the school domain, low commitment to school was an important predictor, while within the family domain, parental attitudes favourable to antisocial behaviour were important. A number of protective factors were also found to be important predictors of gang membership. At the peer-individual level, gang members were less likely than non-gang members to report high levels of social skills or pro-social values and attitudes. Katz and Fox found that exposure to a greater number of risk factors increased the likelihood of gang membership, while exposure to a larger number of protective factors reduced the likelihood of gang membership.

Data collected by the United Nations Development Programme (n = 1,595 adults in Trinidad and Tobago) also allowed for an assessment of risk factors. Important predictors included income, community cohesion, societal cohesion and informal social control. Community cohesion was measured by four items (Cronbach's alpha=0.871), including "living here gives me a sense of community" and "the associations/relationships that I have with the people in this neighbourhood/community mean a lot to me", with responses ranging from strongly agree to strongly disagree. Societal cohesion was measured by twenty items (Cronbach's alpha=0.866), including "I feel like I belong in this country" and "I feel loyal to the people of this country". Informal social control was measured by three items that assessed the likelihood that community members would intervene in situations in which others required assistance (Cronbach's alpha=0.828). Items included "a suspected case of domestic violence" and "a fight breaking out in front of your house with someone being beaten", with responses ranging from very unlikely to very likely. Dependent variables were the presence of gangs, gang problems in the neighbourhood and the level of gang violence. These were assessed by asking the following questions: "Is there a criminal gang (or gangs) in your neighbourhood?", "To what extent is there a criminal gang problem in your neighbourhood?", and "To what extent has your neighbourhood experienced gang violence?" It was found that lower income was related to a higher likelihood of gang presence in neighbourhoods. Income, however, was not related to gang problems and gang violence. Community cohesion, as well as societal cohesion, suppressed gang problems and gang violence in neighbourhoods. More specifically, high levels of each type of cohesion were related to low levels of gang problems and gang violence. Notably, each type of cohesion exhibited independent influence on gang problems and violence. Informal social control was found to exhibit a suppressive effect on gang violence. This may indicate that informal systems of control reduce gang violence, but it could also indicate that higher levels of gang violence exert a suppressive effect on informal systems of behaviour regulation. Further research is required to validate and extend the findings of Katz and Fox (2010) and the UNDP (2012). Such research will indicate which factors are the most important

to address when developing preventive strategies for dealing with gang formation and violence in Trinidad and Tobago.

Secondary prevention strategies should focus on communities with a high
gang presence and high rates of criminal offending. The spatial distribution of
crime in Trinidad and Tobago exhibits a high degree of stability, and available
data quickly point to those communities that are high crime areas. The data used
to compile divisional statistics contain the addresses of each offence committed.
Such datasets can be used to determine which police station districts and which
communities within each district are responsible for a disproportionate number of violent offences. An examination of the addresses for all murders for the
period 1 January 2009 to 31 October 2011, for example, indicate that the police
station districts with the highest number of murders are Besson Street (243, or
19 per cent of the national total for that period),[10] Arima (99), West End (78)
and Morvant (68). The communities with the highest number of murders are
Laventille (172, or 13.4 per cent of the national total for that period), Diego
Martin (66) and Morvant (53). Statistics from the range of serious crimes can be
employed to identify those communities that should be targeted for sustained
intervention.

Data on the spatial distribution of crime should be used in conjunction
with data on the prevalence of gangs in various communities when attempting
to specify the locations for secondary prevention strategies. The most recent
data that can be used to ascertain the location of gangs derive from a nationally
representative sample of persons who were interviewed by the United Nations
Development Programme in November 2010. Of the persons who responded
"yes" to the question "Is there a criminal gang (or gangs) in your neighbourhood?" (n = 222 or 13.9 per cent of the sample), the majority were located in the
communities of Port of Spain, Bonaire, San Fernando and Arima. These data,
in conjunction with the data in figure 3.3, indicate the locations with a higher-
than-average gang presence. As with primary prevention strategies, secondary
prevention should focus on risk factors that are relevant to the communities
and persons who are identified as being at risk. The factors relevant to such
communities and persons are not necessarily the same ones that are relevant
to the population at large. Empirical research must be conducted using at-risk
samples to determine what approaches must be taken to address the problems
of gangs and violence.

In designing and administering gang and crime prevention strategies, it is
important to be aware of unintended negative outcomes that can occur as a
result. In Trinidad and Tobago, one strategy which has had an adverse effect in

communities with gangs relates to the provision of part-time unemployment relief to residents. More specifically, the Unemployment Relief Programme (URP) provides employment for unskilled persons where such persons are engaged in cleaning various neighbourhoods. For reasons that are not entirely clear, where communities have known criminal gangs, the funding for such projects is channelled and disbursed to workers through various gang leaders. This may have occurred because other persons in such communities may not challenge gang leaders for the headship of such programmes, or because governments may have seen this as a way of diverting gangs away from illegal activities. What has occurred instead is that gangs and gang leaders have been empowered to control various communities to the point where they can provide assistance and resources to community members, in turn getting their support and respect. In the latter part of 2011 and early 2012, gang rivalries erupted in an effort to control such contracts. Many gang leaders and members have been murdered, sometimes by persons within their own gangs, as such persons vie for control of URP contracts and funding. One solution to this is to remove the control of such resources from gang members and leaders. These resources could be controlled by a central authority that is empowered to supervise the work that is done and administer payment. Another failed intervention strategy in Trinidad and Tobago involves the use of mediated truces (Maguire 2012). Empirical evidence indicates that truces can actually assist in the development of relationships between rival gangs, making them more potent or, when truces fail, can escalate the rivalries to a level beyond that which existed prior to the truce.

Another preventive strategy important in the case of Trinidad and Tobago relates to addressing proximate risk factors – the events that immediately precede and cause violent acts. Many of the preventive strategies listed above will have medium- to long-term effects, but in the short term, interventions are needed to de-escalate a potentially violent or fatal event prior to its occurring. The Chicago CeaseFire approach uses this strategy and should be considered for use within Trinidad and Tobago. CeaseFire focuses on changing the behaviour of a small number of carefully selected members of the community, specifically, those with a high chance of either "being shot or being a shooter" in the immediate future. Violence interrupters work on the street, mediating conflicts between gangs and intervening to stem the cycle of retaliatory violence that threatens to break out following a shooting. Outreach workers counsel young clients and connect them to a range of services. CeaseFire is built upon a coherent theory of behaviour that specifies how change agents could be mobilized to address some of the immediate causes of violence: norms regarding violence, on-the-spot decision-making by individuals at risk of triggering violence, and the perceived risks and costs of involvement in violence among the targeted population. Although there are a range of potential interventions where gang-related violence in Trinidad and Tobago is concerned, addressing the proximate causes of gang violence is an important strategy which would complement long-term preventive interventions.

In Trinidad and Tobago, suppressive and law enforcement strategies are given priority over preventive measures. Such strategies have met with little success in the fight against gangs, crime and violence. There is an absence of coordination between the bodies responsible for crime reduction and other institutions that provide mechanisms for primary prevention. Establishing such linkages can provide opportunities for preventive measures without substantially increasing the financial burden on the Ministry of National Security and other law enforcement agencies. As an example, although education may increase levels of civility in the population and by extension reduce crime and violence, it does so only as a by-product because there is no purposive strategy to use the education system as a mechanism to reduce crime and violence. Purposeful strategies can be developed and implemented within the education system such that youths develop attitudes, values and skills that make them less predisposed to using violence and engaging in criminal activity. The same applies to other systems that are capable of reaching families and communities, for example community organizations and youth groups. Such an approach will enhance the effectiveness of the Ministry of National Security and other similar agencies and allow them to capitalize on the strengths, reach and resources of other institutions in the fight against gangs and violence.

Although a preventive approach may inhibit the formation of new gangs, it may not sufficiently hinder the continuance of established gangs. Suppressive approaches may be more relevant within this context. Suppressive strategies are reactive in nature and rely on criminal law and the weight of legal sanctions to be effective. Suppressive mechanisms can include arrests, prosecution, fines, imprisonment, seizure of property and other such strategies. Suppressive strategies may serve to incapacitate gang members, deter gang members who have been convicted (specific deterrence) and deter persons who may become involved in gangs (general deterrence). When gang members are successfully prosecuted, incapacitation should be coupled with rehabilitative strategies, and there should be a simultaneous emphasis on reducing the social and economic conditions that predispose gang formation and criminal offending. Suppressive strategies should also attempt to cut off the funding available to gangs. In Trinidad and Tobago, state funding is channelled to gangs through legitimate projects, such as the Community-Based Environmental Protection and Enhancement Programme and the Unemployment Relief Programme (UNDP 2012). Such funding aids in the legitimization of gangs and contributes to their continuance. Note that suppressive strategies will not be successful without the simultaneous use of preventive strategies. For example, if imprisoned gang members are released back into a society or community where there are no legitimate opportunities and where the social and environmental conditions encourage gang membership, then it is unlikely that such persons will desist from future offending.

Gangs represent an extremely difficult problem in Trinidad and Tobago. The gang issue is one that must not be ignored because the problem may escalate to the point where gangs cannot be eradicated. This chapter demonstrates a link between gangs and violence, and argues that the use of suppressive strategies should be complemented by preventive strategies in the fight against gangs in Trinidad and Tobago. Preventive strategies should be focused at the individual, community, national and other relevant levels and should be based on factors that have been empirically linked to gang formation and violence.

Notes

1. These data were gathered by the United Nations Development Programme (UNDP) for the 2012 Caribbean Human Development Report. The current author was national consultant for Trinidad and Tobago for this publication. The present study is the first to examine those data that pertain specifically to gangs in Trinidad and Tobago.
2. According to the Crime and Problem Analysis branch of the Trinidad and Tobago Police Service.
3. These data derive from n = 264 respondents for whom ages were known.
4. Trinidad and Tobago is divided into nine police divisions. There are approximately seventy-eight police stations within these divisions.
5. Police station districts refer to the area of jurisdiction of each police station.
6. Data which indicate whether or not other major crimes are gang related are not available from the Ministry of National Security.

7. Comparison of the rank ordering of gangs and crimes according to police division was used to determine which crimes are most closely associated with the location of gangs.

8. Crime figures indicate the percentage of crime that occurred in each Police Division. Data upon which these calculations are based are available from the author upon request. Data source: Ministry of National Security.

9. In this study, "high-risk schools" were defined as those identified by the Trinidad and Tobago Ministry of Education as having a disproportionate number of students living in high-crime areas or schools with a high number of delinquent incidents.

10. As of March 2012, there are seventy-seven police station districts within the nine police divisions in Trinidad and Tobago. A total of 1,281 murders occurred in Trinidad and Tobago for the period 1 January 2009 to 31 October 2011.

References

Brantingham, P.J., and F.L. Faust. 1976. "A Conceptual Model of Crime Prevention". *Crime and Delinquency* 22(3): 284–96.

Cloward, R., and L. Ohlin. 1960. *Delinquency and Opportunity.* New York: Free Press.

Katz, C.M., and D. Choate. 2010. *Diagnosing Trinidad and Tobago's Gang Problem.* Phoenix: Arizona State University, Center for Violence Prevention and Community Safety, School of Criminology and Criminal Justice.

Katz, C.M., D. Choate, and A. Fox. 2010. "Understanding and Preventing Gang Membership in Trinidad and Tobago". *Crime and Justice Analysis* 31 (December).

Katz, C.M., and A. Fox. 2010. "Risk and Protective Factors Associated with Gang-involved Youth in Trinidad and Tobago". *Pan-American Journal of Public Health/ Revista Panamericana de Salud Pública* 27(3): 187–202.

Katz, C.M., and E.R. Maguire. 2006. *Reducing Gang Homicides in the Besson Street Station District.* Report, Arizona State University, Phoenix.

Katz, C.M., E.R. Maguire, and D. Choate. 2011. "A Cross-National Comparison of Gangs in the United States and Trinidad and Tobago". *International Criminal Justice Review* 21(3): 1–20.

King, W.R. 2012. "Estimating and Investigating Gang Homicide in the Caribbean: Lessons from Trinidad and Tobago". Presentation at the Symposium on Gangs and Gang Violence in the Caribbean. School of Public Affairs, American University, Washington, DC, 17 February. http://www.american.edu/spa/djls/caribbean-gangs-presentations .cfm.

Klein, M., F. Weerman, and T. Thornberry. 2006. "Street Gang Violence in Europe". *European Journal of Criminology* 3(4): 413–37.

Maguire, E.R. 2012. "Preventing Gang Violence in the Caribbean: Problems and Prospects". Paper presented at the Symposium on Gangs and Gang Violence in the Caribbean, School of Public Affairs, American University, Washington, DC, 17 February. http://www.american.edu/spa/djls/caribbean-gangs-presentations.cfm.

Montoute, A. 2010. "Violence and Insecurity in Trinidad and Tobago: The Impact of Gang Violence". Paper presented at the Institute of International Relations, University of the West Indies, St Augustine, Trinidad, 13 December.

UNDP. 2012. *Caribbean Human Development Report: Human Development and the Shift to Better Citizen Security*. United Nations Development Programme, New York.

UNODC (United Nations Office on Drugs and Crime) and World Bank. 2007. *Crime, Violence, and Development: Trends, Costs and Policy Options in the Caribbean*. Report 37820. Washington, DC: World Bank.

Wells, W., C.M. Katz, and J. Kim. 2010. "Firearm Possession among Arrestees in Trinidad and Tobago". *Injury Prevention* 16.

4 | Entrepreneurial Experiences of a Jamaican Posse in the South Bronx

CHRISTOPHER A.D. CHARLES AND BASIL WILSON

Strain theory argues that individuals who encounter societal obstacles to their legitimate attempts to attain societal goals often experience a tension that sociologists have labelled "strain". If a societal goal is internalized by individuals or groups and then their efforts to achieve it are thwarted by societal obstacles, attaining that goal can become more important than the means used. According to Akers and Sellers (2009), strain can cause individuals to turn to criminal activity as a means of accumulating wealth when legitimate means fail. In the latter part of the twentieth century, undereducated and semi- or unskilled young male Jamaicans fit the profile of a cultural group that could become vulnerable to strain.

From the early 1960s through the early 1970s, members of politically affiliated Jamaican criminal gangs, fresh from fighting political "wars" on behalf of the People's National Party and the Jamaica Labour Party, emigrated from Central Kingston to the United States (Headley 1996; Wilson 1980). Most of them landed and regrouped in the Bronx in New York State. The Peyton Place Posse became one of the more influential gangs in this area. Although not all of the posse members had criminal pasts in Jamaica, most members became underground entrepreneurs in the illegal marijuana and crack-cocaine market in an attempt to reduce strain after they were unable to find the good jobs they had expected to find in the United States.

Very little research has been conducted to determine how posse members fared as entrepreneurs in the United States' illicit drug market (Gunst 2003; Harrison 1989; Joseph 1999; Taniguchi, Ratcliffe and Taylor 2011). This chapter extends the prior research on gang members as entrepreneurs and seeks to understand the members of the Peyton Place Posse as entrepreneurs in the illegal narcotics market as they pursued the American Dream. Specifically, we explore the reasons for posse members entering the illicit drug market and review their successes and failures in pursuit of capital accumulation. We begin with a synopsis of strain theory, and how gangs operate in the illegal drug market. The foregoing is followed by a brief discussion of the characteristics of the Bronx, New York. Next, we present a synopsis of the Peyton Place Posse. Finally, we use strain theory to explain the posse's entrepreneurial experiences and outcomes in the illegal narcotics market.

Strain Theory

The quest for a better life in America makes strain theory an appropriate analytical framework for understanding the activities of the posse members in the United State. The ethos of the American Dream transcends class. The typical resident or citizen believes that appropriating the achievement orientation and working hard in competition with others will lead to financial success. Capital accumulation is the index of social worth, integrity and societal success. This pervasive ethos ignores the fact that many people experience conditions such as poverty, inequality and a lack of opportunity that restrict socio-economic mobility. This mobility is further mediated by social structure factors, such as race, social class and gender (Akers and Sellers 2009; Messner and Rosenfeld 2006).

Members of the poor working class, driven by the achievement orientation, experience frustration and anger when they cannot achieve material well-being, despite their hard work. Often uneducated and unskilled or semi-skilled, they do not have the means to achieve their socially sanctioned goals. Unrelenting poverty and struggling to survive economically will convince most that the obstacles to the realization of their dreams are insurmountable (Akers and Sellers 2009; Messner and Rosenfeld 2006).

Repeated frustration and anger resulting from a disjuncture between ends and means create strain. This dialectic causes some members of the working-class poor to give up the belief that conventional hard work will bring financial rewards. Some of these people will commit crimes to reduce that strain. Young people in these circumstances sometimes reduce the strain they experience by joining criminal gangs (Akers and Sellers 2009; Messner and Rosenfeld 2006).

Gangs in the Drug Market

According to Daniels and Adams (2010), the decision to join a gang is related to social disorganization in the community, a lack of positive adult role models and intense material deprivation. When youth experience an absence of personal validation from their families, a gang may be an attractive substitute as a source of income, security, recreation, oppositional identity, social solidarity and respect (Gibbs 2000). However, critical incidents during adulthood may force some gang members to re-evaluate their childhood decision to join a gang (Daniels and Adams 2010).

Recently, the shift in the labour market (in the United States and elsewhere) from unskilled and semi-skilled blue-collar jobs to jobs that require college education has become a factor in the gravitational pull of gangs for less-educated young adults. The de-industrialization of the inner city and lack of stable blue-collar employment pushes many unskilled youth into the drug market economy, as the drug culture emerges and communities become marginalized (Fagan 1996). Hagedorn (1994b) found that older gang members are not necessarily committed to long-term participation in the drug economy – many would prefer full-time, legitimate jobs, even with parsimonious wages, but they become intermittently involved in illegal drug sales because of the spasmodic contractions of the formal labour market. These conditions are present worldwide. The global proliferation of gangs and the culture of gangsterism result from glaring inequalities extant in first world and third world countries. The *favelas* in Brazil, the *barrios* in Mexico, the townships in South Africa and the garrison communities in Jamaica all create the material conditions for the existence of gangs.

The marginalization of certain segments of the populace universally triggers a culture of resistance (Hagedorn 2008). The level of general delinquency is higher in a structured gang of youths compared with that of a group of delinquent youths (Bouchard and Spindler 2010). Gang members are significantly more likely than non-gang members to be perpetrators and victims of personal and property crimes (Fox, Lane and Akers 2010).

Howell and Decker (1999) identified a link between gangs, guns and violence, finding that youth gangs not only had a penchant for guns and violence, but that they were involved in drug trafficking. Gangs have undergone a transformation from preoccupation with neighbourhood turf to a fixation on capital accumulation, leading them to deal in illegal drug distribution (Coughlin and Venkatesh 2003). Illegal drug sales and violence have become hallmarks of contemporary urban gangs (Bouchard and Spindler 2010). Some gangs have explicitly organized as profit-making entities for the sale of illegal drugs. However, there is no difference in the amount of drug sales by gang members and non-gang members (Duran 2010). The more organized drug gangs have developed a chain of command, and individual members are assigned well-defined roles and functions. Such gangs are able to control and protect their housing projects and drug turfs from rival gangs. Residents doing business in the gang-controlled projects pay "taxes" to the gang leaders (Venkatesh 2009).

The illegal drug market is a turbulent environment in which vertically organized and inflexible gangs are likely to fail. Drugs are sold more often than not from loosely organized neighbourhood-based operations; these vary based on the stability of the drug market and how lucrative those markets are. The complexity of a gang's drug operation and the degree to which drug sales are centred in the neighbourhood market are inversely related. The level of gang operations also varies based on the ethnicity of the gang members (Hagedorn 1994a).

The spatial contestation of gangs in the drug market drives the gun-related homicide rate among urban youth (Cohen et al. 1998). Homicides occur primarily in the geographical space where gang members conduct business. The crime rate is usually highest on street corners and in open air drug markets, that is, sites of cut-throat economic competition. Invariably, the crime rate is higher wherever illegal drugs are distributed and multiple gangs operate (Taniguchi, Ratcliffe and Taylor 2011). There is a real danger that the values and culture of adolescent street gangs who rob and intimidate will spread as the members of the gang approach adulthood (Gavriliuk 2011).

Some drug markets in a gang set space are controlled by incarcerated adult gang members. This transforms youth gangs operating in the gang set space into extensions of the incarcerated members. There is a prevalence of gang members in prisons that are becoming more sophisticated and disruptive. The absence of rehabilitation programmes is undermining the intervention strategies used to control such gangs (Winterdyk and Ruddell 2010). From prison, they remain able to protect property rights, enforce the sale of illegal drugs and adjudicate disputes in the drug markets. This remote control increases the rate of incarceration and recidivism among urban youth who have become gang members in response to declining economic opportunities (Skarbek 2011; Valdez 2005).

The Diamond gang comprised second generation Puerto Ricans in the United States who had dropped out of conventional society and found solace and ethnic identity in belonging to the gang. Members of the gang felt neglected and rejected by the larger society and were able to generate income by the gang's involvement in the drug trade on the streets. The United States is not creating the opportunities to provide adolescents and young minority adults with whole-some choices. However, some gang members became disillusioned with the gangster life in the Diamonds and returned to the conventional world (Padilla 1996).

Gangs differ in terms of their structure and their impact on crime patterns, so it is important that law enforcement agencies understand the gangs in their jurisdiction, as different gangs require different responses (Klein and Maxson 2001). Gang members also migrate, such as when gang members take short trips to engage in drug sales and expand their criminal network, visit family, temporarily move, and make other movements during gang wars or crackdowns by law enforcement agencies. There are more permanent movements, such as a court placement or when a gang member moves individually or with family to a new area (Maxson 1998).

Policing and crime control in relation to gangs have been politicized since 11 September 2001 terrorist attacks on the United States and the development of moral panic. This politicization and moral panic threaten civil liberties of urban youth within the context of the rule of law (Morgan, Dagistanil and Martin 2010).

There is also the possibility of gang members, at the behest of the gang leader, to change their modus operandi as a criminal organization and morph into a social movement (Brotherton and Barrios 2004).

There is usually a spike in homicides in some cities when police dismantle the dominant gang in the housing projects because rival gangs start to fight each other over the drug turf that was controlled by the dismantled gang (Hagedorn and Rauch 2007).

The social organization of some local gangs prevents them from developing transnational ties with other criminal organizations. Sometimes the intra-gang structure and inter-gang relations reveal a contractor arrangement driven by weak, market-like ties and criminal social capital (Pih, Hirose and Mao 2010).

Youth street gangs can become transnational criminal organizations due to the regular flow of emigrants from other countries to the United States (Cruz

2010). The gang literature does not offer much information about one such gang, the Jamaican posse or its entry into the US illegal drug market. Jamaican posses in the United States are exemplars of street gangs with transnational linkages and criminal social capital (Gibson and Wilson 2003; Joseph 1999).

The foregoing outline of the creation of gangs and their operation in the illegal drug market is related to the operation of Jamaican posses. The members of the Jamaican posses in the United States come from socially disorganized and marginalized garrison communities of Kingston and Lower St Andrew. The high rates of unemployment in Jamaica since political independence and the high rates of poverty and unemployment in the inner city have led to oppositional identity, a culture of resistance against the social order. Some of the gang members from the inner city garrison communities migrated to the United States. These uneducated and unskilled young men entered the illegal drug market because they were unemployable and engaged in violent spatial contestations with rival Jamaican and African American gangs. These gang members did not become a social movement because their illegal activities were for financial accumulation rather than social change. The Jamaican posses contributed to the spike in gun-related homicides in New York City because of the violent struggle with rival gangs to control the illegal drug markets. We now turn to a brief synopsis of the spare literature on the Jamaican posses.

Jamaican Posses

During the general elections of 1967, 1972, 1976 and 1980, members of criminal posses fought violent political wars on behalf of the People's National Party and the Jamaica Labour Party. After the elections, these individuals were considered political and legal liabilities, and were "assisted" by their political benefactors to travel overseas (Headley 1996; Lacey 1977; Wilson 1980). The pipeline of criminals from Jamaica to the United States is still active (Charles 2009; Charles and Beckford 2012). Those who left Jamaica for the United States maintained ties with their local gangs, communities and political parties in Jamaica (Gunst 2003; Joseph 1999). The transnational character of the posses expanded their reach and resources beyond what might have otherwise have been the case. The posses entered the marijuana and crack-cocaine trade in the inner cities of the United States beginning in the late 1960s, leveraging organized and ruthless paramilitary skills honed in the Jamaican political wars (Lacey 1977; Wilson 1980).

By the 1980s, forty Jamaican posses had formed in the United States. Posses that took their names from politically affiliated communities in Jamaica were reportedly responsible for some four thousand US homicides. The murders occurred as a consequence of inter-gang rivalries for control of the drug market, robberies by rival gangs, petty feuds and the settling of old political scores that had their genesis in Jamaica (Gibson and Wilson 2003; Joseph 1999). Posses generally supported their homeland communities with a portion of the profits from their illegal drug trade, and they shipped guns back for inter-community and intra-community wars (Gunst 2003; Gibson and Wilson 2003).

In the 1980s, many of the violent drug posses were dismantled by a joint federal and state task force. The posses have resurfaced, operating clandestinely to avoid attracting the attention of US law enforcement agencies (Charles 2002, 2004, 2010; Gibson and Wilson 2003; Gunst 2003). The Peyton Place Posse, the subject of this chapter, operated in the South Bronx.

The South Bronx

The Bronx is the poorest of the five boroughs of New York City. Between 2006 and 2010, the annual per capita income in the Bronx was just over half that for New York State (US$17,575 vs. US$30,948). In the same period, the poverty rate in the Bronx was twice that for New York State (28.4 vs. 14.2 per cent). Only about one-fifth (20.7 per cent) of Bronx residents were homeowners compared with more than one-half (55.2 per cent) of residents state-wide. Multi-unit housing accounted for 89.1 per cent of Bronx residential units compared with 50.6 per cent of residential units for New York State (US Census Bureau 2012). The numbers for the South Bronx reflect even worse conditions, which have been present for decades.

Poverty and the immiseration of marginalized groups precipitated the vast destruction of South Bronx housing stock from the 1970s to the mid-1980s (Glazer 1987). Despite poverty and run-down communities, however, residents of the South Bronx still maintain informal networks of social control in their day-to-day interactions (Rengifo 2007).

There is also health disparity between New York City whites and South Bronx African Americans and Latinos. The problem is exacerbated by South Bronx residents' deep mistrust for the health system, their perception of being treated disrespectfully by health care staff, and communication difficulties between the two groups (Kaplan et al. 2006). The high rate of teenage pregnancy in the South Bronx demands parenting and education programmes to help curb the problem, but prevention programmes that fail to account for disorganized families, high rates of substance abuse, poverty and poor education fail to make a difference (Davis et al. 1986).

Despite being involved in criminal activities, users of illegal drugs in the Bronx provide some forms of sustenance for each other. Widespread use of drugs in the Bronx reinforces negative behaviour. The harsh environment and differences in the quality of the drugs available cause users to share needles, placing them at risk for HIV infection (Grund et al. 1992).

About two-thirds (68.8 per cent) of the population of persons twenty-five years and older in the Bronx were high school graduates between 2006 and 2010, compared with 84.4 per cent of this age group state-wide (US Census Bureau 2012). Moral panic is embedded in the community narratives about the lower Bronx, which are fuelled by media reports of blighted local communities. Bronx residents argue that their communities are viewed by outsiders as socially disintegrated, poor and violent (Diaz 2010). Within the local narrative, minority males in particular are considered dangerous, suffering from ecological contamination – they are deemed criminals because they live in crime-ridden communities. The killing of Amadou Diallo is a case in point; the unarmed African immigrant was shot forty-one times by police officers who assumed that Diallo had a gun when he reached for his wallet (Grant 2003).

All of these problems have existed in the Bronx for decades. The collective characteristics of the South Bronx communities – poor housing, homicides and other crimes, moral panic, failing schools, high rates of poverty and unemployment, very low wages, substance abuse, high rates of teen pregnancy, and the resultant ecological contamination in socially disorganized communities – provide a context for understanding the strain that influenced members of the Peyton Place Posse to gravitate to the illegal drug market. This study seeks to answer this question: For members of the Peyton Place Posse, did gang membership and entrepreneurship in the underground drug market effectively relieve their economic strain?

Method

Sample and Procedure

For this study, we chose a purposive sample of eight members of the South Bronx Peyton Place Posse who were willing and able to discuss their recollections and to give us an in-depth understanding of the gang. Specifically, they could tell us about themselves and other gang members in the illegal drug market, and how they were affected by that market. Basil Wilson, the second author of this chapter, was acquainted with posse members. They trusted him and were willing to tell him their stories.

Initially, Wilson contacted a few former group members about their possible interest in participating in a study of the posse. Those contacts then circulated the request, with the request that anyone interested get in touch directly with Wilson. To those who volunteered, he explained the study and informed them of their rights as participants. Eventually eight posse members consented to be interviewed. Rather than tape recordings, at the request of the participants, interview notes were taken to document the discussions.

From 2010 through 2012, we conducted eight in-depth retrospective interviews with the posse members. In addition to collecting demographic data, we asked about the origins of the posse and their pre-drug-market relationships, and about how the group organized and structured itself to enter the drug market. The interviews also explored outcomes: What happened to the posse and its members given circumstances such as cut-throat competition with other groups, members' incarceration or avoidance of incarceration, deportation, killings and crack addiction? Finally, we asked whether members had invested money gained from the sale of illegal narcotics and whether they had achieved the long-term goal of capital accumulation.

All identifiers related to the participants were removed from the interview notes to guarantee anonymity and confidentiality. Afterward, we reviewed the notes several times, identifying the most relevant themes and issues and focusing on important events, the decisions and behaviours of posse gang members, and the community and the illegal drug market in general.

Findings and Discussion

Between 1968 and 1973, the majority of the members of the all-male Peyton Place Posse were Jamaican immigrants who had settled in the South Bronx, a borough of New York City. According to the interviewees, many of them had been childhood friends back in Central Kingston, attending St Mathews School on Victoria Avenue. They came to the United States from the communities of Tel Aviv, Southside, Rae Town and Browns Town in Central Kingston, which were low-income communities that suffered from intense material deprivation, where capital accumulation and upward mobility for the poor were limited.

Some posse members were helped to emigrate by political entities in Jamaica that found their continuing presence after their participation in violent election battles on behalf of those entities a political liability. Others had families residing in the United States who were willing to file resident alien petitions on their behalf. Earlier immigrants articulated a narrative to their marginally employed or unemployed relatives back in Jamaica, promoting the American Dream and asserting that it was "easier to make it in America". Poverty at home with no opportunity to improve oneself motivated many to emigrate. The perception that life was "too hard" in Jamaica influenced those without other means to enter the United States, travelling through the Bahamas illegally on private boats.

Arriving in the United States, the new immigrants were determined to change their circumstances. As one posse member told us, "When I first came to this country, I first worked as a welder at the World Trade Center, but I find the money small and it wasn't anything like what I could make on the streets" (personal interview, 16 January 2011). Even those without US family ties saw emigration as a way to reduce the strain they were experiencing in Jamaica. This movement was primarily a young man's endeavour; the average age of Peyton Place Posse members in 1973 was about twenty-five years.

In 1962, Jamaica gained political independence from England. Most Jamaicans had high expectations for a better life as citizens of an independent nation. Conversely, however, poverty increased throughout Jamaica's first decade of independence (Lacey 1977).

Poverty was the push factor that influenced posse members to leave Jamaica, where the chance of economic success was limited, for the United States, where achieving economic success seemed more likely.

Motivational Context

Upon arrival in the United States, the Jamaicans faced several obstacles to their dreams of "making it". First, they lacked the college education and skills that would have prepared them for decent-paying jobs in the competitive US labour market. Moreover, they were black males who, at the time, were stigmatized as dangerous and lazy. Although many applied for jobs in the labour market, they were unsuccessful and became frustrated. Over time, some pursued the promise of wealth accumulation offered by the underground economy and entered the illegal drug market. Not all of the immigrants associated with the posse made this choice.

The gang included about twenty core members who made their living by selling drugs, but about ten peripheral members refrained from participating directly in drug sales. They held legitimate jobs, while indulging with their core-member peers in smoking marijuana and other social activities. Peripheral members did not emerge from the gang experience unscathed, however. For example, one steadily employed peripheral member was addicted to crack for many years, until he finally kicked the habit in the early 1990s. Although profitable drug sales provided economic relief for many core posse members, the dangerous nature of drug markets produced its own variant of strain. The posse had to remain hypervigilant to protect itself from rival gangs and to stay constantly one step ahead of law enforcement.

Within a few months of beginning operations in the lucrative illegal drug markets, posse members were acquiring the kind of money that typical working-class Jamaican immigrants in the United States would take years to acquire. These drug entrepreneurs with their newly found wealth lived lavishly, buying consumer goods that set them apart from other working-class immigrants from the Caribbean. Our interviewees described a life of driving expensive cars, purchasing exquisite clothing and partying with a bevy of pretty women. One posse member boasted, "When you check it out, everyone on the corner was decked out with fine clothing, expensive jewellery and late-model motorcars. When we visited clubs, we drank the most expensive champagne" (personal interview, 5 Novemebr 2010). Fast money from the illegal narcotics market was used by posse members, not only to reduce the strain they experienced as new immigrants, but also to flaunt their financial success.

Transnational Linkages

Some Peyton Place Posse members who were dealing in the open drug markets of the 1970s and 1980s maintained close ties with the communities in which they were raised. The gang members had a commitment to purchase homes for parents in particular and relatives in general. Some made financial contributions to the communities in which they grew up. One member said, "When Mr. C was alive and drugs were flowing, he was always willing to help members of the Central Kingston community" (personal interview, 15 October 2009). For example, during lucrative times, one member (since deceased) purchased a fishing boat for colleagues hustling on the seas in Central Kingston; he was also instrumental in resurfacing a soccer field in Brown's Town in Central Kingston. Some members of the posse paid for other residents of Central Kingston to enter the United States illegally. One member bought a house for his mother in the middle-class community of Havendale; another bought a home for his mother in the working class community of Rockfort. These and similarly acquired homes served as refuges for those who were forced to return to Jamaica through deportation.

Such remittances, as well as the sending of barrels of clothing and food, a small fraction of the total wealth generated by posse members, reduced the economic strain of family members and friends still living in Jamaica who were unemployed or in low-paying jobs. These criminals were concerned about the economic well-being of their relatives and friends. Commitment to helping family members and communities in Jamaica was quite typical for Jamaican posses operating in New York City and elsewhere in the United States. These posses were all affiliated with a politicized community in Jamaica. The Peyton Place Posse members were unlike the other posse members in two ways: they did not ship illegal guns to their communities in Jamaica, and their communities did not provide a constant supply of new gang members for their New York operations.

Organizational Structure

The majority of this group of new Jamaican immigrants lived in proximity in the South Bronx. They naturally coalesced as a gang, in part because of their prior close friendship ties back in Jamaica. The posse was named after a social club, Peyton Place, which was near the location where members conducted illegal drug operations. Posse turf in the South Bronx was based on 168th and 169th Streets, between Fulton and Third Avenues. From the late 1960s through the 1980s, Peyton Place Posse members sold illegal drugs there in gates and on street corners.

In the 1970s, during the embryonic stages of the posse's marijuana business, formally employed gang members on the periphery of the posse supplied start-up capital for the drug sales. The relationship between core posse members and those on the periphery was quite fascinating. Friendships persisted even though the two sub-groups occupied different worlds. Those on the periphery worked in the legitimate economy as bus drivers, electricians and cab drivers. They ventured to gang haunts only to participate in the rituals of smoking marijuana, sharing crack and attending dances. Some peripheral members succumbed to crack addiction, but they still managed to refrain from becoming involved in illegal drug dealing. The presence of the peripheral members provided crucial social support and encouragement for the core members who accumulated wealth through crime.

As the posse's enterprise became more expansive, access to suppliers became critical. One posse member with a supply connection to a Cuban source shared his proceeds with other members. In general, however, the business was quite Darwinian, and the migration of gang members involved short trips for drug sales. Gang members scrambled to make money in the open and competitive drug markets with every man for himself. They quickly adopted the American achievement orientation toward individualism, as they competed on the way to the top of the scale of wealth accumulation. Demand for illegal drugs was so great during this time that the assumption prevailed that there was no upper limit to potential sales – more sellers, they believed, would simply bring more buyers to the market.

As marijuana gave way to cocaine and crack cocaine in the 1980s as the drugs of popular choice, the financial stakes escalated and the nature of the business became increasingly chaotic and dangerous. The lucrative enterprise attracted rival gangs who targeted those who were successful in the illicit marketplace. Posse members began acquiring guns for defence against competing drug gangs whom they considered to be "preying vultures". In an interview with an influential core group member, he mentioned that in the early days of the posse there was an attempt by another member of the gang to play the role of don with a centralized leadership structure. He stated, "We made it clear to him that we were not into any donsmanship, we don't want any leader, when you have a gun every man is a leader" (personal interview, 5 June 2011).

In response to the crack epidemic, law enforcement raised its game as well. In the late 1980s, local and federal law enforcement agencies started cracking down hard on drug markets. Selling illegal drugs with impunity as a means of accumulating wealth and the prevalence of open markets came to a screeching halt at the end of the 1980s.

The Role of Crack-Cocaine Addiction

By the 1980s, marijuana declined as the drug of choice. Cocaine and crack were in great demand on the streets of New York and sales were skyrocketing. At the same time as their customers, the majority of Peyton Place Posse members were becoming crack addicts. This became a significant obstacle to reaching their

"American Dream" goal. The crack culture encouraged extreme highs, bountiful sex and cut-throat control of the crazed drug markets. With all of their attention focused on protecting their markets, supplying their own habits and simply staying alive, addicted posse members were not investing the capital that passed through their hands for the future. One member stated, "I blew over $800,000 during the heights of the crack epidemic" (personal interview, 20 March 2012). Another said, "I squandered over $200,000" (personal interview, 5 June 2011).

Violence in the Illegal Drug Market

The Peyton Place Posse was subject to continuous violent confrontations with rival African American and Jamaican gangs who challenged their control of the lucrative drug turf. In their quest to reduce economic strain through crime, posse members invited strain of another kind – that associated with facing the daily threat of death in the illegal drug market. Shootings, some fatal, during inter-gang conflicts and robberies were not uncommon. One peripheral member of the posse expressed this insight: "Once the gun was introduced, it changed everything. Those who possessed 'weed gates' were constantly fearful of robbers who preyed on them. One killing led to another" (personal interview, 10 August 2012).

The unremitting threat of robberies by rival gangs led to a breakdown of trust and constant tensions among the gangs. During this period, three Peyton Place Posse members were indicted and convicted for murder; each received a sentence of twenty-five years to life and served twenty-two years in state prison before being deported to Jamaica along with two other known posse enforcers.

Violence related to age-old disputes and reprisal killings also occurred among the gangs. Shortly after one posse member emigrated from Jamaica to the United States, his brother invited him to a dance in Brooklyn that was attended by other posse members and Brooklyn gang members. The new immigrant was dancing with his brother's girlfriend when a member of a rival gang punched him in his face because of a long-standing feud. A fight ensued, and shots were fired. The posse left Brooklyn in a hurry.

Drug markets by their nature are exceedingly violent. The Peyton Place Posse comprised members who had intentionally embraced a subculture of violence to support their pursuit of capital accumulation. The Peyton Place Posse members were like members of other Jamaican posses that engaged in a scale and pattern of violent crimes beyond that of the African American and Latino drug gangs, which attracted the attention of law enforcement agencies. In the 1970s, the gang members purchased guns from gun dealers in Connecticut. The gun of choice was the "Saturday night special", but by the late 1980s, the "special" was replaced by the semi-automatic 9-millimetre pistol, which was far more lethal. Posse members believed that success in the illegal drug market was paramount and that it should be achieved by any means necessary, even by the use of lethal violence. In February 1988, a drug kingpin killed a police officer in Queens (a borough of New York City), which triggered a major crackdown on the illegal drug market. The administration of Mayor Ed Koch went after open drug markets in Harlem, the South Bronx and elsewhere to reduce moral panic in New York City.

Outcome

Were Peyton Place Posse members able to effectively relieve their strain by pursuing capital accumulation through criminal entrepreneurship? In the United States, posse members were determined to do exactly that. In the 1970s, they generated substantial income from marijuana sales. In the 1980s, demand for crack and crack cocaine opened possibilities for accumulating serious capital, although being involved in that business meant being exposed (as perpetrators and victims) to increasing violence and death. Nonetheless, posse members were relatively successful in defending their drug turf and market from rival gangs. Although some were sending a portion of that capital to Jamaica to assist relatives and friends, those remittances were a small fraction of the wealth they were accumulating and had little impact on their financial security. In the 1980s and a little beyond, posse members were awash in the fast money generated by the crack epidemic, positioned to secure their individual financial futures.

In the 1990s, the gang as a group began to falter. This period coincided with an exponential increase in homicides in New York City that sparked a New York Police Department crackdown on open drug markets. This crackdown was in conjunction with a federal task force created to dismantle the posses. For example, in 1990 there were over two thousand homicides in New York City; five hundred of those homicides took place in the Bronx. The arrests of three key posse members for murder signalled the disintegration of the gang. Even so, posse members had enjoyed many years of making a great deal of money by this time. Did their successful criminal entrepreneurship give them financial security?

For three members of the posse, it seems that the answer was yes. A small number of posse members did use their profits to amass personal wealth. These individuals tended to be college educated or to possess above-average street savvy. For them, as for others, the informal job market had proved more lucrative than the formal job market, which invariably offered minimum wage. These members operated in the drug market at the wholesale level rather than the more volatile retail level. They found ways to launder money and to invest in stocks, real estate and other productive financial instruments. When they could, they made an exodus from the underground economy and functioned as legitimate businessmen. One educated member said, "I operated at the wholesale level and never became involved in the retail level so many people did not know me on the streets. Once I was in a position to leave the game and invest in legitimate assets, I ceased that opportunity and made my exodus" (personal interview, 5 June 2011).

In other words, one could say, they took the money and ran. The non-career posse criminals reduced strain by making their money and then exiting from the criminal life, investing their wealth, improving their standard of living and achieving some degree of upward social mobility. These gang members felt that they had made enough money to significantly improve their lives, so it was time to leave the gang. Those who left the gang migrated from the Bronx and bought houses in the suburbs. Two of the three members who left the gang for good subsequently became involved in small-scale drug sales elsewhere, and the other did not re-enter the illegal narcotics market. One of the two former gang members who was still involved in small-scale drug dealing also established a legitimate business in Jamaica. The long-standing friendship among posse members, the individualist ethic, the loose organizational structure and the absence of a central authority in the gang meant that the non-career posse criminals could leave the organization without being killed.

The majority of posse members, however, failed as entrepreneurs, and remained career criminals as long as the possibility lasted, perhaps lacking the knowledge, skills and discipline to make the kinds of choices made by their more business-savvy colleagues. Most posse members held the worldview of the Caribbean immigrant population that making it in America included acquiring real estate. The purchase of a house and the ability to pay the mortgage were indicators of success, a goal that was difficult to achieve in Jamaica for the average working-class person. Home ownership was a goal for most members, but one that few realized. The career criminals tended to spend lavishly rather than invest for the future; as quickly and abundantly as they made money, they squandered it. Operating day to day on the streets, they were subject to all of the violence, interpersonal betrayal and trauma of their trade. Most of all, they related their downfall to the fact that most of them used the products they sold and so fell prey to all of the problems associated with cocaine and crack addiction.

The Peyton Place Posse failed as entrepreneurs in the illegal drug market in the United States between the early 1970s and the late 1980s. The majority of posse members failed to reduce strain that they experienced in Jamaica and continued to experience in the United States as new immigrants who sought the America Dream. The gang members exited the illegal narcotics market because some were murdered, some left the life of crime, some became drug addicts, and some were convicted because of the action of law enforcement agencies. Today, it is ironic and, perhaps, symbolic that the two housing projects in the South Bronx where the Peyton Place Posse once practised a highly lucrative drug trade have since been reduced to rubble.

Conclusion

This chapter has contributed to gang literature with an analysis of the criminal entrepreneurial experience of a Jamaican posse (gang) that chased the "American Dream" as a way of relieving economic strain, and of the role of crack addiction in the demise of that gang. The conclusions we can draw from such a study are necessarily limited and not generalizable. Our sample was purposive; only a few gang members consented to be interviewed, and their views may or may not reflect those of the majority. Moreover, the interviews were conducted more than two decades after the demise of the gang. Post-event information, recall and discussion of the events over that period will have affected their original reconstructed memories.

We do know that, for better or worse, the crack era of 1985 to 1989 led to the ruin of the Peyton Place Posse. Posse members moved from selling marijuana in the 1970s to the much more profitable and volatile business of selling cocaine and crack in the 1980s, as the demand for those drugs increased in the inner cities. Only a few posse members were able to amass and successfully hold on to wealth during this period. These few were perceived to have successfully reduced their strain by leaving the posse, laundering and investing illicit capital, improving their standard of living and, in short, by achieving upward social mobility.

For the rest, crack addiction seems to have derailed the pursuit of the American Dream as envisioned by the Peyton Place Posse. Most of the abundant capital accumulated from their criminal activities was essentially squandered. The core members of the posse, with few exceptions, were devoured by the criminal lifestyle. Some met an early death. At least five others spent a large portion of their lives behind bars in state prisons; for some, a prison sentence possibly saved them from crack addiction or from death on the streets. For much of their adulthood, those posse members lived lives of criminality. In the sunset of their lives, while being interviewed, some expressed regret at having chosen to chase their dreams through illicit drug markets.

Their failure was in large part due to crack addiction. The stress of the drug trade, the subsequent addiction of gang members to crack, and inter-gang violence resulting in deaths of some members and the incarceration of key gang members for murder together led to the demise of the Peyton Place Posse by the late 1980s. The devastating impact of crack addiction and the subsequent financial ruin of a large number of the posse members led to a derailment of their dreams of beating the system.

The crackdown on the illegal drug markets in general and the Jamaican posses in particular in the United States in the 1980s led to the institutionalization of organized crime in Jamaica. The various Jamaican posses moved their headquarters backed to Jamaica because of the crackdown in the United States, and they had political support from some politicians, some police officers and some residents in garrison communities. These alliances made the gangs formidable security threats at home. The gangs still sell illegal drugs in the United States, but without the spotlight, fanfare and bling of the 1980s because it is good business sense to stay below the radar of law enforcement agencies in the United States.

Policy Recommendations

1. There should be a reintegration programme in Jamaica supported by the government, private sector and nongovernmental organizations to facilitate the re-entry of deportees into society so they can be productive citizens, thereby reducing economic strain.
2. Governments and law enforcement agencies should break the link between political institutions and criminal gangs. The New York Police Department was able to disrupt the Peyton Place Posse relatively easily because the gang members did not have political protection in New York as they did in Jamaica.

3. Successful entrepreneurs in the illegal narcotics market who were never involved in committing violence and homicides and who are willing to leave the illegal drug market and stay out of criminal activities should be facilitated by the authorities after a punitive tax is levied on their accumulated wealth.

4. Governments and law enforcement agencies should not see gang membership as homogenous because all gang members do not have the same level of involvement in the gang. A distinction should be made between peripheral gang members who engage in social activities with gang members and core gang members. The latter group should be pursued by law enforcement agencies because they are the ones engaged in criminal activities.

5. Further and deeper collaboration between local and overseas law enforcement agencies is needed in order to effectively respond to transnational criminal gangs.

References

Akers, R.L., and C.S. Sellers. 2009. *Criminological Theories: Introduction, Evaluation and Application*. New York: Oxford University Press.

Bouchard, M., and A. Spindler. 2010. "Groups, Gangs, and Delinquency: Does Organization Matter?" *Journal of Criminal Justice* 38(5): 921–33.

Brotherton, D., and L. Barrios. 2004. *The Almighty Latin King and Queen Nation: Street Politics and the Transformation of a New York City Gang*. New York: Columbia University Press.

Charles, C. 2002. "Garrison Communities as Counter Societies: The Case of the 1998 Zeek's Riot in Jamaica". *Ideaz* 1(1): 29–43.

Charles, C.A.D. 2004. "Political Identity and Criminal Violence in Jamaica: The Garrison Community of August Town and the 2002 Election". *Social and Economic Studies* 53(2): 31–74.

———. 2009. "Violence, Musical Identity, and the Celebrity of the Spanglers Crew in Jamaica". *Wadabagei: A Journal of the Caribbean and Its Diaspora* 12: 52–79.

———. 2010. "The Reintegration of Criminal Deportees in Society". *Dialectical Anthropology* 34(4): 501–11. doi:10.1007/s10624-010-9205-7.

Charles, C.A.D., and O. Beckford. 2012. "The Informal Justice System in Garrison Constituencies". *Social and Economic Studies* 61: 51–72.

Cohen, J., D. Cork, J. Enberg, and G. Tita. 1998. "The Role of the Drug Markets in Local Homicide Rates". *Homicide Studies* 2(3): 241–62.

Coughlin, B.C., and S.A. Venkatesh. 2003. "The Urban Street Gang after 1970". *Annual Review of Sociology* 29: 41–64.

Cruz, J.M. 2010. Central American Maras: "From Youth Street Gangs to Transnational Protection Rackets". *Global Crime* 11(4): 379–98.

Daniels, D., and Q. Adams. 2010. "Breaking with Township Gangsterism: The Struggle for Place and Voice". *African Studies Quarterly* 11(4): 45–46.

Davis, J.K., R. Fink, A. Yesupria, and R. Lala. 1986. "Teenage Pregnancy in an Urban Hospital Setting". *Journal of Community Health* 11(4): 259–67.

Diaz, R.. 2010. *Moral Panics and Community Narratives: The Case of the Bronx*. PhD dissertation, New School University.

Duran, R.J. 2010. "Gang Organization: Slangin' Gang Bangin' and Dividin' By Generation". *Latino Studies* 8(3): 373–98.

Fagan, J.. 1996. "Gangs, Drugs and Neighborhood Change". In *Gangs in America*, edited by Jeffrey Fagan, 39–74. Thousand Oaks, CA: Sage.

Fox, K.A., J. Lane, and R.L. Akers. 2010. "Do Perceptions of Neighborhood Disorganizations Predict Crime or Victimization? An Examination of Gang Member Versus Non-Gang Member Jail Inmates". *Journal of Criminal Justice* 38(4): 720–29.

Gavriliuk, V.V. 2011. "The Gopniks as a Phenomenon in the Youth Community". *Russian Education and Society* 53(1): 28–37.

Gibbs, J.T. 2000. "Gangs as Alternative Transitional Structures: Adaptations to Racial and Social Marginalizations in Los Angeles and London". *Journal of Multicultural Social Work* 8(1–2): 71–99.

Gibson, C., and B. Wilson. 2003. "Jamaican Posses and Organized Crime." *Wadabagei: A Journal of the Caribbean and Its Diaspora* 6(1): 43–64.

Glazer, N. 1987. "The South-Bronx Story: An Extreme Case of Neighborhood Decline". *The Policy Studies Journal* 16(2): 269–76.

Grant, O.B. 2003. "Forty-One Shots in the Dark: Race, Rational Choice Theory and the Death of Amadou Diallo". Conference paper, Society for the Study of Social Problems.

Grund, J.-P.C., L.S. Stern, C.D. Kaplan, N.F. Aadrians, and E. Drucker. 1992. "Drug Use Contexts and HIV-Consequences: The Effect of Drug Policy on Patterns of Everyday Drug Use in Rotterdam and the Bronx". *Journal of Addiction* 87(3): 381–92.

Gunst, L. 2003. *Born Fi Dead: A Journey through the Yardie Underworld*. New York: Canongate.

Hagedorn, J.M. 1994a. "Neighborhood, Markets, and Gang Drug Organization". *Journal of Research in Crime and Delinquency* 31(3): 264–94.

———. 1994b. "Homeboys, Dope Fiends, Legits, and New Jacks". *Criminology* 32(2): 197–219.

———. 2008. *A World of Gangs: Armed Young Men and Gangster Culture*. Minneapolis: University of Minnesota Press.

Hagedorn, J.M., and B. Rauch. 2007. "Housing, Gangs and Homicides: What Can We Learn from Chicago?" *Urban Affairs Review* 42(4): 435–56.

Harrison, F.V. 1989. "Drug Trafficking in World Capitalism: A Perspective on Jamaican Posses in the United States". *Social Justice* 16(4): 115–31.

Headley, B. 1996. *The Jamaican Crime Scene: A Perspective*. Washington, DC: Howard University Press.

Howell, J.C., and S.H. Decker. 1999. "The Youth Gangs and Drugs: Drugs and Violent Connection". Juvenile Justice Bulletin.

Joseph, J. 1999. "Jamaica Posses and Transnational Crimes". *Journal of Gang Research* 6(4): 41–47.

Kaplan, S.A., N.S. Calman, M. Golub, J.H. Davis, C. Ruddock, and J. Billings. 2006. "Racial and Ethnic Disparities in Health: A View from the South Bronx". *Journal of Health Care for the Poor and Underserved* 17(1): 116–27.

Klein, M.W., and C.L. Maxson. 2001. *Gang Structures, Crime Patterns, and Police Responses*. Report of the US Department of Justice. https://www.ncjrs.gov/pdffiles1/nij/grants/188511.pdf.

Lacey, T. 1977. *Violence and Politics in Jamaica: 1960–1970*. Manchester: University of Manchester Press.

Maxson, C.L. 1998. "Gang Members on the Move". *Juvenile Justice Bulletin*. http://www.ojjdp.gov/jjbulletin/9810_1/intro.html.

Messner, S.F., and R. Rosenfeld. 2006. *Crime and the American Dream*. New York: Wadsworth.

Morgan, G., S. Dagistanil, and G. Martin. 2010. "Global Fears, Local Anxiety: Policing, Counterterrorism and Moral Panic over Bikie Gang Wars in New South Wales". *Australian and New Zealand Journal of Criminology* 43(3): 580–99.

Padilla, F.M. 1996. *The Gang as an American Enterprise*. New Brunswick, NJ: Rutgers University Press.

Pih, K.K., A. Hirose, and K. Mao. 2010. "Gangs as Contractors: The Social Organization of American Taiwanese Youth Gangs". *Trends in Organized Crime* 13(2–3): 115–33.

Rengifo, A.F. 2007. *Neighborhood Effects and Informal Social Control: Examining the Role of Social Networks in the South Bronx*. PhD dissertation, City University of New York.

Skarbek, D. 2011. "Governance and Prison Gangs". *American Political Science Review* 105(4): 702–16.

Taniguchi, T.A., J.H. Ratcliffe, and R.B. Taylor. 2011. "Gang Set Space, Drug Markets, and Crime around Drug Corners in Camden. *Journal of Research in Crime and Delinquency* 48(3): 327–63.

United States Census Bureau. 2012. *Bronx County Quick Facts from the US Census Bureau*. http://quickfacts.census.gov/qfd/states/36/36005.html.

Valdez, A. 2005. "Mexican American Youth and Adult Prison Gangs in a Changing Heroin Market". *Journal of Drug Issues* 35(4): 843–67.

Venkatesh, S. 2009. *American Project: The Rise and Fall of a Modern Ghetto*. Cambridge, MA: Harvard University Press.

Wilson, B.W. 1980. *Surplus Labour and Political Violence in Jamaica: The Dialectics of Political Corruption in Jamaica*. PhD dissertation, City University of New York.

Winterdyk, J., and R. Ruddell. 2010. "Managing Prison Gangs: Results from a Survey of US Prison Systems". *Journal of Criminal Justice* 38(4): 730–36.

5 | Differences in Delinquency, Victimization and Risk, and Protective Factors for Gang and Non-Gang Youth from Trinidad and Tobago and the United States[1]

CHARLES M. KATZ AND ANDREW M. FOX

O ver the last several decades, much research has been conducted on gangs, gang membership and gang-related crime and delinquency within developed nations. Scholars have spent substantial time and resources examining such issues as the prevalence of gang membership, risk and protective factors associated with gang membership, neighbourhood-level factors associated with gang-related problems, the organizational structure and group processes associated with gangs, and the contributions made by gangs and gang membership to criminality.

This body of research has relied on a wide variety of qualitative and quantitative methodologies. For example, case studies of gangs in England (Smithson, Monchuk and Armitage 2012), Norway (Lien 2005) and Canada (Descormiers and Morselli 2011) have provided rich, thick depictions of gang organizational structure and associated group processes; in-depth interviews with gang members in the Netherlands (van Gemert and Fleisher 2005), France (Fiori-Khayat 2008) and Australia (White 2008) have detailed the role of ethnicity and gender in gangs and have provided insight into the reasons that youth join gangs. Surveys of the police and other state institutions in Russia (Salagaev et al. 2005), the Netherlands (Weerman 2005) and the United States (Egley, Howell and Moore 2010) have estimated the number of gangs and gang members; surveys of school youth in Germany (Huizinga and Schumann 2001), Italy (Blaya and Gatti 2010; Haymoz and Gatti 2010), France (Blaya and Gatti 2010) and Switzerland (Haymoz and Gatti 2010) have compared gang and non-gang youth in terms of socio-demographic characteristics, delinquency, victimizations, and risk and protective factors.

Cumulatively, this body of literature has substantially changed policies and practices in developed nations. Initially, it placed pressure on policymakers and practitioners to recognize the existence of gangs. Policymakers in American and European communities, however, tended to deny the existence of gangs and their associated problems (Huff 1990; Esbensen and Maxson 2012), which delayed the implementation of prevention programming. This failure to appropriately prevent gang formation resulted in a de facto reliance on suppression strategies that might have otherwise been unnecessary.

Over time, this body of literature dispelled many of the myths associated with gangs and gang members. Popular media outlets, when they did acknowledge gang problems, often characterized gangs as violent organized groups composed primarily of urban minority male youth who united in order to profit from illicit enterprises such as drug trafficking, human trafficking and fraud. A vastly different perspective has emerged through systematic research, which has led to increasingly informed policymaking. Cumulatively, gang research in developed nations has increased our knowledge about the scope and nature of gang-related phenomena and has fostered the development and implementation of data-driven comprehensive strategies designed to prevent, intervene in and suppress gangs, gang membership and gang-related crime. As noted in chapter 1, much less is known about gangs and gang-related phenomena in developing nations, and particularly in the Caribbean.

Understanding gangs in the Caribbean context is important for a number of policy-related reasons. First, the Caribbean has one of the highest rates of violence in the world. A recent report by the United Nations Office on Drugs and Crime indicated that when examining worldwide criminal justice data, the Caribbean had the second highest homicide rate out of nineteen sub-regions, just behind Southern Africa (Malby 2010). A number of international organizations have attributed much of the increase in the regional homicide rate to a rising gang problem (Franco 2005).[2] Also, effective and efficient state-based mechanisms of formal social control are largely absent from Caribbean nations; anecdotal evidence suggests that the concomitant lack of formal social control and the increased presence of gangs in these nations presents a challenge to state sovereignty (Manwaring 2007; Townsend 2009). Manwaring reported, for example, that *posses* (gangs) have largely replaced the state as the primary source of formal social control in a few of Jamaica's urban poor *garrisons* (neighbourhoods). Gangs, he argues, help provide many basic services, such as education, police, courts, medical assistance and jobs for Jamaican residents. Understanding gangs and their impact on communities and their contribution to violence is an important first step toward designing effective, efficient and equitable responses that will enhance the rule of law and democratic institutions.

There are also more academically relevant reasons for studying gangs in the Caribbean. As noted above, we know little about whether the gang literature, predominately based in the United States and Europe, can be generalized to gangs in the Caribbean. If researchers determine that gangs, gang member-ship and gang crime in much of the rest of the world and in the Caribbean are quite similar, then we can discount the probability that characteristics unique to the Caribbean are the most prominent aspects contributing to its gangs and gang-related problems. Conversely, if researchers determine that Caribbean gangs, gang membership and gang crime differ in meaningful ways from those in other parts of the world, then we can further explore whether those differences may be attributable to historical, cultural, political and/or economic differences between the nations (Kohn 1987, 716). Gang scholars have long argued that poverty, unemployment, disorder and violence are strongly correlated with the prevalence of gangs, gang members and gang crime. These social-structural problems are more pronounced in developing nations, particularly when con-trasted with the problems in developed nations such as the United States. If such social-structural factors are related to gang phenomena, then we should observe the differences between youth from developed and developing nations with respect to the prevalence of gang membership, the reasons for gang join-ing, the risk and protective factors associated with gang membership, and types and seriousness of delinquency.

In this chapter, we are interested in understanding the scope and nature of the gang problem in Trinidad and Tobago from self-reported data obtained from school-aged youth, rather than from data obtained from the police or from external respondents based on their impressions of a site. In other words, we are interested in understanding the problem from Trinidadian school youth themselves, rather than from third parties who interact with youth. Addition-ally, we supplement this data with self-report data obtained from a sample of school youth in Arizona (United States). We use the data from Arizona not to make direct comparisons between Trinidad and Tobago and Arizona, but rather to contextualize the findings from Trinidad and Tobago. We hope that our research serves as an initial step toward a more empirical understanding of Trinidadian gang membership, delinquency and victimization.

The present study explores four major questions: (1) the proportion of youth who are involved in gangs, including the socio-demographic characteristics associated with self-reported gang membership; (2) the experiential differences with delinquency, drug use and victimization between gang and non-gang youth; (3) when and why youth join gangs; and (4) the risk and protective factors associated with gang membership.

Research Design

This study relies on self-report data collected from independent samples of youth enrolled in and attending school in Trinidad and Tobago and Arizona.[3] The sample from Arizona includes 21,317 respondents who completed the Arizona Youth Survey in Arizona in 2006. The sample from Trinidad and Tobago included 2,292 respondents who participated in the Trinidad and Tobago Youth Survey, also in 2006. To be clear, while we label respondents as being from either Arizona or Trinidad and Tobago, we do not claim that our data are generalizable to each nation as a whole; they reflect only the sites from which they are drawn. This issue is perhaps more germane for the Arizona sample from the United States where there are greater nationwide economic, geographic and cultural differences that could be related to our research questions. One limitation of the present study is the uncertainty of its ability to generalize findings and apply them to the wider regions from which the samples were drawn.

Study Areas

Trinidad and Tobago. The Republic of Trinidad and Tobago is a two-island nation located about eleven kilometres from the northeastern coast of Venezuela, between the Caribbean Sea and the North Atlantic Ocean. Trinidad and Tobago obtained independence from Great Britain in 1962. It remains a member of the Commonwealth of Nations and continues to be highly influenced by British culture and law. Although Trinidad and Tobago was once an agrarian society, over the past thirty years it has become one of the wealthiest and most industrialized Caribbean countries, largely due to petroleum production and the provision of regional finance. It recently reported one of the highest gross national incomes per capita and the second fastest growing economy in all of the Caribbean, Central America and South America (Dubinsky and Derrick 2007). Per capita GDP is about US$28,400. The nation is composed of about 1.26 million people, of whom 40 per cent are East Indian, 37.5 per cent are African, 20.5 per cent are Afro-Indian, and 2 per cent are white, Chinese or from another ethnic group.

Education in the Republic of Trinidad and Tobago is compulsory for all children ages six to twelve; after completing primary school, students may continue to secondary school, vocational studies or craft training, or they may end their formal education (Marlow-Ferguson 2002). At the time of this study, just over 72 per cent of youth ages twelve to eighteen were enrolled in secondary school, 90 per cent of whom attended school daily (UNICEF 2009). According to data provided by officials at the Educational Planning Division of the Ministry of Education in Trinidad and Tobago, dropout rates among school-attending youth were low – approximately 1 per cent of students dropped out of school during the 2005–2006 school year. Dropout rates did vary slightly by gender and form (grade), with 1.3 per cent of males and less than 1 per cent of females dropping out. The highest dropout rate (2.34 per cent) was found for form five (tenth grade in the United States) males. We made several inquiries about enrolment and absenteeism in schools that were participating in the study. Several officials in the Ministry of Education in Trinidad and Tobago stated that such data were not routinely collected, and the enrolment data that were available were not necessarily accurate. School officials estimated that 5 to 10 per cent of students were absent from school on any given day.

Arizona, United States (AZ). Arizona is located in the southwestern part of the United States, bordering the nation of Mexico and proximate to the Californian metropolitan areas of Los Angeles and San Diego. Arizona has grown substantially over the past decade; from 2000 through 2010, the population increased from about 5.1 million to about 6.4 million residents. About 58 per cent of the population is white, 30 per cent is Hispanic, 4 per cent is black, and the remaining 8 per cent is American Indian, Asian or another race (US Census 2012). The state's primary economic drivers are manufacturing, mining and tourism; its per capita GDP is about US$41,000.

In Arizona, education is compulsory between the ages of six and sixteen. On average, in the 2005–2006 school year, about 81 per cent of Arizona's children attended school daily.[4] About 4.7 per cent of youth dropped out of school that year; dropout rates varied by gender, ethnicity and grade level, with males being more likely to drop out than females (5.3 per cent vs. 4.1 per cent). In

2005–2006, about 9.1 per cent of American Indians dropped out compared with 6.1 per cent of Hispanics, 4.8 per cent of African Americans, 3.1 per cent of whites and 1.8 per cent of Asians. With respect to dropout rates by grade, only about 1.5 per cent of seventh and eighth graders dropped out of school compared with 4.5 per cent of ninth graders, 5.3 per cent of tenth graders, 6.7 per cent of eleventh graders and 9.4 per cent of twelfth graders (Franciosi 2007).

Sampling Design

Trinidad and Tobago sample. Our sample from Trinidad and Tobago relied on data obtained through the 2006 Trinidad and Tobago Youth Survey (TTYS), one of several data collection initiatives funded by the Trinidad and Tobago Ministry of National Security for the purpose of diagnosing the nation's violent crime problem. The TTYS target population was defined as third and fifth form students (equivalent to US eighth and tenth grades) attending *urban, high-risk* public schools. *Urban* public schools were those located within the nation's five urban school districts. *High-risk* schools were those that had been identified by the Ministry of Education as having a high number of delinquent incidents or a disproportionate number of students living in high-crime areas. Sixty-seven public schools were located in urban districts (the Tobago school district did not qualify) and twenty-seven of those were identified as high risk. Of them, twenty-two schools (81.5 per cent) agreed to participate in this study. That response rate was typical in comparison to international standards (Gfroere, Wright and Kopstein 1997; Kellerman et al. 2003; Prais 2005; Wild et al. 2003), but was high compared to studies conducted in other developing nations (Bulmer 1993).

Arizona sample. The data from Arizona (United States) was collected through the 2006 Arizona Youth Survey (AYS) project. A cross-sectional stratified sampling strategy was used to determine the sample for the AYS in order to ensure that a proportionate number of schools and students were surveyed from each of Arizona's fifteen counties. Only schools enrolling students in the eighth, tenth and twelfth grades were eligible. Schools were categorized based on school size (small, medium, large) and by grade(s) served (eighth grade only; tenth and twelfth grades; eighth, tenth and twelfth grades). Schools were then randomly selected to participate in the study from within each county by school size and type. Of 1,142 eligible schools, four hundred were invited to participate. (If a school declined to participate, another school from the same county and category was randomly selected to replace it.) Of four hundred schools invited to participate, 362 accepted, for a school-level response rate of 90.5 per cent. Compared with the response rates for similar school-based studies, this response rate was high (Johnston, O'Malley and Bachman 2002).

To improve the comparability of the two samples, we restricted analysis of the US-based sample to students enrolled in the eighth and tenth grades who attended schools in designated urban areas as determined by the 2000 US Census. The ultimate US-based sample for this study included 21,317 eighth and tenth grade students attending one of the 136 Arizona public secondary schools that met our final criteria.

Survey Instrument and Data Collection

The survey instrument used for both sites was developed as part of the Six-State Consortium, a larger project led by the Social Development Research Group at the University of Washington (United States). The Consortium's goal was to develop an instrument that could be used to examine risk and protective factors associated with youthful misbehaviour. We chose this instrument for Trinidad and Tobago because the measures had been validated for use in the international community (Beyers et al. 2004; Brook et al. 2006; Fairington 2004; Farrington 2006; Harachi et al. 2003; Hemphill et al. 2004) and because it was scheduled to be used in Arizona, allowing us to make cross-site comparison of identically measured constructs. The instrument contained questions that measured thirty risk factors and thirteen protective factors within four domains: community, school, family and peer/individual. The survey instrument also measured levels of alcohol and drug use and delinquency (Arthur et al. 2002; Hawkins, Catalano and Miller 1992). However, the instrument was slightly modified for use by Trinidad and Tobago youth. Specifically, we sought the advice of key stakeholders employed by the Ministry of Education on how we might alter the instrument slightly to reflect the regional language and culture (that is, monetary units, social activities and names of examples of pro-social organizations).

The survey instrument was administered to all eligible students in attendance on a specified day between March and June 2006 in Trinidad and Tobago and between February and April 2006 in Arizona. On the day the survey was administered, all students who were present were given a copy of the survey instrument. As a consequence, our sample excludes youth that were not enrolled in school or missing from school and those in hospitals or committed to detention facilities on that particular day. In both countries, if students who were present did not wish to participate in the study, they were instructed to turn it in without answering any questions.[5] Likewise, students were instructed that if they did not want to answer a specific question, they were not to provide an answer to that question.

With respect to our Arizona-based sample, student participation rates were estimated to range from about 97 to 100 per cent at participating schools. Our high response rates were largely a consequence of the passive parental consent procedures; these were carried out in both sites. The Trinidad and Tobago Ministry of Education stated that they did not collect the kind of data that would report student-level participation in the study, and that if any schools did collect such data, it would not necessarily be accurate. Although we could not collect data to calculate response rates in Trinidad and Tobago, when interviewed, school officials indicated that on any given day 5 to 10 per cent of students would be absent.

Measures

Gang involvement served as the primary outcome variable for the present study. Measuring gang membership through self-identification is the most common method for identifying gang members (Klein and Maxson 2006). This is typically operationalized by the researcher asking the respondent through a survey instrument, "Have you ever belonged to a gang?" or "Do you currently belong to a gang?" However, these questions may be problematic because recent research suggests that the word *gang* is not universally understood by youth across nations. For example, in Europe some researchers have argued that use of the term gang in survey research has yielded unreliable results because the term is understood by European youth in the broader context of having a tight relationship with a group of friends (Blaya and Gatti 2010; Esbensen and Weerman 2005). On the other hand, substantial evidence from the United States (Esbensen et al. 2001; Webb, Katz and Decker 2006) and initial findings from the Caribbean (Ohene, Ireland and Blum 2005; Katz and Fox 2010; Katz, Maguire and Choate 2011; Wells, Katz and Kim 2010) suggest that the term gang is commonly understood to mean street-oriented youth who engage in criminal behaviour as part of their group identity and has been successfully employed in survey research as a method for respondents to self-identify gang status.

In the present study, gang membership was measured in both surveys through the question "Have you ever belonged to a gang?" Response options included "No", "No, but would like to", "Yes, in the past", "Yes, belong now", and "Yes, but would like to get out." Guided by prior research, we categorized respondents into two groups. Respondents who reported current or previous gang membership were categorized as gang members for the present study and respondents who did not self-report any gang involvement were categorized as non-gang members. Because we were examining the relationship between gang involvement and delinquency, we did not further restrict our gang sample to individuals who self-reported delinquency. As noted by Curry, Decker, and Egley (2002, 281), "This measurement strategy avoided the potential tautology of establishing the relationship between membership and delinquency in our operational definition."

Both surveys collected demographic information for the respondent including attributes such as gender, age and ethnicity. Respondents from Trinidad and Tobago were classified as African, East Indian, Afro-Indian and other and Arizona respondents were classified as white (non-Hispanic), black, Hispanic and other. The instrument in both studies collected information related to whether the gang had a name, the number of gang friends the respondent had, the age at which the respondent first became involved with a gang and his or her reason for joining a gang. Respondents' involvement in delinquency and victimization was captured through a series of questions asking the number of times in the past twelve months that they had engaged in or experienced acts of delinquency (that is, violence, property crimes, and drug and alcohol use) or victimization. Categorical response options were provided to the respondent: "Never", "1–2", "3–5", "6–9", "10–19", "20–29", "30–39", and "40+". We created nine scales from these questions: (1) violence, (2) property, (3) drug sales, (4) arrest, (5) lifetime alcohol use, (6) thirty-day alcohol use, (7) lifetime drug use, (8) thirty-day drug use and (9) victimization. (For the scales and their individual questions, see appendix 5A.)

Both projects measured the presence of risk and protective factors among the respondents. Specifically, questions measuring thirty risk factors and thirteen protective factors were included in both instruments. (For risk and protective factors and each of their properties by domain, see appendix 5B.) Guided by prior research, we calculated a score for each respondent by averaging responses across questions within each factor.[6] Scales were initially constructed using all questions used by the Social Development Research Group. After scale construction, some of the scales were altered (that is, questions were dropped) due to lack of internal reliability. In the end, all multiple-question scales used in the multivariate analysis demonstrated internal reliability (as measured by

Cronbach's alpha). (For questions and response categories used to construct the risk and protective factor scales and information on each scale's internal reliability, see appendix 5B.) Respondents who scored in the upper third for a particular risk or protective factor were coded as "1", indicating that the respondent was at elevated risk (or protection) for the factor. Respondents who scored elsewhere in the distribution were coded as "0", indicating that they were at low risk (or protection) for the factor.[7]

Limitations to Methodological Design

The present study exhibits a number of methodological strengths, including the use of the same instrument with the same measures, identical procedures for administering the instrument to students, and the use of data collected during the same time period. Still, the methodological design of the present study suffers from a number of limitations. First, our samples excluded students from private schools and students who were dropouts, sick, truant or otherwise absent from school on the day the survey instrument was administered. This might have resulted in an underrepresentation of high-risk youth in both samples. Second, the two research sites have different compulsory education laws with respect to the ages at which youth are required to attend school. Youth in Trinidad and Tobago are permitted to drop out four years earlier than Arizona youth. This might have resulted in a lower percentage of older high-risk youth being included in the sample from Trinidad and Tobago compared with the Arizona-based sample. Third, data used for the present study were not collected as part of a planned research project; as a consequence, the two sampling designs were methodologically unique. Specifically, the Arizona sample was based on a stratified sampling strategy while the sample from Trinidad and Tobago was composed of a purposeful sample focused on high-risk urban youth. Although we were able to address one issue by eliminating non-urban schools from the Arizona-based sample, we were unable to restrict the Arizona sample to include only high-risk schools. This difference between the two samples might bias the results of the present study by overestimating the problem in Trinidad and Tobago. With that said, the sample from Trinidad and Tobago was fairly robust. Specifically, 28.2 per cent of all public schools on the island of Trinidad (twenty-two of seventy-eight) were included in the sample. Therefore, while the Trinidadian schools included in the sample represented those at higher risk in the nation, they represented a sizable proportion of all schools on the island. Nevertheless, we believe that the differences in the two sampling designs are important and should be used to contextualize the findings presented below.

Last, recent research suggests that caution should be taken when applying risk and protective factors developed in the United States to other countries (Maguire, Wells and Katz 2011). One author of the present study found that after imposing measurement factors from the United States onto a population of youth in Trinidad and Tobago, there were several issues concerning the construct validity of the community risk and protective factors. To partially address this issue and to ensure internal reliability of the risk and protective factors, we removed any question that lowered the internal reliability of the measure in either sample. Furthermore, we disaggregated a small number of risk and protective factors in order to increase construct specificity based on the authors' examination of the internal reliability of the measures. For example, in the United States, two constructs – alcohol use and marijuana use – were combined into the same scale. In Trinidad and Tobago, however, perceptions of alcohol use were not the same as for marijuana use, so we used two separate scales for those constructs. This strategy allowed us to create the same constructs for each sample so that the findings from Trinidad and Tobago could be compared to data from the United States.

Findings

Proportion of Youth Involved in Gangs

Table 5.1 displays the sample characteristics of school youth from Arizona (n = 21,317) and from Trinidad and Tobago (n = 2,292). In both Arizona and Trinidad and Tobago, the samples were more female than male: that is, 52.8 per cent of the Arizona sample and 60 per cent of the Trinidad and Tobago sample were female. Youth in Trinidad and Tobago were more likely to report having ever been a member of a gang (12.5 per cent compared with 7.6 per cent). Gang-involved youth were more likely to be male in both countries, with 57.4 per cent in Arizona and 59.1 per cent in Trinidad and Tobago. In Trinidad and Tobago, gang-involved youth were older than non-gang youth (15.6 years compared with 15.3 years); they were also older than the sample of youth from Arizona. In Arizona, gang and non-gang youth were different in terms of race and ethnicity,

Table 5.1. Demographic characteristics of non-gang and gang school youth

	United States			Trinidad and Tobago		
	Non-Gang	Gang	Total	Non-Gang	Gang	Total
Gender (%)[a, b]						
Female	53.7	42.6	52.8	62.8	40.9	60.0
Male	46.3	57.4	47.2	37.2	59.1	40.0
Age (%)[a, b, c]						
13 or younger	28.1	23.7	27.8	1.0	0.6	0.9
14 years old	32.8	43.7	33.6	20.9	12.2	19.9
15 years old	18.8	16	18.5	38.6	38.8	38.7
16 years old	19.4	14.4	19	26.8	31.1	27.4
17 or older	1.0	2.1	1.1	12.6	17.1	13.2
Mean age (SD)[b, c]	14.3 (1.1)	14.3 (1.1)	14.3 (1.1)	15.3 (1)	15.6 (1.1)	15.4 (1.1)
Race/ethnicity (%) [a]						
White	53.3	22.7	50.9			
Black	4.7	5.8	4.8			
Hispanic	30.8	54.6	32.6			
Other	11.2	16.8	11.7			
African				42.0	38.1	41.5
East Indian				23.5	21.3	23.3
Afro-Indian				14.5	17.5	14.9
Other				19.9	23.1	20.3
N[c]	19,689 (92.4%)	1,628 (7.6%)	21,317 (100%)	2,006 (87.5%)	286 (12.5%)	2,292 (100%)

[a]Significant differences at $p < .05$ within US between gang/non-gang.
[b]Significant differences at $p < .05$ within TT between gang/non-gang.
[c]Significant differences at $p < .05$ between countries' gang members.

with gang-involved youth (22.7 per cent) less likely than non-gang youth (53.3 per cent) to be white and more likely to be black (5.8 per cent compared with 4.7 per cent), Hispanic (54.6 per cent compared with 30.8 per cent) or other (16.8 per cent compared with 11.2 per cent). In Trinidad and Tobago, however, ethnicity did not differ between gang and non-gang youth. About 42 per cent of the total Trinidadian sample was African, 23.3 per cent was East Indian, 14.9 per cent was Afro-Indian and 20.3 per cent self-reported being some other race or ethnicity, and those percentages remained nearly the same for each group when the sample was separated into gang and non-gang youth.

When and Why Youth Join Gangs

Table 5.2 presents our findings related to the mean age that youth self-reported joining a gang and their self-reported reasons for joining. Youth in Arizona reported being significantly younger (average age 12.3 years) at first gang involvement than youth in Trinidad and Tobago (average age 12.9 years). Most youth in the Arizona sample reported first becoming involved with a gang between the ages of 10.73 and 13.93 years, while youth in Trinidad and Tobago first reported becoming gang-involved between the ages of 11.13 and 14.77 years.

Self-reported reasons for joining a gang varied significantly between the two sites. Gang-involved youth in Arizona were most likely to join for protection or safety (33.5 per cent), while gang-involved youth in Trinidad and Tobago were most likely to join for friendship (42 per cent). About 6 per cent of youth in both countries joined because a family member was in a gang. About 11 per cent of gang-involved youth in Arizona and 8 per cent in Trinidad and Tobago joined their gang to make money, while 20.3 per cent of Arizona gang members and 14.7 per cent of gang members in Trinidad and Tobago joined for some reason other than the ones specified.

Table 5.2. When and why do school youth join a gang?

	United States	Trinidad and Tobago
Age of first involvement* – Mean (SD)	12.33 (1.60)	12.95 (1.82)
Reason for joining gang (%)*		
Protection/safety	33.5	29.4
Friendship	28.4	42.0
Parent(s) in a gang	2.0	2.1
Sibling(s) in a gang	4.8	3.8
Make money	10.9	8.0
Other	20.3	14.7

*p < .05

Youth Experiences with Delinquency, Drug Use and Victimization

Table 5.3 displays the magnitude of the differences in delinquency, drug use and victimization between school youth in Trinidad and Tobago and Arizona. In both sites, gang-involved youth were significantly more likely to self-report all types of delinquency, drug and alcohol use, and victimization (as indicated by a ratio of greater than one). For some of the measures of delinquency, drug use and victimization, the magnitude between gang and non-gang youth was surprisingly similar for the two sites. For instance, in both samples, gang-involved youth reported about 6.5 times more violent behaviour, about 4 times more property crime and about 2 times more lifetime and thirty-day alcohol use than non-gang youth.

For drug-related offences, the magnitude of the differences between gang members and non-gang members was significantly higher among youth from Trinidad and Tobago. For instance, while Arizona gang youth were about 7.7 times more likely than non-gang youth to sell drugs, gang youth from Trinidad and Tobago were about 10.8 times more likely than non-gang youth to sell drugs. Arizona gang-involved youth were 3.2 times more likely than non-gang youth to have ever used marijuana and about 4.1 times more likely to have used marijuana in the past thirty days. Gang-involved youth from Trinidad and Tobago were about 5.4 times more likely than non-gang youth to have ever used marijuana and about 7.8 times more likely to have used marijuana in the past thirty days. While gang youth in the Arizona-based sample were arrested almost 7.8 times more often than non-gang youth, gang youth from Trinidad and Tobago were arrested about 3.1 times more often than non-gang youth. The data showed no significant difference in either sample between gang and non-gang victimization rates. Specifically, when compared to non-gang youth, gang youth were 4.3 times more likely to be victimized in Arizona and 3.5 times more likely in Trinidad and Tobago.

We also examined self-reported delinquency, drug use and victimization between gang members in Trinidad and Tobago and Arizona. Gang members in Arizona self-reported significantly higher levels of property crime, drug sales and marijuana use when compared with gang members in Trinidad and Tobago. For instance, Arizona gang members reported about 2.5 times the property crime, about two times the drug sales and about two times the marijuana use (ever and thirty-day use) than gang members in Trinidad and Tobago. On the other hand, gang members from Trinidad and Tobago were about 50 per cent

Table 5.3. Self-reported delinquency and victimization among gang and non-gang school youth

	United States			Trinidad and Tobago		
	Gang to Non-Gang Ratio	Non-Gang	Gang	Gang to Non-Gang Ratio	Non-Gang	Gang
Violence[a, b]	6.69	0.50	3.32	6.52	0.53	3.48
Property[a, b, c]	4.39	0.92	4.04	4.63	0.34	1.58
Drug Sales[a, b, c]	7.67	0.12	0.92	10.75	0.04	0.43
Arrest[a, b, c]	7.75	0.08	0.62	3.13	0.30	0.93
Lifetime alcohol use[a, b, c]	1.88	1.56	2.94	1.65	2.16	3.57
Thirty-day alcohol use[a, b]	2.69	0.52	1.40	2.39	0.61	1.46
Lifetime marijuana use[a, b, c]	3.20	0.69	2.21	5.44	0.19	1.01
Thirty-day marijuana use[a, b, c]	4.08	0.24	0.98	7.77	0.06	0.48
Victimization[a, b]	4.28	0.25	1.08	3.46	0.35	1.20

[a]Significant differences at $p < .05$ within US between gang/non-gang.

[b]Significant differences at $p < .05$ within TT between gang/non-gang.

[c]Significant differences at $p < .05$ between countries' gang members.

more likely to have been arrested and reported about 20 per cent more alcohol use in their lifetime than the Arizona-based sample of gang members. There were no significant differences between gang members in Trinidad and Tobago and Arizona with respect to violence, thirty-day alcohol use and victimization.

Risk and Protective Factors Associated with Gang Membership

Tables 5.4 and 5.5 present our findings with respect to the relationship between gang status and risk (table 5.4) and protective factors (table 5.5).[8] The first model predicts gang membership for the Arizona-based sample and the second model for the Trinidadian-based sample. The third model shows the findings for all youth and the interaction between the risk and protective factors and the site where they are reported. The main effect for each risk and protective factor was also estimated in the third model, but the findings are not reported here, given the difference in main effect interpretation when interactions are included.[9]

Risk and Protective Factors Associated with Gang Membership in Trinidad and Tobago

Analyses of data from respondents in Trinidad and Tobago indicated that two risk factors and no protective factors in the community domain were significantly related to gang involvement. Respondents who reported residential mobility (OR 1.36) and those who reported an elevated risk of perceived availability of handguns in their communities (OR 2.63) were significantly more likely to be gang involved. No risk or protective factors in either the school or family domains reached statistical significance. In the peer-individual domain, two risk and two protective factors were significantly associated with gang involvement. Those who reported early initiation of antisocial behaviour (OR 2.16) and those who were at risk for the intention to use drugs (OR 2.28) were significantly more likely to self-report being gang-involved. Additionally, those youth who reported elevated levels of social skills (OR 0.44) and interaction with pro-social peers (OR 0.67) were significantly less likely to be involved in a gang.

Risk and Protective Factors Associated with Gang Membership in Arizona (United States)

Analyses of data from the Arizona-based sample indicated that within the community domain, three risk factors (table 5.4, model 1) and one protective factor (table 5.5, model 1) were associated with gang involvement. Respondents who reported low neighbourhood attachment were less likely to be gang members (OR 0.85). Additionally, respondents who reported an elevated risk of community disorganization (OR 1.82) and residential mobility (OR 1.65) were significantly more likely to be gang involved. We also found that respondents who reported opportunities for pro-social involvement in their community (OR 0.85) were less likely to be involved in a gang.

In the school domain, both risk factors and neither of the protective factors were significantly related to gang involvement among the Arizona sample. Arizona gang-involved youth were more likely to report academic failure (OR 1.70) and less likely to report low commitment to school (OR 0.81). Within the family domain, four risk factors and one protective factor were associated with gang involvement among the Arizona-based sample. The odds of being a gang

Table 5.4. Risk factors for gang membership among school youth

Domains and scales	AZ			TT			Country X R&P[b]		
	b	se[a]	OR	b	se	OR	b	se	OR
Risk Factors									
Community									
Low neighbourhood attachment	-0.17	(0.07)	0.85 *	0.04	(0.14)	1.04	0.19	(0.16)	1.21
High community disorganization	0.60	(0.07)	1.82 **	0.13	(0.14)	1.13	-0.39	(0.16)	0.68 *
Mobility	0.50	(0.67)	1.65 **	0.30	(0.11)	1.36 **	-0.18	(0.14)	0.83
Laws and norms favourable to drugs	0.17	(0.09)	1.18	-0.12	(0.15)	0.89	-0.23	(0.19)	0.80
Perceived availability of handguns	0.60	(0.06)	1.83	0.97	(0.13)	2.63 **	0.45	(0.16)	1.56 **
Perceived availability of drugs	-0.02	(0.09)	0.98	-0.14	(0.21)	0.87	-0.11	(0.24)	0.90
School									
Academic failure	0.53	(0.08)	1.70 **	0.17	(0.14)	1.18	-0.42	(0.18)	0.66 *
Low commitment to school	-0.21	(0.07)	0.81 *	-0.32	(0.22)	0.73	-0.17	(0.24)	0.84
Family									
Family history of antisocial behaviour	0.36	(0.08)	1.43 **	0.16	(0.18)	1.17	-0.17	(0.20)	0.85
Poor family management	0.04	(0.07)	1.04	0.17	(0.21)	1.19	0.08	(0.23)	1.09
Family conflict	-0.13	(0.07)	0.88	0.07	(0.20)	1.07	0.16	(0.21)	1.17
Parental attitudes favourable towards drug use	0.25	(0.08)	1.28 **	0.05	(0.23)	1.05	-0.22	(0.26)	0.80

Continued...

Table 5.4. Risk factors for gang membership among school youth (*continued*)

Domains and scales	AZ			TT			Country X R&P[b]		
	b	se[a]	OR	b	se	OR	b	se	OR
Parental attitudes favourable towards alcohol use	-0.17	(0.08)	0.84 *	0.04	(0.19)	1.04	0.17	(0.22)	1.18
Parental attitudes favourable towards antisocial behaviour	0.22	(0.08)	1.24 **	0.05	(0.23)	1.05	-0.23	(0.26)	0.79
Peer-individual									
Rebelliousness	0.35	(0.07)	1.42 **	0.11	(0.22)	1.12	-0.28	(0.25)	0.75
Early initiation of antisocial behaviour	0.74	(0.07)	2.09 **	0.77	(0.15)	2.16 **	0.11	(0.19)	1.12
Early initiation of drug use	0.37	(0.07)	1.45 **	0.20	(0.14)	1.22	-0.21	(0.17)	0.81
Early initiation of alcohol use	0.32	(0.08)	1.38 **	0.16	(0.20)	1.17	-0.21	(0.22)	0.81
Attitudes favourable to antisocial behaviour	0.12	(0.07)	1.13	0.27	(0.16)	1.30	0.19	(0.18)	1.20
Attitudes favourable to drug use	-0.28	(0.10)	0.76 *	-0.18	(0.18)	0.83	0.04	(0.21)	1.04
Attitudes favourable to alcohol use	0.01	(0.10)	1.01	-0.29	(0.20)	0.75	-0.15	(0.25)	0.86
Intention to use drugs	0.22	(0.07)	1.24 **	0.83	(0.17)	2.28 **	0.54	(0.18)	1.72 **

Intention to use alcohol	-0.04	(0.07)	0.96	0.08	(0.19)	1.08	0.23	(0.23)	1.26
Perceived risk of drug use	-0.13	(0.07)	0.88	0.21	(0.18)	1.24	0.42	(0.20)	1.52 *
Antisocial peers	0.83	(0.08)	2.29 **	0.28	(0.19)	1.33	-0.46	(0.22)	0.63 *
Peers use drugs	-0.04	(0.08)	0.96	0.14	(0.15)	1.15	0.17	(0.18)	1.18
Peers use alcohol	-0.09	(0.08)	0.92	-0.05	(0.16)	0.95	0.09	(0.18)	1.09
Rewards for antisocial involvement	0.10	(0.07)	1.11	0.25	(0.17)	1.29	0.14	(0.19)	1.15
Depression	0.17	(0.07)	1.19 *	0.21	(0.14)	1.24	0.09	(0.17)	1.09
Sensation seeking	-0.16	(0.10)	0.85	0.24	(0.16)	1.28	0.44	(0.20)	1.55 *

*p < .05; **p < .01

[a] All standard errors are robust standard errors adjusted for clustering on the respondents' school.

[b] Country X R&P model reports interactions between the dichotomous country variable (coded "0" for Arizona [US] and "1" for Trinidad and Tobago) and the risk or protective factor of interest. For risk factors, odds ratios greater than one (positive beta) indicate a stronger association in Trinidad and Tobago compared with the United States, and odds ratios less than one (negative beta) indicate a stronger association in the United States compared with Trinidad and Tobago.

Table 5.5. Protective factors for gang membership among school youth

Domains and scales	AZ			TT			Country X R&P[b]		
	b	se[a]	OR	b	se	OR	b	se	OR
Protective Factors									
Community									
Opportunities for pro-social involvement	-0.16	(0.08)	0.85 *	0.09	(0.14)	1.09	0.29	(0.17)	1.34
Rewards for pro-social involvement	0.20	(0.07)	1.22	-0.07	(0.16)	0.93	-0.22	(0.19)	0.81
School									
Opportunities for pro-social involvement	-0.02	(0.07)	0.98	0.19	(0.20)	1.21	0.20	(0.23)	1.22
Rewards for pro-social involvement	0.00	(0.08)	1.00	-0.14	(0.17)	0.87	-0.12	(0.20)	0.89
Family									
Family attachment	0.06	(0.09)	1.06	0.07	(0.17)	1.07	0.17	(0.19)	1.18
Opportunities for pro-social involvement	0.06	(0.09)	1.07	0.06	(0.20)	1.06	-0.07	(0.25)	0.93
Rewards for pro-social involvement	-0.31	(0.13)	0.74 *	-0.18	(0.27)	0.84	-0.30	(0.24)	0.74

Peer-individual

	β	(SE)	OR	β	(SE)	OR	β	(SE)	OR
Religiosity	0.04	(0.08)	1.04	0.06	(0.13)	1.06	0.03	(0.15)	1.03
Social skills	-0.18	(0.11)	0.84	-0.82	(0.25)	0.44**	-0.72	(0.32)	0.49*
Belief in the moral order	-0.21	(0.10)	0.81*	-0.36	(0.20)	0.70	-0.17	(0.24)	0.85
Pro-social involvement	-0.15	(0.08)	0.86	0.05	(0.16)	1.06	0.14	(0.19)	1.15
Rewards for pro-social involvement	0.25	(0.08)	1.28**	0.35	(0.18)	1.41	0.21	(0.21)	1.24
Interaction with pro-social peers	-0.07	(0.09)	0.93	-0.41	(0.20)	0.67*	-0.35	(0.23)	0.70
N		18,712			2,206			20,918	
McFadden's r-square		0.239			0.240			0.242	
Nagelkerke r-square		0.293			0.314			0.298	

*p < .05; **p < .01

[a] All standard errors are robust standard errors adjusted for clustering on the respondents' school.

[b] Country X R&P model reports interactions between the dichotomous country variable (coded "0" for Arizona [US] and "1" for Trinidad and Tobago) and the risk or protective factor of interest. For protective factors, odds ratios greater than one (positive beta) indicate a stronger association in the United States compared with Trinidad and Tobago, and odds ratios less than one (negative beta) indicate a stronger association in Trinidad compared with the United States.

member increased for those who reported a family history of antisocial behaviour (OR 1.43), parental attitudes favourable toward drug use (OR 1.28) and parental attitudes favourable toward antisocial behaviour (OR 1.24). The odds of being gang-involved decreased, however, for those who reported parental attitudes favourable toward alcohol use (OR 0.84). Respondents who reported receiving rewards from their family for pro-social involvement were less likely to be involved in a gang (OR 0.74).

In the peer-individual domain, eight risk and two protective factors were significantly associated with gang involvement in the Arizona-based sample. Respondents who reported rebelliousness were more likely to be gang involved (OR 1.42). Additionally, those who reported early initiation of antisocial behaviour (OR 2.09), drug use (OR 1.45) and alcohol use (OR 1.38) were more likely to be gang involved. Interestingly, those who reported attitudes favourable to drug use (OR 0.76) were less likely to be gang involved. Respondents who reported an intention to use drugs in the future (OR 1.24) and those who had antisocial peers (OR 2.29) were more likely to be gang involved. Additionally, those who were at risk for depression (OR 1.19) were more likely to be gang involved. While respondents who reported belief in the moral order (OR 0.81) were significantly less likely be gang involved, those who reported rewards from one's peers for pro-social involvement (OR 1.28) increased the likelihood that a youth would be gang involved.

Differences in Risk and Protective Factors Associated with Gang Membership Across Sites

We tested whether a risk and protective factor predicted gang involvement similarly across samples by running a series of interactions. In tables 5.4 and 5.5, model 3 presents the findings from these interactions. By interacting each risk and protective factor with the dichotomous site variable, we examined whether the risk and protective factors for gang involvement were significantly different between the two sites. The site/country variable was coded "0" for Arizona and "1" for Trinidad and Tobago; thus, for risk factors odds, ratios greater than one (positive beta) indicate a stronger association in Trinidad and Tobago, while odds ratios of less than one (negative beta) indicate a stronger association in Arizona. For protective factors, odds ratios greater than one (positive beta) indicate a stronger association in Arizona, and odds ratios less than one (negative beta) indicate a stronger association in Trinidad and Tobago.

Our analyses indicated that seven risk factors (table 5.4, model 3) and one protective factor (table 5.5, model 3) were more strongly associated with one site than the other. For instance, while high community disorganization was more strongly associated with gang involvement in Arizona, the perceived availability of drugs was more strongly associated with gang involvement in Trinidad and Tobago. In the school domain, academic failure was a significantly stronger predictor of gang involvement in Arizona when compared with Trinidad and Tobago. In the peer-individual domain, three risk factors were more strongly associated with gang involvement in Trinidad and Tobago, while one risk factor was more strongly associated with Arizona. Intention to use drugs, perceived risk of drug use and sensation seeking were all more strongly associated with gang involvement in Trinidad and Tobago. The presence of antisocial peers, on the other hand, was more strongly associated with gang involvement in Arizona. One protective factor, having social skills, resulted in significantly more protection from gang involvement in Trinidad and Tobago than in Arizona.

Discussion and Conclusion

This chapter examined the scope and nature of the gang problem in Trinidad and Tobago, and placed these findings in the context of those found in Arizona (United States). Using self-report surveys of youth in both sites, the current chapter examined the prevalence of gang membership, the characteristics of the gang members, the rate of involvement in delinquency and victimization among gang members and non-gang members, and the relationship between risk and protective factors and gang involvement. Understanding gang membership in the context of youth from different countries will inform both policy and theory. Many policies and theories that address gang-related issues are based on findings from the United States; it is unknown how similar those gang-related phenomena are in different contexts, especially the Caribbean.

To summarize the findings, the rate of gang membership was higher in Trinidad and Tobago compared with Arizona. Specifically, 12.5 per cent of youth in Trinidad and Tobago compared with 7.6 per cent of youth from Arizona reported having ever been a gang member. In terms of age, gang members in Trinidad and Tobago were slightly older than non-gang members; however, there was no difference in age between gang and non-gang members in Arizona. The most frequently cited reason for joining a gang in Arizona was protection or safety, while in Trinidad and Tobago the most-cited reason was friendship. In terms of delinquency and victimization, gang members were more likely to be involved in delinquency and drug use and more likely to be victimized than non-gang members in both countries. The ratio between gang and non-gang members was surprisingly similar in both countries. Even though the frequency of involvement in delinquent activities was different between sites, gang members were significantly more likely than non-gang members to engage in such activities in both countries. This finding suggests that the consequences of gang membership are just as detrimental in Trinidad and Tobago as they are in Arizona (United States).

The findings on risk and protective factors indicate that there were a number of factors that were significantly more likely to be related to gang membership in one of the two sites. The risk factors of high community disorganization, academic failure and antisocial peers were stronger predictors in Arizona, while in Trinidad and Tobago the perceived availability of handguns, intention to use drugs, perceived risk of drug use and sensation seeking were more related to gang membership. The presence of social skills was a significantly stronger protective factor in Trinidad and Tobago compared with Arizona.

These findings will help to inform policy decisions and provide additional evidence for gang-related theory. In terms of policy, one of the most important findings is that the sources of gang membership are not necessarily the same – the reasons for joining and the risk factors for gang membership are not identical for both countries. This is important to policymakers for a number of reasons. First, many gang intervention and prevention programmes are based on research from the United States and Western Europe. Policymakers should not necessarily adopt these programmes without first confirming that the programmes address the underlying risk factors for their specific context. Many responses that might be the solution to gang problems in the United States will not necessarily be the solution to the gang problems in the Caribbean. Second, the current study suggests that the behaviours and consequences associated with gang membership *are similar* among gang members in both countries. Gang members in both countries were significantly more likely to be involved in delinquency, suggesting that gang members are an important group upon which to focus resources. Policymakers in the Caribbean, however, must ensure that their response to the gang problem matches the causal factors associated with gang membership in the Caribbean.

The findings from the current chapter also have a number of different theoretical implications. First, three risk factors that were associated with gang membership in the Arizona sample (community disorganization, academic failure and antisocial peers) were significantly less likely to be related to gang membership in Trinidad and Tobago. These findings indicate that gang membership in Arizona is related to structural issues, but this is not necessarily true in Trinidad and Tobago. Gang membership in Arizona corresponds with community and scholastic deficiencies. Gang formation, as with many community and societal ills, is the result of a complex process that is unique to the country's development and history. The mechanisms at work at the macro level have to be understood in each context. For example, the development social disorganization theory has a long history tied to American cities. The theory was born out of the new ecological understanding of crime in Chicago at a time in American history when, due to European immigration and the industrial revolution, mass societal transformations were taking place (Sampson and Groves 1989; Shaw and McKay 1931). In brief, social disorganization theory suggests that high rates of residential turnover, poverty and racial and ethnic heterogeneity forming out of rapid urban growth translate to strained social institutions, which then result in crime. Obviously this theory is uniquely tied to American communities, and we are only now beginning to understand its applicability to other parts of the world. Researchers should continue to unpack the complex mechanisms at play in other countries, which will require both the construction of new theories and the alteration of old ones. In sum, this chapter suggests that some structural- and individual-level theories and explanations might not translate to developing nations such as Trinidad and Tobago. Obviously more research must be done on this topic.

Second, among the sample from Trinidad and Tobago, our study found that family risk and protective factors were unrelated to gang joining. It might be that such family-based theoretical constructs on which the risk and protective model are based (that is, family bonding and attachment, social learning, control) have limited influence in the Caribbean or are mediated through alternative pathways. Theories must be developed that help identify the causal mechanisms at work in communities, families, schools and peer groups in the Caribbean, if in fact these mechanisms are different than in the United States. Context matters, and theoretical development based on the unique characteristics of the Caribbean is important.

Third, the findings suggest that gang and non-gang members in Trinidad and Tobago are more polarized in terms of drug use and attitudes toward drugs than in the United States. Overall, drug use is lower among youth in Trinidad and Tobago; however, use and intention to use are more related to gang membership in Trinidad and Tobago. This raises the age-old question of selection versus influence (also called facilitation) among gang members in the Caribbean. Are individuals who use drugs and are favourable towards drug use more likely to join a gang, or do individuals learn about and adapt their perceptions after joining a gang? Researchers should investigate the selection, facilitation and enhancement models as outlined by Thornberry et al. (2003) through longitudinal research. Doing so would not only allow policymakers to develop more effective and efficient prevention and intervention strategies aimed at reducing gang participation but would also allow researchers to better understand the causal pathways leading youth towards gang participation.

Future research should also continue to compare the causes and correlates of gang membership across contexts. The current chapter supports the fact that gang researchers need to examine the sources of gang membership in different contexts. Future research should use a similar approach to understand the similarities and differences of risk and protective factors between gang members in different parts of the world. Further, once these differences have been identified, researchers must then engage in more detailed studies to better understand the mechanisms at work in different countries. Diagnosing the extent and nature of a country's gang problem is the essential first step in developing an effective and efficient response to gangs.

Appendix 5A: Scale items and reliability

Variable	Items	Response categories and coding scheme	Range	Mean (SD)	Cronbach's alpha
Violence	Handgun carry frequency (12 months)	Never = 0, 1-2 = 1, 3-5 = 2, 6-9 = 3, 10-19 = 4, 20-29 = 5, 30-39 = 6, 40+ = 7	0–35	0.71 (2.46)	0.786
	Attack to harm (12 months)	Never = 0, 1-2 = 1, 3-5 = 2, 6-9 = 3, 10-19 = 4, 20-29 = 5, 30-39 = 6, 40+ = 7			
	Attack with a weapon (12 months)	Never = 0, 1-2 = 1, 3-5 = 2, 6-9 = 3, 10-19 = 4, 20-29 = 5, 30-39 = 6, 40+ = 7			
	Taken handgun to school freq (12 months)	Never = 0, 1-2 = 1, 3-5 = 2, 6-9 = 3, 10-19 = 4, 20-29 = 5, 30-39 = 6, 40+ = 7			
	Use weapon or force to steal (12 months)	Never = 0, 1-2 = 1, 3-5 = 2, 6-9 = 3, 10-19 = 4, 20-29 = 5, 30-39 = 6, 40+ = 7			
Property	Stole something worth < $50 (TT$300) (12 months)	Never = 0, 1-2 = 1, 3-5 = 2, 6-9 = 3, 10-19 = 4, 20-29 = 5, 30-39 = 6, 40+ = 7	0–28	1.10 (2.95)	0.736
	Stole something worth > $50 (TT$300) (12 months)	Never = 0, 1-2 = 1, 3-5 = 2, 6-9 = 3, 10-19 = 4, 20-29 = 5, 30-39 = 6, 40+ = 7			
	Vehicle theft frequency (12 months)	Never = 0, 1-2 = 1, 3-5 = 2, 6-9 = 3, 10-19 = 4, 20-29 = 5, 30-39 = 6, 40+ = 7			

Continued...

Appendix 5A: Scale items and reliability (*continued*)

Variable	Items	Response categories and coding scheme	Range	Mean (SD)	Cronbach's alpha
	Tried to steal from a building (12 months)	Never = 0, 1-2 = 1, 3-5 = 2, 6-9 = 3, 10-19 = 4, 20-29 = 5, 30-39 = 6, 40+ == 7			
Drug Sales	Drug selling frequency (12 months)	Never = 0, 1-2 = 1, 3-5 = 2, 6-9 = 3, 10-19 = 4, 20-29 = 5, 30-39 = 6, 40+ == 7	0-7	0.17 (0.87)	
Arrest	Arrest frequency (12 months)	Never = 0, 1-2 = 1, 3-5 = 2, 6-9 = 3, 10-19 = 4, 20-29 = 5, 30-39 = 6, 40+ == 7	0-7	0.12 (0.57)	
Victimiza-tion	Threatened/injured with a weapon (12 months)	Never = 0, 1-2 = 1, 3-5 = 2, 6-9 = 3, 10-19 = 4, 20-29 = 5, 30-39 = 6, 40+ == 7	0-7	0.33 (1.04)	
Lifetime alcohol use	Lifetime alcohol use frequency	Never = 0, 1-2 = 1, 3-5 = 2, 6-9 = 3, 10-19 = 4, 20-39 = 5, 40+ = 6	0-6	1.73 (1.99)	
30-day alcohol use	30-day alcohol use frequency	Never = 0, 1-2 = 1, 3-5 = 2, 6-9 = 3, 10-19 = 4, 20-39 = 5, 40+ = 6	0-6	0.60 (1.15)	
Lifetime drug use	Lifetime drug use frequency (marijuana/cocaine)	Never = 0, 1-2 = 1, 3-5 = 2, 6-9 = 3, 10-19 = 4, 20-39 = 5, 40+ = 6	0-12	0.75 (1.65)	
30-day drug use	30-day drug use frequency (marijuana/cocaine)	Never = 0, 1-2 = 1, 3-5 = 2, 6-9 = 3, 10-19 = 4, 20-39 = 5, 40+ = 6	0-12	0.28 (0.97)	

Appendix 5B. Risk and protective factor descriptives

Domains and Scales	Items	Range	Cronbach's Alpha	
Risk Factors			AZ	TT
Community				
Low neighbourhood attachment	2	1–4	0.832	0.612
High community disorganization	5	1–4	0.813	0.685
Mobility	1	1–3	NA	NA
Laws and norms favourable to drugs	5	1–4	0.748	0.709
Perceived availability of handguns	1	1–4	NA	NA
Perceived availability of drugs	2	1–4	0.722	0.741
School				
Academic failure	1	1–4	NA	NA
Low commitment to school	7	1–5	0.765	0.627
Family				
Family history of antisocial behaviour	8	1–5	0.799	0.773
Poor family management	8	1–4	0.822	0.787
Family conflict	3	1–4	0.758	0.676
Parental attitudes favourable towards drug use	1	1–4	NA	NA
Parental attitudes favourable towards alcohol use	1	1–4	NA	NA
Parental attitudes favourable towards antisocial behaviour	3	1–4	0.734	0.644
Peer-individual				
Rebelliousness	3	1–4	0.786	0.726
Early initiation of antisocial behaviour	1	0–8	NA	NA
Early initiation of drug use	1	0–8	NA	NA
Early initiation of alcohol use	2	0–8	0.560	0.608
Attitudes favourable to antisocial behaviour	5	1–4	0.802	0.747
Attitudes favourable to drug use	1	1–4	NA	NA
Attitudes favourable to alcohol use	1	1–4	NA	NA
Intention to use drugs	1	1–4	NA	NA
Intention to use alcohol	1	1–4	NA	NA
Perceived risk of drug use	3	1–4	0.747	0.750

Continued...

Appendix 5B. Risk and protective factor descriptives (*continued*)

Domains and Scales	Items	Range	Cronbach's Alpha	
Antisocial peers	6	0–4	0.811	0.650
Peers use drugs	1	0–4	NA	NA
Peers use alcohol	1	0–4	NA	NA
Rewards for antisocial involvement	3	1–5	0.765	0.818
Depression	4	1–4	0.832	0.841
Sensation seeking	3	1–6	0.712	0.521
Protective Factors				
Community				
Opportunities for pro-social involvement	3	1–4	0.585	0.641
Rewards for pro-social involvement	3	1–4	0.865	0.769
School				
Opportunities for pro-social involvement	5	1–4	0.584	0.722
Rewards for pro-social involvement	4	1–4	0.679	0.708
Family				
Family attachment	4	1–4	0.747	0.700
Opportunities for pro-social involvement	3	1–4	0.765	0.714
Rewards for pro-social involvement	4	1–4	0.750	0.644
Peer-individual				
Religiosity	1	1–4	NA	NA
Social skills	4	1–4	0.633	0.524
Belief in the moral order	4	1–4	0.705	0.770
Pro-social involvement	1	0–7	NA	NA
Rewards for pro-social involvement	1	1–5	NA	NA
Interaction with pro-social peers	5	0–4	0.665	0.549

Average AZ alpha = .740
Average TT alpha = .692

Notes

1. Funding for this research was provided in part by the Ministry of National Security of Trinidad and Tobago. The points of view expressed in this paper are those of the authors alone and do not represent the official policies or positions of the Ministry of National Security or the Trinidad and Tobago Police Service. This research was approved by the Human Subjects Protection committee at Arizona State University (IRB protocol #0702001609 and #0706001954).
2. This information also comes from personal communication with Christopher Hernandez-Roy, Director of the Department of Public Security, Organization of American States, 25 April 2009.
3. A body of research is emerging on the validity of self-report data that was obtained from gang members who participated in both school-based (Esbensen et al. 2001) and arrestee-based studies (Katz et al. 1997; Webb, Katz and Decker 2006). This body of research suggests that these methodologies are some of the most valid and robust for understanding gangs, gang membership and gang-related problems.
4. See data at http://www.ombudsman.com/pdfs/AZ_Results.pdf.
5. In Arizona, passive consent procedures were used to obtain consent from parents of children attending the selected schools. Very few parents refused to allow their child to participate in the study. In Trinidad, parental consent is not required for surveys administered by school officials.
6. Some items were required to be reverse-coded before scale construction.
7. There are advantages and disadvantages associated with dichotomizing predictor variables. Prior research indicates that dichotomizing risk and protective factors is beneficial as long as it increases interpretability (meaningful interpretations of odds ratios) and reduces error-associated skewed variables. Additionally, although use of dichotomized predictors limits the amount of variation in a variable, it rarely affects the substantive findings (Farrington and Loeber 2000). For an explanation of the cut point chosen for the present study, see Bond et al. (2005).
8. The risk and protective factors were estimated in the same model, but are presented separately because of page size limitations.
9. All the risk and protective factors were mean centred in the third model to reduce any potential multi-collinearity.

References

Arthur, M.W., J.D. Hawkins, J.A. Pollard, R.F. Catalano, and A.J. Baglioni Jr. 2002. "Measuring Risk and Protective Factors for Substance Use, Delinquency, and Other Adolescent Problem Behaviors: The Communities That Care Youth Survey". *Evaluation Review* 26: 575–601.

Beyers, J.M., J. Toumbourou, R. Catalano, M. Arthur, and D. Hawkins. 2004. "A Cross-National Comparison of Risk and Protective Factors for Adolescent Substance Use: The United States and Australia". *Journal of Adolescent Health* 35: 3–16.

Blaya, C., and U. Gatti. 2010. "Deviant Youth Groups in Italy and France". *European Journal of Criminal Justice and Policy Research* 16: 127-44.

Bond, L., J.W. Toumbourou, L. Thomas, R.F. Catalano, and G. Patton. 2005. "Individual, Family, School, and Community Risk and Protective Factors for Depressive Symptoms in Adolescents: A Comparison of Risk Profiles for Substance Use and Depressive Symptoms". *Prevention Science* 6(2): 73–88.

Brook, J., N. Morojele, K. Pahl, and D. Brook. 2006. "Predictors of Drug Use among South African Adolescents". *Journal of Adolescent Health* 38: 26–34.

Bulmer, M. 1993. *Social Research in Developing Countries: Surveys and Censuses in the Third World*. New York: Routledge.

Curry, D., S.H. Decker, and A. Egley. 2002. "Gang Involvement and Delinquency in a Middle School Population". *Justice Quarterly* 19(2): 275–92.

Descormiers, K., and D. Morselli. 2011. "Alliances, Conflicts, and Contradictions in Montreal's Street Gang Landscape". *International Criminal Justice Review* 21(3): 297–314.

Dubinsky, C., and C. Derrick. 2007. *Latin America and the Caribbean: Selected Economic and Social Data*. Washington, DC: United States Agency for International Development.

Egley, A. , J.C. Howell, and J.P. Moore. 2010. *Highlights of the 2008 National Youth Gang Survey*. Washington, DC: Department of Justice, Office of Justice Program, Office of Juvenile Justice and Delinquency Prevention.

Esbensen, F.A., and C. Maxson. 2012. "The Eurogang Programme of Research and Multimethod Comparative Gang Research". In *Youth Gangs in International Perspective: Results from the Eurogang Programme of Research*, edited by F. Esbensen and C. Maxson, 1–16. New York: Springer.

Esbensen, F.A., and F. Weerman. 2005. "Youth Gangs and Troublesome Youth Groups in the United States and the Netherlands: A Cross-National Comparison". *European Journal of Criminology* 2(1): 5–37.

Esbensen, F.A., L.T.Winfree Jr, Ni He, and T.J. Taylor. 2001. "Youth Gangs and Definitional Issues: When Is a Gang a Gang, and Why Does It Matter?" *Crime and Delinquency* 47(1): 105–30.

Fairington, A. 2004. "Communities That Care: A Case Study of Regeneration from Wales". *The Eurogang Programme of Research and Multimethod Comparative Gang Research* 14(1): 27–36.

Farrington, D. P. 2006. *Childhood Risk Factors and Risk Focused Prevention*. Cambridge: University of Cambridge.

Farrington, D. P., and R. Loeber. 2000. "Some Benefits of Dichotomization in Psychiatric and Criminological Research". *Criminal Behavior and Mental Health* 10: 100–22.

Fiori-Khayat, C. 2008. "Ethnicity and Juvenile Street Gangs in France". In *Street Gangs, Migration and Ethnicity*, edited by F. van Gemert, D. Peterson, and I. Lien, 156–72. Portland: Willan Publishing.

Franciosi, R. 2007. *Dropout Report 2006*. Arizona Department of Education: Phoenix.

Franco, A.A. 2005. Testimony of Adolfo A. Franco on 20 April 2005, US House of Representatives Subcommittee on the Western Hemisphere. http://commdocs.house. gov/committees/intlrel/hfa24054.000/hfa240540f.htm.

Gfroere, J., D. Wright, and A. Kopstein. 1997. "Prevalence of Youth Substance Use: The Impact of Methodological Differences between Two National Surveys". *Drug and Alcohol Dependence*. 47: 19–30.

Harachi, T.W., J.D. Hawkins, R.F. Catalano, A.M. Lafazia, B.H. Smith, and M.W. Arthur. 2003. "Evidence-Based Community Decision Making for Prevention: Two Case Studies of Communities That Care". *Japanese Journal of Sociological Criminology* 28: 26–37.

Hawkins, J.D., R.F. Catalano, and J.Y. Miller. 1992. "Risk and Protective Factors for Alcohol and Other Drug Problems in Adolescence and Early Adulthood: Implications for Substance Abuse Prevention". *Psychological Bulletin*. 112: 64–105.

Haymoz, S., and U. Gatti. 2010. "Girl Members of Deviant Youth Groups, Offending Behaviour and Victimisation: Results from the ISRD2 in Italy and Switzerland". *European Journal on Criminal Policy and Research* 16(3): 167–82.

Hemphill, S.A., J.W. Toumbourou, R.F. Catalano, and M. Mathers. 2004. "Levels and Family Correlates of Positive Adolescent Development: A Cross-National Comparison". *Family Matters* 68 (Winter): 28–35. http://aifs.gov.au/institute/pubs/fm2004/ fm68/sh.pdf.

Huff, R. 1990. "Denial, Overreaction, and Misidentification: A Postscript on Public Policy". In *Gangs in America*, edited by C.R. Huff, 310–17. Thousand Oaks, CA: Sage.

Huizinga, D., and K. Schumann. 2001. "Gang Membership in Bremen and Denver: Comparative Longitudinal Data". In *The Eurogang Paradox*, edited by M. Klein, 231–46. Netherlands: Kluwer Academic.

Johnston, L., P.M.O'Malley, and. J.G. Bachman. 2002. "Monitoring the Future: National Survey Results on Drug Use, 1975–2001". University of Michigan.

Katz, C.M., and A. Fox. 2010. "Risk and Protective Factors Associated with Gang Involved Youth in a Caribbean Nation: Analysis of the Trinidad and Tobago Youth Survey". *Pan-American Journal of Public Health/Revista Panamericana de Salud Pública* 27(3): 187–202.

Katz, C.M., E.R. Maguire, and D. Choate. 2011. "A Cross-National Comparison of Gangs in the United States and Trinidad and Tobago". *International Criminal Justice Review* 21(3): 243–62.

Katz, C.M., V.J. Webb, P.R. Gartin, and C.E. Marshall. 1997. "The Validity of Self-Reported Marijuana and Cocaine Use". *Journal of Criminal Justice* 25(1): 31–42.

Kellerman, B., N. Lomuto, J. Machan, and P.A. Minugh. 2003. "Alabama Student Survey of Risk and Protective Factors: Demand and Needs Assessment Studies". Birmingham: Alabama Department of Mental Health and Mental Retardation Substance Abuse Services Division.

Klein, M., and C. Maxson. 2006. *Street Gang Patterns and Policies*. New York: Oxford University Press.

Kohn, M. 1987. "Cross-National Research as an Analytic Strategy". *American Sociological Review* 52: 713–31.

Lien, I. 2005. "The Role of Crime Acts in Constituting the Gang's Mentality". In *European Street Gangs and Troublesome Youth Groups*, edited by S.H. Decker and F. Weerman, 105–28. New York: AltaMira.

Maguire, E.R., W. Wells, and C.M. Katz. 2011. "Measuring Community Risk and Protective Factors for Adolescent Problem Behaviors: Evidence from a Developing Nation". *Journal of Research in Crime and Delinquency* 48: 594–620.

Malby, S. 2010. "Homicide". In *International Statistics on Crime and Justice*, edited by S. Harrendorf, M. Heiskanen, and S. Malby, 7–21. Vienna: United Nations Office on Drugs and Crime.

Manwaring, M.G. 2007. *A Contemporary Challenge to State Sovereignty: Gangs and Other Illicit Transnational Criminal Organizations in Central America, El Salvador, Mexico, Jamaica and Brazil*. Carlisle, PA: Strategic Studies Institute.

Marlow-Ferguson, R. 2002. *World Education Encyclopedia: A Survey of Educational Systems Worldwide*, 2nd ed. Farmington Hills, MI: Thomson Learning.

Ohene, S., M. Ireland, and R. Blum. 2005. "The Clustering of Risk Behaviors among Caribbean Youth". *Maternal and Child Health Journal* 9(1): 91–100.

Prais, S.J. 2005. "Two Recent (2003) International Surveys of Schooling Attainments: England's Problems". National Institute of Economic and Social Research Discussion Paper No. 258. London: National Institute of Economic and Social Research.

Salagaev, A., A. Shashkin, I. Sherbakova, and E. Touriyanskiy. 2005. "Contemporary Russian Gangs: History, Membership, and Crime Involvement". In *European Street Gangs and Troublesome Youth Groups,* edited by S.H. Decker and F. Weerman, 169–92. New York: AltaMira.

Sampson, R., and W.B. Groves. 1989. "Community Structure and Crime: Testing Social Disorganization Theory". *American Journal of Sociology* 94: 774–802.

Shaw, C.R., and H.D. McKay. 1931. *Report on the Causes of Crime*. Washington, DC: Government Printing Office.

Smithson, H., L. Monchuk, and R. Armitage. 2012. "Gang Member: Who Says? Definitional and Structural Issues". In *Youth Gangs in International Perspective*, edited by F. Esbensen and C. Maxson, 53–69. New York: Springer.

Thornberry, T., M.D. Krohn, A.J. Lizotte, C.A. Smith, and K. Tobin. 2003. *Gangs and Delinquency in Developmental Perspective*. Cambridge: Cambridge University Press.

Townsend, D. 2009. *No Other Life: Gangs, Guns and Governance in Trinidad and Tobago*. Geneva Small Arms Survey. Geneva: Graduate Institute of International and Development Studies.

UNICEF. 2009. At a Glance: Trinidad and Tobago. http://www.unicef.org/infobycountry/stats_popup5.html.

US Census Bureau. 2012. "State and County Quick Facts". 2012. Data derived from "Population Estimates", "American Community Survey", "Census of Population and Housing", "State and County Housing Unit Estimates", "County Business Patterns", "Non-Employer Statistics", "Economic Census", and "Survey of Business". http://quickfacts.census.gov/qfd/states/04000.html.

van Gemert, F., and M. Fleisher. 2005. "In the Grip of the Group". In *European Street Gangs and Troublesome Youth Groups,* edited by S.H. Decker and F. Weerman, 11–31. New York: AltaMira.

Webb, V., C.M. Katz, and S.H.Decker. 2006. "Assessing the Validity of Self-Reports by Gang Members: Results from the Arrestee Drug-Abuse Monitoring Program". *Crime and Delinquency* 52(2): 232–52.

Weerman, F. 2005. "Identification and Self-Identification: Using a Survey to Study Gangs in the Netherlands". In *European Street Gangs and Troublesome Youth Groups*, edited by S. H. Decker and F. Weerman, 129–46. New York: AltaMira.

Wells, W., C.M. Katz, and J. Kim. 2010. "Firearm Possession among Arrestees in Trinidad and Tobago". *Injury Prevention* 16(5): 337–42.

White, R. 2008. "Weapons Are for Wimps: The Social Dynamics of Ethnicity and Violence in Australian Gangs". In *Street Gangs, Migration and Ethnicity*, edited by F. van Gemert, D. Peterson, and I. Lien, 140–55. Portland: Willan.

Wild, T., L. Ragan, C. Pim, A. Roberts, H. Pazderka-Robinson, T. Horne, and P. O'Hara. 2003. "Tobacco Use among Alberta Youth: Results from the Alberta Youth Tobacco Survey". University of Alberta, Edmonton.

6 | Diagnosing Gang Violence in the Caribbean

CHARLES M. KATZ AND EDWARD R. MAGUIRE

Gang violence has become a serious problem in many Caribbean islands. A recent report from the United Nations Development Programme highlights the corrosive effects of gangs and gang violence in the region (UNDP 2012). More than half of homicides in some Caribbean nations are now thought to be gang-related (Hill 2012; Katz and Choate 2006). In a recent survey of citizens in seven Caribbean nations, 29 per cent of respondents reported that their neighbourhoods have experienced some level of gang violence. This finding ranged from a low of 18.3 per cent in Barbados to a high of 43.1 per cent in St Lucia (UNDP 2011). Many Caribbean islands have been shaken by specific incidents of gang violence, often newsworthy due to the innocence of the victim or the sheer audacity of the offence. For instance, in January 2007 masked gang members stormed the home of a female police constable in Trinidad and murdered her, along with her husband, her daughter and a family friend (Seelal 2007). In July 2010, a fourteen-year-old tourist was killed in the US Virgin Islands when she was caught in the crossfire between warring gangs (Sloan 2010).

Unfortunately, gang violence has only recently been acknowledged as a major problem in many Caribbean islands (UNDP 2012; Seepersad 2013). Policymakers and criminal justice officials have been slow to address gangs and gang violence in the region and often neglect to take these issues seriously until pressured to do so by the media and the public (Harriott 1996; Katz and

Choate 2006; Katz 2008; Moncrieffe 1998). With gangs contributing to soaring violent crime rates in several Caribbean nations and territories it is becoming increasingly difficult for public officials, community members and academics to ignore the problem. Yet the region still grapples with the question of how best to address gang violence.

Because gangs have instilled a general sense of alarm in residents, many Caribbean nations and international development organizations, such as the United Nations Development Programme, the Organization of American States and the various development banks, have launched discussions (or in some cases, pilot projects) focused on how to address the gang problem in the Caribbean. Many of these discussions focus on large-scale social issues associated with human development in the Caribbean, including unemployment, concentrated disadvantage, poor education and family-related problems. Often referred to as "root causes", these factors are the "usual suspects" that are often used to explain the growth and diffusion of gangs and gang violence in the Caribbean (Katz and Fox 2010; Katz, Maguire and Choate 2011; Maguire et al. 2008; Robotham 2003; UNDP 2012). While thinking broadly about the root causes of gangs, crime and violence is certainly important, there is often an underlying sense of pessimism or hopelessness in these discussions. A commonly heard refrain at international meetings is that it will take a generation to address gang violence in the Caribbean. When examining the sources of the gang problem in the Caribbean from a root cause perspective, it is tempting to conclude that it will take at least a generation to solve these issues because changing deeply ingrained social and economic issues is ambitious, difficult and time-consuming work.

However, there is a simple, practical and evidence-based alternative way to view these issues. This point of view is routinely ignored in most discussions about how to reduce gang violence in the Caribbean. Instead of focusing solely on root causes, criminologists also focus heavily on "proximate causes" of violence. Proximate causes are those factors that influence violence but are closer or more proximate to the violent event than root causes. Proximate causes can often be identified by thinking about the motive and the means for the offence. For instance, in homicides carried out by rival gangs using firearms, both the firearm and the gang conflict can be thought of as proximate causes. If we think in terms of proximate causes instead of root causes, the scope of the problem – and the complexity of potential solutions – becomes smaller and more manageable. Continuing on with the previous example, shifting focus to these two proximate causes might result in the design of a set of interventions capable of reducing the gang conflict and addressing the use of illegal guns to carry out acts of violence.

There has been relatively little thoughtful discussion on launching effective short-term and intermediate-term measures to address gang violence in the Caribbean (Maguire 2012; for exceptions, see Harriott 2009; Deosaran 2004, 104–28).

With few exceptions, the response to gangs thus far in the Caribbean has been characterized by poor leadership, weak financial support, stale thinking and an absence of urgency. Jurisdictions often adopt ill-advised programmes and policies. For instance, gang scholars have argued for many years that overly aggressive street suppression strategies have the unintended consequence of increasing cohesion and rebellion among gang members and those who are loyal or sympathetic to them (Klein 1995a). Similarly, the use of gang truces or peace treaties between gangs is endemic throughout the Caribbean, despite existing evidence suggesting that these approaches typically generate a short-term reduction in violence followed by a long-term increase (Klein 1995b; Kodluboy and Evenrud 1993; NGCRC 1995; Ordog et al. 1995). Truces and treaties are often negotiated by politicians. Yet, close relationships between political officials and gang leaders serve to legitimize gangs in the eyes of the populace, including aspiring gang members, and to elevate gang leaders to the status of community leaders (UNDP 2012). There is little scientific evidence to support many of the approaches that are used instinctively throughout the region. Some of these practices, like extrajudicial killings of gang members by police, undermine the rule of law and probably do more to worsen the gang problem than to help solve it (Manwaring 2007; UNDP 2012). Finally, well-intentioned but uninformed NGOs often contribute to the chaotic landscape of gang violence programming in the region by ignoring interventions with a strong record of success and recommending or funding generic interventions that are neither evidence-based nor sufficiently focused.

As noted in earlier chapters, gang experts often classify strategies to address gangs and gang violence into three categories: prevention, intervention and suppression. Prevention attempts to keep youth out of gangs. Intervention focuses on dealing with youth once they are already in gangs by encouraging them to leave the gang, providing them with new skills that provide alternatives to gang life, or encouraging them to moderate their behaviour if they decide to stay in the gang. Suppression involves making use of the formal criminal justice system to arrest, prosecute and otherwise control gangs. As a general principle, comprehensive efforts to address gangs and gang violence consist of a balance between prevention, intervention and suppression.

As with much of the world, the most common and instinctive approach to dealing with gangs in the Caribbean is suppression (UNDP 2012). The intellectual support for suppression strategies comes from deterrence theory, which holds that punishments or sanctions are most effective when they are severe, swift and administered with certainty. A *specific deterrent* effect occurs when a sanction (such as imprisonment) discourages the offender from offending again or reduces the severity of their future offences. A *general deterrent* effect occurs when a sanction imposed on some people leads others not to commit crime (Klein 1995a). In the developed world, suppression strategies typically focus criminal justice resources on gang members through the use of such practices as targeted and specialized police patrols, intelligence databases, aggressive prosecution strategies and enhanced sentences for those who are convicted (Katz 1997, 2001, 2003; Katz and Webb 2003, 2006; Webb and Katz 2003). Suppression is a vital component for addressing gang violence, provided that it is used in a strategic, focused and just manner and constitutes just one part of a more comprehensive approach.

For suppression strategies to work well, they need to effectively deter and incapacitate gangs. Unfortunately, deterrence and incapacitation do not function well in the Caribbean. Punishments may be severe in some instances, but they are neither swift nor certain. This is why "tough on crime" political rhetoric about corporal and capital punishment in the Caribbean is often just a distraction from the more important reforms that need to be instituted in the region. The real problem is that the likelihood of offenders actually receiving these tough sanctions is too low to substantially deter or incapacitate those weighing the costs and benefits of committing a crime. If politicians aim to reduce crime and violence, they need to focus on methods that will improve swiftness and certainty, not severity. The police in some Caribbean nations face numerous challenges in building effective cases against violent offenders. Some of these challenges are the result of deficiencies in the police agencies themselves, and indeed the police are often blamed for failures of the justice system. Some of these challenges, however, result instead from deficiencies in other parts of the justice system, especially crime laboratories and the courts. Due to these systemic problems – together with the well-known tendency of gangs to intimidate and kill witnesses against them – police face an often insurmountable set of obstacles in trying to build criminal cases against gang members. As a result, gang suppression efforts in the Caribbean often amount to little more than aggressive harassment policing.

Most Caribbean nations lack the basic institutional capacity to respond effectively to gangs. They do not have the *analytical capacity* to systematically track the identities of gangs and gang members; the overall number of gangs, gang members and gang-related offences; the nature of conflicts and alliances

between gangs; and the criminal behaviour carried out by gangs (Katz and Choate 2006; Maguire and Bennett 2008; UNDP 2012). Despite recent advances by
some police agencies, most still lack the analytical capacity to engage in intelligence-led or predictive policing, in which police use crime analysis to predict when and where certain offences (like retaliatory shootings) are going to
happen and then mobilize rapidly to prevent these incidents (Beck and McCue
2009; Maguire and Bennett 2008). Furthermore, as evidenced by the region's
low clearance rates, many also lack the *operational capacity* to identify offenders, arrest them and build successful criminal cases against them, particularly
for cases involving gang members (Maguire et al. 2010).

Developing these analytical and operational capacities throughout the Caribbean is vital for at least three related reasons. First, it will help nations focus
scarce resources in a way that is most likely to generate efficient and effective
results. Criminologists have discovered that a small number of offenders, victims, groups and places are responsible for a disproportionate share of crime
and violence. Communities and agencies that have the capacity to identify these
outliers can focus resources where they are needed most, which will generate
the greatest impact.

Second, enhancing these capacities will help police find legal ways to hold
offenders accountable, thus firmly establishing the rule of law and sustaining
their own legitimacy. When the public loses faith in the government's ability to
control serious crime, the police lose legitimacy and citizens begin to rely on
them less. Citizens may choose not to report a crime committed against them
or choose not to cooperate with an investigation as a victim or as a witness. In
this way, police illegitimacy can undermine deterrence and weaken the rule of
law (see, for example, Adams 2012; Maguire, Bennett and Harriott 2014; Reisig
and Lloyd 2009). If people don't cooperate with police, fewer crimes get solved,
clearance rates drop and offenders become emboldened. Enhancing the analytical and operational capacities of police will increase their legitimacy, which in
turn, will help to slow and eventually reverse this downward spiral.

Third, when police are ineffective in controlling gangs and violence, residents may begin to work around the police and rely instead on informal illicit
means of social control. In some of the most troubled Caribbean neighbourhoods, residents do not call the police to discipline their children or teens;
instead they call the neighbourhood gang leader or the don. Serious deficits
in police legitimacy create a vacuum that enables gang leaders to step into
the social control role ordinarily reserved for police (Clarke 2006; Deosaran
2004). Gang leaders in Trinidad bragged to us that there were no rapes in their

neighbourhoods because they had forbidden them. They also told us that they administered harsh beatings to people who carried out unsanctioned robberies or kidnappings. One gang leader explained how he rescued a victim kidnapped by one of his own gang members because the member did not have permission to carry out the offence. They claimed to regulate who could commit crime, which victims could be targeted and where the offences could be carried out.

As the gang's informal social control function begins to take root, gang leaders may establish a basic set of rules to be followed within the community and use violence to punish those who violate these rules (Arias and Rodrigues 2006). These systems of informal social control can become sophisticated, with the establishment of community courts led by gang leaders and attended by local elected officials (Charles 2012; Harriott 1996, 2003, 2008, 2009; Katz and Choate 2006; Leslie 2010; Sives 2002). Gang leaders, community residents, political officials and police all told us that gang leaders provided food, jobs, money and other resources to the downtrodden. As evidenced most dramatically by the massive outpourings of people and emotion at funerals for slain gang leaders, in some Caribbean communities these leaders have developed Robin Hood personas. Although no data exist concerning the extent of these phenomena in the region, a recent survey of citizens in seven nations provides some insights (UNDP 2011). Overall, 14.5 per cent of respondents agreed that dons should be used as agents of crime control to reduce the crime rate. This figure ranged from a low of 7.9 per cent in Barbados to a high of 23.9 per cent in Suriname. In some communities, half the respondents thought dons should be enlisted to help reduce crime. While these dynamics are not the norm in all Caribbean communities, there is evidence that these imbalances are found in some of the region's most troubled communities.

All of these complex issues point to the need for Caribbean nations to take stock of their gang problems. This means carrying out structured diagnoses, not only of the gang problem itself, but also of their own capacity to address the gang problem. The purpose of this chapter is to outline the basic steps involved in carrying out a systematic diagnosis of the gang problem in a specific jurisdiction. This diagnosis involves two parts, one external and one internal. The external component calls for an attempt to understand the nature of the gang problem itself, particularly with regard to gang violence. The internal component involves assessing the analytical and operational capacity of the state and its partners to address the gang problem. In order to contextualize these issues, we provide a framework for thinking about how to improve a jurisdiction's capacity to address gang violence over the short, intermediate and long term.

We illustrate these principles and ideas by describing a project we carried out in the Republic of Trinidad and Tobago to diagnose the nature and causes of a serious outbreak of gang violence and to propose potential solutions.

Diagnosing an Outbreak of Violence in Trinidad and Tobago

In 2004, we began teaching a course in Trinidad on strategic crime control to a group of middle managers in the police service. What started as a university course eventually led to an ambitious and wide-ranging project, the bulk of which occurred between 2005 and 2010. The project involved carrying out a comprehensive diagnosis of the outbreak of violence in Trinidad and Tobago, recommending potential solutions and evaluating the agencies' responses to those recommendations. Edward Maguire established a multidisciplinary team of scholars and practitioners to execute the project; Charles Katz served as the team's lead on gang-related issues. The project was large and involved many facets, but for our purposes here we will focus on just two parts: (1) diagnosing the causes of the nation's outbreak of violence and (2) diagnosing the capacity of the criminal justice system and other entities to address the violence.

Figure 6.1 illustrates the annual number of homicides in Trinidad and Tobago from 1988 to 2008. After many years of relative stability in homicides, the outbreak of violence began around 2000. Although policymakers and police leaders understood that homicides were increasing, most of them were unaware of vital details associated with the outbreak in violence.[1] Our analysis of TTPS data indicated that the escalation in the homicide rate was sudden and dramatic and represented something very different from the minor fluctuations in violence that had occurred in prior years. Root cause explanations for crime are often more appropriate for explaining changes that unfold more slowly than those in figure 6.1. Proximate cause explanations are typically more suitable for explaining rapid changes in crime because the causes themselves sometimes evolve rapidly. As we began to familiarize ourselves with the nature of crime and gangs in Trinidad and Tobago, we learned that the rapid increase in violence had much more to do with changes occurring among gangs than with sudden changes in poverty, education, employment or other major social issues. It is evident that certain key events among street gangs led to increased conflict between gangs, and each new violent incident prompted a series of others as a cycle of retaliation set in.

Although government and police leaders knew that homicides were increasing, this awareness did not result in any major changes in criminal justice policies

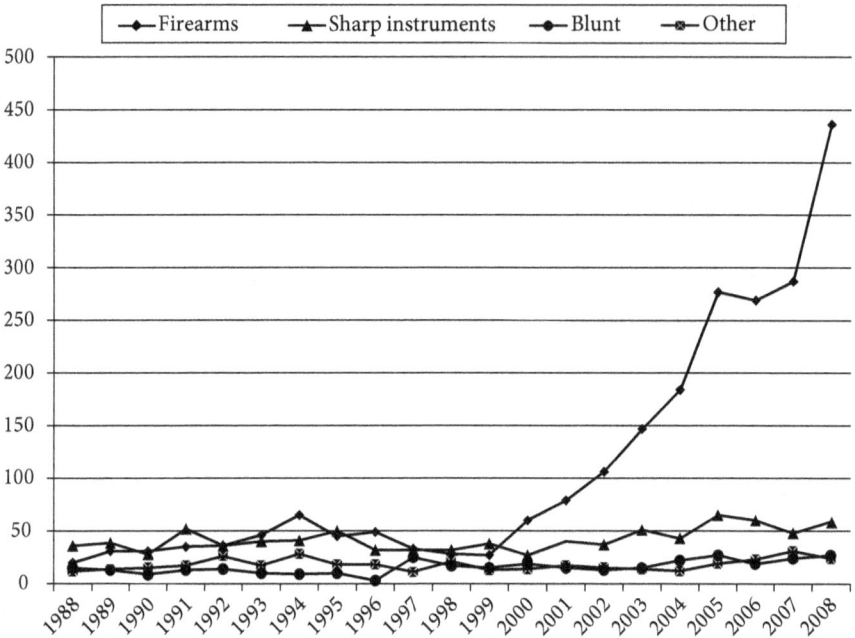

Figure 6.1. Homicides by weapon type, 1988–2008

or practices. At the time we began our diagnosis in 2005, the police were still relying on the same tools they had used throughout the first five years of the homicide increase. Moreover, the police were still hampered by serious deficiencies in other parts of the criminal justice system, particularly the nation's crime lab and courts. It quickly became clear to us that the system was broken because it was incapable of generating a sufficient baseline of deterrence to steer people – especially those involved in street gangs – away from crime and violence. These observations highlighted the need for a thorough diagnosis of the nation's "network of capacity" to control gangs and violence (Moore 2002, 338). Our diagnostic process included an examination of the violence problem itself and the nation's capacity to address it.

Our diagnosis of the nation's outbreak of violence contained many components, some directly related to gangs and others only indirectly related. In this section, we discuss the three aspects of our diagnostic process most directly related to gang violence: violent places, violent gangs and violent gang members. Due to space limitations, we do not address other aspects of our diagnosis, including those focused on firearms and drugs (see, for example, Kuhns and Maguire 2012; Wells, Katz and Kim 2010).

The Role of Violent Places

Our initial analysis of 2005 homicide data revealed substantial variation in homicides by geographic area (Katz and Maguire 2006). While the national homicide rate was 34.5 per 100,000 persons,[2] seven of the nation's sixty-six police station districts had substantially higher homicide rates. As seen in table 6.1, the most extreme was the Besson Street Station District which covers the Laventille area; this district had a homicide rate of 249 per 100,000 persons, about seven times the national average. About 62 per cent of the nation's homicides in 2005 occurred in only seven station districts. About 25 per cent of the homicides took place in the Besson Street station district alone, followed by about 8 per cent in Morvant, 7.8 per cent in West End, 6 per cent in Belmont and Arima, 4.7 per cent in St James, and 4.4 per cent in Carenage (2006).

We further examined violent places using a gang expert survey. In January 2006, we provided a batch of surveys to each district commander in the TTPS and asked them to forward a survey to the most senior criminal investigations department officer in each station district, or to the officer whom they believed had the most knowledge about gangs in each district.[3] Our gang expert survey was modelled after the Eurogang Expert Survey, which was created to collect data on the scope and nature of gang problems from police officers and other individuals with gang expertise in Europe (van Gemert 2005).

Table 6.1. Homicides and homicide rates by station districts in 2005

Station district	Homicides (Number)	Population	Homicide rate per 100,000 persons
Besson Street	96	38,513	249
Morvant	31	28,233	110
West End	30	31,588	95
Belmont	23	22,624	102
Arima	22	38,521	57
St James	18	16,729	108
Carenage	17	9,096	187
National	385	1,114,772	34.5

Source: Katz and Maguire 2006.

Our findings indicated that in 2006, Trinidad and Tobago had about ninety-five gangs and 1,269 gang members. The police experts noted that the majority of the gangs (74.2 per cent) were formed in 2000 or later. (Note that 2000 was the same year that the homicide outbreak began.) We also found that the vast majority of police districts (86.5 per cent) reported zero, one or two gangs and either no or few gang members. This study indicates that the nation's gangs and gang members were concentrated most heavily in the Port of Spain area in communities with above-average homicide rates. The Besson Street station district reported the largest number of gangs and gang members and also had a homicide rate three times greater than the next most violent police station district. As shown in table 6.2, five station districts, all with high levels of violence, were home to 50 per cent of the nation's gangs and about 70 per cent of the nation's gang members.

Criminologists have shown that spatial concentrations of violence occur at multiple levels of aggregation, from larger units like metropolitan areas or cities to much smaller units like street corners or blocks (Maguire et al. 2008; St Jean

Table 6.2. Districts with the greatest number of gangs and gang members

		Gangs (Number)	Gang Members (Number)
Five station districts with most gangs			
	Besson Street	19	385
	San Juan	8	130
	Sangre Grande	8	90
	St Joseph	7	55
	Belmont	6	165
Five station districts with most gang members			
	Besson Street	19	385
	Belmont	6	165
	San Juan	8	130
	Carenage	4	100
	Sangre Grande	8	90

Source: Katz and Choate 2006.

2007; Weisburd et al. 2004). Understanding these localized ecologies of violence is crucial for clarifying the nature of a violence problem and designing targeted solutions (Katz and Schnebly 2011). In this case, we first identified station districts that had experienced a disproportionate share of violence or had a substantial presence of gangs and gang members. Within those station districts, as illustrated in figure 6.2 below, we identified gang territories and spatial concentrations in homicides. Identifying these kinds of spatial patterns provides practical information that can be used to optimize the deployment of prevention, intervention and suppression strategies that are a good match for the location (Maguire et al. 2008).

The Role of Violent Gangs

Following our analysis of the spatial distribution of homicides and its relation to gangs and gang members, we began to look more closely at the role of gangs,

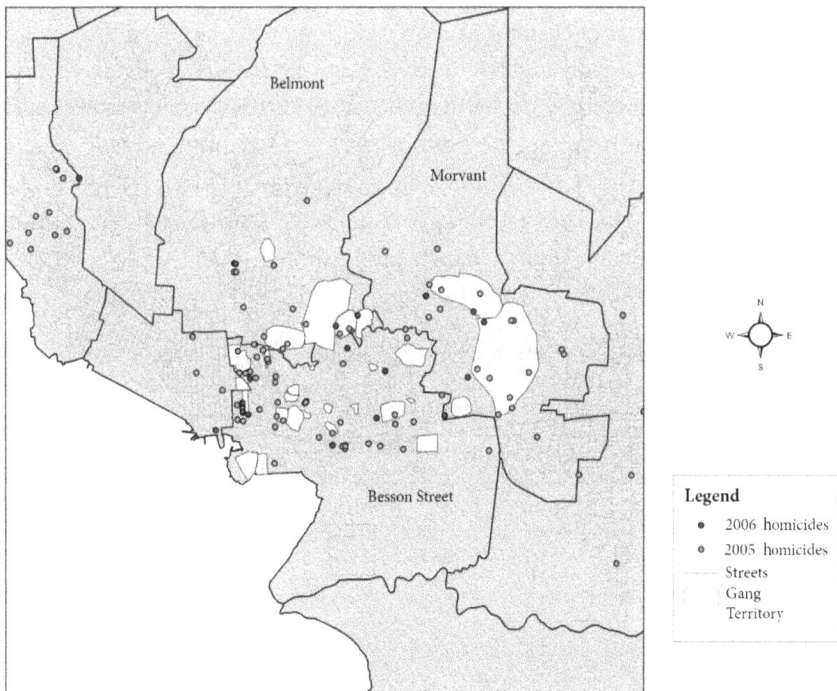

Figure 6.2. Gang territories and homicides, Belmont, Morvant and Besson Street

particularly in the Besson Street station district (Katz and Maguire 2006). Informal interviews with Besson Street officers revealed that most of the homicides in the community were committed by violent gangs. Besson Street's Criminal Investigation Division (CID) officers gave us access to intelligence files on the individuals they suspected were contributing heavily to violence within the community. The intelligence was recorded on forms that are similar to field contact cards used by police officers in the United States. These files provided us with basic information such as date of birth, ethnicity, gender, address, aliases and gang affiliation for suspects in the Besson Street station district. We used these files to identify the gang affiliations of suspects and victims involved in homicides.[4]

Ninety-six homicides were recorded in the Besson Street district between 1 January 2005 and 26 January 2006. Table 6.3 shows the gang affiliation for suspects and victims in these cases. We found that about 33 per cent of homicide victims and 59 per cent of the homicide suspects were gang members. Taken together, about 63 per cent of homicides involved either a victim or suspect who was a known gang member.

Next, we identified all of the gangs that were linked to each particular homicide as either suspects or victims in each case. Figure 6.3 contains the results from a basic social network analysis showing which gangs were involved in homicides. Gangs are denoted by capital letters, and the arrows depict suspect and victim affiliation. For example, the bottom left corner shows that gang G was suspected in six homicides: one in which the victim was a police or prison officer, two in which the victims were members of rival gangs (gangs C and P) and three in which the victims' gang affiliations were unknown. The analysis showed that

Table 6.3. Victim and suspect gang affiliation for homicides in the Besson Street Station District, 1 January 2005–26 January 2006

	Victim		Suspect		Victim or suspect	
	Number	%	Number	%	Number	%
Not affiliated with a gang	43	44.8	30	31.2	30	31.2
Gang member	32	33.3	57	59.4	60	62.5
Unknown	21	21.9	9	9.4	6	6.3
Total	96		96		96	

Source: Katz and Maguire 2006.

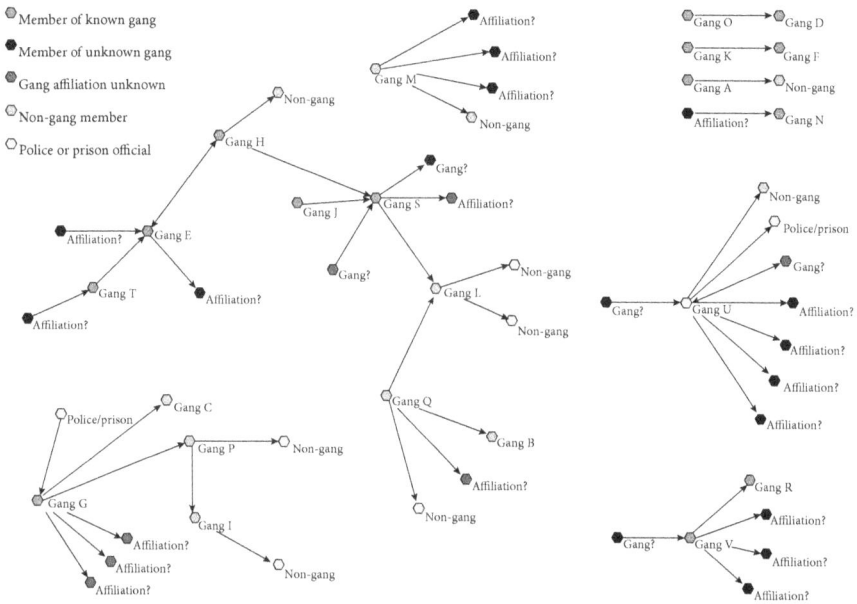

Figure 6.3. Network of homicides involving known gang members, 2005–2006

some gangs were substantially more involved in violence than others. Some gangs participated primarily in violence associated with localized feuds with another gang (that is, gangs F and K); while others participated in more robust violent networks involving a number of gangs (that is, gang S versus gangs J, H and L). We identified twenty-eight gangs active in or around the Besson Street station district, twenty-two of which were involved in at least one homicide during the period of our data collection.

Table 6.4 shows that seven gangs were disproportionately involved in homicides in the Besson Street Station District. These seven gangs were either involved as suspects or victims in about 63 per cent of the homicides in the district. A vital step in any thorough diagnosis of crime is to identify these types of patterns, which we refer to as *concentrations* of violence. Identifying concentrations of violence can provide a form of actionable intelligence enabling policymakers and practitioners to make informed decisions about where and how to allocate their resources.

Earlier, we discussed the differences between solutions that emerge from root cause thinking and those that emerge from proximate cause thinking. The finding that some gangs are more involved in violence than others serves as a useful example of those differences. Root cause theorists set their aims high in

Table 6.4. Gang-involved homicides in the Besson Street Station District by victim and suspect affiliation, 1 January 2005–26 January 2006

Gang	Homicide Suspects (Number)	Homicide Victimizations (Number)	Total (Number)	%
E	2	8	10	12
V	6	3	9	11
U	7	1	8	10
H	6	1	7	9
S	3	3	6	7
T	4	2	6	7
G	6	0	6	7

Source: Katz and Maguire 2006.

the name of crime prevention with goals such as eliminating gangs, reducing poverty and improving access to education. These are laudable and ambitious goals. A proximate cause theorist might focus first on the gangs that are involved in the greatest share of violence with the understanding that addressing those gangs will generate the largest and quickest return on investment. This is akin to a triage strategy in emergency medicine: First stop the bleeding and then address those issues that require a longer-term follow-up. To be clear, this is not an either-or proposition. A comprehensive strategy for reducing gang violence will address *both* root causes and proximate causes over the short, intermediate and long term.

The Role of Violent Gang Members

We also sought to examine whether there were chronic offenders in the Besson Street district who were disproportionately responsible for acts of crime and violence. For this analysis we relied again on the Besson Street intelligence dataset that we described earlier, which identified individuals as gang or non-gang involved, and we matched the police intelligence with criminal history record information obtained from the TTPS Criminal Records Office.[5]

Our analysis first revealed that there were major differences in criminality between gang and non-gang members. For example, as seen in table 6.5, while

Table 6.5. Per cent ever arrested by gang status

	Non-gang member (N = 878)		Gang member (N = 368)	
	Number	%	Number	%
Ever arrested	177	20.2	189	51.4
Ever arrested by crime type				
Violent offence	91	10.4	116	31.5
Firearms related	76	8.7	95	25.8
Drug sales	28	3.2	56	15.2
Drug use/possession	70	8.0	86	23.4
Property offence	67	7.6	51	13.9
Sex crime	16	1.8	10	2.7
Other	50	5.7	46	12.5

Source: Katz and Choate 2006.

about 20 per cent of non-gang members had ever been arrested, about 51 per cent of identified gang members had ever been arrested for at least one offence. When compared with non-gang members, gang members were about five times more likely to have ever been arrested for drug sales; three times more likely to have ever been arrested for a violent crime, firearms-related crime, and drug use or possession; and approximately twice as likely to have ever been arrested for a property offence, sex crime or other crime.

Further analysis also revealed that a small but substantial number of gang members were chronically involved in criminal activity. As seen in table 6.6, just over 6 per cent (n = 24) of gang members had been arrested eight or more times. Likewise, 7.3 per cent (n = 27) of gang members had been arrested four or more times for a violent crime, 2.4 per cent (n = 9) of gang members had been arrested three or more times for drug trafficking, and about 5 per cent (n = 18) of gang members had been arrested three or more times for possession of a gun or ammunition.

We further examined the impact of chronic offenders on crime in the Besson Street station district by comparing the proportion of chronic offenders in different categories to the proportion of arrests they generated. Across each category, a small proportion of chronic offenders was responsible for generating a

Table 6.6. Frequency of arrest among gang members by offence type (N = 372)

All offence types		Number	%
	0 times	183	49.2
	1 time	57	15.3
	2 to 7 times	108	29.0
	8+ times (chronic)	24	6.5
Violent crime			
	0 times	256	68.8
	1 time	42	11.3
	2 times	34	9.1
	3 times	13	3.5
	4+ times (chronic)	27	7.3
Drug trafficking			
	0 times	316	84.9
	1 time	36	9.7
	2 times	11	3.0
	3+ times (chronic)	9	2.4
Possession of gun or ammunition			
	0 times	278	74.7
	1 time	52	14.0
	2 times	24	6.5
	3+ times (chronic)	18	4.8

Source: Katz and Maguire 2006.

much larger proportion of arrests when compared to gang members who were not chronic offenders (see table 6.7). For instance, 6 per cent (n = 24) of gang members were responsible for generating almost 40 per cent of all arrests among the sample. This pattern was most striking for chronic violent offenders. Just over 7 per cent (n = 27) of gang members were responsible for 50 per cent of all arrests for violent offences in the sample. Likewise, 2.4 per cent (n = 9) of gang members were responsible for 33 per cent of arrests for drug trafficking, and

Table 6.7. Chronic offenders and their contribution to crime (N = 372)

	Gang Members (#)	Gang Members (%)	Total Arrests (#)	Total Arrests (%)
Chronic offenders	24	6.4	298	38.7
Other offenders	348	93.6	472	61.3
Chronic violent offenders	27	7.2	149	50.0
Other offenders	345	92.3	149	50.0
Chronic drug traffickers	9	2.4	29	33.3
Other offenders	363	97.6	58	66.7
Chronic gun/ammo possession offenders	18	4.8	62	38.3
Other offenders	354	95.2	100	61.7

Source: Katz and Maguire 2006.

about 5 per cent (n = 18) of gang members were responsible for about 40 per cent of all arrests for possession of a gun or ammunition.

Summary

In summary, the initial phase of our diagnostic process revealed that violence in Trinidad and Tobago was concentrated in a small number of places, groups and people. About two-thirds of the nation's homicides took place in just seven of the nation's sixty-six station districts we examined. Additional analyses not reported here identified much smaller concentrations of violence at the block or street level within these districts (Maguire et al. 2008). Within the most violent police station district (Besson Street), 63 per cent of the homicides involved a known gang member. Moreover, these homicides were not spread evenly or randomly across all the gangs in the district. Only seven gangs were responsible for about two-thirds of all homicides in the community. A similar pattern was observed for gang members. About 7 per cent of gang members were responsible for about 50 per cent of violent crime in the district. The idea that violence is concentrated is something of a criminological axiom, and these patterns are typical for communities experiencing outbreaks of violence. These concentrations of violence provide a clear point of departure for launching effective prevention, intervention and suppression efforts.

These findings suggest that targeted strategies focused on the right places, groups and people can generate a disproportionate impact on violence. For instance, research shows that when police focus their efforts on crime "hot spots", they can achieve sizeable reductions in violence (see, for example, Braga, Papachristos, and Hureau 2012; Sherman 1995; Sherman and Weisburd 1995).[6] Similarly, repeat offender programmes that target chronic offenders have been found effective (Abrahamse et al. 1991; Martin and Sherman 1986). For instance, one study showed that when police focused their efforts on seizing guns from chronic offenders, every gun removed from the street reduced the number of subsequent gun crimes by three (Sherman and Rogan 1995). More recently, evaluations of focused deterrence strategies have shown that increasing the threat (both actual and perceived) of formal sanctions against high-risk violent offenders and violent groups is effective in reducing violence (Braga and Weisburd 2012; Kennedy 2009; McGarrell, Chermak, and Wilson 2006). All of these effective interventions rely heavily on crime analysis and gang intelligence to help police and other officials identify and focus their efforts on the right places, groups and people. Research demonstrates clearly that focused strategies can generate rapid impacts on crime and violence.

Long-range efforts that seek to address the root causes of crime and violence are important and can play a useful role in comprehensive strategies to address gangs and violence. However, there appears to be a prevailing mindset among many people in the region that these are the *only* meaningful approaches. The implicit critique seems to be that dealing with proximate causes represents a "Band-Aid" solution that only addresses the symptoms of a larger problem with deeper roots. We have no inherent objection to strategies that seek to ameliorate root causes, as long as these efforts are evidence based (when possible) and are otherwise well conceived. But we object to the notion that addressing root causes is the only effective way to address violence. Thus we urge policymakers to take proximate causes seriously as well. Addressing proximate causes means identifying concentrations of violence, such as those we have identified here, and implementing targeted solutions intended to address them.

Some crime control strategies in the region, such as the state of emergency implemented in Trinidad and Tobago in August 2011, ignore these concentrations, relying instead on unfocused and generic approaches. Generic solutions that ignore concentrations of violence are typically less effective and more expensive than those that are more focused on the places, groups and people most responsible for the problem. Moreover, depending on the manner in which they are carried out, generic solutions can also alienate the public and diminish the perceived legitimacy of police agencies (Kochel 2009; Sherman 1993). As we will show in the next section, when police agencies do not take deficits in their perceived legitimacy seriously, they not only alienate the public, but they further reduce their own crime control effectiveness.

Diagnosing the Capacity to Address Violence

Knowing the nature and causes of a community's violence problem is only one part of the equation. Having the organizational and inter-organizational capacity to use that information properly and administer appropriate and effective solutions is also vital. Thus, we examined not only the gang and violence problems in Trinidad and Tobago, but also the nation's capacity to address these issues. We audited existing gang violence prevention, intervention and suppression strategies and gauged their potential for effectiveness. In general, we found that little attention was paid to implementing evidence-based gang prevention and intervention programming (Katz, Choate, and Fox 2010). Instead, the nation's strategies for addressing gang violence were heavily oriented toward a narrow range of suppression activities. Using a variety of qualitative and quantitative data sources, we examined the capacity of the Trinidad and Tobago Police Service (TTPS) and other agencies to address gangs and gang violence. We summarize our findings in three sections: (1) structures and strategies for addressing violent crime, (2) methods for holding violent offenders accountable, and (3) public perceptions of state capacity to address violent crime.

Structures and Strategies for Addressing Violent Crime

A central element of our diagnosis involved determining whether the TTPS had the appropriate structures, operational strategies, internal management practices and external partnerships to prevent and deter violent crime. This involved an assessment of the agency's capacity to perform basic policing functions (patrol, investigations, emergency response and so on) as well as its capacity to adopt innovative evidence-based strategies. This portion of our diagnosis was complex and we do not have the space to discuss it fully here. Instead we provide three examples that focus on the capacity of the TTPS to (1) investigate homicides; (2) process physical evidence; and (3) collect, maintain and disseminate gang intelligence.

Investigating Homicides

It was clear from the beginning that the TTPS did not have sufficient structures or processes in place to investigate homicides or other forms of violent crime successfully. We interviewed people throughout the police service and associated agencies about the low detection rates and tried to understand the processes that the TTPS uses when investigating homicides and the decision process used to determine who leads the case. We learned that the TTPS did not have clear lines of accountability or responsibility for homicide investigations. Station house Criminal Investigative Division (CID) investigators assigned to police stations were often responsible for conducting homicide investigations, with investigators from the homicide unit playing an auxiliary role and assisting with homicide investigations when asked. If a CID officer was not available, either an officer from within the station district or an officer from the homicide unit took the lead in the investigation. We found that CID investigators were overburdened with large caseloads for many different types of offences; they reported to us that it was difficult for them to focus on homicide cases. These inconsistent structures and processes created significant obstacles for the successful investigation of homicides in Trinidad and Tobago. We discuss two examples below.

First, we found that many investigators in both CID and the Homicide Bureau lacked the proper training to conduct a homicide investigation. Similarly, the unsystematic methods used to assign cases to investigators resulted in inexperienced officers leading many homicide investigations without structured opportunities to learn from their more experienced colleagues. As seen in figure 6.4, the typical homicide was investigated by an officer who had almost no homicide investigation experience, and there were very few seasoned homicide investigators in the TTPS Homicide Bureau (Katz and Maguire 2005). Figure 6.4 shows that of 462 homicides, 48.5 per cent (n = 224) were investigated by an officer who had never investigated a homicide before. More than 75 per cent of homicides were investigated by officers who had conducted two or fewer homicide investigations in the past. Given that investigators lacked prior training and experience, it was not surprising that as the homicide problem worsened, detection rates dropped.

Second, there was little accountability in the investigation of homicides in the TTPS. No single person or organizational unit within TTPS was held

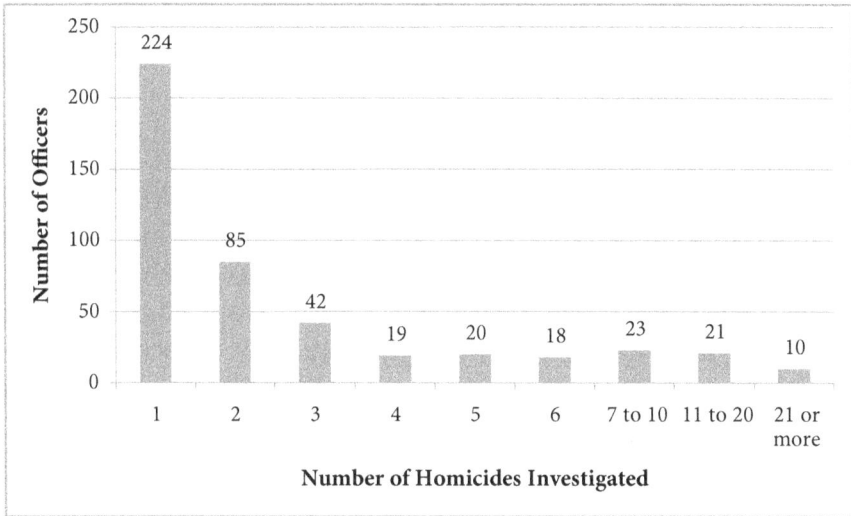

Figure 6.4. Investigator experience investigating homicides

accountable for homicide investigations. This resulted partially from a lack of clear understanding about who was actually responsible for homicide investigations. CID investigators argued that station district commanders and the homicide unit had ultimate responsibility for homicide investigations. Station district commanders argued that station district investigators and homicide unit investigators, neither of whom fell under the command of station district commanders, had ultimate responsibility for homicide investigations. Administrators and investigators from the Homicide Bureau claimed that they were an auxiliary unit that assisted with homicide investigations when asked, and that station house commanders and CID investigators were ultimately responsible for homicide investigations. In short, none of the key stakeholder groups took clear responsibility for the investigation of homicides in Trinidad and Tobago. Homicides were investigated collaboratively by the CID and the homicide unit, and there were no clear lines of responsibility or accountability that could be used to improve sagging performance.

Limited Capacity to Process Physical Evidence

We also found that it was difficult for police officers to investigate homicides because the TTPS and the Forensic Science Centre (FSC) had limited capacity to process physical evidence. Police agencies with a well-developed capacity to address violent crime have structures and policies in place that enable them to locate, collect, transport, analyse and store physical evidence for use by the police and courts. We found that as the homicide problem in Trinidad worsened, the FSC's organizational capacity to process evidence was unable to persist at the same pace. There was no system in place to prioritize the processing of evidence and as a result, evidence was processed in the order that it was received. Little attention was paid to the severity of the crime, its potential for solvability or its relevance to a case. For example, firearms-related violence had escalated rapidly by 2005 and the FSC had developed a backlog of 2,058 firearms cases. At the time, our analysis determined that the FSC was able to process just over two hundred firearms cases per year, which meant that at its current pace it would take the FSC ten years to process the current backlog of firearms cases. This did not include any new firearms-related evidence that would need to be processed (Maguire and King 2013; Maguire et al. 2010, 391–92).

We also found other serious and fundamental problems associated with the evidence-processing capacity of the TTPS. Observations of homicide scenes showed that crime scenes were routinely unsecured; citizens and nonessential police personal were permitted to enter and walk through them. On occasion, evidence that was collected at crime scenes was packaged in whatever containers might be found nearby, including used bags from fast food restaurants. We also observed that sometimes, the individual who collected the evidence neglected to submit it to the FSC. Likewise, evidence collected by the police was often not properly catalogued or stored in a secured setting. For instance, evidence was often stored in locations that were exposed to the elements (such as flooding, heat, dirt, debris). Conversely, results from evidence processed appropriately often did not make it back to the investigating officer. For example, we found that only 31 per cent of IBIS ballistic imaging reports were routed to the correct detective (King and Wells 2008; Maguire and King 2013).

Gang Intelligence

Finally, we found that the TTPS did not have a well-developed capacity to understand and respond to its gang problem. Many police agencies have specialized gang units or similar structures that are responsible for coordinating and directing the agency's gang-control efforts through the use of gang intelligence (Katz et al. 2012; Katz, Maguire and Roncek 2002). In the TTPS, there was no formal entity responsible for gang-related issues. The CID maintained profiles of gangs and gang members, but the quality of this information varied widely by station district. For instance, one district established informal methods for collecting and maintaining gang intelligence by photographing gang members and consolidating that information in thousands of Microsoft Word files. This information was crude in the sense that it was difficult to search and analyse, but the CID officers who put this information together had managed to amass considerable expertise and intelligence on gangs in their district. We visited another district known for its intense level of gang violence, and CID officers there informed us that there were no gangs. This information conflicted with everything we had heard about the gang problem in this district from a number of credible sources. Consequently, because they argued there were no gangs, there was no gang intelligence.

In short, there was no formal or centralized structure to gather, analyse and disseminate gang intelligence. Certain individuals and units within the TTPS had developed localized pockets of expertise on gangs, but this expertise seemed to emerge as a result of individual initiative, not as a result of any concerted strategic effort on the part of the TTPS. The agency did not have any established mechanisms by which its personnel could develop highly technical skills and sophisticated intelligence through training and experience. This lack of training was detrimental to the larger police organization and rendered it incapable of developing a sound plan for addressing gangs and gang violence. The agency lacked sufficient policies and protocols for collecting, maintaining and disseminating gang-related intelligence that would allow the agency to implement intelligence-led policing practices and allocate resources appropriately.

Gang intelligence is important for other more basic reasons as well. Many of the same factors that are associated with violent gang conflict also inhibit the ability of the police to intervene successfully using traditional investigative methods. Gang members do not typically contact the police to resolve a conflict because doing so could result in loss of status and expose them to the risk that police will discover their illegal activities (Katz et al. 2011). Citizens in neighbourhoods with gang problems are also reluctant to call the police out of fear of gang reprisals or because they have a poor perception of the police (Adams 2012; Johnson 2006; UNDP 2012). As a consequence, the most typical police approach to gang violence in Trinidad and Tobago was a reactive response to specific incidents that had already occurred, rather than a proactive response such as intervening in disputes between gangs to prevent impending violence. The TTPS simply did not have the intelligence networks required to intervene effectively in gang conflicts until after these conflicts had generated significant levels of violence.

Police officials and researchers have identified gang intelligence as one of the most powerful tools in the fight against gang violence (Bureau of Justice

Assistance 1997; Jackson and McBride 1996; Katz 2003; Katz, Webb, and Schaefer 2000). For instance, in January 2013 the chief of the Washington, DC Metropolitan Police Department attributed part of that city's dramatic reduction in homicides (to levels not seen since 1963) to the use of gang intelligence to prevent retaliatory shootings (Simon 2013). Likewise, police-based gang intelligence systems serve as the cornerstone for some of the most innovative and effective violence reduction strategies. Absent a structured and strategic approach to dealing with gangs – including a coordinated and well-trained cadre of gang experts and a defensible gang intelligence system – the TTPS struggled to keep up with the sudden increases in violence. They were constantly playing catch-up, relying primarily on reactive approaches rather than thoughtful, proactive and focused approaches to those places, gangs and gang members that were disproportionately responsible for the nation's outbreak of violence.

Methods for Holding Violent Offenders Accountable

The proportion of homicides solved by a police agency (usually referred to as its clearance rate or detection rate) is often considered a bellwether for measuring its overall performance. There are two reasons for this. First, taking a human life is typically thought of as the most serious type of offence. Second, homicide statistics tend to be recorded more accurately than other offence types. Police agencies with high homicide detection rates are more likely to realize three criminological benefits: (1) incapacitating offenders, thereby reducing the probability that they will commit another homicide; (2) creating a culture of general deterrence, whereby citizens know that if they were to commit a homicide they would be apprehended; and (3) promoting a feeling among the population of "just desserts", or the sense that justice is being done, which establishes confidence in the police and the justice system. High homicide detection rates are a vital ingredient for ensuring that the police are viewed as legitimate in the eyes of the public. All three of these criminological benefits, through different causal mechanisms, are likely to reduce the overall level of homicide. Agencies with low homicide detection rates are often viewed as ineffective because they are unable to perform one of the most vital functions of the police – holding offenders accountable for taking human life.

As seen in figure 6.5, homicide detection rates in Trinidad and Tobago declined dramatically from 1999 to 2008. In 1999, homicide detection rates were above 70 per cent. By 2008, they had fallen to about 15 per cent. This precipitous drop

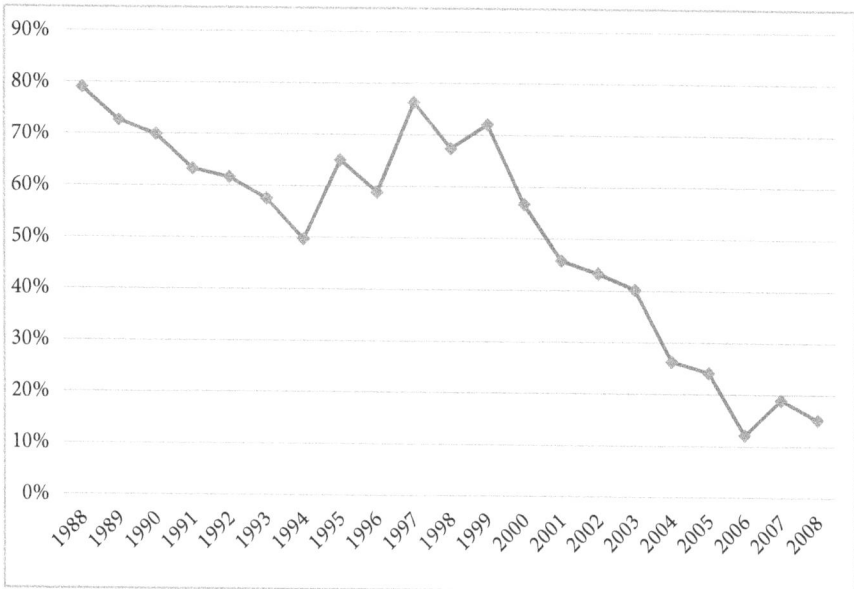

Figure 6.5. Homicide detection rates in Trinidad and Tobago, 1988–2008

clearly signalled the mounting problems in the management of homicide investigations in the TTPS. For the general public, this pattern revealed itself through the relentless drumbeat of media coverage that expressed concerns about the TTPS and the government ministry that oversees it, the Ministry of National Security. For the offender community, particularly within gangs, this pattern revealed itself every time a murderer walked free. The drop in homicide detections sent a clear message that the state was no longer able to hold violent offenders accountable for taking human life.

While homicide detection rates were low for homicides in general, detectives told us that gang-related homicides were particularly difficult to solve. We looked into this issue by examining the outcomes of the thirty-two homicides involving a gang member victim in the Besson Street station district over a thirteen-month period. Of the thirty-two homicides, only three resulted in an arrest and none resulted in a conviction. Gang homicide cases are difficult to investigate, particularly in an environment where the public no longer trusts the police. Detectives told us they often knew the identity of the suspect, but witnesses were rarely willing to assist the police because they feared retaliation. As Adams (2012, 283) notes, "With witnesses 'out of the way', offenders face negligible odds of conviction even if they are arrested and tried for their crimes." Capacity issues in the TTPS and the FSC were compounded by further issues in the courts, which together led to negligible conviction rates. According to Adams (2012), only five of the 1,247 murders that occurred in Trinidad and Tobago from 2003 to 2006 resulted in a conviction, for a conviction rate of 0.4 per cent. The inability of the criminal justice system to arrest and convict most homicide offenders reinforced the public's distrust in the government's capacity to protect it. This worked to embolden offenders who learned that in spite of political rhetoric to the contrary, they could get away with murder.

Public Perceptions of State Capacity to Address Violent Crime

Based on the surveys of residents and interviews with key community stakeholders, we further examined the capacity of the police and other parts of the criminal justice system to control gangs and violence. Survey data revealed that residents had serious doubts concerning the capacity of the police and courts to handle these issues. In 2006, we launched three waves of face-to-face interviews with approximately six hundred randomly selected residents in Belmont, located in East Port of Spain. In Gonzales, a troubled Belmont community, we found that about 85 per cent of residents reported hearing gunshots in their neighbourhood at least once in the past thirty days, but only about 7 per cent of those who heard gunshots reported it to the police (Johnson 2006). When asked why, more than 70 per cent strongly agreed that people who report crimes committed by gang members to the police are likely to suffer retaliation. Similarly, almost 80 per cent of respondents stated that the police did not respond quickly when people ask them for help. These findings resonate strongly with those reported by Adams (2012), whose research on a different Trinidadian neighbourhood found that residents felt like "prey."

A recent citizen survey conducted by the United Nations Development Programme revealed similar findings (UNDP 2011). Only about 10 per cent of survey respondents in Trinidad and Tobago were confident in the ability of the police to control gang violence. This figure was the lowest of the seven Caribbean countries included in the survey; the average for the other six nations was 26.7 per cent. Confidence levels for Trinidadian respondents living in neighbourhoods with gangs were even lower (4.5 per cent). Perhaps even more troublesome were residents' perceptions about corruption in Trinidad and Tobago's judicial system. About 63 per cent of residents in neighbourhoods with gangs believed that judges in the nation were corrupt, 76.6 per cent believed that the judicial system was corrupt, and 56 per cent believed that powerful criminals would go free (UNDP 2011).

Interviews with key community stakeholders in Belmont provided further insights. They explained that the institutions of formal social control (such as the police and prosecutors) were no longer entrusted with ensuring their safety. Instead, residents living in gang-controlled communities were relying instead on the local gang leader to provide social control. For example, one stakeholder told us: "Gangs bring down crime. They instituted a community court that meets weekly where young males are punished and given strokes. . . . One to two local councillors have gone to the courts to observe their practice." Another explained, "Gangs are the first ones to respond to crime, the police are incompetent; they take too long and never finish the work. If you go to the gang leader you know they will take care of you." Still another said, "If you live in a community where there is gang cohesion you are more safe because they [protect you.] . . . Gangs provide safety, create jobs . . . give people food, give mothers milk for their babies" (Katz 2007).

Police sometimes view public attitudes toward police as dispensable and somehow unrelated to their ability to control crime. A wide-ranging body of research dispels this notion, including recent research in Trinidad and Tobago. For instance, based on interviews with residents in a troubled Trinidadian neighbourhood, Adams (2012, 278) notes that police are viewed as "incompetent, brutal, and a 'waste of time'". As a result, residents no longer trust the police, and therefore are no longer willing to call the police or to serve as witnesses in criminal proceedings. Similarly, a comprehensive study of seventy-three neighbourhoods in thirteen TTPS station districts found that police behaviour had "important consequences for neighbourhoods" (Kochel 2009, 197). The study found that neighbourhoods with higher quality police services also report higher levels of collective efficacy and less crime and disorder. Conversely, when neighbourhoods experience (or perceive that they experience) higher levels of police misconduct, this is associated with lower legitimacy for legal institutions, less collective efficacy, and increased crime and disorder in the neighbourhood.

Finally, based on a national youth survey in Trinidad, Johnson and her colleagues (Johnson et al. 2008, 244) reported that only 34.6 per cent of respondents viewed police as respectful, only 36.1 per cent believed police were fair and neutral, and more than half (56.8 per cent) believed police accepted payments from criminals. As expected, youth from disorganized communities view police in a more negative light than youth from other communities. The authors concluded that as these youth aged, the TTPS would continue to have difficulty developing the positive police-community partnerships that are necessary for effective policing. The research evidence is clear: The police must have the trust and cooperation of the public to be effective in controlling crime and violence.

Summary

In conclusion, we found that police and other parts of the criminal justice system in Trinidad and Tobago lacked the capacity to control gangs and violence. The police rarely made arrests in gang homicides, and when they did make an arrest, prosecutors were seldom successful in securing a conviction. Homicide investigators had little training and experience in investigating homicides, let alone more complex gang homicides. Capacity problems in the TTPS were compounded by similar capacity issues in the nation's crime lab and the courts. The crime lab was unable to keep up with the increase in firearms and ballistic evidence submitted by the police, and structural issues in the courts wasted police officers' time and allowed proceedings to drag on endlessly. We also found that the general public had little confidence in the police and the courts to protect them and expressed serious concerns about police misbehaviour and the general lack of police responsiveness. Residents in some high-crime communities instead placed their faith in gang leaders to maintain social control, a phenomenon that has led some observers to argue that gangs in the Caribbean threaten the basic sovereignty of the state (Manwaring 2007). As police legitimacy declines, people are less willing to report crime to the police, cooperate with police investigations and serve as witnesses in court, thus perpetuating a downward spiral in the ability of police to control crime.

Conclusion

Violence ebbs and flows over place and time. Criminologists spend considerable effort generating, testing and modifying theories to account for these natural variations in crime and violence. Rapid increases in violence like the outbreak experienced in Trinidad and Tobago, however, are well outside the range of what is ordinarily considered natural variation. These outbreaks of violence cannot usually be understood based solely on explanatory variables featured prominently in most theories of crime. Social factors like age, sex, race, education or the economy often move too slowly to explain sudden or rapid increases (and decreases) in violence. Thus, in order to understand outbreaks of violence, it is necessary to look beyond the root causes of crime. A proper diagnosis of a violence outbreak means looking carefully at those places, times, groups and individuals that generate the greatest share of violence. This process involves the use of crime analysis to identify concentrations or patterns of violence. These patterns are vital for designing effective prevention, intervention and suppression strategies for reducing violence.

Our diagnosis revealed that the problem in Trinidad and Tobago was concentrated in a number of specific ways. The homicide outbreak primarily involved male offenders and victims, most of them young men of African descent, who were either members or affiliates of criminal street gangs. Their weapon of choice was guns (Wells, Katz, and Kim 2010; also see St Bernard 2009), unlike the cutlasses, razors or sticks used by earlier generations of Trinidad's gangs (Meeks 1999). These homicides were spatially concentrated at multiple levels within certain station districts, neighbourhoods, blocks and street corners (Maguire et al. 2008). Even within the universe of gangs, certain gangs appeared to commit violence or to be violently victimized more often than others. These intense concentrations of violence in Trinidad and Tobago serve as a useful point of departure for developing targeted solutions. Because these solutions are focused intently on the places and people most responsible for the violence, they are likely to be more efficient and more effective than generic or unfocused solutions.

Our diagnosis also revealed that Trinidad and Tobago was struggling with serious organizational and inter-organizational issues that limited its capacity to address violent crime in general and gang violence specifically. Five years after the outbreak of violence emerged, the nation continued to rely on the same structures and strategies that had already proven ineffective in reducing gang violence. Prevention and intervention efforts directed specifically at gangs were sporadic and unsystematic and did not rely on evidence-based practice. Police rarely made arrests in gang-related homicides and shootings, though even when they did, offenders were rarely convicted. The TTPS had weak accountability mechanisms in place for homicide investigations, and officers lacked the training and experience needed to investigate homicide cases, especially those involving gangs. The nation's evidence-processing capacity was quickly swamped by the outbreak of violence leaving investigators with even fewer resources at their disposal to investigate cases, particularly those involving guns. The nation also lacked the appropriate structures and strategies for collecting, analysing and distributing gang intelligence to aid in its suppression and intervention efforts. Without reliable gang intelligence, the TTPS was unable to engage in proactive policing practices, relying instead on less effective reactive approaches.

After completing the initial phase of our diagnosis, we made a number of recommendations intended to improve the effectiveness of Trinidad and Tobago's criminal justice system in preventing and controlling violence, especially gang-related violence. The full details of all our recommendations are beyond the scope of this chapter but we will mention some of them briefly. Some of our recommendations were warmly embraced and were implemented to varying degrees, while others were ignored or were implemented only on the surface while the agency continued engaging in traditional practices. For instance, all of the approaches we've discussed in this chapter require police agencies to develop a sophisticated analytical capacity that enables them to develop a deep understanding of crime patterns and the agency's effectiveness in addressing those patterns. Thus, we recommended the creation of the Crime and Problem Analysis (CAPA) Branch. Today CAPA is the largest and most well-trained crime analysis unit in the region. We also recommended the creation of a full-service homicide unit with appropriate training and accountability structures, a gang unit with both an intelligence and operational function, reforms in forensic evidence processing by the FSC and the TTPS, a series of strategic problem-solving initiatives, and the launch of an award-winning community-policing demonstration project. These recommendations were intended to increase the capacity of the TTPS and its partner agencies to address violence (with a particular emphasis on gang violence) while simultaneously improving the fractured relationship between the TTPS and communities.

Although only some of our recommendations were implemented, the Government of Trinidad and Tobago deserves credit for investing in a comprehensive diagnosis of its outbreak of violence and financing its own capacity to address that outbreak. It is rare for governments to open themselves up to such intensive external scrutiny. Our diagnosis resulted in a clear understanding of the nature of violence in Trinidad and Tobago, the reasons why it increased so rapidly, where it was being carried out and by whom, and what to do about it. Unfortunately, knowing what to do about violence is only one piece of a complex puzzle. Crime is an issue about which everyone has an opinion. In Trinidad and Tobago, we encountered a contentious political atmosphere in which citizens, the media and people in positions of authority disagreed vehemently with one another about the way forward. Moreover, extensive turnover in leadership, both within the TTPS and other agencies and in the government more generally, made it difficult to implement change based on the results of our diagnosis. Our experience in Trinidad and Tobago highlights the complexity of the reform process.

Gangs and violence are among the most pressing issues in the Caribbean. Research suggests that "one size fits all" solutions do not work particularly well for addressing these issues. Three ingredients are vital for successfully addressing violent crime in the Caribbean. The first is carrying out a proper diagnosis of the nature and causes of violence, as well the capacity of the jurisdiction to address these issues. The second is designing a set of focused initiatives based on the results of the diagnosis; these initiatives should include prevention, intervention, and suppression components. The third, and perhaps most challenging is marshalling the political, fiscal and civic commitment to carry out these initiatives.

Notes

1. The TTPS had the seeds for developing better knowledge systems about gangs and gang violence in the sense that specific individuals in the TTPS were well versed in these issues. For instance, we very quickly discovered a police sergeant in a high-crime community who was a virtual walking database of gang-related issues. We also found analysts who were able to successfully track gang members and gang offences. However, these were isolated individuals who did not have sufficient rank or authority to influence agency policy, so they toiled away quietly in their own corners of the agency. As a result of a general lack of capacity, during the time of our research, the TTPS could never *reliably* provide basic and vital information such as the share of homicides that were gang-related or gang-motivated.

2. Several population estimates for Trinidad and Tobago are available. The national homicide rate varies according to which population estimate is selected as the denominator. The population estimates we use in this chapter are derived from the individual-level census data file provided to us by the Central Statistical Office.

3. The first round of data collection yielded thirty-nine returned instruments. Due to the lower than desired response rate, senior TTPS officials recommended that we hold in-person meetings with all selected respondents to increase the response rate. These meetings were held over a one-week period in May 2006 until a respondent from each station district had completed the survey instrument. This strategy resulted in a response rate of 100 per cent (n = 66).

4. We reviewed these data during regularly scheduled meetings with Besson Street CID officers. At these meetings, we provided CID officers with printouts containing basic descriptive information on homicides that occurred within the district from 1 January 2005 through 26 January 2006. For each homicide, the printouts contained the case ID number, the victim's name, the date of the homicide and a short narrative describing the circumstances of the homicide. When we met with the officers, we

discussed each homicide incident and determined whether the suspect or victim was a gang member and, if so, the nature of their gang affiliation.

5. At the time, the TTPS had not established a formal method for documenting persons as gang members; however, Besson Street intelligence officers were using a number of processes based on local custom and knowledge to identify and document gang members. The first step involved in identifying an individual as a gang member is observing his or her affiliations and activities with known gang members or gang leaders. Observed affiliation can take place in a number of different ways. For example, the individual could be (1) an employee working on a job site run by a known gang leader; (2) a neighbourhood cab driver regularly used by gang members; (3) a roommate of a known gang member; (4) a spouse, girlfriend or partner of a known gang member; (5) a close family member of a known gang member; (6) a person who regularly associates with a gang member or leader; (7) a person who arrives at the station on behalf of any gang member who has been arrested; (8) a person who arrives at the station at the instruction of the court for the purpose of having his "whereabouts" book signed by an officer; or (9) a person who shows up in court to support any gang member. Following the observation of an individual affiliating with a gang member or leader, Besson Street gang intelligence officers determine where the individual lives or routinely spends time. If the individual lives or spends a substantial amount of time in the same area that their associate claims as its territory, the intelligence officer interviews the individual to make a final determination of gang membership. During the interview, intelligence officers question the individuals about their friendship networks and gang affiliation to make a final assessment of whether or not the individuals are gang members. Note that at the time of our work, gang members in Trinidad and Tobago did not tend to be secretive or deceptive about their gang affiliation.

6. Our time in the Caribbean suggests that although the term "hot spots" is used widely, that usage is not consistent with the way criminologists use the term. In the Caribbean, the term is often used to refer to entire communities, cities or police jurisdictions. Sherman (1995, 36) defines hot spots as "small places in which the occurrence of crime is so frequent that it is highly predictable, at least over a 1-year period". Hot spots can vary in size from an individual address or street corner to a street block or a whole neighbourhood, but in general hot spots are small.

References

Abrahamse, A.F., P.A. Ebener, P.W. Greenwood, N. Fitzgerald, and T. E. Kosin. 1991. "An Experimental Evaluation of the Phoenix Repeat Offender Program". *Justice Quarterly* 8(2):14168.

Adams, R. 2012. "'We Are Like Prey': How People Negotiate a Violent Community in Trinidad and Tobago". *Race and Justice* 2(4): 274–303.

Arias, E.D., and C.D. Rodrigues. 2006. "The Myth of Personal Security: Criminal Gangs, Dispute Resolution, and Identity in Rio de Janeiro's Favelas". *Latin American Politics and Society* 48(4): 53–81.

Beck, C., and C. McCue. 2009. "Predictive Policing: What Can We Learn from Wal-Mart and Amazon about Fighting Crime in a Recession?" *Police Chief* 76(11): 18.

Braga, A.A., A.V. Papachristos, and D.M. Hureau. 2012. "Police Programs to Prevent Crime in Hot Spot Areas". *Crime Prevention Research Review, No. 7*. Washington, DC: US Department of Justice, Office of Community Oriented Policing Services.

Braga, A.A., and D.L. Weisburd. 2012. "The Effects of Focused Deterrence Strategies on Crime: A Systematic Review and Meta-Analysis of the Empirical Evidence". *Journal of Research in Crime and Delinquency* 49(3): 323–58.

Bureau of Justice Assistance. 1997. *Urban Street Gang Enforcement*. Washington, DC: Government Printing Office.

Charles, C.A.D. 2012. "The Informal Justice System in Garrison Communities and the Retreat of the Jamaican State". Paper presented at the Conference on Law and Justice in the Commonwealth Caribbean: The Post-Independence Experience, Jamaica. 3 February.

Clarke, C. 2006. "Politics, Violence and Drugs in Kingston, Jamaica". *Bulletin of Latin American Research* 25(3): 420–40.

Deosaran, R. 2004. "A Portrait of Crime in the Caribbean: Realities and Challenges". In *Caribbean Security in the Age of Terror: Challenge and Change*, edited by I.L. Griffith, 104–28. Kingston: Ian Randle.

Harriott, A. 1996. "The Changing Social Organisation of Crime and Criminals in Jamaica". *Caribbean Quarterly* 42(2/3): 54–71.

———. 2003. "The Jamaica Crime Problem: New Developments and New Challenges for Public Policy". In *Understanding Crime in Jamaica: New Challenges for Public Policy*, edited by A. Harriott, 1–12. Kingston: University of the West Indies Press.

———. 2008. *Organized Crime and Politics in Jamaica: Breaking the Nexus*. Kingston: University of the West Indies Press.

———. 2009. *Controlling Violent Crime*. Kingston: Grace, Kennedy Foundation.

Hill, S. 2012. "The Rise of Gang Violence in the Caribbean". Presented at the Symposium on Gangs and Gang Violence in the Caribbean, American University, Washington, DC. 17 February.

Jackson, R. K., and W.D. McBride. 1996. *Understanding Street Gangs*. Incline Village, NV: Copperhouse.

Johnson, D. 2006. "Results from the Gonzales IMPACT Study". Unpublished report, George Mason University.

Johnson, D.,W.R. King, C.M. Katz, A. Fox, and N. Goulette. 2008. "Youth Perceptions of the Police in Trinidad and Tobago". *Caribbean Journal of Criminology and Public Safety* 13(1, 2): 217–53.

Katz, C.M. 1997. "Police and Gangs: A Study of a Police Gang Unit". PhD dissertation, University of Nebraska at Omaha.

———. 2001. "The Establishment of a Police Gang Unit: An Examination of Organizational and Environmental Factors". *Criminology* 39(1): 37–75.

———. 2003. "Issues in the Production and Dissemination of Gang Statistics: An Ethnographic Study of a Large Midwestern Police Gang Unit". *Crime and Delinquency* 49(3): 485–516.

———. 2007. "Institutional Capacity, Informal Social Control, and Their Influence on Illicit Opportunities in the Caribbean". Presented at the Global Future Forum sponsored by the Central Intelligence Agency and Privy Council, Ottawa, Canada.

———. 2008. "The Scope and Nature of the Gang Problem in Antigua and Barbuda". Unpublished paper, Arizona State University.

Katz, C.M., and D. Choate. 2006. "Diagnosing Trinidad and Tobago's Gang Problem". Presented at the Annual Meeting of the American Society of Criminology, Los Angeles.

Katz, C.M., D. Choate, and A. Fox. 2010. "Understanding and Preventing Gang Membership in Trinidad and Tobago". Fairfax, VA: Crime and Justice Analysts, Inc.

Katz, C.M., and A. Fox. 2010. "Risk and Protective Factors Associated with Gang Involved Youth in a Caribbean Nation: Analysis of the Trinidad and Tobago Youth Survey". *Pan-American Journal of Public Health/Revista Panamericana de Salud Pública* 27(3): 187–202.

Katz, C.M., A. Fox, C. Britt, and P. Stevenson. 2012. "Understanding Police Gang Data at the Aggregate Level: An Examination of the Reliability of National Youth Gang Survey Data". *Justice Research and Policy* 14(2): 103–28.

Katz, C.M., K. Fox, V.J. Webb, and J. Shaffer. 2011. "Understanding the Relationship between Violent Victimization and Gang Membership". *Journal of Criminal Justice* 39: 48–59.

Katz, C.M., and E. Maguire. 2005. "Improving Homicide Detection Rates in Trinidad and Tobago". Manassas, VA: George Mason University.

———. 2006. "Reducing Gang Homicides in the Besson Street Station District". Phoenix: Arizona State University.

Katz, C.M., E.R. Maguire, and D. Choate. 2011. "A Cross-National Comparison of Gangs in the United States and Trinidad and Tobago". *International Criminal Justice Review* 21(3): 243–62.

Katz, C.M., E.R. Maguire, and D. Roncek. 2002. "The Creation of Specialized Police Gang Units: A Macro-Level Analysis of Contingency, Social Threat and Resource-Dependency Explanations". *Policing: An International Journal of Police Strategies and Management* 25(3): 472–506.

Katz, C.M., and S. Schnebly. 2011. "Neighborhood Variation in Gang Member Concentrations". *Crime and Delinquency* 57(3): 377–407.

Katz, C.M., and V.J. Webb. 2003. "Police Response to Gangs: A Multi-Site Study". Phoenix: Arizona State University West.

———. 2006. *Policing Gangs in America*. New York: Cambridge University Press.

Katz, C.M., V.J. Webb, and D.R. Schaefer. 2000. "The Validity of Police Gang Intelligence Lists: Examining Differences in Delinquency between Documented Gang Members and Non-Documented Delinquent Youth". *Police Quarterly* 3(4): 413–37.

Kennedy, D.M. 2009. *Deterrence and Crime Prevention: Reconsidering the Prospect of Sanction.* New York: Routledge.

King, W.R., and W. Wells. 2008. "The Use of Forensic Ballistic Information by the Trinidad and Tobago Police Service". Manassas, VA: George Mason University.

Klein, M.W. 1995a. *The American Street Gang.* New York: Oxford University Press.

———. 1995b. "Street Gang Cycles". In *Crime,* edited by J.Q. Wilson and J. Petersilia, 217–36. San Francisco: Institute for Contemporary Studies.

Kochel, T. 2009. "Legitimacy as a Mechanism for Police to Promote Collective Efficacy and Reduce Crime and Disorder". PhD dissertation, George Mason University.

Kodluboy, D.W., and L.A. Evenrud. 1993. "School-Based Interventions: Best Practice and Critical Issues". In *The Gang Intervention Handbook,* edited by A.P. Goldstein and C.R. Huff, 257–99. Champaign, IL: Research Press.

Kuhns, J.B., and E.R. Maguire. 2012. "Drug and Alcohol use by Homicide Victims in Trinidad and Tobago, 2001–2007". *Forensic Science, Medicine, and Pathology* 8(3): 243–51.

Leslie, G. 2010. "Confronting the Don: The Political Economy of Gang Violence in Jamaica". Small Arms Survey: Geneva.

Maguire, E.R. 2012. "Preventing Gang Violence in the Caribbean: Problems and Prospects". Presented at the Symposium on Gangs and Gang Violence in the Caribbean. Washington, DC: American University. 17 February.

Maguire, E.R., and R.R. Bennett. 2008. "Introduction: Special Issue on Criminal Justice Research in Trinidad and Tobago". *Caribbean Journal of Criminology and Public Safety* 13(1–2): xii–xxxiv.

Maguire, E.R., R.R. Bennett, and A. Harriott. 2014. "The Antecedents of Informal Social Control: Evidence from Seven Caribbean Nations". Paper. American University, Washington, DC.

Maguire, E.R., and W.R. King. 2013. "Transferring Criminal Investigation Methods from Developed to Developing Nations". *Policing and Society: An International Journal of Research and Policy* 23(3): 346–61.

Maguire, E.R.,W.R. King, D. Johnson, and C.M. Katz. 2010. "Why Homicide Clearance Rates Decrease: Evidence from the Caribbean". *Policing and Society* 20(4): 373–400.

Maguire, E.R., J.A. Willis, J. Snipes, and M. Gantley. 2008. "Spatial Concentrations of Violence in Trinidad and Tobago". *Caribbean Journal of Criminology and Public Safety* 13(1, 2): 44–83.

Manwaring, M.G. 2007. *A Contemporary Challenge to State Sovereignty: Gangs and Other Illicit Transnational Criminal Organizations in Central America, El Salvador, Mexico, Jamaica and Brazil.* Carlisle, PA: Strategic Studies Institute.

Martin, S.E., and L.W. Sherman. 1986. "Selective Apprehension: A Police Strategy for Repeat Offenders". *Criminology* 24(1): 155–73.

McGarrell, E., S. Chermak, and J. Wilson. 2006. "Reducing Homicide through a 'Lever-Pulling' Strategy". *Justice Quarterly* 23(2): 214–31.

Meeks, B. 1999. "NUFF at the Cusp of an Idea: Grassroots Guerrillas and the Politics of the 1970s in Trinidad and Tobago". *Social Identities* 5(4): 415–39.

Moncrieffe, D. (1998). *Gang Study: The Jamaican Crime Scene*. Kingston: Criminal Justice Research Unit, Ministry of National Security and Justice.

Moore, M.H. 2002. "Creating Networks of Capacity: The Challenge of Managing Society's Response to Youth Violence". In *Securing Our Children's Future*, edited by G. Katzmann, 338–85. Washington, DC: Brookings Institution.

NGCRC (National Gang Crime Research Center). 1995. *Gang Prevention and Gang Intervention: Preliminary Results from the 1995 Project GANGPINT*. National Needs Assessment Gang Research Task Force.

Ordog, G.J., W. Shoemaker, J. Wasserberger, and M. Bishop. 1995. "Gunshot Wounds Seen at a County Hospital Before and After a Riot and Gang Truce: Part Two". *Journal of Trauma-Injury Infection and Critical Care* 38(3): 417–19.

Reisig, M.D., and C. Lloyd. 2009. "Procedural Justice, Police Legitimacy, and Helping the Police Fight Crime: Results from a Survey of Jamaican Adolescents". *Police Quarterly* 12: 42–62.

Robotham, D. 2003. "Crime and Public Policy in Jamaica." In *Understanding Crime in Jamaica: New Challenges for Public Policy*, edited by A. Harriott, 197–238. Kingston: University of the West Indies Press.

Seelal, N. 2007. "Girl, 5, Sees Family Killed". *Trinidad and Tobago Newsday*, 24 January.

Seepersad, R. 2013. "Crime in the Caribbean." In *Gangs in the Caribbean*, edited by R. Seepersad and A.M. Bissessar, 2–35. Newcastle: Cambridge Scholars Publishing.

Sherman, L.W. 1993. "Defiance, Deterrence and Irrelevance: A Theory of the Criminal Sanction". *Journal of Research in Crime and Delinquency* 30: 445–73.

———. 1995. "Hot Spots of Crime and Criminal Careers of Places". In *Crime and Place*, edited byJ.E. Eck and D. Weisburd, 35–52. Washington, DC: Police Executive Research Forum.

Sherman, L.W., and D.P. Rogan. 1995. "Effects of Gun Seizures on Gun Violence: 'Hot Spots' Patrol in Kansas City". *Justice Quarterly* 12(4): 673–93.

Sherman, L.W., and D. Weisburd. 1995. "General Deterrent Effects of Police Patrol in Crime 'Hot Spots': A Randomised, Controlled Trial". *Justice Quarterly* 12(4): 625–48.

Simon, R. 2013. "Washington, DC Finishes 2012 with Fewer than 100 Homicides". *Los Angeles Times*, 1 January.

Sives, A. 2002. "Changing Patrons, from Politician to Drug Don: Clientelism in Downtown Kingston, Jamaica". *Latin American Perspectives* 29: 66–89.

Sloan, G. 2010. "Shooting Death of Cruiser in Virgin Islands Comes as Killings There Soar". *USA Today*, 19 July.

St Bernard, G. 2009. "Demographics, Youth Firearms and Reported Homicide in Trinidad and Tobago: A Socio-Demographic Perspective". *Caribbean Journal of Criminology and Public Safety* 14(1, 2): 81–109.

St Jean, P.K.B. 2007. *Pockets of Crime: Broken Windows, Collective Efficacy, and the Criminal Point of View*. Chicago: University of Chicago Press.

UNDP. 2011. *UNDP Caribbean Citizen Security Survey 2010* (database). Produced and distributed by United Nations Development Programme, New York.

UNDP. 2012. *UNDP Caribbean Human Development Report 2012*. New York: United Nations Development Programme.

van Gemert, F. 2005. "Youth Groups and Gangs in Amsterdam: A Pretest of the Eurogang Expert Survey". In *European Street Gangs and Troublesome Youth Groups,* edited by S.H. Decker and F.W. Weerman, 147–68. New York: AltaMira.

Webb, V.J., and C.M. Katz. 2003. "Policing Gangs in an Era of Community Policing". In *Policing Gangs and Youth Violence*, edited by S.H. Decker, 17–49. Belmont, CA: Wadsworth.

Weisburd, D., S. Bushway, C. Lum, and S.M. Yang. 2004. "Trajectories of Crime at Places: A Longitudinal Study of Street Segments in the City of Seattle". *Criminology* 42(2): 283–322.

Wells, W., C.M. Katz, and J. Kim. 2010. "Firearm Possession among Arrestees in Trinidad and Tobago". *Injury Prevention* 16: 337–42.

7 | Violence Reduction as Gang Reduction

Suppression and the Case of the Shower–Presidential Click

Anthony Harriott

Gang-related violence in its many forms and motivations has been the source of the rapid, persistent and long-term increases in Jamaica's homicide rates in the period after 1980 (Harriott 2003, 2008a). Levy (2009) depicts the problem of gang violence in its garrison form as being particularly problematic at that time. Since 2009, however, Jamaica's homicide count has declined significantly, that is, by some 35 per cent by the end of 2012. Indeed, the reported frequency counts for violent crimes, with the exception of rape, have significantly declined.[1] These outcomes have been largely due to the recent push for systematic gang control and (gang) violence reduction efforts led by law enforcement.

Jamaica's recent gang-control efforts have not only impacted the rates of violent crimes, but have also impacted public confidence in law enforcement and, perhaps most importantly, community self-efficacy. The power of the gangs has been weakened but not broken; their income streams have been disrupted but not terminated; their relationships with the political parties may be under greater public scrutiny but the gangs still enjoy political protection and community support. Things are not as they were prior to 2010; advances have been made.

The significant decline in Jamaica's rate of violent crime (even if it is not lasting) and the associated processes emphasize the importance of conducting a comprehensive study designed to inspect these drastic changes. This chapter is not that study. Here, a rather limited but central aspect of this story is explored. This study recounts the most recent method for addressing the gang problem, the use of violence control as a more deliberate and purposeful form of gang control. This chapter explores the approach to reducing gang violence in Jamaica, reports the resulting outcomes and communicates lessons that have been drawn from the experience. This is done by focusing on the states' attempt to respond to a single organized crime entity.

The crime entity which has drawn the most intense attention of the state is the Presidential Click. After the state initiated the operation against the Presidential Click, the rate of serious crimes immediately began to decline, and this decline may eventually be regarded as a crucial turning point in both the state and country's violence reduction effort. The Presidential Click is not a typical criminal group, but rather a high intensity and *high impact* case. It is one of the most powerful, oldest and most resilient criminal groups in Jamaica, and even has links to national power circuits via its alliance to one of the nations' major political parties. The Click is further connected with global criminal networks that enable the exploitation of illegal opportunities beyond Jamaica's borders. While the group has both licit and illicit sources of income, at its core, their wide range of illegal activities demonstrates their tendency towards violent entrepreneurialism.

The Presidential Click has an exceptional relationship with the host community that it is deeply embedded in. The nature of this relationship consists of high levels of cohesion, stable leadership and, for the most part, uncontested leadership transitions. Most of all, the Presidential Click is known for its use of violence as a disciplinary tool in the maintenance and replication of the garrison phenomenon, its violent conflicts with other groups and with law enforcement, and the exploitation of its reputation for violence to extract protection fees and various forms of tribute and rent from its victims including other criminals.[2] Many regard this Jamaican organized crime group as one that most closely approximates what Anton Blok (1974) describes as mafia.[3] Its exceptionality and intensity, not its representativeness, make this case useful and illuminating for purposes of this discussion of the response of the state. By targeting powerful and difficult cases in their anti-gang campaign, the state has consequently brought most of the gang and organized crime control issues into the sharpest possible relief.

Context is an important aspect in the explanation of these developments; it may help to better situate and understand both the changes in strategy and the violence reduction outcomes. The histories of the gangs, their changing relationships with the political parties and with their host communities, the character of their communities and their relationships to the major institutions of the society or polity – that is, the histories of social exclusion but political inclusion – are all useful for understanding and evaluating the responses of the state. Space does not permit such an elaborate preliminary to the main thrust of this chapter. Much has been written on these issues in earlier chapters, and chapter 1 provides some account of elements of the Jamaican context. Here, the discussion of context is largely restricted to the immediate circumstances and factors that contributed to the elaboration of Jamaica's gang prevention and control strategy, and, in even more limited ways, to the national and community contexts of the state's responses and unfolding of this strategy in the case that is discussed below.

Gangs generally escalate crime, particularly violent crime (Klein 1971; Fagan 1989; Huff 1996; Curry 2000; Bennett and Holloway 2004; Small Arms Survey 2010; Melde and Esbesnen 2011). Organized crime tends to be increasingly criminally productive and in many settings, more violent than ordinary street gangs. There is considerable evidential support for these claims in the context of the Caribbean (Harriott 2003; Katz and Fox 2010; CHDR 2012). It is well documented that the types of criminal activities that organized crime and gangs engage in, such as drug trafficking, drug dealing, extortion, protection rackets and the protection of territory, tend to generate violence. However, it is not just the activities themselves that generate violence. In fact, the social dynamics of the group generally heighten the criminal productivity of its members relative to their prior rates of criminality, as well as the criminality of non-gang offenders. These group processes, especially those that elevate violent offending, have been much discussed elsewhere (Jankowski 1991; Thornberry 1998; Klein and Maxson 2006; Moxson 2011) and include "an oppositional culture, group identity and cohesion, and status processes that encourage violent responses to signs of disrespect or challenges to the group" (Moxson 2011, 159). The degree of groupness (measured in terms of cohesiveness), the dimensions of groupness (such as identity), and other group characteristics (such as territorial attachments) help to better explain the process by which gangs and organized crime enhance criminal productivity (Hennigan and Sloane 2013). Moreover, because Jamaican gangs are predominantly composed of young risk-taking, status-seeking, rank-ordered males, a layer of gender dramaturgy may be added to these group dynamics. High gang density adds to the risk of inter-gang violence or gang "wars" as they are revealingly called in Jamaica.[4] When gangs are affiliated with political parties, the risk of inter-gang violence, especially during election campaigns, tends to increase its intensity and geographic scope. Connectedness to power, especially power in the state via political parties whose membership and influence permeate the state institutions and civic organization, provides a large pool of enablers and thereby increases access to opportunities. The political party-gang nexus also insulates the gangs from law enforcement and permits impunity. Gangs often provide benefits and services that ought to be provided by the state (though they often use the resources of the state), which builds social support for these gangs or at least contributes to a permissiveness that negates much of the community level social control. Gang control, reduction and prevention are thus presented with many challenges.

This study argues that despite the difficult nature of the problems and the incapacities of the response mechanisms of the state, important advances have been made in gang control. These advances include a coincidence (coordination would be a further advance) of gang suppression with social prevention, which has yielded a generalized reduction in violent crimes. This reduction in violent crime is significant because, unlike past moments of violence reduction, it cannot be explained by developments in the underground or any other factors aside from the efforts of the state. There are many competing explanations that attempt to explain the reduction; however, none of them are credible. For example, localized peace-making efforts preceded this period, but they cannot adequately explain the national outcomes. There have been no significant changes in the opportunities for violent crimes to occur, and the general demand for homicidal violence in the society has not shifted either. Neither have there been any appreciable changes in root or distal causes of violent crimes that would account for a decline in their rates. For example, in the context of decades of economic stagnation compounded by a profound economic crisis, youth unemployment and underemployment remain chronic and, after a period of promise, inequality is again deepening.[5] Access to legitimate opportunities remains rather limited. The dynamics of gang violence itself and the concept of cycles of gang violence (Klein 1995a, 112–19; Klein 1995b) or cycles of retaliatory violence (Jankowski 1991) as an explanation of the decline in violent crimes may also be discounted. Particular gangs and their communities may exhibit these cycles, but an examination of the aggregate data for the country does not reveal that such patterns have national impact on cycles of violence.

The impact has been a steady increase in the homicide rate (unless there is a hidden long-range impact that is just revealing itself) with inter-group violence being the main escalator of a steadily upward long-term trend in the homicide rate (Harriott 2003).[6] In the case of Jamaica, the strong features of a subculture of violence may explain the absence of clearly discernable cycles in the national aggregated crime statistics that are, for example, associated with revenge killings (Harriott 2003, 2008a). The subculture adds intensity and may perhaps shorten the cycles of dyadic inter-group violence. Thus, when the death toll from inter-group violence is aggregated annually, the cycles that dyads of groups in conflict display are not visible over as long of a period as the one under review (excepting as short periods of decline lasting no more than a year). In 2010, a trend which lasted for almost thirty years was disrupted. The available evidence suggests instead, that the lower rates of serious crimes are the consequence of law enforcement's targeted focus on the major gangs in the country. It has created an opportunity for Jamaica to break the power of these groups and to bring its crime problem, or at least its violence problem, under greater control improving its security situation.

The rest of the chapter is organized as follows: first, the strategy is described, then the decline in murders and its association with more effective gang control is discussed, and finally, the operation against the Presidential Click is examined.

Jamaica's Gang Prevention and Control Strategy

Gangs have become more prevalent, gang density is fairly high and, although many are short lived (as is reflected in the constantly changing police estimates of their number), a large number of gangs are fairly durable. At the end of 2010, the police estimated that there were 210 "criminal gangs" in Jamaica. As gangs are by definition groups that engage in criminal activity, the use of the word "criminal" as a descriptor is unnecessary. It is, however, used by the police and others to distinguish these groups from other problematic groups which may be gang-like in appearance but are not actual gangs, such as "corner crews" (see Levy et al. 2012). If we may nevertheless persist with the confusion, the Jamaica Constabulary Force (JCF) estimated that there were twenty-nine non-criminal gangs.[7] Police estimates indicate that during the decade of 2000–2010, gang prevalence increased and has since continued to increase.[8] The spatial distribution of these gangs suggests a high degree of concentration in the primate city of Kingston, in addition to considerable prevalence in other cities as well. Of the 210 actual street gangs, 53 per cent (112) were located in the city of Kingston, in the parishes of Kingston and St Andrew.[9] Approximately 5 per cent (10) were located in the city of Montego Bay. Nationally, gang density (which is expressed as the number of criminal gangs per square mile) was 0.05. Gang density for the city of Kingston was much higher than 0.64.[10] Most gangs are territorial and many are either party affiliated or prone to being caught up in political mobilizations and thus are particularly conflict prone. As noted in chapter 1, some gangs predate Jamaica's independence in 1962. Some of Montego Bay's gangs are similarly durable, having survived for at least fifty years. In some parts of the country, and in some sections of its cities, the gang problem is deeply rooted and chronic and in others it is emergent. The challenges of responding are thus neither simple nor uniform.

Territorial gangs tend to openly display their political affiliations and influence. They participate in internal party leadership contests, in electoral campaigns and in ongoing political mobilizations and efforts by the parties to win elections and form the political administration (Lacy 1977; Headley 2002; Harriott 2008b; Sives 2010). Gangs exercise influence and power in the communities, and in some instances are their communities' rule-makers and rule-enforcers via the provision of services traditionally supplied by the state, such as welfare and security. Their power and influence are visibly expressed in some communities; for example, certain gangs provide assistance to parents in outfitting their children for school, guarantee free utilities by force of arms and the open display of weapons, instil the general belief among residents of their host communities that they are protective of them, and establish "jungle courts" that impose punishments on rule violators (Harriott 2008a; Jaffe 2012; Charles and Beckford 2012). The more powerful groups that are nestled in garrison communities tend to exercise increasing control over different dimensions of residents' lives. Their methods of rule involve both the coercive and authoritative generation of compliance. The more successful leaders of these groups enjoy a measure of referent power among marginalized youth often extending beyond their own communities, which contributes to the reproduction of the gang.

Where the relationships between the more powerful gangs and territorially based organized crime networks and the political parties are strong, their relationship with the governing party and state is typically that of a partnership. It is a partnership that affects a particular type of system inclusion and rule in the inner-city or ghetto communities (Harriott 2008b). However, a second aspect of the process occurs when organized crime groups and street gangs use criminalization to penetrate both political parties and the state. This partnership allows gangs and the state to influence each other. Perhaps with a bit of exaggeration, Jaffe characterizes this partnership as the expression of a hybrid state (Jaffe 2012). The state is not the garrison writ large. It is important to inspect the degree of state capture by organized crime and various types of criminal interests (as distinct from the more traditional forms of corrupt influences) and the extent to which this process has transformed the very character of the state. It would be evident that the character of the state has changed if the composition of a dominant coalition in the political administration includes these criminal interests, and if this dominant coalition has the ability to impose its will on the behaviour of the institutions of the state. Historically, organized crime networks have often had influence in the governments' dominant coalitions, but this is quite different from being a part of that coalition. Were the latter to occur, the state would become more predatorily extractive and more likely to protect and offer immunity to these criminal interests. These influences and tendencies are present, but they are not sufficiently developed in their measurable expressions in order to support the conclusions that the state has become predatory in character and has been captured and led by a dominant coalition that includes organized crime and/or street gang formations or other criminally oriented interests.[11]

In the garrison communities, however, the form of rule can be described as a "hybrid state", though this is not sufficiently scaled up nationally to warrant such a generalized characterization of the state. It is this relationship that makes the responses of the political administration and state to the gangs so complicated and compromised. State resources are used to support and sustain gangs but conversely allocated to control the gangs. Political administrations tend to claim support for "tough" anti-gang legislation, but in the past they displayed little effort to apply these laws methodically. Moreover, where the capabilities for effectively applying or enforcing these laws have been lacking, little enthusiasm has been displayed for developing them. The legal symbols that come from the legislative agenda are therefore not usually taken as signifiers of any sort of resolve to respond more effectively to violent crime (for example, legislation which provides for the forfeiture of assets that are derived from illegal activities). As such, they risk becoming additional symbols of the blustering impotence and masked complicity of the political administrations and, by extension, the state. Unused or misapplied, these intended expressions of strength and resolve are converted into their opposites because they are incapable of following through with their plans.

Instead, the state decided to respond with the strategy of gang-truce-making as opposed to traditional crime-fighting responses, which provides evidence that particular gangs have accumulated significant power to influence the government; this failure to respond appropriately may indicate the further weakening of both the criminal justice system and the state itself. Peace truces are usually adopted where gang violence continues unabated despite the efforts of the state, which are primarily suppressive law enforcement but may also include attempts to buy peace. The signing of peace treaties between gangs in different sections of the city of Kingston has a long history from the conflict years of the 1970s to the present (Jackson 2008; Brown 2009). Since then, truces have been signed and broken and re-signed in several communities across that city. Truces are not a part of the written strategy described in legislation, but they are negotiated by the Peace Management Initiative (PMI), which is a state-supported agency. Often times, the two major political parties are involved and may even play leading roles in brokering these truces (see "Two Killed in West", *Gleaner*, 23 May 2001, and "Streets Still Blocked – But Truce Reached in Central Kingston", *Gleaner*, 22 November 2001). The parties are represented on the PMI, which allows them to become involved in peace truces as members; however, they may also negotiate truces independently of the PMI.

In some communities, the gangs enjoy considerable power and at times become so intoxicated by their power that they overreach. At the community level, this may take the form of invading the private lives of community residents and demanding sexual favours of the women and children, or inflicting excessive and unjust punishment on members of the community whom they think have violated the rules. When this occurs, people may ask their political party leaders (not the police) to seek a remedy or attempt to restrain the gang. The gang leaders may either comply or resist, and those who resist risk overreaching their power, which could result in dire consequences. Criminal activities outside of the host community may also be overreaching, such as in the "lotto scam" case, which victimizes United States citizens and consequently makes these groups and networks targets of US law enforcement. In the Christopher Coke case, barricading the community of Tivoli Gardens (the host community of the Presidential Click) as if in open warfare with the state and engaging in attacks on several police stations precipitated the state of emergency and an assault on the Presidential Click. Gang overreach may reduce or even strip away political protection and invite a sharp-edged reaction from law enforcement. In 2010, this sharp-edged state response was undertaken with some success. Jamaica has, as noted earlier, made some recent and more generalized advances in gang reduction and control. These outcomes are the results of prior work and learning.

The Strategy

This prior experience and learning are encapsulated in Jamaica's anti-gang strategy and plan. Before this development, and with the exception of the National Security Policy (NSP) (Government of Jamaica 2007), the Ministry of National Security, often in response to advocacy by the JCF, implemented policy as a knee-jerk reaction, typically in response to a focusing event. In the past, such efforts would have been considered piecemeal and lacking in coherence or clear strategic vision. Jamaica has witnessed a substantial advance resulting from the creation of a written set of policies, such as a new 2012 edition of the NSP and an anti-gang policy. It registers advances in leadership and offers an approach that is grounded in a better appreciation of the complexities of the problem.

However, other factors may also account for this development, such as access to (grant) resources for the purpose of policy formulation. The existence of a written anti-gang policy perhaps results from the institution of a sharper line between operations and policy and, similarly, between the domains of the police commissioner and the minister of national security. In order for the minister and the political executive as a collective to have and maintain their influence on police operations, this influence must now travel as policy and with greater formality than in the past.[12] This finding clearly indicates that progress has been made regarding political influence in the police force, although much still depends on who holds the commissioner and minister's offices. In addition to the acuteness of the problem of gang violence, the above are some of the factors accounting for the development of an anti-gang strategy.

The basic conceptual elements of a framework for gang prevention and control are outlined in the previous chapter and need not be repeated here. Some of these ideas inform the discussion of the Jamaican experience and the Anti-Gang Strategy and Plan (AGSP) that is described below.

According to the AGSP, its guiding "philosophy" is a community-based approach to gang reduction. The community-based approach may be interpreted as developmental and democratic in orientation. It is "developmental" in that there is some commitment to solving the social problems that are associated with gang formation, and it is "democratic" because community inclusion and participation are accepted principles that may, for example, be extended to involvement in new forms of local police accountability. The AGSP states, "The crux of this Community-Based Gang Reduction (CBGR) Philosophy (strategy) is that it combines building enforcement capacity within the JCF with increased coordination, facilitation and awareness of social programmes likely to prevent or inhibit gang activity. As the strategy matures, the process of safety through enforcement is replaced with safety through 'development'" (Amiot and Foster 2011, 6).

The AGSP's Community-Based Gang Reduction Model represents the specification and operationalization of the "guiding philosophy". This approach finds evidential support in the extant research conducted on community-level factors that account for offending or gang activity (Thresher 1927; Sampson and Groves 1989; Fagan 1996), gang membership (Pyrooz, Fox and Decker 2010; Katz and Fox 2010) and the control and prevention effects of community action (Bursik and Grasmick 1993; Papachristos and Kirk 2006; McGarrell et al. 2012), and such potential effects in the Caribbean (CHDR 2012). In its various programmatic expressions, the community-based approach has shown results elsewhere (McGarrell et al. 2012). This approach to gang prevention would be useful in Jamaica because it is home to territorially rooted gangs that enjoy strong community support. Both community workers in the state system and researchers who ground their work in deep and methodical community consultations generally advocate for this type of approach (Levy et al. 2012). The AGSP is less intense in its advocacy, but recognition of the importance of community clearly instructs the strategy.

The Community-Based Gang Reduction Model may have been somewhat inspired by Wyrick (2006). Given its aspiration for comprehensiveness and most importantly, the integration of community policing with social interventions, the model could have benefited from the thinking that informed The Little Village Project and the work of Irving Spergel (2007). The model represents "gang reduction through enforcement working together with gang reduction through development". It describes the model as follows, "On the left side, enforcement brings gang members into the judicial system; and on the right, social programmes (development) draw gang members and potential gang members out of the gang. It is important to note that the model uses two-way arrows on the left to indicate that enforcement does not necessarily induce gang members to leave the gang; it may only temporarily prevent their participation" (Amiot and Foster 2011, 9).

This way of thinking about gang reduction suggests that it is important to recognize the importance of law enforcement, yet also accept its limits. Historically, law enforcement and policymakers each accept this reality. Recognition of the limits of law enforcement and its more doubtful partner "crime fighting" finds expression among station-level officers in various ways, but perhaps most sharply and promisingly is the conclusion that if one gang member is killed or imprisoned he is quickly replaced by new recruits. Station-level officers recognize the limits of law enforcement and the impact of crime fighting; they understand the bleak reality that removing gang members does not solve the problem because other members quickly replace them.

The real advance in thinking is reflected in taking the next step, that is, the elaboration of a more comprehensive approach that integrates intervention and social prevention with law enforcement. The importance of this approach is better appreciated if the relationships between gangs and communities are understood. A considerable amount has recently been written on these relationships (Charles 2002; Harriott 2008b; Figueroa, Harriott and Satchell 2008; Levy 2009; Charles and Beckford 2012; Jaffe 2012; Levy et al. 2012). The fact that a community-based approach to gang reduction and prevention is being advocated and taken as strategy by the JCF represents another important element in the advances in thinking and practice. However, law enforcement tends to mainly rely on its experiences. The advances in thinking are based on the processing of these experiences.

The main elements of the Jamaican AGSP are (1) building the capacities of the JCF; (2) creating new specialized units, reshaping organizational structures and improving internal coordination within law enforcement; (3) vertical prosecution; and (4) community-development-oriented prevention. It is suggested that building the capacity of the JCF to more effectively reduce gang violence and gang prevalence involves the creation of specialized structures, specialized training for the operatives who function within these structures, improved intelligence gathering, and easier and wider user access to intelligence reports and assessments. The perennial issue of improving the capabilities in different branches of the forensic sciences is also an aspect of the AGSP. A second important element is that the design of systems ensures the reliable and on-time delivery of laboratory outputs and that police investigators are able to use these outputs effectively. The problem is not just one of capacity, but greater coordination across agencies, and greater accountability within these agencies. Moreover, greater accountability is required.

The final element of this aspect of the strategy is developing the capacity to better investigate gang-related financial crimes, such as money laundering and asset concealment. This is a glaring problem, which is made worse by inadequate records on assets forfeiture held by the JCF and the Office of the Director of Public Prosecutions. This is evident in the cases of Christopher Coke and the Presidential Click.

When confronted with a new problem or the escalation of an old problem, the JCF typically forms a new response unit that is dedicated to dealing with that problem. To the extent that new units deepen specialization, cultivate the needed competences, and promote responsibility or ownership of a problem and the accompanying accountability for its solution, then such units may help to better advance the work of the police. However, accompanying the creation of these units are the dangers of duplicating effort, generating conflicting lines of responsibilities within the force and increasing the human resource requirements for internal administration. The JCF already has an Organized Crime Investigation Division (OCID) and crime-type specialized units such as the Transnational Crime and Narcotics Division, the Lotto Task Force and the Financial Investigations Division which investigate specific activities of organized crime groupings and networks. The police force also has structures in place dedicated to investigating the individual leaders of organized crime groupings and gangs or "high value targets". This is the stated purpose of the Major Organized Crime and Anti-Corruption Task Force (MOCA). This organizational landscape illustrates the problem of overlapping missions without some of the benefits of specialization. In the case of the gang problem, despite aforementioned risks, there is a level of justification for the creation of new specialized structures as parts of a coordinated response capability.

The structural changes described in the AGSP include (1) the establishment of a gang unit within the OCID, (2) a dedicated uniformed gang enforcement unit in each of the nineteen geographic (police) divisions and (3) one company of the Mobile Reserve, to be a designated Gang Response Unit. This last unit is noteworthy as it would reduce the dependence of the JCF on the Jamaica Defence Force (JDF) and could potentially improve officer accountability for conduct during violent confrontations with gangs, as only one organization and one chain of command would be involved.

Ineffective gang and organized crime investigations and prosecutions are glaring weaknesses in the work of the criminal justice system. This is evidenced by the long careers that, until recently, several gang leaders have enjoyed and the low conviction rates on gang violence and gang crime more generally. Vertical prosecution is one of the proposed remedies for this problem. This involves close collaboration between law enforcement and prosecutors during the investigative stage of a case and "remain[ing] attached to a particular case until its final disposition" (Amiot and Foster 2011, 34). The purpose is to improve the quality of the investigations, system efficiency and the chances of just convictions. Investigator and prosecutor collaboration has been discussed frequently for several years, and there have been some actual interactions via what is called a Court User Group. Vertical prosecutions are able to advance and structure these interactions and processes in a more efficient way.

There are some potential dangers and moral hazards associated with close police and prosecutor collaboration. The danger is that prosecution bias may be introduced at an early stage in the investigative process that effectively selects and pursues suspects on a presumption of guilt, thus foreclosing on alternatives. The focus on seeking convictions compromises the premise of justice. Policing ought to be so concerned with justice that its processes are designed to safeguard it as both process and outcome. Police-prosecutor collaboration may nevertheless help to raise the standards of investigation. It is thus best viewed as involving risks to be managed rather than as entailing such great dangers that it is to be completely avoided at all cost.

The AGSP integrates law enforcement and social prevention and interestingly proposes a coordination mechanism for doing so. More generally, it highlights the need for "empowered" implementation mechanisms. This rightly suggests that plans usually remain plans and that they risk being ignored unless the empowerment occurs. The actual approach to social prevention will be described in the cases that are discussed below. An interesting advance in thinking is the belief that government ought to respond in more "joined-up" ways and that the various programmes should be mutually reinforcing. Thus, for example, national youth policy ought to be alert to the problem of delinquency and youth gangs; new community development programmes should be more deliberate and explicit about crime prevention and be better coordinated with CBP; and school support programmes such as the Programme of Advancement through Health and Education (PATH) should be better directed to ensure family stability and reduced delinquency. Community development and other programmes that are intended to have crime-reduction outcomes ought to have crime-prevention-specific and gang-specific components when applicable. These programmes should be better coordinated and state agencies directed to operate in more "joined-up" ways. The essential elements needed for a more effective gang control and prevention strategy are present in official thinking, planning and practice. The challenges are related to programme design, the scale of operations, consistency and coordination within government and across government and nongovernment agencies, internal accountability, and the efficient use of resources for problem-solving rather than in pursuit of electoral outcomes or narrow departmental interests.

Although having a written strategy represents a considerable advance, there are some deficiencies and gaps within it. The strategy integrates law enforcement with social crime prevention; however, the challenges of integration are best overcome if these challenges and the integrative principles are explicitly stated and thus taken into account. These challenges of integration ought to (and may indeed) include integrating formal and informal social control. If such a foundational principle is expected to be at work but is not explicitly stated, then it is unlikely that any effort to achieve this goal would be pursued methodically. For example, the effective integration of these two elements would entail reconciling the different perspectives on gangs by two opposing viewpoints. On one hand, law enforcement and crime-fighters tend to adopt a tough approach to gang members but, on the other, the community workers are development oriented and often open to viewing gang members as community defenders and valued armed actors. In order for the community development approach to succeed, social facilitation to be eschewed and social control stimulated, then the attitudes of the community members toward gangs have to be taken into account and transformed. This further complicates matters and inserts obstacles to integration by creating tension among the different types of actors who must make the strategy succeed. This means that the tensions between the police and other actors have to be managed, and the punitive and non-punitive responses have to be balanced. For example, if organized crime and gang members are allowed an exit, then the challenge is to effectively link this with robust law enforcement that makes it difficult for persons who take this option to play manipulative double games to the advantage of their gangs. If this is done successfully, then gang exits are further encouraged not just by the pull factors but by an increasing push as the risk of remaining in the gang is increased.

Another challenge is to treat citizen participation in anti-gang programmes as a valued element. If participatory structures are able to exert the power of the community, then they may become important agents for gang prevention and, in doing so, may build citizen support for law enforcement. Such support is most effective when police authorities are able to resist the temptation to control and to channel citizens into structures that provide uncritical support for the police and that are not particularly keen on police accountability to the communities.

A good anti-gang strategy should ensure that the various programmes that operationalize this strategy are consistent with the risk factors and causes (proximate and distal) of the problem. This means making individuals (at risk) more

resilient in addition to making communities more resilient. It may not be sufficient to assume that doing community development (and youth development)
adequately focuses on the sources of the problem. A major gap in the strategy comes from the social and political legitimization of the gangs and how to
appropriately respond to this reality.[13] This issue is discussed in the next chapter. Moreover, on matters of security, there is often a gap between written policy and actual policy and between what is intended and what is implemented.
These deficiencies, which accompany the advances, have consequences for the
achieved outcome.

Advances and Results

As noted earlier, since 2010, Jamaica's gang-control efforts have had strik-
ingly positive results, which makes these efforts worthy of examination. These
national results are, however, treated rather tentatively as background to the
discussion of the case that is presented below. This is somewhat different from
making claims regarding the efficacy of Jamaica's anti-gang strategy. Any such
conclusive claims must await rigorous evaluation, which may come after a
longer period of substantial decline in the rates of gang-related crimes.

  At the time of writing, Jamaica had experienced three consecutive years of
decline in its homicide rate and rate of violent crimes (2010–2012). In 2009,
Jamaica's homicide rate was 62 per 100,000 citizens, and in 2012 it had declined
to 40.3 per 100,000.[14] Western Kingston, which has had high rates of homicide and is the home territory of some of Jamaica's most powerful and resilient organized crime groups and street gangs, including the Presidential Click,
experienced a sharp reduction of its reported homicide count during the period
2008–2012 (see figure 7.1). The murder rate for the area is very sensitive to gang
violence.

  Cycles of gang violence are evident in this locality and are clearly revealed
in the crime statistics for this area.[15] The volatility of the homicide and shooting
series that is presented in figure 7.1 and, more specifically, the sharpness of the
decline and increase in the frequency counts, the short durations of the changes,
and the similarity in the behaviour of the homicide and shooting counts all reveal
the effects of gang activity. There are three time points that depict sharp reductions in homicide and shootings. These are 2001, 2005–2006 and 2008–2012.
These moments of decline may be explained by gang truces and agreements that
were negotiated between the major organized crime groupings in the area for

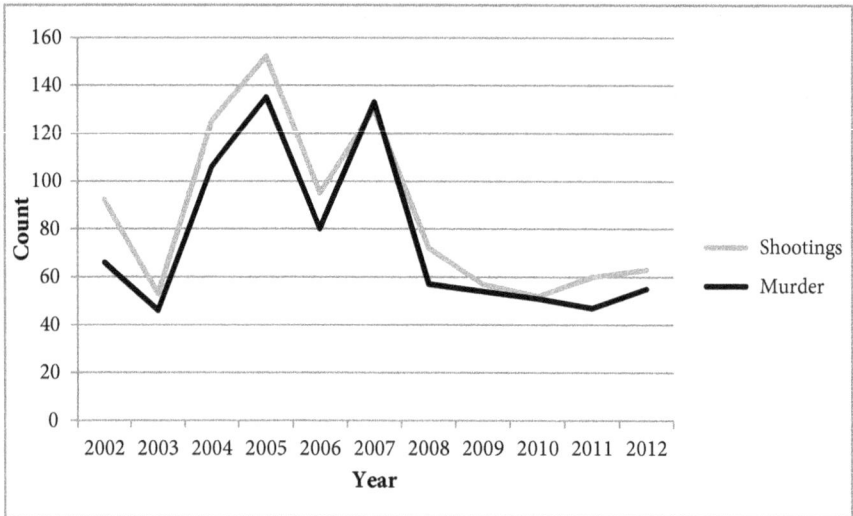

Figure 7.1. Sensitivity of murders and shootings in Western Kingston to gang violence, 2002–2012

Source: Statistics Division of the Jamaica Constabulary Force.

purposes of better exploiting criminal opportunities (2001[16] and 2006[17]), and gang suppression and intervention efforts of the police and military (2008–2012).

Gang truces which may be occasioned by various developments including access to legitimate economic opportunities, community pressures for peace and police suppression operations, are usually momentary in their effects, leading to the volatility of the homicide and shooting counts that is depicted in figure 7.1. Since 2008, however, there has been a more prolonged period of gang suppression and prevention activities in some locales. If the homicide rate for Western Kingston is sensitive to gang activity, the national homicide rate has become similarly sensitive to the levels of gang violence (which is not to be equated with cycles of gang violence).

Much of the reduction in the national homicide rate is therefore attributed to the decline in gang-related violence. According to the official police reports, in 2009, gangs accounted for 52 per cent of all homicides that occurred in Jamaica, while in 2010, this was dramatically reduced to 28 per cent (see figure 7.2). When 2009 is contrasted with 2011, a 51 per cent decline in gang-related homicides was associated with a 26 per cent decline in the homicide count. For the period 2009–2011, there is an evident association between the reduction in the homicide rate and the reduction in gang-related homicides. For the

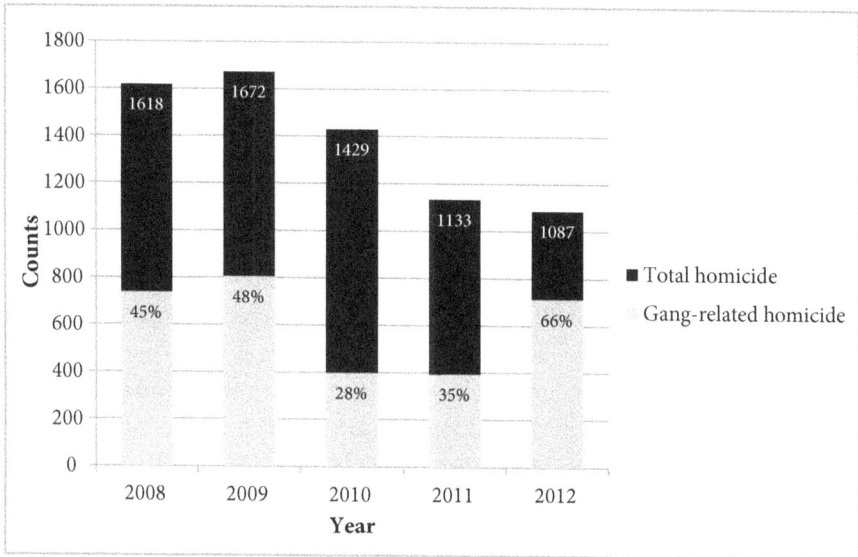

Figure 7.2. Decline in homicides, 2008–2012

Source: Economic and Social Survey of Jamaica for 2008–2011; and for 2012, the JCF Statistics and Information Management Unit (which is the source for the *Economic and Social Survey of Jamaica*). For 2012, the numbers given are regarded as provisional.

period 2009–2012, using the same data source, this association between the reduction in gang-related homicides and the reduction in the national homicide rate remains, but appears to be less strong than expected.[18] These changes are depicted in figure 7.2. At face value, these data suggest that between 2011 and 2012 reversals in gang prevention and control may have occurred (as evidenced by the apparent dramatic increase in gang-related homicides that reportedly occurred in 2012) and that other categories of homicide may more fully account for the overall decline in the homicide rate.[19]

The apparently sharp increase in the category of gang-related homicides in 2012 relative to 2011 may be accounted for by the changes in the categorization and coding of homicides, particularly the treatment of the category "undetermined". Immediately prior to these years, for example, in 2008, the "undetermined" category accounted for approximately 7 per cent of the cases. In 2010, this category rose to 29.5 per cent, and in 2012, it declined again to 2.4 per cent. It is a volatile category, and its volatility most directly affects the "gang-related" category. The sharp decline in the undetermined category accounts for the sharp increase in gang-related homicides in 2012. Many of the undetermined cases seem to be consistent with gang-related killings, but there is usually not enough information to make a clear determination. Some coders may thus load the undetermined cases into the gang-related category, while others may be more guarded in their conclusions. Sharp changes in the volume of cases that are assigned to the latter category may be explained by this type of action rather than any sharp shift in gang violence. A greater reliability in the coding of these data is required before the true patterns are more fully revealed.[20] In the absence of more accurate and reliable data, we must simply make the best of what is available. Despite the difficulties with the data, it is reasonable to make the claim that a large percentage of the decline in the homicide rate during the period under review may be accounted for by the reduction in gang-related killings.

Although the changes in data coding explain the magnitude of the increase in gang-related murders in 2012, an increase in this category of murder may have occurred. If so, it suggests that the process of controlling gang violence is a difficult one and may not result in a steady downward trend. There has been gang fragmentation, as is reflected in an increase in the number of gangs, and violent competition for leadership within some gangs. These data should not be interpreted to signify a resurgence of gang violence (and power), but rather that there is a potential that this could occur quite quickly.

Advances in Law Enforcement Responses

The JCF has reported that gang activity has been disrupted, and their capabilities have been degraded. The intensive gang policing during the 2010 state of emergency and the death and detention of many of their leaders and members did indeed disrupt their activities. The JCF recalibrated its gang suppression tactics and introduced some new elements. The problem was given focused attention. Gang members were targeted more accurately as a result of improved intelligence gathering and analysis. The JCF established a permanent and more active presence in some of the gang-dominated communities and in so doing, contended with the gangs for territory and the support of the residents. Law enforcement practices continue to display many weaknesses, including deficiencies in investigative practices. Thus, the reduction in the rate of violent crimes has not been accompanied by a proportionate increase in the cleared-up rates. For example, during the period under review (2009–2012), while the homicide count declined by 35 per cent, the cleared-up rate increased by only 12 per cent (from 29 per cent in 2009 to 41 per cent in 2012);[21] there has been no noticeable change in the appallingly low conviction rates. As a part of the corrective strategy outlined in the AGSP, as noted earlier, vertical prosecutions are planned but have not yet been implemented. The police force, however, has a newfound momentum. This situation contrasts with the lethargy of the period before 2010.

These advances in gang control are yet to be consolidated. Gang fragmentation and increasing gang violence in the tourism-dependent parish of St James reveals the flexibility of gang formations.[22] The constant income shifts and violence-generating activities demonstrate that any gang-control strategy should not focus narrowly on gang activities, but should include the primary sources of gang resilience, that is, their relationships to the parties and to communities (Harriott 2008b). This point is now acknowledged in the National Security Policy of the Government of Jamaica (Government of Jamaica 2012, 30).

The Benefits of Prior Police Reform

The recent (since 2010) advances in gang control have their antecedents in earlier efforts. The operations against Coke and the Presidential Click/Shower were not the first attempts to break up or dismantle a major gang. In 2005, Donald Phipps, the then-leader of the Spanglers, was convicted in a Jamaican court, and authorities subsequently seized the opportunity to degrade the power of that gang. Earlier, Operation Kingfish was launched with the objective to methodically investigate the major gangs, and in particular, their transnational operations. Its operatives and officers were all vetted for integrity, because corruption tends to compromise the investigation of wealthy and politically connected suspects. Kingfish relied on the United Kingdom's support and collaboration, and saw initial success. After Kingfish, the anticorruption measures within the JCF as a whole were deepened. More systematic use of technology in the investigation of serious crimes and new legislation has provided investigators with powerful tools which may be used against organized crime and gangs more generally. An example of this is the Proceeds of Crime Act (although there has not been much success in applying this act) and the seizure of the cash and wealth of powerful criminals such as Phipps and Coke demonstrate successful legislation against gangs. Prior to the operation against Coke and the Presidential Click, the JCF was positioned to provide a better response to gangs, including improved investigation of them.

Prior to Operation Kingfish, anti-gang efforts coincided with anti-violence efforts – if violence was reduced, very little follow-through for gang reduction and control occurred. Since then, this approach has been changed. The response to gangs has become more methodical with more explicit anti-gang objectives. The next logical step in this direction is to alert citizens of consequences of gang wars and develop systematic and accountable efforts towards preventative actions. The PMI does much of this type of activity, and if the police were similarly to become more preventive in orientation, the result would be even further reductions in gang violence or at least in gang "wars".[23] Fortunately, sources indicate that the police are moving toward preventive action (personal communication with a senior JCF officer, February 2013.)

The Benefits of Prior Coordination and Advances in Social Prevention

Similarly, prior advances in social crime prevention and interagency coordination were required to make such an approach successful. In 2003, the Jamaican government established the Anti-Crime Initiative, a group composed of representatives of several agencies who were involved in either crime suppression or prevention or who were involved in work that was relevant to these efforts.[24] At least ten state agencies participated in this early project. Both the JCF and the JDF were supportive and were actively involved in the various projects. Urban communities and schools served as the main sites of intervention.

Shifts in thinking that favour social crime-prevention programmes have occurred among policymakers and law enforcement and among the general population. Data from the Caribbean human development project on citizen security (see CHDR 2012) indicate large majority support for social crime prevention among a representative sample of the Jamaican population (n = 2,000). These crime prevention strategies include support for improved access to opportunities via education (95 per cent), better integration of the communities of the urban poor (93 per cent), and actual opportunity creation as employment (98 per cent).[25] There is a strong orientation to social justice among the population, which is further evidenced by the work of Powell (2004). This thinking influences governments through public policy and emphasizes a community-development approach to the gang problem as evidenced by new programmes such as the Citizen Security and Justice Programme (CSJP) and the Citizens Security Initiative (CSI).[26]

Considerable advances in problem solving are represented by the new-found line of thought that views the role of community and the reintegration of communities as critical to gang reduction and prevention. This has resulted in interventions that are not designed exclusively for gang-attached youth, but which are available to them. The upshot of this approach is the development of programmes that provide greater access to opportunity and projects that provide pathways to work and enter the mainstream of society – albeit not smooth pathways. Multiple state agencies, private sector actors, churches, educational institutions and other non-government groupings have attempted to form partnerships to aid these efforts. Much has been done and much is to be learned about these interventions.

There have been corresponding advances in the creation of organizational structures that are able to support social crime prevention. These structures include the aforementioned CSI, the CSJP, the crime prevention unit within the Ministry of National Security, the Community Security and Safety Branch of the JCF and the PMI. Infrastructure includes monitoring and evaluation capabilities in the form of a crime observatory within the Ministry of National Security. Building an observatory and using the method of routine evaluations would provide the information needed for better programme design and improved accountability and learning. This aspect is still in its rudimentary stages and has not yet impacted learning, innovation and programme effectiveness. Indeed, the pressure of managing the crime problem places demands on the observatory for information that is useful for operational purposes. This risks diverting the services of the observatory to the provision of tactically useful information only. Nevertheless, at the community level there are structures that could facilitate the coordination of programmes and that give voice to the leaders and residents of the affected communities.

Intervention and prevention work are more directed toward members of the communities than toward the at-risk and gang-involved subpopulations within these communities. Despite the distinction that is made or implied in the JCF strategy, intervention and prevention are indistinguishable in practice. In some communities, especially the garrison communities, there are good reasons for this, including the rootedness of the gangs there. In the case of the Spanglers (which is discussed in chapter 8), many of the young men in the gang's host community viewed themselves as Spanglas, and members of the gang regard the community as an extension of the gang.[27] This reveals the reality of shared experiences and merged identities.[28]

Joined-up or coordinated programmes rely on good working partnerships. State and non-state actors have been working together for the prevention of gang violence, which demonstrates an improved understanding of partnerships. Old tensions between them, however, remain and are based on the idea that states are corrupt and ineffective, and thus NGOs are better fitted to execute these types of programmes. External agencies may at times unwittingly fuel these tensions by funding local NGOs as competitors with the state. This idea is inappropriate when applied to community-level gang prevention and may be generally counterproductive in citizen security.[29] If a community approach is accepted, then it is easier to see that the different actors all bring value to this process. Perhaps, in this regard, some lessons have been learned. Partnerships that unite the efforts of state and non-state actors, especially with the inclusion of empowered community structures, present the opportunity for formal and informal control to become mutually reinforcing. This is critical to success in gang control and prevention. This, as noted earlier, ought to be an underlying principle that informs violence-reduction and gang-prevention programmes and provides a basis for partnerships and coordinating efforts across state and non-state agencies.

As noted earlier, there have been instances where suppression and social prevention coincide. First, there were advances on both but on parallel rather than intersecting tracks. The two approaches coincided in the early 2000s, and especially after the conviction of Donald Phipps in 2006, produced a measure of coordination and integration within several communities. The ingredients for success were thus present prior to the operation against the Presidential Click and the extradition of Coke. At the time, the major remaining problem was the lack of political consensus, often stated as a lack of "political will" to seriously tackle the problem where it mattered. This problem was momentarily resolved during the Coke crisis.

The community approach to gangs is complicated by a number of realities. These realities include, first, party-competitive politics. The communities of the urban poor are terrains within which party politics are enacted. This may present special difficulties when gangs are party affiliated and whole communities are similarly aligned to the same party, thereby resulting in strong gang–community–party affinities. The second is police operations that result in abusing citizen rights and consequently complicating the integration of suppression and social prevention. Advances in community-based policing could help to minimize these difficulties. The third reality is a measure of community crime dependence. In conditions of crime dependence, collective efficacy may facilitate crime rather than supporting social control. This emphasizes the importance of power shifts in some communities as a condition of effective social control and of making the communities less hospitable to gangs. It is against this backdrop that the case of the Presidential Click is examined.

The Presidential Click

In this section, the state's response to the Presidential Click is presented as an instance of how the state's anti-gang strategy was actually enacted.[30] The Presidential Click and its home community are but sites of state responses that illuminate the difficulties, the opportunities and the promising approaches being taken to the problem. The story is written to highlight the general points that may be useful for similar cases.

In 2010, the Presidential Click was perhaps the most powerful organized crime grouping in Jamaica. It is a highly structured community-based group that is very cohesive; its core is composed of members who reside or who resided in Tivoli Gardens at some point during their criminal careers. The Presidential Click also includes affiliate members and units that are drawn from the neighbouring communities. These are satellite units of the group that are treated as subordinates. This aspect of its structure with its accompanying power relationships tends to generate internal conflicts. Beyond these two layers of the Presidential Click is a much less cohesive transnational network. This larger network is called the Shower Posse.[31] The Presidential Click may thus be viewed as a distinct part of the Shower Posse, which is a loose transnational organized crime network. In the group's heydays of the 1980s, there were no distinctions by name between the entity that was located in Jamaica and the nodes that operated abroad. The entire conglomeration was called the Shower. The later distinctions by name suggest a weakened trans-border multi-nodal Shower and a more cohesive and national Presidential Click.

The Presidential Click is itself somewhat complicated. Like some of the other major territorial organized crime groups, it operates at different levels. It appears to have three distinct tiers. At the first level, which may be considered to be its base, it incorporates ordinary street criminals who are resident in its territory, but these recruits continue to function as ordinary street criminals. The Presidential Click simply co-opts them, enables them and controls them. These recruits are required to turn the loot from robberies and other street crimes over to the leader of the Presidential Click and, in return, they are given a percentage of whatever they present to the group. They are effectively treated as if they are contract workers or employees. As individuals, their returns may not compensate for their individual efforts, but they have the advantage of the protection of the Presidential Click. A former operative of the Click to an American court described this relationship as follows:

Q. Were you good at robbing?
A. Yes, sir.
Q. And after you had carried out a robbery what did you do with the proceeds of that robbery?
A. Sir, give Dudus, the boss.
Q. You would give him the proceeds of that robbery?
A. Yes, sir.
Q. And these were robberies that occurred outside of Tivoli in different communities around Jamaica?
A. Yes.
Q. And after you gave the defendant the proceeds of these robberies what would he do?
A. Sir, like I come back the next day and get like – I get like five grand, sir, or ten grand.
Q. So he would pay back from the proceeds?
A. Yes, sir.
Q. What percentage of proceeds would he give you back? Typically?
A. Sir, like I could have nothing.
Q. Less than you had robbed?
A. Yes, sir.
Q. A lot less than you had robbed?
A. Yes, sir.
Q. What was your understanding about what would happen if you robbed without permission?
A. Get killed.
Q. Was that one of the rules of the system?
A. Yes, sir.[32]

The relationship between lower-level group operatives and don or crime boss, and the related practices described above are known to exist among other organized crime groups that also operate in the western section of the city.

At this level, the operations of the vaunted Presidential Click resemble the depictions of criminal wretchedness in a novel written by Charles Dickens. Christopher Coke, the crime boss, resembles Fagin of *Oliver Twist*, but instead of running a group of child pickpockets who must master the craft of removing wallets unnoticed, he runs a gang of young robbers who relieve victims of their valuables at gunpoint. Fagin's recruits began their course of training with practice in how to stealthily remove a handkerchief from someone's pocket. Coke begins his induction of new recruits with instructions on how to use a gun.[33]

The operations of the Presidential Click are, however, more complex. This group not only exploits its lower-level street operatives, it enlists them in order to control its territory as a criminal monopoly enterprise. These methods are designed for the control of territory. Street criminals are incorporated into "the system" (which is how the processes of criminal production and internal group control are known) as a method of dominance of territory and control of the population as a part of a local political monopoly.

At the second level of functioning, the Presidential Click is able to use its territorial monopoly and its national and transnational networks to exploit criminal and corrupt opportunities at and beyond the street level. At this level, it operates as a criminal enterprise that engages in the supply of illicit goods and services. It monetizes its reputation for violence via extortion and protection rackets, and exploits drug markets at home and abroad. It appears to be able to do these things successfully and with immunity from law enforcement. On this basis, it is able to project its power and influence locally and nationally. The Presidential Click resembles the mafia at this level.

At the third level of functioning, the Presidential Click crosses into legal activity. Here it uses its political relationships to exploit corrupt opportunities in the state sector, typically but not exclusively in construction. Using its reputation for violence, it fixes the prices of construction materials from its suppliers and in various ways imports criminal methods into the world of normal business. Elsewhere, I list some of its contracts with various state agencies (Harriott 2008b). At this level of its operations, the Presidential Click tries to pass as corrupt politically facilitated business – that is, as normal "businessmen" – and they name their occupations as such.

Also at this level, there are complex organizational requirements that are derived from running a transnational network, corrupting state officials and probing new opportunities, participating in national elections and managing front firms, among other activities. At this level, the group presents a more sophisticated image.

Given the limited access to information, in trying to understand the Presidential Click there is the risk of being like the blind man who mistakes a part of the elephant for the whole. A familiar level of its activity may be mistaken for the whole. Earlier, in this chapter the Presidential Click was characterized by what may be considered as its core feature, that is, violent entrepreneurship. This feature operates at every level of its functioning. It is therefore reasonable and analytically useful to characterize the group in this way, but it should also be viewed through the three complex levels of operation described above. This configuration is largely imposed by its territoriality, monopolistic ambitions and politics.

These latter characteristics, which are not uncommon to Jamaican organized crime, are sources of their power and influence but also of their vulnerability. For example, the lower-level street operatives that were victimized by the group's controlling activities were the ones who eventually gave the US District Court damning evidence against Christopher Coke.

The Presidential Click/Shower has a long history, and is deeply rooted in the community of Tivoli Gardens in the western sector of Kingston, which it helped to transform into what is called a garrison community.[34] Christopher Coke was (and is) the executive president or leader of the Click, the then-symbolic president of the Shower, and also president or suzerain of Tivoli Gardens and the neighbouring communities within its gravitational field.[35]

Tivoli Gardens is estimated to have a population of some 10,094 persons.[36] The entire community was erected after the slum that was built on the land and occupied by supporters of the then-opposition party, was cleared. Seaga (2009), in his unmistakable style, describes the place as it was prior to the construction of Tivoli Gardens, as the "rectum" of the city and a "haven for every known criminal in the city" (pp. 153–54).

Since then, there has been much state investment in that community. Patrick Bryan has catalogued the level of investment (2009, 150–51). Over one thousand houses, several high-rise apartment buildings, several small parks, a community centre, a youth centre, clinics, a maternity centre, day nurseries, a secondary school and playfields were all built primarily with state funds, including loan funds. To these facilities were added other elements of a comprehensive welfare system that was not enjoyed by other communities until other garrisons were built. Initially, even the electricity bills of residents were paid by the Jamaican state via the Social Development Commission (SDC).[37] The new neighbourhood was fully incorporated into the political system as a politically homogenous community that was intensely and enduringly loyal to its patrons. Indeed, it was viewed by Seaga (2009, 163) in geopolitical terms as deterrence to territorial advances by the opposition PNP.

The garrison community is thus not an ungoverned space; rather, it may be argued that the garrison community is the product of a form of governing marginalized communities.[38] Neither is it spatially remote; it is an urban phenomenon that is most prevalent in the administrative capital of the country. It was erected in a socially marginalized space where multiple overlapping subcultures (of violence, of inner-city) and behavioural norms have stood in tension with the mainstream and modal conduct norms. Nevertheless, in many ways the garrison community is tied to, and indeed self-identifies as a part of, the cultural mainstream. In this sense, it is not socially remote. It largely circumvents the institutions of the criminal justice system, makes its own rules and engages in self-policing, but it is not politically remote. It is rather a product of the political system and competes and cooperates within it. Tivoli Gardens is a garrison community that is co-governed by one of the main political parties that alternates in government and holds a monopoly on political power and influence in the community in association with a crime monopoly with gang or organized crime grouping. Both share in rule-making and rule enforcement and in the allocation of resources (state and otherwise) to the community. State agencies serve these communities, typically under the direction of the monopoly-holding party.[39] Conflicts arise between gang/community and law enforcement when this compact is breached. In the case of Tivoli Gardens, gang leaders participate fully and openly in the political life of the community and are recognized as an important component of the community leadership. Prior to 2010, they had the political influence, the armed capability and the system of armed defence to regulate community access and to dissuade the police from engaging in normal police work (patrol and investigation) within the community.

Christopher Coke led the Presidential Click, and the last four leadership transitions that have occurred within this group were successions of one member of the Coke family by another. The organization has become a family business with a hereditary leadership, which is a source of resilience when there are available male heirs, but a potential weakness and vulnerability to fragmentation when one cannot be found. The hereditary line is particularly in danger under extraordinary conditions that do not allow time for adaptability and adjustments and therefore do not permit the emergence of an acceptable leader.

The operation, or rather the campaign, against the Presidential Click, has already progressed through several phases. These are (1) the preliminary phase which began with the request for extradition through the resolution of the political issues and the two-party agreement on the state of emergency; (2) the military operation in Tivoli Gardens; (3) the national campaign; and (4) the attempts to consolidate Tivoli as a normal community.

The First or Preliminary Phase: The Political Manoeuvres

For a weak criminal justice system that operates in a context of persistently high rates of violent crimes, properly targeting the problem is essential for case success as well as for policy success. Targeting for effective violence prevention and control is based on the well-established idea that violence usually exhibits clear patterns of concentration and of escalation. The spatial mapping of violence and gang network mapping and analysis are but two of the tools that are available for ascertaining these patterns. In the case of Jamaica, it is established that many of the violent crimes and most of the homicides are group perpetuated. Of the group-perpetuated violence, the respective contributions of the few organized crime groups and networks, on one hand, and youth and neighbourhood street gangs on the other, have not been properly determined. The available evidence however suggests that organized crime is the major contributor of the homicide rate. Moreover, of these organized crime groups, the territorially based ones and in particular those that are based in the garrison communities are the most problematic. Targeting for success should therefore involve ending the immunity of the garrisons.

Poorly targeting groups and the communities in which they operate may simply increase the problems of police and state legitimacy. A negative instance of gang suppression and poor targeting is El Salvador where in the five-year period beginning with the passage of its Mano Dura law in 2003 and ending in 2008, the prison population increased from six thousand to twelve thousand, that is, by 100 per cent with some 40 per cent of prisoners being alleged gang members.[40] Moreover, in 2005, following the passage of the anti-gang laws (Super Mano Dura), of the fourteen thousand suspected gang members who were arrested in that year, some ten thousand were released (Seelke 2007, 3). Despite these efforts, El Salvador's homicide rate continued to increase during and beyond this period of Mano Dura suppression.

In Jamaica, political affiliation and the associated protection has compromised the ability of authorities to properly target some of the more powerful gangs. Coke was targeted by American law enforcement. In May of 2010, an American extradition order for Coke triggered a crisis that enveloped the Jamaican political administration and contributed to the prime minister's resignation and the electoral defeat of the then-ruling party.

The response of the political administration put Coke at the centre of a conflict between the two countries. Given the power disparity between Jamaica and the United States, this conflict presented huge risks to the government. Despite these political risks and moral hazards, the Jamaican administration appeared to have stonewalled the process for a lengthy period, thereby further demonstrating the political influence and power of the Presidential Click.

Its influence within the ruling party was evidenced by the view (reportedly expressed in private by the then-minister of national security to the then-commissioner of police) that the extradition of Coke "would bring down the government" (Henry 2011). This view encapsulates the ambivalence in relation to the crime problem that may be found in the political elite. Gang influence and power further reinforces this ambivalence and impulse to inaction. In the case of Coke and the Presidential Click, the minister's reported comment revealed a fear of large-scale destabilizing (even if momentary) violence and its national and local, and political and economic, consequences. This narrative may have been compelling enough to partially explain the prime minister's expressed willingness "to put his career on the line for the rights that are enshrined in the constitution" by resisting the request for the extradition of Coke (Spaulding 2013).

This was a backstage narrative that was perhaps intended to make common ground with the security forces. The front-stage narrative that was intended for the general public was that the government's objection to the extradition was grounded in law. The request by the United States was found to be in violation of the procedures that were specified in the Mutual Legal Assistance Treaty (MLAT).

There were perhaps real differences between the two governments, or at least important elements within these governments, on attitudes to Jamaican law and perhaps even law in general. The Jamaican experience with legally problematic extradition requests suggests that US officials may have different approaches to the law than some of their Jamaican counterparts. The dominant position among US officials is to view the law as a tool for solving social problems such as transnational drug-trafficking and for prosecuting the more general war on drugs (see Kohler-Hausmann 2010). To the extent that law does not serve these purposes, it is regarded as being dysfunctional. It underplays the importance of due process and may even regard it (that is, a set of specific procedural rules, not necessarily the abstract idea) as an impediment to case-solving and problem-solving. This is a form of legal instrumentalism that is associated with the crime-control perspective.[41] Procedural law, particularly Jamaican procedural law, should therefore not restrain or shackle the effort to control transnational crime. Indeed, as early as in 2004, the US authorities expressed some impatience with the lengthy legal process which they claimed could take two to five years, especially when appeals were made (US Dept. of State 2004). The disregard for lawful procedure was evident in the case of Richard Morrison (in 1991), who was also a leader of the Shower. In that case, legally required procedures were violated, but with fewer tensions and perhaps a greater convergence of views between the Jamaican and US governments.[42] There were other instances of this problem.[43]

Procedural justice is an important issue, and getting representatives from powerful countries and other external actors to comply with national laws is a matter of national self-respect. Political administrations are expected to uphold the rule of law, but in the case of the order to proceed with the extradition of Coke, these were perhaps secondary concerns. The events revealed that the Presidential Click and JLP alliance was not simply a matter of corruption of politics or even the criminalization of politics but also, and perhaps more importantly, a manifestation and acknowledgement of the power of the Presidential Click and of organized crime more generally, which politicians believed that they had to appease and protect. The fear of violence was realized. However, with hindsight, it was not the power of the Presidential Click, but the resistance to the extradition of its leader that helped to bring down the government.

The resistance within the political administration precipitated civic mobilization and political reaction within the country. The private sector via its representative organization (the PSOJ) withdrew from the Social Partnership that was and is an important forum for building social consensus on vital policy issues and partnership between government, private sector, trade unions and other civil society actors. The trade unions similarly withdrew. A new civic organization consisting of several important civil society actors including representatives of church organizations, various business organizations and other influential actors was formed and began campaigning on this issue of the extradition. The experience of other countries that have been similarly besieged by high levels of violence generated by organized crime suggests that civic activism helps to bring about a turn of events and forces more concerted state actions.

This proved to be true for Colombia where a movement for peace developed that was directed against both the narco-violence of organized crime and the interminable armed conflict between the guerrilla groups and the military (see Dudley 2006) and Italy where an "anti-mafia social movement" emerged and may have had some impact on the weakening of the mafia (Stille 1996; Johnson and Soeters 2008). Civic activism had played an important role by increasing the political cost to the government of any continued stonewalling of the extradition request. The administration became increasingly embattled and isolated. On 18 May 2010, the extradition order was signed (see "Coke Extradition Request Signed", Gleaner, 18 May 2010.).

After the order was signed to proceed with the extradition, Tivoli Gardens quickly became a fort. The roads into that community were barricaded, and sandbagged and gun emplacements were erected on buildings and in support of some of the barricades. The protective role of the community quickly became evident. On 20 May 2010, just two days after the extradition order was signed, some eight hundred to a thousand women from the community, all dressed in white, marched in support of Coke.[44] The demonstration was well organized, which suggested that the Presidential Click possessed political craft and a high degree of control.

The demonstration actively showed community support for Coke. It appears that its immediate purpose was to counter the police narrative, which claimed that the residents of the community were hostages to the Presidential Click. Their supporting evidence was that their cell phones had been seized by the gang so that they could not communicate with the security forces and others outside of the community. According to some of the spokespersons, the police and military were conducting an "information war" against them. This information war was seen as the prelude to the armed battle with the security forces. The counternarrative was that this was an attempt to further stigmatize the community. Community mobilization was implemented to demonstrate active support for Coke in its emotional intensity while also revealing the rational bases of this support. Thus some of the placards that were held by the demonstrators read: "Dudus (Coke) a wi Prime Minister," "We will die for Dudus," "Wi can walk a night, wi can leave wi door open, all because of Dudus". Even a representative of the dog population in the community was made to appear as a pro-Dudus demonstrator (see "Willing to Die for 'Dudus'", *Jamaica Observer*, 21 May 2010). The symbolism was clear: all of Tivoli, including the animals, was freely, fully and faithfully in support of Coke.

Such seemingly intense support for a particular criminal organization is invariably accompanied by a profound distrust of the police. Distrust of the police was thus a recurring theme of the demonstrators. Mobile phones were displayed to the press to make the point that the security forces misrepresented their situation. They were not hostages, but should be regarded as free actors who supported their don. And as the police could not be trusted, Coke should not surrender *to them*. It follows from this line of argumentation that resistance to Coke's arrest was thus justified.

While the United States appeared to narrowly target Coke the individual, by barricading the community and initiating an armed resistance to his arrest, Coke presented the security forces with the opportunity to widen the targets of the operation. He inadvertently made the Presidential Click and its supporters in the community of Tivoli Gardens the targets of law enforcement.

The Second or Violent Confrontational Phase

Extradition always had the potential to trigger a new phase in the violence of organized crime groupings. Groups that are excluded, or included but without much influence on national policymaking, may use corruption as a means of altering policies that negatively affect them. They may also resort to violence. Old and powerful organized crime groups, such as the Presidential Click, historically combine the manipulation of corrupt motivations of their targets and use of their channels of political influence with leveraging their reputations and capabilities for violence, in order to get the outcomes that they desire. As extradition involves the will of a powerful external actor that is beyond the reach of their direct political influence and ability to corrupt, then great pressure must be directed at the Government of Jamaica as the intermediate actor. Under certain conditions (such as a moment of inflamed conflict between the two parties and when the gang leader who is targeted for extradition is affiliated with the party that is in opposition), this could conceivably involve a very challenging episode of violence that may be more protracted than the one that is being discussed here. This type of violence would be directed primarily at the political administration as part of a design to bend its will and prevent it from acceding to a specific extradition request, or complying with its treaty obligations, or to change its policy on extradition, or to hasten the electoral defeat of the ruling party. In areas where policy-targeted actors have histories of violence and the capability to deliver it, violence may be used as an event veto or a policy veto. In Colombia, in the 1980s and 1990s, extraditions triggered narco-terrorism, which targeted politicians, judges, police and military personnel, and other state and government officials by using indiscriminate means of violence such as bombs (see Thoumi 2003, 203–7).

As noted elsewhere (Harriott 2008b), the threat to the Jamaican state was and is primarily internal via a corrupt erosion of its institutional capabilities and character. This was confirmed by the events that were associated with the extradition of Coke. The extradition proceedings upset the arrangements and the particular relationship between the Presidential Click and the JLP and forced an open confrontation with the Presidential Click.[45]

The Presidential Click initiated the violent stage of the process. Fourteen police stations in the city were attacked. These actions demonstrated the offensive capability of the Presidential Click and may have been intended to confirm the fears that any attempt to enter Tivoli Gardens would result in a major violent clash extending well beyond that community and even beyond the city of Kingston.

The armed confrontations with the security forces illuminated the capabilities of the Presidential Click and its neighbouring allies. The large gun and improvised explosive device (IED) finds were already noted in chapter 1. Given Jamaica's small size, these capabilities suggest that groups such as the Presidential Click may be rightly viewed as potential national security threats (see Government of Jamaica 2012).[46] Its garrison safe haven, access to resources on a large scale from multiple sources, its alliances and relationships, and state mimicking activities, all contributed to enabling this level and quality of threat.

The results of the violent confrontation with the security forces were seventy-one persons dead (revised from seventy-three)[47] including one soldier.[48] Six constables and fourteen soldiers and an unknown number of gang members and bystander citizens were injured by gunfire, and shrapnel injured another four soldiers.[49] The economic costs were estimated to be in the billions of Jamaican dollars (Buddan 2011).

An analysis of the available information on the dead revealed that they were from eight of Jamaica's fourteen parishes. Only 33 per cent were residents of Tivoli Gardens. Some 30 per cent were from neighbouring communities. Others were from distant cities such as Montego Bay, which is in the western end of the island, distant towns such as Morant Bay in the east, and distant villages such as Devon in central Jamaica.[50] It is reasonable to suggest that fighters were represented among the dead. The wide geographic representation of the "fighters" confirms the fairly extensive mobilizable network of the Presidential Click.[51] One of these, Cedric Murray of the Stone Crusher group, which was one of the more violent organized crime groups in the city of Montego Bay, left behind a diary which revealed an unsurprisingly high degree of commitment to his crime career and a surprisingly strong loyalty to "the Coke family".[52]

Some new features in the response of the state marked the operation. The operation was pushed to the point of a collapse of the armed resistance and a rout of the Presidential Click. Moreover, the security forces did not withdraw from the community, thereby allowing a return to the status quo ante. The community remains occupied by the police. Political conditions made these outcomes possible, and subsequently, political protection was lost. Prior to this, such operations would end in a stalemate with the security forces withdrawing from the community without achieving their objectives. This was the case in 2001 when twenty-three persons were killed.[53] Stalemate would be achieved by political mobilization around claims that such operations were motivated by partisan political considerations or that the behaviour of the police and military was partisan. For this reason, they were excessive and even careless in their use of violence. The point here is not whether the latter is or is not an accurate claim, but rather that, true or false, such claims are employed at critical times in order to neutralize the operations of the security forces and or limit the accomplishment of their goals.[54]

In 2010, it was difficult to politicize the military-police operation as partisan victimization by the security forces. Moreover, the political efforts to block the arrest and extradition of Coke had failed prior to the operation. Any further effort at open political mobilization along these lines during the operation would have been exceedingly risky for a prime minister and ruling party. Former prime minister and former member of parliament for Western Kingston Edward Seaga nevertheless sharply criticized then-prime minister and member of parliament, Bruce Golding, for "abandoning" the community and for not stopping the operation (which he had the legal authority to do). Thus, former prime minister Seaga (2009) continued: "You must remember that the Member of Parliament is also the Prime Minister and he is the one who makes the decision . . . *He can make the decision to stop it.* Why is he not doing so? But I can only tell you that since he has become Prime Minister he has neglected the area."

According to Seaga (2009), "What was happening in Tivoli was bringing out the problem of this country – the coalition of the classes against the masses. It does not matter how many poor people died down there." For him, the operation was literal class warfare against the poor (*Jamaica Observer*, 30 May 2010, 6–7). By this line of argument, Golding had failed to act in a manner that was consistent with past patterns of politically intervening to prevent a breach of the defences of Tivoli Gardens and an overrun of the Presidential Click. The fighters of the Presidential Click may have counted on the operation of June 2010 to follow this pattern. This seems to have been the expectation. In his diary, Cedric Murray notes, "On the Day of war . . . all hell broke loose . . . *more than we expect* but yet still again babylon[55] prove how they are even worst [*sic*] than the gunman" ("Diary of a Killer: Gangster Longed to Go Out with Woman", *Jamaica Observer*, 3 September 2010). Golding had also failed to effectively employ the political victimization and class victimization narratives in defence of the Presidential Click and Tivoli Gardens. The script had been written. The problem was Golding's unwillingness or inability to follow it, not the criminality of the Presidential Click.

The occupation of the community by the police created the opportunity to de-garrison it. The community was no longer closed to law enforcement, but it remained closed to the competitor political parties. The Opposition PNP saw an opportunity; however, this was not an opportunity for an agreement to end the garrison phenomenon, but rather to end the particular garrison of Tivoli.[56]

Such a posture invited defensiveness on the part of their competitor party, the JLP, which would have lost its monopoly. This moment may have been a missed opportunity to truly erode the garrison communities. Even though the political elite failed to fully grasp the moment, if even just the first step of opening up the community to law enforcement were to succeed, it could possibly improve the country's crime situation by ending immunity from law enforcement.

The rout of the Presidential Click and the degrading of its capabilities and organizational capacities removed any immediate possibility of it continuing to be a national security threat. The Presidential Click and the Shower network have a long history of violence, access to the means of violence and a protective community or staging area from which to launch any violent operation. They administered the everyday violence that maintained and projected their power in the community via their brand of informal justice. They commercially exploited their reputation for violence through extortion and protection rackets, and they are known for using violence in support of the political/electoral goals of the party to which they were affiliated. They also provided a safe haven for members of allied gangs. Suppressing the Presidential Click and the Shower network was thus a big effort against violent crimes. The challenge was to seize the opportunity that was presented by the operation against the Presidential Click and to transform the operation into a national campaign against gangs and garrison communities and for violence reduction.

The Third or Post-Extradition Phase: A National Anti-Gang Campaign

It was quickly evident that the goal of the security forces was not simply to capture Coke. They proceeded to take control of Tivoli Gardens and hoisted the national flag on one of the tall buildings in that community. The hoisting of the national flag symbolized a claim to previously uncontrolled (by law enforcement) territory and may have signified an agenda that included ending the garrison phenomenon or initiating a process of de-garrisonization.[57] The operation in Tivoli Gardens also quickly progressed into an anti-gang (or at least an anti-gang violence) campaign that went beyond Tivoli Gardens. The state of emergency and the momentary political and social consensus provided the opportunity for this phase of the operation-turned-campaign. It is this going beyond Tivoli Gardens and pursuing a national campaign that explain the subsequent general decline in violent crimes nationally.[58]

The national campaign targeted the most powerful and violent gangs and organized crime groupings, arrested gang leaders and operatives in mass numbers, seized the cash and assets of selected gang leaders, and implemented community-based or targeted social prevention strategies. This last element will be discussed in the next case, as it was not very pronounced in the response efforts in Tivoli Gardens.

Any attempt to significantly reduce gang violence by degrading the capabilities and breaking the power of a group such as the Presidential Click, demands the arrest of its leaders and main operatives; it also necessitates moving beyond national boundaries and similarly arresting important members of its transnational network.[59] Such an approach had earlier served to pacify the gangs of Port-au-Prince in Haiti and sharply reduced the then-frequent kidnappings and reversed the increasing murder rate.[60] Moreover, following an armed clash with the security forces in which some seventy persons were killed, mass arrests were inevitable. The state of emergency provided the legal basis for these arrests.

Approximately forty-six hundred persons were detained and processed during the period of the campaign, which began and ended with the state of emergency, that is, 23 May to 22 July 2010 ("Amnesty Backs Tivoli Commission of Enquiry", *Jamaica Observer*, 23 May 2011).[61] Those detained included some one thousand persons from Tivoli Gardens and the larger West Kingston area.[62] Many of the leaders of territorially based organized crime groups and street gangs were arrested in addition to lower-level operatives and gunmen. What was most revealing about the "high value" detainees was the state of their records. Several had rather bare criminal records.[63] The pattern of detentions suggests that the security forces did a broad sweep rather than retaining a strict focus on the gang leaders, main enablers and killers.

Police appeared to select targets without the influence of party competitive politics, because gangs aligned with either party were suppressed. Claims of political bias therefore did not enter the discussion and did not contribute to unravelling the political consensus. Broadening the scope of the campaign threatened sections of the society and leadership of the political parties. Politicians dissented and eventually changed their positions because the broad sweep detained too many persons for too long. Many detainees were simply processed and released without being charged.

Police excess occurred despite the safeguards that were put in place by the political administration. These safeguards included an independent tribunal, which heard appeals by detainees. In some instances, these appeals were successful and the appellants were released. This approach reflects a new sensitivity to the abuse of power. It represents an advance in the use of suppression on a national scale and the administration of states of emergency. Such safeguards are likely to promote the use of this extreme measure to curb ordinary criminality, but only if it proves to be effective as a safeguard against the abuse of power.

Fuelled by the excessive detentions and high death toll, objections to the national anti-gang campaign thus took the form of objections to the state of emergency. These objections empowered the security forces, particularly their freedom to detain suspects. At the levels of society and polity, the traditional method of gang-crime suppression by means of the state of emergency, collapsed. The distrust of a security apparatus with extraordinary powers was too great. The opposition PNP called for an end to the state of emergency and the ruling JLP agreed ("State of Emergency To Be Lifted", *Gleaner*, 20 July 2010). The state of emergency was terminated on 22 July 2010.

With the end of the state of emergency, the national anti-gang campaign may have lost some of its momentum, but the police were able to continue the campaign by adjusting some of their tactics. If criminal suspects could not be taken off the streets, their assets could be taken from the banks. Assets forfeiture has been named as a critical aspect of the anti-gang strategy of law enforcement (Amiot and Foster 2011, 29–32).[64] Effective assets forfeiture may powerfully show that criminal success, and particularly flaunting or advertising a criminal lifestyle, may be temporary and will invariably trigger a criminal investigation. If successful, assets forfeiture would reduce the referent power of gang leaders and reduce their ability to employ corrupt means to further accumulate wealth and to purchase immunity from law enforcement.

Given the difficulties with the investigation of gang-related street crimes, the police attempted to go after the criminally acquired money and wealth of gang leaders. In pursuit of this goal, the mothers and girlfriends of these suspects were arrested on the grounds that they were the holders of these funds and assets (typically held in bank accounts and as homes and vehicles). Criminally acquired wealth hidden in business and co-mingled with legitimate funds presented additional (capability/capacity) challenges for the JCF. This type of action, when viewed in the context of the law enforcement seizure initiative, marked a new level of effort and determination as well as some administrative progress with the formation of an Assets Recovery Agency.

These actions also revealed the weakness and incapacities of law enforcement as the above-described effort resulted in little success with assets forfeiture. An attempt was made to seize cash held by Justin O'Gilvie, an alleged business partner of Coke, via some of the companies that are suspected to be controlled by Coke, such as Incomparable Enterprises Limited and Bulls Eye Security Services. In 2012, the Supreme Court of Jamaica ruled, however, that Justin O'Gilvie be freed and the cash returned to him (Gayle 2012). Earlier in the same year, the court similarly ruled that cash which had been seized from Donald Phipps, the then-leader of another organized crime grouping (the Spanglers), be returned to him ("Millions to 'Zeeks'", *Gleaner*, 23 October 2012). Taken together, these developments are a major setback for law enforcement, whose efforts seem to be focused on seizing cash. Cash seizures are usually the outcome of opportunities presented during raids and interceptions. They are not typically the result of investigations, hence leading to the difficulties in court. Asset seizures require investigations that are intended to result in the forfeiture of the targeted assets. Law enforcement suffers from capacity problems and inexperience in this field of investigation. These problems must be solved if the recent advances in crime control are to be consolidated.

Despite the problems, a bold action was taken by the security forces. The assault on powerful gangs and the politically unbiased prosecution of the national campaign resulted in increased confidence in the police. At the end of 2010, some 77 per cent of a sample representing Jamaica's population reported that they had "a great deal" or "some amount" of confidence in the police to "effectively control crime" in the country (CHDR 2012, 106). The level of confidence in the "ability of the police to control gang violence", however, remained fairly low at 23.4 per cent (p. 85). The more general levels of confidence in the JCF have since fallen, but they remain much higher than the traditional very low of the previous decade (Harriott et al. 2013; Powell et al. 2006, 27). The high levels of generalized confidence have resulted in increased citizen participation in gang-crime suppression. For example, in 2010, there was a 100 per cent increase in calls to Crime Stop, most of which were reports on illegal weapons.[65] Some 10 per cent of these calls resulted in gun finds and/or arrests. The performances of the JCF and JDF during the national anti-gang campaign have yielded benefits that have not quickly evaporated. Important among these benefits are animating itself and the general population. The challenge is to further consolidate these gains.

The Fourth Phase: Consolidation?

Consolidating the gains of the campaign, that is, the reduction in serious crimes and the reduced capabilities and power of the major gangs and organized crime groupings in the country, entails first, the prevention of gang dominance of the communities. For Tivoli Gardens, this means, "de-garrisoning" that community. The garrison is a form of local political administration.[66] De-garrisoning a community therefore means changing its form of political administration or local regime type and, with this, the relationship of community to the state and the methods and structures of community governance. It involves ending the Presidential Click's participation in the political administration of the community and abolishing the structures of its co-rule including its "courts". For this to occur, the power of that group must be broken and its relationship to the locally dominant political party and important political actors who facilitate access to state resources and protection as immunity from law enforcement scrutinized and severed.[67] It also means ending the collective benefits that the community derives from crime, normalizing its relationship with law enforcement and better integrating the community.[68]

The garrison is the outcome of interactions between interested parties with shared interests including the political party which enjoys a monopoly, the gangs that enjoy a crime monopoly and the residents who, as a collective, enjoy many benefits that no other member of society is able to.[69] De-garrisoning is thus a very difficult task as it involves confronting the political parties which are powerful national institutions, in addition to confronting the members of these communities who are active agents in its maintenance and reproduction.

At the core of the administration of the garrison is self-help policing and "justice". Ending self-policing is thus an important aspect of de-garrisoning. For the police, the major challenge of this fourth phase reaches beyond community occupation to normal policing based on a measure of community consent and cooperation. This means, in the first instance, replacing the range of services that the gang provided. These replacement services should be provided with approximate responsiveness and efficiency. Gang-provided security was efficient and effective. There were channels of communication between the gang leaders and the residents of the community through which incidents of criminal victimization of community members could be and indeed were reported, and punishment was swift, certain, severe and unencumbered by law. Some of these cases are described in Charles and Beckford (2012). Consequently, the reported (and actual) crime rate was known to be very low. Thus, to the extent that the expectations of the community are based on the standards of efficiency and effectiveness that they had known under the community administration of the Presidential Click, the police would have great difficulty meeting that standard and winning the confidence of the people. In these community settings, introducing normal police should not mean operating at the normal standards of effectiveness. These communities demand a higher standard.

The JCF has established a permanent post in Tivoli Gardens, which is located at the former office of the former president of the Presidential Click. Initially, the strength of the post was eighty-five constables yielding a police density of 1:118. Later, and at the time of writing (in 2013), the police density in that community was reduced to 1:174, which is higher than the national police density (1:237).[70] The place is not highly overpoliced. The force requirements to de-garrison these communities and effect a local regime change may be attended by initial abuses of power but do not appear to threaten Jamaica's democracy.[71] Once these communities are "normalized" by routing the dominating criminal group and forming the right relationship with the population, the personnel requirements for police, even community policing, may not be beyond the resources that are already available to the JCF. This experience has been generalized. Small units are now being permanently placed in the high-crime communities across Jamaica. These permanent posts may be used as launching pads from which to pacify the communities. They present the JCF with an opportunity to consolidate a new relationship with these communities on the basis of better service, open channels of citizen participation and direct accountability.

Nevertheless, there are difficulties in meeting the expectations of the people. Residents have publicly voiced complaints that the crime rate in the community of Tivoli Gardens has been increasing since the extradition of their "president" and the transition from gang-provided security to police-provided security ("Dudus' Shadow Stalks: Leadership Vacuum Evident West Kingston Residents Say", *Gleaner*, 30 September 2012, A4). Anti-police manifestations include children throwing garbage and rocks at the police from rooftops ("Police Under Attack in Tivoli", *Gleaner*, 5 March 2011); a shunning of voluntary interaction with the police, especially by young males; and the general treatment of the police as alien and unwanted occupiers. These developments confirm that a change in citizen-police relations and in the style of policing these communities is an important element in the attempts to consolidate the advances that have been made in this and other similar communities. Much is required of both the police and the citizens.

The people within the community and beyond its borders anticipated these troubles. Interestingly, a *Gleaner* poll suggested that 69 per cent of the population felt that crime would increase if Coke were extradited ("We Are Doomed: Extraditing Coke Will Drive Up Crime", *Gleaner*, 15 June 2010).[72] This level of

community (and national) permissiveness adds to the difficulties of consolidation as de-garrisoning the community. The operation and the high death toll, the
feeling of isolation, and tensions with the rest of society may have been expected
to foster a greater community cohesion that enfolds the criminal structures.
And yet the people, particularly the larger national population, despite their
permissive attitude toward Coke and those gang leaders that offer protective
and other services, also condemned the administration's apparent defence of
Coke. These are the complexities of the Jamaican situation. It is not just governments that are given to ambivalence, but also sections of the population. People
tolerate and even support the gangs because of the services that they provide,
even though they seem to prefer a better alternative.

Crime has its obvious social and economic costs, but it also has its benefits.
Among other things, consolidating change as de-garrisoning turns upon the
ability of the state to demonstrate to these communities that the benefits of
crime are less than the benefits of normalization. The community has suffered
loss of benefits that were attributable to crime. These include the loss of some
sources of income, for example, from entertainment events that were made
possible because the Presidential Click guaranteed the protection of the event.
The loss of welfare benefits affects the entire community. For example, while
(as noted in chapter 1) prior to 2010 less than 1 per cent of households paid
electricity bills, since then, all are required to pay because the gang is no longer
able to block the collection efforts of the power company (JPS). However, the
greatest loss comes from the loss of protection and security. Jaffe (2012) arrives
at a similar conclusion based on her work in the neighbouring community
of Mathews Lane in the period after Donald Phipps (the former leader of the
Spanglers, an organized crime grouping based in that community) was arrested
and imprisoned. The groups that are most at risk of victimization stand to lose
the most. This includes the women who are at risk of being raped. The gangs
have a reputation for protecting the female residents of their communities. This
partly explains the support that these gangs, including the Presidential Click,
enjoy among women. Security is highly valued, particularly by the more vulnerable subpopulations. Women therefore feel that they have a lot to lose if the
gang is destroyed.

In order to compensate for a perceived loss of security, the state must protect
the residents of the community, including its more vulnerable groups. Policing
by permanent presence and introducing a new relationship to these communities based on respect for citizens' rights and accountability would offset the
loss of gang protection. It would also add freedom from the abuses of the gang

including its "right" of sexual access to the young women of the community. Community must on balance become a winner in the process of de-garrisoning. Security, greater freedom of political choice, freedom from the arbitrary rule of the garrison bosses, and better integration into formal social opportunity structures hold the possibility for a better life.

Gang members should also have the possibility to become winners while the gang as a group becomes a big loser. Gang reduction strategies may be more effective when they involve elements that are specifically designed for the rehabilitation and integration of gang members. This element is not present in the case of the Presidential Click. The short-term outcomes for the Presidential Click included:

- The loss of its leader and his exposure as a "drug kingpin". Coke's appearance in a court of law permitted some exposure of his activity. This does not happen to a similar degree when gang leaders are killed and when some plea bargains are struck, thereby sealing the case. Exposure tarnishes their image. Coke was now an "international drug lord" with responsibility for various atrocities.
- The loss of reputation as inviolable and unassailable.
- Loss of information to the police who now know a lot more about the gang.
- Loss of dominance of the community, including the power to make rules and enforce them. This loss of dominance is symbolized by the presence of a police post at the office of the "president".
- The risk of loss of assets.
- Gang fragmentation. The group has been split. It is clear that the Presidential Click will need time to recover, and it may never return to having the power and dominance in the community that it had.

Interventions that are directly aimed at supporting gang members who wish to leave the gangs and to end their criminal careers are an important aspect of consolidation. Gang intervention, when applied to groups that are at the apex of the illegal opportunity structure, such as the Presidential Click, presents gang-exit programmes with the issue of how to generate worthwhile replacement income and alternate opportunities for gang members. To be effective and lasting, interventions should include this element. This problem is, however, overestimated and thus viewed as the major obstacle. There are two related impediments. First, the income, and thus the income replacement, are overestimated. The available evidence on the wages of lower-level operatives and police estimates of the personal assets of the leaders of selected organized crime groupings suggest that income distribution in the underground economy is characterized by great inequality. It further suggests that income inequality in the underground sector of the economy may be even greater than inequality in the formal sector. There are thus similar feelings of unjust treatment and mobility constraints in both sectors. This inequality is, for example, revealed in the stratification in Tivoli Gardens where location in the hierarchy of the Presidential Click may be predicted from the material comforts of the apartments and other status markers. The level of inequality would have been more glaring if the palatial homes of the leaders of the Click and previous leaders were to be removed from the upper-middle-class areas of the city and relocated in Tivoli Gardens. Those at the bottom of the gang's hierarchy earn very little. As a general rule, their income is less than proceeds of their individual efforts; for example, robberies are put into a pool of funds that is then administered by the leader.[73] The only way for these low-level operatives to access a much larger share of the funds that they illicitly acquire, they must "rob" the "president" by withholding some of these funds. In so doing, they place their lives and the welfare of their families at risk. Those at the bottom live very precarious lives.

Given the relative weights of the risks and rewards that are presented to those gang operatives who are at the base of these groups, it is not so difficult to develop effective gang-exit interventions for them. The challenge has less to do with the quantum earned, and more to do with the lack of alternatives for earning an income. Many gang-involved persons are unprepared for employment and functioning in conventional contexts of mutual support, interdependence and trust, that is, where there are no enemies and where they are stripped of their subcultural status-giving identities and roles. They are required to habituate themselves to new patterns of interaction with others. This is not simply a matter of cultivating new social skills. It may present those who are deeply invested in subcultures with more profound issues, such as having to grapple with their notions of authenticity.

Given these and other legitimate political considerations, in the wake of the Tivoli Gardens operation of 2010 and the dislocation of the people, emergency "jobs" were provided to residents of that community by the local government authorities ("Cemetery Clean-Up May Meet Early Death", *Gleaner*, 16 June 2010). They resembled temporary patronage jobs that are understood by all to be patronage jobs. They do not make the behavioural change demands of conventional jobs.

More generally, these responses are unable to resolve the problems that accompany the potential to reinforce criminality by making the state responsible for replacing crime-dependent income and welfare. Political administrations have not yet resolved the problem of responding to crime-related crises in ways that avoid signalling that violence may be a way of getting attention and accessing resources on the terms of those making the demands. One way of solving this problem is by enabling gang-involved youth and members of gang-dominated communities so that they may have greater and more equal access to opportunities, while not unfairly overallocating resources to these communities, as employment- and business-related grants. In the case of the garrison communities, as is indicated above, because of their close ties to the political parties and ability to leverage their political capital, the evidence points to their privileged access to state resources (relative to other communities of the urban and rural poor).

The second impediment is the belief that replacement income must be better than the income that would be gained from middle- to high-end illegal opportunities. Several gang members wish a different life. They would take lower-paying jobs as a part of a pathway out of gangs and crime. In a recent study of street gangs in Kingston, Levy found a preference for and willingness to participate in legitimate income-earning projects (Levy et al. 2012). Similar findings have been produced elsewhere. Hagedorn "found that older gang members are not necessarily committed to long-term participation in the drug economy – many would prefer full-time legitimate jobs, even with low wages" (Hagedorn 1994).[74] This finding is particularly true for members of common street gangs that are not involved in high-income rackets, but it also holds true for lower-level operatives in organized crime groupings like Presidential Click.

The willingness to take lower-paying legitimate income may be increased by coordinating this option with suppression that targets the illegal opportunity structures. By increasing the risks that are associated with illegal income-generating activity, the limited legitimate opportunities may become relatively more attractive options. Social interventions and deterrence are thereby made to operate together, and therefore, more effectively. Using the logic of deterrence may, therefore, also make the case for a comprehensive approach.[75]

Gang interventions, however, require more than income replacement. Other problems, especially the security concerns of gang members, have to be solved. They need programmes that help them to adapt to conventional lives. It is necessary to pave the pathway to a new life in society, and this involves considerable problem solving and a more comprehensive approach.

After the operation of May 2010 and the accompanying national and international attention that was given to Coke and the more general gang problem, the political administration advocated for a more comprehensive approach to violence reduction.[76] As then-prime minister Golding noted in a statement that was delivered during a sitting of parliament:

> Rooting out the criminal networks and changing the culture of garrison politics cannot be achieved purely by law-enforcement efforts. That is a necessary part of the process but it has to be accompanied by a programme of transformation to fill the space now occupied by dons and crime practitioners, to provide for the people in these vulnerable communities a new pathway of hope and opportunity. The state must reassert both its authority and responsibility in these communities. But it must be a helpful – not hostile – state.[77]

This programme of transformation has not materialized in Tivoli Gardens, although the "one hundred communities" programme holds some promise for that community. Tivoli remains largely a case of suppression and demonstrates both its successes and its limits. This case therefore remains highly susceptible to reversals. Indeed, after the initial post-2010 disorganization and fragmentation, by 2013 (that is, at the time of writing) the Presidential Click had begun to regroup. This process of re-grouping was occurred in the phase of an intense battle for the leadership of the group. Leadership succession battles were at first an intra-family contest between Christopher Coke's son and his senior brother. A challenge from the kin of an earlier leader added to the level of violence as two violent campaigns were being fought: one for succession by contenders within the Coke kinship group, and the other for a takeover of the group by members of a re-emergent family that was associated with the leadership of the group prior to the rise of the Cokes.[78] Both families claim hereditary rights to the leadership of the group. The latter conflict is likely to increase the cohesiveness, and thus the resilience, of the group. Ultimately, it is the internal relationships of the group and its relationship with the community and the political party to which it is affiliated that are the primary sources of its strength – not its armed capabilities, income streams or even its organizational complexity. Organized crime groupings that have deep and strong ties and enjoy significant community support are not easily "dismantled".

Conclusion

The Coke case instantiates strategy prior to its written form as the AGSP. There are gaps between practices and the written strategy. The actual practices described here provide a basis to further refine strategy and perfect practice. The advances that have been made are not just the outcomes of muddling through. There have been advances in thinking, in institutional configuration and capabilities, in building partnerships, in programme design and perhaps even in the implementation of these programmes. Future success depends on supplementary learning and better implementation. There is much experience that may be further distilled for valuable lessons.

Aspects of the anti-gang strategy appear to account for the violence reduction outcomes. Targeted gang suppression has yielded positive results, but control and prevention have moved beyond suppression as a stand-alone approach to a more integrated strategy that incorporates deterrence-driven, social prevention. This approach is likely to yield a more sustainable reduction in the rates of violent crimes, as long as the programmes are not too ambitious and do not overextend the resources of the implementing institutions. There have been considerable advances in the development of institutions that are able to design and implement social interventions. Several such organizations now exist within and beyond the state. If properly coordinated, programme implementation may become more effective.

Improved community integration has presented opportunities for de-garrisoning the gang-dominated communities. For these extreme but high-impact cases, breaking crime dependency, improving access to legitimate opportunities and increasing attachment to the helping and opportunity-creating institutions which operate in the mainstream of the society appear to result in greater commitment to conventional norms and means of achieving one's life goals.

If these processes described in this chapter are to be consolidated, both the state and the people must seek changes. In all of the communities, there were significant sections of their populations and an emergent leadership that were willing to work for change in concert with external actors, particularly the state agencies. Because the power shifted from gangs to pro-social community elements, greater participation of the people via democratic participatory channels is likely to stimulate a more robust informal social control that is directed against delinquent and gang-affiliated youth.

The case of Coke, the Presidential Click and Tivoli Gardens encapsulates the advances, the difficulties and further possibilities for violence reduction and gang prevention and control in Jamaica. The advances in strategy have yielded lower rates of violence and a decline in the power and influence of the gangs. Gang suppression has had immediate and significant impact and in concert with social prevention programmes, these results have been sustained over three years. This period is not a long time. There may be reversals before Jamaica arrives at a turning point in its efforts to control its violence and gang problems. The prevention programmes are yet to be evaluated, but their independent impact is expected to be more medium-term in helping to consolidate the gains from suppression. The Jamaican authorities should seek to further refine their anti-gang strategy, as well as look beyond it. For an instance of a more comprehensive approach to gang control and prevention, we next turn to a discussion of the case of the Spanglers of Mathews Lane (see chapter 8).

Notes

1. The source of this data is the statistics unit of the Jamaica Constabulary Force (JCF). The annual statistical reports of the JCF are published in the *Economic and Social Survey of Jamaica*. It is estimated that only 20 per cent of all crimes are reported to the police, but the reporting of violent crimes much more closely approximates the true rates. Thus, for example, at least 95 per cent of all homicides enter the police statistics. Crime trends may be validated using multiple time-point observations from victimization survey data. The LAPOP Survey of 2012 (Harriott et al. 2013) and the Jamaica Victimization Survey of 2012 may be used to externally validate the decline in reported serious crimes. There is every indication that both support the claim that serious crimes have declined since 2010.

2. To borrow from the language of economics, the supply of violence is inelastic. It is thus appropriate to refer to the return on protection rackets as rent.

3. Multiple sources confirm the violent entrepreneurial character to this group including the transcript of Coke's sentencing hearing: C5M9COK1, *United States District Court, Southern District of New York, United States of America v. Christopher Michael Coke* 07CR0971 (RPP).

4. In high-violence areas inter-gang violence may have consequences for entire sets of communities and may truly endanger the lives and dislocate the daily routines of the populations, including work and school attendance. Such violence is warlike in its consequences.

5. The data source is the World Bank, which reports a Gini index of 59.9 for 2011, as cited in Harriott et al. (2013, 43).

6. Long cycles are not yet observable and in any event would not be attributable to retaliatory dynamics. Deeper long-range processes would have to be probed, perhaps processes that are associated with the subculture of violence and/or the formation of large monopoly-holding gangs such as the Presidential Click.

7. These would also perhaps be what Levy et al. (2012) call "corner crews".

8. The increases after 2010 may be partly due to gang fragmentation after the assault on the major territorial organized crime groups and street gangs by law enforcement. Even though it is occurring in the context of a decline in the power and influence of

the major gangs and organized crime groups, it underscores the delicate state of the moment and the possibility of early reversals in the gang-control efforts of the state.

9. The JCF/National Intelligence Bureau estimates of the number of gangs tend to fall within this range. At the time of writing (2013), according to the Government of Jamaica NSP (2012), the estimate was 250 "gangs". Parts of St Andrew are rural but most gangs are in the urban areas which are parts of the city.

10. This calculation is based on the aggregated areas of the parishes of Kingston and St Andrew, which include rural areas. City-level information was not available. Gang density is therefore grossly underestimated.

11. Obika Gray (2001, 2004) has proffered a characterization of the state as "parasitic". This position has much merit, but the supporting evidence that has been presented is still rather thin.

12. The undue political influence on the police force has not ended, but instead, it has declined because an unwilling police commissioner has the force of law on his or her side.

13. It is understandable that the JCF would wish to avoid any discussion of such openly political issues.

14. Computed using homicide counts that were provided by the JCF and the population estimates published in the Economic and Social Survey of Jamaica for the respective years.

15. Frequency counts are used as they are quite suitable for making the points that are made here.

16. In 2001, the Presidential Click and the Spanglers negotiated an agreement that divided the downtown area of the city of Kingston for purposes of criminal exploitation. The major gangs were later all allocated exploitable territory with clear boundaries. This had the effect of reducing gang violence. I thank Tarik Weeks for helping me to confirm and date this agreement.

17. Localized police gang-suppression efforts were already fairly intense and may also have contributed to the decline in violent crimes.

18. Unlike with the aggregated homicide statistics, the data on this category of homicide are of doubtful reliability. There are issues of definitional and coding consistency. They are nevertheless helpful for a rough estimation of the problem and trends.

19. The difficulty with the analysis of the data reported above (as supporting evidence for the claim that the reduction in gang-related homicides in the main accounts for the decline in the homicide rate) is that while the homicide counts are reliable and accurate (they represent at least 95 per cent of the homicide count), the subcategories such as gang-related murder are not reliable. They at best crudely capture the broad picture.

20. I did this for an earlier period but not for the period under review in this chapter.

21. The JCF provided the data, but the author is responsible for any error of computation.

22. In 2012, gang-related murders accounted for 69 per cent of all murders in St James. The corresponding proportion for the city of Kingston was 71 per cent.

23. Being proactive here means responding to gang-related violence in ways such that retaliatory violence by the aggrieved party is avoided and the violence is not escalated. Letting gang members kill each other is not a solution to the gang problem. It promotes feelings of impunity among gang members.

24. I was kindly permitted to see the minutes of its meetings.

25. Computed by the author.

26. At the time of writing, the latter was merged with the former.

27. The promotional material of the group at times uses the spelling "Spanglas".

28. Robust community participation carries the risk of political pressure for the redirection of resources to where they may not yield the best gang-control outcomes.

29. Small NGOs typically do not have the expertise to properly design such programmes, nor do they have the project management and evaluation competences. Like the state agencies, they therefore contribute best as partners in a cooperative effort.

30. These operations and programmes preceded the elaboration of the strategy in its written form as JCF 2011.

31. The use of the word Click reveals the US influences on the gang. It is a term used and made popular by gangs whose members are predominantly of Hispanic origin or ancestry.

32. See C5M9COK1 *United States District Court, Southern District of New York, United States of America v. Christopher Michael Coke* 07CR0971 (RPP), 64–65.

33. See C5M9COK1 *United States District Court, Southern District of New York, United States of America v. Christopher Michael Coke* 07CR0971 (RPP), 46.

34. See Figueroa (1994) for a discussion of this phenomenon.

35. It is not clear to this author that the Shower as a transnational network has a single leader. There is however evidence in the court records to support the view that Christopher Coke was revered and treated as leader-like. It is for this reason that Coke is described as the symbolic (not executive) leader of the Shower.

36. At the time of writing, this was the best available estimate. The 2001 census was already twelve years old, and the new census is not yet available. The estimate is based on survey methodology and was done in 2011 by the Social Development Commission, Governrnent of Jamaica; see the *Tivoli Gardens Community Profile*, March 2012. It is unlikely that the population of Tivoli Gardens could have grown so rapidly over the period since the 2001 census. Despite the exactness with which it is presented, the 2010 estimate should be taken as just that, an estimate. Less rigorous estimates are as high as twenty thousand persons.

37. This was learned from personal communication on March 2013, with a former executive officer of the SDC who administratively authorized these payments.

38. Conceivably, a neighbourhood could be garrisoned. Community, as entailing a fair measure of cohesiveness, a shared sense of belonging, and common identity, is thus not a necessary precondition for a garrison.

39. The community of Tivoli Gardens and the constituency of Western Kingston have been represented by two prime ministers and three party leaders. This level of representation has given Tivoli Gardens privileged access to the resources of the state.
40. These data are presented in Rodgers and Muggah (2009, 309).
41. It could also be argued that such an approach is inspired by or at least is consistent with the much celebrated American pragmatism. If an approach or method works in terms of achieving a desired outcome, then it is justified. This tendency is also evident in the post-9/11 public debate on the use of torture against terrorism suspects which has been occurring in the United States.
42. Morrison's notice of appeal was "misplaced" by the staff at the Registry at the Court of Appeal. The Jamaican government attempted to correct the problem by call for the return of Morrison but the US government did not comply. For additional information, see Spaulding (2013).
43. In the case of Norris Barnes, an alleged drug trafficker, the extradition process was completely circumvented, and he was simply spirited out of the country.
44. The population of females is estimated to be some eleven thousand. The demonstrators therefore represented more than 10 per cent of the adult women.
45. The strains in the relationship between party and gang were personalized and described as a strain in the relationship between Coke and Golding. This set the stage for an easy restoration of the old party Presidential Click/Shower relationship.
46. The Presidential Click was not a security threat in the sense of being an independent political actor operating outside of the political system/institutions and seeking to challenge it by use of force. It was and is a within-system actor. It was a security threat in the sense that it demonstrated the ability to direct violence at law enforcement as a means of blocking state actions against it and was able to do this on a scale that was national in its impact.
47. There are various estimates of the death toll. The initial number of seventy-three included persons who were killed outside of the area of the operation but were considered to be related deaths. This subgroup includes two police officers. The official number given by the security forces is therefore seventy-one to seventy-three, depending on how the count is done. The list of the dead that was made available to me is that of sixty-nine civilians. There have been reports of missing persons who are presumed to be dead. The final count is therefore likely to be higher than the seventy-one. The Office of the Public Defender (2013, 58) claims to have identified seventy-six known civilians who were killed during the operation.
48. The high death toll has sullied the operation. The Office of the Public Defender has been probing the alleged excessive use of violence and abuses of power by the security forces.
49. The JDF Headquarters provided these facts on the JDF casualties on 30 September 2013. The Report of the Office of the Public Defender (2013, 23) cites police sources as reporting the number of security personnel injured (on 24 May 2010) as

six. Police sources have confirmed that six constables were injured. The number of injured soldiers was not included in that count.

50. Thirteen of the dead were unidentified.

51. A list of the dead and some basic demographic data on their ages, sex and place of residence among other items were kindly given to the author by the JCF on my request. This was done in 2010. The computations are based on these data.

52. Although where group cohesion and high loyalty may be expected, Jamaican criminals are not generally known for this virtue. As is the case in the larger society, criminal groups typically display low levels of trust. Loyalty is usually associated with trust, not distrust. Excerpts from Murray's diary were published in "Diary of a Killer: Gangster Longed to Go Out with Woman", *Jamaica Observer*, 3 September 2010.

53. As noted above, there have been several accounts of this event, with various estimates of the death toll. For example, see the Report of the Commission of Inquiry (2002) into the "Upsurge of Violence since May 2001 in the Kingston Metropolitan Area".

54. For one such instance, see "Reneto Adams: More Lives Than a Cat", *Jamaica Observer*, 24 June 2012.

55. Typically used to refer to the police.

56. There were also contrary and more constructive vices, but these were not are pronounced in the news media.

57. As noted earlier, garrisons are not ungoverned territory. They have access to state services. It is law enforcement that is blocked. De-garrisonization would thus include, among other things, eliminating the informal gang-controlled enforcement and punishments and normalizing policing in this and other similar communities. For a discussion of de-garrisoning, see the report of the National Committee on Political Tribalism (1997).

58. The state of emergency was not extended beyond the parishes of Kingston, St Andrew and St Catherine, but the campaign was extended to other parishes. It is noteworthy that the resurgence of gang-related violence began in the city of Montego Bay. Perhaps because of its tourism dependence, the state of emergency was never extended to that city.

59. Truce-making for example, may temporarily reduce gang violence but does not alter the power relations and may even increase the power of the participating gangs. There were arrests of members of the Shower network in Canada, which suggests possible coordination with Canadian law enforcement. See "Canadian Police Arrest Alleged Shower Posse 'Big Fish'", *Jamaica Observer*, 4 May 2010.

60. A senior officer in the United Nations Stabilization Mission in Haiti (MINUSTAH) gave data on reported crimes during this period to me.

61. On 14 July 2010, the count was 4,181. A later count by the JCF was 4,600.

62. Some 980 persons were detained within the first five days of the operation in Tivoli Gardens. We may assume that all of these persons were detained in Tivoli Gardens and its neighbouring areas. See Amnesty International (2010).

63. A sample of the records of these "high-value" detainees was reviewed by the author. These were kindly made available to me by the JCF on my request.

64. The AGSP discusses the issue of financial crimes but is particularly interested in the independence of the investigative organizations. It does not explicitly discuss assets forfeiture, but this is implied.

65. See the Report of Crime Stop to the Committee on National Security of the Private Sector Organization of Jamaica. The report is recorded in the minutes of the committee.

66. This idea needs further development and systematization, but that project is for another place and time.

67. See Harriott 2008b for further discussion of this issue.

68. The report of the National Committee on Political Tribalism (1997) puts a broader perspective on how to de-garrison these communities. The discussion in this chapter is narrower in scope and is limited to gang control and prevention.

69. Garrison benefits are not to be confused with benefits to the poor. If free housing and utilities were benefits to the poor, then all poor, both urban and rural, would have an equal chance of accessing them.

70. These data on police strength were provided by the JCF. At the time of writing in 2013, police strength including the Island Special Constabulary Force was 11,425.

71. This conclusion holds true particularly if members of the security forces are held accountable for the abuses.

72. This is a rather high percentage of the population. It may be correct but in its magnitude, it does not triangulate well with other related survey results including Harriott and Lewis with Nelson and Seligson (2013). I do not intend for this measurement to be taken in its exactness.

73. Personal communication.

74. I thank Charles and Wilson (in this volume) for bringing this article to my attention.

75. A practical difficulty here is that the criminal justice system generates little general deterrence effects. Any such approach would therefore require robust police reform. One of the consequences of having a chronic violence and gang problem is that in crafting an effective response, many things have to be done conjointly with limited resources.

76. Such an approach fitted with the political motivation to move resources into the community to quiet dissension and consolidate political power.

77. In "PM's Latest Words on West Kingston", *Gleaner*, 3 June 2010. http://jamaica-gleaner.com/gleaner/20100603/news/news3.html.

78. During the 1970s, what subsequently became known as the Shower was ably led by Claudius Mossop. After his violent death in 1977, he acquired folk-hero status among youth in Tivoli Gardens. His name lends credibility to any challenge for the leadership of the Presidential Click/Shower by members of his family.

References

Amiot, M., and R.E. Foster. 2011. *Jamaica Constabulary Force: Three Year Anti-Gang Strategic Plan*. Sponsored by the European Commission in consultation with the MNS and JCF. http://www.nypd2lapd.com/sitebuildercontent/sitebuilderfiles/three yearantigangstrategy.pdf.

Amnesty International. 2010. *Jamaica: A Long Road to Justice? Human Rights Violations under the State of Emergency*. Bulletin 40, 29 May. London: Amnesty International Publications.

Bennett, T., and K. Holloway. 2004. "Gang Membership, Drugs and Crime in the UK." *British Journal of Criminology* 44: 305–23.

Blok, A. 1974. *The Mafia of a Sicilian Village, 1860–1960: A Study of Violent Peasant Entrepreneurs*. Prospect Heights, IL: Waveland.

Brown, I. 2009. "Rival Gangs Commit to Ending Conflict in Trench Town". *Jamaica Observer*, 4 March. http://www.jamaicaobserver.com/news/147035_Rival-gangs-commit-to-ending-conflict-in-Trench-Town.

Bryan, P. 2009. *Edward Seaga and the Challenges of Modern Jamaica*. Kingston: University of the West Indies Press.

Buddan, R. 2011. "Decline, Stabilisation or Growth". *Gleaner,* 15 May. http://jamaica-gleaner.com/gleaner/20110515/focus/focus4.html.

Bursik, R., and H. Grasmick. 1993. *Neighborhoods and Crime: The Dimensions of Effective Community Control*. New York: Lexington.

Charles, C. 2002. "Garrison Communities as Counter Societies: The Case of the 1998 Zeeks' Riot in Jamaica." *Idez* 1(1): 29–43.

Charles, C., and O. Beckford. 2012. "The Informal Justice System in Garrison Communities." *Social and Economic Studies* 61: 51–72.

CHDR 2012. *Human Development and the Shift to Better Citizen Security: Caribbean Human Development Report 2012*. New York: UNDP.

Curry, G.D. 2000. "Self-Reported Gang Involvement and Officially Recorded Delinquency". *Criminology*, 28(4): 1253–1274.

Dudley, S.T. 2006. *Walking Ghosts: Murder and Guerrilla Politics in Colombia*. New York: Routledge.

Fagan, J. 1989. "The Social Organization of Drug Use and Drug Dealing among Urban Gangs". *Criminology*. 27: 633–69.

———. 1996. "Gangs, Drugs and Neighborhood Change." In *Gangs in America*, 2nd ed., edited by R. Huff, 39–74. Thousand Oaks, CA: Sage.

Figueroa, M. 1994. "Garrison Communities in Jamaica 1962–1993: Their Growth and Impact on Political Culture". Paper presented at conference, Democracy and Democratization in Jamaica: Fifty Years of Adult Suffrage, Kingston, 6–7 December 1994.

Figueroa, M., A. Harriott, and N. Satchel. 2008. "The Political Economy of Jamaica's Inner-City Violence: A Special Case?" In *The Caribbean City*, edited by R. Jaffe, 94–122. Kingston: Ian Randle.

Gayle, B. 2012. "Supreme Court Clears O'Gilvie". *Sunday Gleaner,* 16 December, D11.

Government of Jamaica. 2007. *National Security Policy for Jamaica – Towards a Secure and Prosperous Nation.* Kingston: Jamaica Information Service.

———. 2012. "A New Approach: National Security Policy for Jamaica 2012". Prepared for the Ministry of National Security by A. Clayton, University of the West Indies, Mona.

Gray, O. 2001. "Rethinking Power: Political Subordination in Jamaica". In *New Caribbean Thought: A Reader*, edited by B. Meeks and F. Lindahl, 210–31. Kingston: University of the West Indies Press.

———. 2004. *Demeaned but Empowered: The Social Power of the Urban Poor in Jamaica.* Kingston: University of the West Indies Press.

Hagedon, J.M. 1994. "Homeboys, Dope Fiends, Legits, and New Jacks". *Criminology* 32(2): 197–219.

Harriott, A. 2003. "Social Identities and the Escalation of Homicidal Violence in Jamaica". In *Understanding Crime in Jamaica: New Challenges for Public Policy*, edited by A. Harriott, 89–112. Kingston: University of the West Indies Press.

———. 2008a. *Bending the Trend Line: The Challenge of Controlling Violence in Jamaica and the High Violence Societies of the Caribbean.* Kingston: Arawak.

———. 2008b. *Organised Crime and Politics in Jamaica: Breaking the Nexus.* Kingston: Canoe.

Harriott, A., and B. Lewis, with K. Nelson, and M. Seligson. 2013. *The Political Culture of Democracy in Jamaica and in the Americas, 2012: Towards Equality of Opportunity.* LAPOP/ Vanderbilt University.

Headley, B. 2002. *A Spade Is Still a Spade: Essays on Crime and the Politics of Jamaica.* Kingston: LMH Publishing.

Hennigan, K., and D. Sloane. 2013. "Improving Civil Gang Injunctions: How Implementation Can Affect Gang Dynamics, Crime and Violence". *Criminology and Public Policy* 12(1): 7–42.

Henry, P. 2011. "Nelson said Coke Extradition Would Topple Gov't – Lewin". *Jamaica Observer*, 4 February.

Huff, C.R. 1996. "The Criminal Behavior of Gang Members and Non-Gang At-Risk-Youth". In *Gangs in America*, edited by C.R. Huff, 75–102. Thousand Oaks, CA: Sage.

Jackson, J. 2008. "Ceasefire: August Town Gangs Sign Historic Truce". *Gleaner,* 26 June. http://jamaica-gleaner.com/gleaner/20080626/news/news3.html.

Jaffe, R. 2012. "The Hybrid State: Crime and Citizenship in Urban Jamaica". Unpublished article, submitted to *American Ethnologist.*

Jankowski, M. 1991. *Islands in the Street: Gangs and American Urban Society.* Berkeley: University of California Press.

Johnson, Hume, and J. Soeters. 2008. "Jamaican Dons, Italian Godfathers and the Chances of a Reversible Destiny". *Political Studies* 56(1): 166–91.

Katz. C.M., and A. Fox. 2010. "Risk and Protective Factors Associated with Gang Involved Youth in a Caribbean Nation: Analysis of the Trinidad and Tobago Youth Survey." *Pan-American Journal of Public Health* 27(3): 187–202.

Klein, M.W. 1971. *Street Gangs and Street Workers.* Englewood Cliffs, NJ: Prentice-Hall.

———. 1995a. *The American Street Gang: Its Nature, Prevalence and Control.* New York: Oxford University Press.

———. 1995b. "Street Gang Cycles". In *Crime*, edited by J.Q. Wilson and J. Petersilia. San Francisco: Institute of Contemporary Studies Press.

Klein, M.W., and C. Maxson. 2006. *Street Gang Patterns and Policies.* New York: Oxford University Press.

Kohler-Hausmann, J. 2010. "The Attila the Hun Law: New York's Rockefeller Drug Laws and the Making of the Punitive State." *Journal of Social History* 44(1): 1–95.

Lacy, T. 1977. *Violence and Politics in Jamaica 1960–1970: Internal Security in a Developing Country.* Manchester: Manchester University Press.

Levy, H. 2009. *Killing Streets and Community Revival: Community Stories (70s–80s).* Kingston: Arawak.

Levy, H., E. Ward, D. Hutchinson, and T. Weeks. 2012. *Youth Violence and Organised Crime in Jamaica: Causes and Countermeasures: An Examination of the Linkages and Disconnections.* Final Technical Report. Unpublished monograph, Institute of Criminal Justice and Security, University of the West Indies/International Development Research Centre.

McGarrell, E., N. Corsaro, C. Melde, N. Hipple, J. Cobbina, T. Bynum, and H. Perez. 2012. *An Assessment of the Comprehensive Anti-Gang Initiative: Final Report*, 20 July. Michigan State University.

Melde, C., and F. Esbensen. 2011. "Gang Membership as a Turning Point in the Life Course". *Criminology* 47(2): 513–52.

Moxson, C. 2011. "Street Gangs". In *Crime and Public Policy*, edited by J.Q. Wilson and J. Petersilia, 158–83. New York: Oxford University Press.

National Committee on Political Tribalism. 1997. *Report of the National Committee on Political Tribalism.* Chaired by the Hon. Justice J. Kerr, commissioned by Prime Minister P.J. Patterson, Kingston, Jamaica.

Office of the Public Defender. 2013. "Interim Report to Parliament: Concerning Investigations into the Conduct of the Security Forces during the State of Emergency Declared May, 2010 – West Kingston/Tivoli Gardens 'Incursion' – The Killing of Mr Keith Oxford Clarke and Related Matters". 29 April.

Papachristos, A., and D. Kirk. 2006. "Neighborhood Effects on Street Gang Behaviour". In *Studying Youth Gangs*, edited by J. Short Jr. and L. Hughes, 63–84. Lanham, MD: AltaMira.

Powell, L.A. 2004. "Mapping Jamaican Perceptions of Distributive Justice: An Equity-Based Heuristic". *Social and Economic Studies* 53(4): 63–88.

Powell, L.A., with P. Bourne, and L. Waller. 2006. *Probing Jamaica's Political Culture: Main Trends in the July–August 2006 Leadership and Governance Survey.* Kingston: Centre for Leadership and Governance, University of the West Indies.

Pyrooz, D., A. Fox, and S.H. Decker. 2010. "Racial and Ethnic Heterogeneity, Economic Disadvantage and Gangs: A Macro Level Study of Gang Membership in Urban America". *Justice Quarterly* 27: 1–26.

Rodgers, D., and R. Muggah. 2009. "Gangs as Non-State Armed Groups: The Central American Case". *Contemporary Security Policy* 30(2): 301–17. doi:10.1080/13523260903059948.

Sampson, R., and W. Groves. 1989. "Community Structure and Crime: Testing Social Disorganization Theory." *American Journal of Sociology* 94: 774–802.

Seaga, E. 2009. *My Life and Leadership Volume 1: Clash of Ideologies 1930–1980.* Oxford: MacMillan.

Seelke, C. 2007. *Anti-Gang Efforts in Central America: Moving Beyond Mano Dura?* Miami: Center for Hemispheric Policy, University of Miami.

Sives, A. 2010. *Elections Violence and the Democratic Process in Jamaica 1944–2007.* Kingston: IRP.

Small Arms Survey Geneva. 2010. *Small Arms Survey 2010: Gangs, Groups, and Guns.* Cambridge: Cambridge University Press.

Spaulding, G. 2013. "Embattled 'Storyteller' Returns". *Sunday Gleaner*, 3 February. http://jamaica-gleaner.com/gleaner/20130203/lead/lead2.html.

Spergel, I. 2007. *Reducing Youth Gang Violence: The Little Village Gang Project in Chicago.* Lanham, MD: AltaMira.

Stille, A. 1996. *Excellent Cadavers: The Mafia and the Death of the First Italian Republic.* London: Vintage.

Thornberry, T. 1998. "Membership in Youth Gangs and Involvement in Serious and Violent Offending". In *The Modern Gang Reader*, 3rd ed., 224–32, edited by A. Eglery Jr., C. Maxson, J. Miller, and M. Klein. New York: Oxford University Press.

Thoumi, F.E. 2003. *Illegal Drugs, Economy, and Society in the Andes.* Washington, DC: Woodrow Wilson Center Press.

Thresher, F. 1927. *The Gang: A Study of 1,313 Gangs in Chicago.* Chicago: University of Chicago Press.

US Department of State. 2004. *2003 INCSR International Narcotics Control Strategy (INCSR).* Annual report to Congress by the US Department of State. WA DC.

Wyrick, P. 2006. "Gang Prevention: How to Make the 'Front End' of Your Anti-Gang Effort Work". *United States Attorneys' Bulletin*, 54: 52–60.

8 | Gang Prevention and Control in Jamaica
Social Prevention and the Case of the Spanglers

Anthony Harriott

The previous chapter highlights the suppression of organized crime group-ings by robust and extraordinary policing measures which were prose-cuted with extraordinary powers and with extraordinary levels of intensity. It also revealed the limitations of this approach. Extraordinary powers cannot be made a permanent feature of policing, even the policing of organized crime. In a highly competitive democracy, it is unlikely that such a situation would be permitted to last. The accompanying abuses of power lead to social and political dissensus, which in turn reduces cooperation with the police, thereby making law enforcement less effective and eventually discrediting extraordinary suppression methods.

In a context of weak local public support for law enforcement and high gang-community cohesion, suppression tactics may initially "dismantle" and fragment the gangs or force them into a state of dormancy as a survival tech-nique, but then they are likely later to regroup and adapt to the new situation. The risk that is associated with this process is a medium-term outcome char-acterized by increased gang cohesiveness and embeddedness in the less resil-ient communities of the urban poor and even a multiplication of the number of gangs.[1] This is a high risk and is likely to occur where the gang problem is chronic. The risk that exclusively suppressive strategies may unwittingly result in even greater social facilitation of criminality occurs where criminal groupings are cohesive and embedded in marginalized communities. The risk is especially heightened when a significant proportion of residents make their livelihoods in the informal sector of the economy with the direct and indirect assistance of the local organized crime network. These are the conditions that exist in the communities that are dominated by Jamaica's most powerful and resilient gangs.

In the tough social conditions of urban Jamaica, truly lasting organized crime and gang suppression rests not just on effective formal social control, but also on the animation of informal social control that is directed at organized crime and gang-involved youth by the home communities of these groups. The experience that will be discussed below suggests that the vitalization of informal control is possible in these communities and that this may be achieved by integrating these communities and empowering them through state assistance.

This is not an argument for a return to an imagined golden age of community, but rather for the bolstering of informal control with formal state control by a responsive and accountable state. If the people are to become more effective agents of social control, they must have a stake in their community and the future of their society. Their stake in these communities may be increased by, for example, ensuring higher rates of home ownership, which in most of the garrison communities could involve privatization of state-owned housing (in which some residents now live at the behest of the local don), better regulation of public spaces and a reduction in public poverty. Making such changes in public policy and achieving the desired social control outcomes are some of the more difficult medium- to long-term issues.

This chapter discusses the enactment of Jamaica's anti-gang strategy as a coordinated suppression and social prevention effort but with emphasis on the latter. The experience reveals the possibilities for sustaining project and programme outcomes based on community self-efficacy. It takes the case of an embedded organized crime grouping, the Spanglers, and examines the importance of community self-efficacy in enabling successful gang control. This chapter complements the previous one, in that if the first highlighted the challenges of suppression and the failure to adopt a truly comprehensive and integrated strategy, this chapter highlights the value of a comprehensive and better-coordinated approach.

There are three strands to the argument that is presented here. Inner-city populations, like the general population, exhibit a strong social justice orientation (Powell 2004). These populations apply this outlook in their narratives about the causes and solutions to crime (UNDP 2012, 160).[2] Inspired by notions of social justice and community development, they became more integrated into the political system and developed a tradition of community activism and organization (Francis 1969; D.T.M. Girvan 1962; N. Girvan 1993; Munroe 1999; Levy forthcoming). Both of these features, a social justice orientation and community activism, are contributory conditions for successful social crime prevention and collective efficacy, and they exist even in the worst gang-dominated areas.

These two influences are, however, double-edged. Social justice may lead to social facilitation of crime especially in contexts of marginalization where criminality may present itself as social banditry by, for example, funding welfare programmes. In these contexts, the investment of criminally acquired funds into community-based enterprises may be cast as "community development". Both ideas may be used as central themes in narratives that justify gang dominance and demobilize the capacity of the dominated community for social control or direct sections of the community in support of a gang-serving system of control and the reinforcement of subcultural norms. This may occur in deep ways such as via social definitions that conflict with legal definitions of crime, including violent and predatory behaviour. Lottery scams and extortion rackets, for example, may be viewed as mere transfers of money and wealth from the rich to the poor (Robinson 2013). Where these narratives are accepted, it becomes easy to enfold the gang in the community as agents of social justice. The more able organized crime groupings and gangs reinforce these narratives with welfare programmes, thereby further strengthening their ties to the communities, which increases their political capital. Thus, if in some settings a social justice orientation may lead to perverse outcomes, histories of community activism and participation in community governance may also be channelled into a competitive politics that is corrupted by the gang-party nexus. This is usually the case in the gang-dominated communities. In these conditions, both social justice narratives and community structures may reinforce the problems.

Correcting the community-state relationship and better integrating the marginalized communities of the urban poor may animate social control. This is a major problem that Jamaica and other Caribbean countries that are faced with high levels of serious gang-perpetuated crimes must solve. The challenge is to better resolve the issues that create a chasm between state and citizen, such as social injustice, disregard for citizens' rights, inadequate access to justice, and the gap between legal and social definitions of crime. Some of these are demands that the system abide by its existing rules, others are demands for modest reforms, and still others are contestations with the system for deeper change in the principles, rules and processes. Making progress in solving these problems and thereby better integrating citizens would energize and make both informal and formal social control easier. In this regard, Jamaica and other Caribbean states are advantaged by small size, enabling fairly intense face-to-face interaction that occurs in different community settings. These close interactions allow for the potential power of informal control, which may be coupled with the power of a decentralized and responsive state. Communities and neighbourhoods may then better hold both their delinquents and the state to account. This is one of the positive lessons learned from the experience in suppressing the Spanglers.

As is the case in chapter 7, here a high-intensity case is used to describe the response of the state. It is an exceptional case with respect to at least three of its features. First, it is exceptional in terms of the characteristics of the group as a target of strategy. The Spanglers is an influential and highly resilient organized crime grouping. This group was targeted while its political sponsor was in power. Due to transgressions that strained its relationships with the party, it lost much of the protection and near immunity that it would normally have enjoyed.[3] Second, there was a rather generous (relative to other communities) allocation of state resources, or state-directed resources, for the prevention and intervention programmes that were delivered in its home community. The risk of gang suppression resulting in a political defection of gang and community is to be minimized. This is an unstated goal of government responses unless the target of the responses to the gang and territorially based organized crime problem is an affiliate of the political opposition. Third is the high-level media attention that was attracted by Donald Phipps (popularly known as Zeeks), the former leader of the group. The press demonstrated its power as an agent of informal social control by effectively becoming a targeting agent. This resulted in a focused response by the police and the political administration. An unresponsive political administration risked paying a political price for its ties to the Spanglers. This risk (along with the above-mentioned overreach of its leader) helped to dislodge the protective shield that its affiliation to the then-ruling party provided the group. Although there was prior experimentation with strategy, this was a test case of the strategy of the state.

There is a danger in generalizing single exceptional cases, even this case and the case of the Presidential Click that is the subject of chapter 7. However, some general principles of policy, programme design and action may be distilled from these experiences. Though, it is important to note that even at this level of abstraction, such principles may be very limited in their applicability – perhaps to territorially based organized crime groupings only. The generalizations with a wider applicability may simply be taken as principles that appear to be useful and processes that may be productive.

The chapter is an analytic description of the enacted anti-gang strategy. Danger accompanies the projection of greater coherence onto the strategy than what actually existed. The approach taken here is not necessarily to document what occurred historically, but to try to understand the processes and to draw lessons from them; this attempt may consequently better inform the design of new projects with similar aims. One may, for example, discern a principle at work even though that principle was not specifically used to inform the design of the programmes, or the programme participants were not consciously working by this principle. Therefore, the material presented may actually be better thought through, more systematic and more coordinated than the actual plans and the reality.

The rest of the chapter is organized in three sections. First, a conceptual map of the chapter is presented. This is followed by a brief description of the Spanglers as the target of strategy and the object of study in the community context. Third and finally, an analytic description of the strategy presented in its different phases and dimensions of the process.

Community Efficacy and Social Control

If gang suppression is to be successful in the gang-dominated communities of Jamaica, it must lead to greater community efficacy. In order to ensure this outcome, gang suppression must be linked to socially integrative action and social prevention programmes. Social prevention is in turn effective if it is deliberate about strengthening social control. This is the case for an integrated approach to the problem of territorial gangs and organized crime groupings.

Social control involves how people respond to deviant behaviour. These responses are related to their notions of right and wrong conduct. Social control, therefore, also entails how people define the types of behaviour that are to be controlled (Horwitz 1990).

Social definitions of what ought to be controlled, however, do not always correspond with legal definitions. Indeed, a divergence between legal and social definitions of crime is evident in the inner-city communities where the gangs operate. Notions of right and wrong are interpreted through the lens of a subculture that may regard, for example, some types of conflict murders as "justice" and some types of predatory victimizing behaviour as amoral, depending on the target of the action. If the target of the action is outside the boundary of belonging (community), then the notion of a wrong may not arise, or it may be invoked in perverse or inverted ways. This divergence presents major challenges for achieving effective social control. There is too little mutual reinforcement of informal and formal social control. Convergence of the definitions of what ought to be named as crime, and therefore behaviour to be controlled, should be regarded as a central crime- and violence-prevention issue. Its resolution remains a major challenge for state and society.

Divergent definitions of crime have their basis in both the historical legacy of an excessively penal style of formal control that unnecessarily criminalized harmless behaviours[4] and the contemporary reality of the marginalization of large sections of the population. Adaptation to the material conditions of marginality will tend to generate its own moral order, which consequently produces a constant contestation of the legal and dominant social definitions of what ought to the controlled.

This problem raises the issue of how the moral order is and how it ought to be protected. As Black (1998) notes, it may be viewed as rightly protected by the state and the laws as well as by citizens. Control may be done in various styles or response types, of which Black identifies four: punitive or penal, conciliatory, compensatory, and therapeutic. State-managed formal control may vary in style, but in general, state involvement entails the use of coercion.

Informal social control is best grounded in accepted values and norms. If these are consensus values and norms, then control simply involves the reinforcement of these norms. Little, if any, manifest coercion is required, and the response styles may therefore be non-coercive. Because Jamaica has a developed subculture of violence and normative contestation, the settings where the subculture is most pronounced require a measure of coercion to bring about normative conformity.[5] This is why any attempt to further animate informal social control in the gang-dominated communities requires the support of law enforcement.

Conduct norms are nevertheless integrative. They prepare people for acceptable interactions with others, that is, interactions that do not result in unnecessary conflicts and violence (at least within the groups to which the subject belongs). Norm violations typically signify a problematic person, and, as others including Horwitz (1990) have noted, norm abidance demonstrates the ability to socially negotiate for the desired social goods. In these senses, people acquire conduct norms not just because they are social beings who wish to be accepted by significant others, but also because they associate these norms with the social skills that are required for achieving their life goals. The acquisition or renewal of conventional conduct norms is, in this sense, anticipatory. If failure in the conventional world of work is anticipated and a life of "survival" in the informal and illegal sectors is expected, then people will reject those norms that are not regarded as useful and instead acquire the relevant skills and conduct norms that are helpful for success in the sectors that are their anticipated destinations.

This case calls for the better integration of urban high-crime communities and the creation of new and improved channels to mainstream opportunities. If those members of the community who exhibit mainstream conduct norms and invest in acquiring the capabilities for work-related success and social mobility have no opportunities, and this condition is chronic and viewed as unjust, then this type of action and process will be regarded as futile. People may then gravitate to the illegal opportunities and be supportive of those who are successfully engaged in these activities, especially if the harms that are associated with these activities are directed outward and the benefits distributed inward. This is the subcultural problem that helps to embed gangs in these communities. Internalizing subculture behaviour in this way signifies further unwanted behaviour to the mainstream. This behaviour set is the outcome of marginalization, and it further obstructs access to legitimate opportunities. At this stage of the process and from the viewpoint of an external observer, it may take on the appearance of self-inflicted exclusion. This process becomes a vicious cycle that progressively deepens the problem as a chronic condition. From the viewpoint of the marginalized, this is an issue of social injustice.

A strong social justice orientation may, as noted earlier, influence the formation of social definitions of harmful behaviour that are contrary to law. In some contexts, violence and even killing, for example, may be regarded as just responses to injustice. This is largely true of retaliatory violence when the initial act of violence was conflict generated – as is often the case with gang violence. Gang culture taps into these beliefs and thereby further weakens informal social control. In the gang-dominated communities, animating informal social control therefore entails contending at the definitional level with beliefs about what ought to be controlled. It means contesting the gang culture; contesting the practices and beliefs about revenge, disrespect (dissing) and the code of protective silence; and non-cooperation with law enforcement. Informal social control is closely related to collective efficacy.

Collective efficacy may be defined as "a link of cohesion and trust with shared expectations for intervening in support of neighbourhood social control" (Sampson and Raudenbush 2001, 2, cited in St Jean 2007, 43). Cohesion and trust are viewed as the building blocks of collective efficacy. Much has been written about the importance of social cohesion as an enabler of individual and collective action (Putnam 2000)[6] and as a protective factor against criminality as the source of a social pressure for conformity (Hirschfield and Bowers 1997; Sampson, Raudenbush and Earls 1997).[7] There are several dimensions to social cohesion. These include a sense of belonging, recognition and respectful treatment by other members of the community and participation in legitimate community organization. More generally, social cohesion involves shared values, identity and institutions – all of which promote amenability to social control. It may be argued that willingness to act is also related to trust, shared values and known rules of action (Sampson 2011). Community organizations therefore matter as repositories of trust, confidence and the capacity for collective action. Expectations and rules of action are often negotiated within these organizations.

It is argued that collective efficacy may return low rates of violent crime even where there is marginalization and considerable social disadvantage (Sampson, Raudenbush and Earls 1997, cited in St Jean 2007). In these settings, collective efficacy should not be confused with community resilience. The latter is adaptive and behaviourally accommodative to an unfavourable power configuration (such as gang dominance), while the former signifies community power and the ability to control violent and other socially harmful behaviour. That collective efficacy returns low rates of violence in these conditions is a promising conclusion that suggests that significant gains in crime control are possible even without resolving the problem of socially integrating the marginalized communities. A recent seven-country study of citizen security also provided some empirical support for this line of reasoning and investigation in the Caribbean by probing the relationship between community cohesion, informal social control and gang presence in communities (UNDP 2012, 79–81). Further research in different contexts is required, however, before drawing any universal conclusions regarding social integration as being simply a catalytic efficacy-enhancing factor or a necessary condition for collective efficacy.

Where there are strong subcultural influences and profound legitimacy problems with the institutions of formal control, attending to the problem of social integration may be of great importance even if it is not a necessity. In the concrete conditions of the gang-dominated marginalized communities of urban Jamaica, developing sustainable crime-control-specific collective efficacy may depend more on a programme of social integration. This, however, does not mean that all of the macro-level structural features of economy and society that give rise to marginalization have to be solved as a precondition for greater social integration in the perhaps shallow terms of having a shared sense of belonging to community and country or even in the deeper sense of having common values and norms common values and norms (whether or not one violates those norms).

Collective efficacy, as Sampson notes, is task-specific (2011, 215), and is also capabilities specific. Many of Jamaica's communities have traditions of collective action, including community self-protection from crime. This type of crime control specific action is, however, largely restricted to Neighbourhood Watch groups and similar groupings that have a reactive "eyes and ears of the police" role, and to spontaneous vigilante action. The communities of the urban poor share this tradition of community action to advance their various interests, but they tend to be less engaged in collective action for public safety. Indeed, this function has in some communities fallen to the dons and gang leaders. Here, the process of developing this crime-prevention-specific efficacy is discussed in detail.

Safety-specific collective efficacy is related to a willingness to work for a better community. Therefore, people must possess a sense of belonging and a stake in the future of their communities or neighbourhoods. They must see their individual futures as being linked to the future of their community. Typically, aspirations for the future include upward social mobility and residential mobility – the idea of having a better future elsewhere. Data from a national survey that was conducted in 2010 indicated that 54.5 per cent of Jamaicans would prefer to live elsewhere, and 52 per cent of the respondents who resided in the city of Kingston similarly wished to be mobile.[8] Many persons who favour residential mobility are, however, unable to move. Moreover, many have a sense of belonging to their communities. When the citizens believe their community has a golden crime-free and orderly past, it indicates hopeful aspirations for the future of their community, even if these beliefs are untrue. These aspirations are linked to a willingness to act and to collectively engage in social control.

In figure 8.1, below, some measures of perceived collective efficacy are presented. Large majorities in Jamaica claim active participation in community activities and organizations. They also perceive that most of their neighbours are willing to engage in the informal control of various types of violent and criminal behaviour. These types of behaviour range from what is often considered private (domestic violence) to those potentially dangerous to a third party (fighting), as well as property crimes.

As Short and Hughes (2010) note, [social capital] and collective efficacy "are of critical importance to such tasks as enhancing legitimate opportunities,

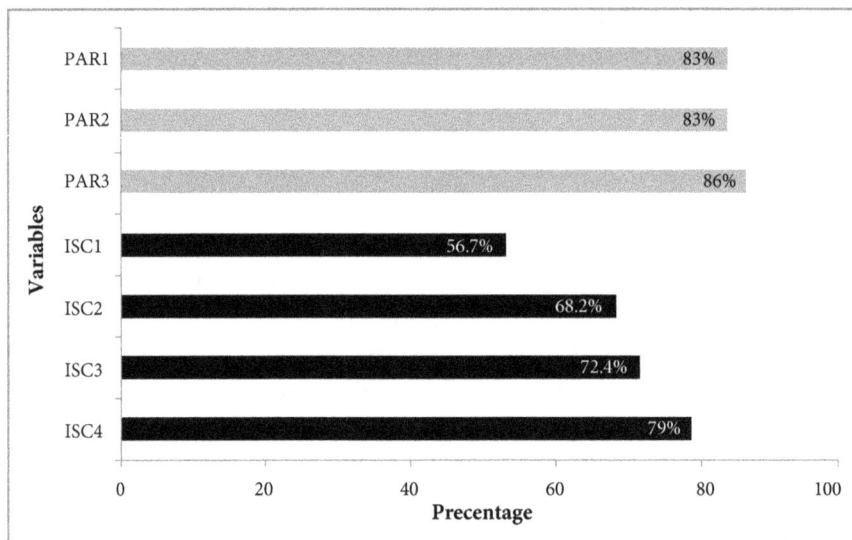

Figure 8.1. Participation and social control

Source: Computed from the dataset for the UNDP 2012

Key:

PAR1 = participation in community activities

PAR2 = involvement in community organization

PAR3 = work with others to improve your community

ISC1 = the perceived likelihood that people from your community would intervene in a suspected case of domestic violence.

ISC2 = the perceived likelihood that people from your community would intervene to stop fighting "in front of your house".

ISC3 = the perceived likelihood that people from your community would intervene in a case of stranger theft from a member of their community.

ISC4 = work with others to reduce violence.

controlling violence and facilitating positive conventional socialization" (p. 133). These may be thought of as axes on which the workings of community programmes, such as the one that is aimed at controlling the Spanglers, turn.

Enhancing collective efficacy and animating informal social control, however, depend on linking it with formal state control and especially the quality of police service. The community must know that it has the support of a reliable and rights-regarding police service. Having enough confidence in the police force to work with them does not necessarily lead to an overreliance on formal control and a subsequent atrophying of informal control. In fact, studies have found the opposite, that is, that working with the police assists and invigorates informal control (Silver and Miller 2004). This viewpoint is referred to as the notion of vertical links (Sampson 2011, 215–16). It also applies to the other service agencies of the state. With such an approach, Jamaica may at least make progress toward de-garrisoning gang-dominated communities such as Matthews Lane.

The Spanglers and the Community[9]

The Spanglers is one of Jamaica's oldest gangs. It has evolved through different formations but maintains a line of continuity to the 1950s, which is demonstrated by its unbroken history of alignment to one of the major political parties (the PNP).[10] Like the Presidential Click, the Spanglers gang has become a family firm. It is transnational and forms linkages by migration and drug trafficking, but it is also deeply rooted in its home community of Matthews Lane.

As is the case with other garrison communities, this community is highly criminogenic yet tends to have low rates of serious crime. Local criminality is disciplined by the dominant organized crime grouping and is directed outwardly rather than inwardly. Therefore, there is little discussion in this chapter of the changes in community crime rates. The impact of the state's anti-gang strategy is not to be assessed in these terms, but rather by its impact on the capability and cohesion of the Spanglers and the gang's relationships in the community.

The Matthews Lane community is located in the commercial district of Downtown Kingston, or the old city centre. It has high poverty and youth unemployment rates and thus may be expected to have low rates of social mobility. Given these structural features of the community, social disorganization theory would anticipate weak social ties and consequently weak informal social control (Sampson 2011). On the other hand, low rates of social mobility may indicate residential stability. Moreover, the community is small with a high population density.[11] As is typical of Kingston's inner-city communities, there is little private space, and much activity takes place on the streets. Social interaction is therefore fairly intense. It is also socially and politically homogenous. Stability, smallness and sameness may be expected to increase the intensity of interaction and the strength of social ties thereby yielding shared values and potentially strong informal social control. Theoretical expectations suggest that the similarity of lived experiences would strengthen common bonds.

The effects of politics further complicate the situation. The party that is dominant in the community has had a positive ideological orientation to social justice. Such tendencies amplify notions of the victimhood of inequality and, as stated above, this may under some conditions favour social facilitation. However, this orientation may also weaken the sense of individual responsibility for one's transgressions. If an ideological orientation to social justice polarizes the society, fails to resolve the deep structural problems and fails to integrate the marginalized poor, it may lead to the unintended outcomes of undermining informal and formal social control. Since its independence in 1963, Jamaica has made considerable social progress, but the society is still viewed as socially unjust (Powell 2004). In many respects it remains socially unjust, as is evidenced by the unimproved high level of inequality (Knight 2008; Harriott et al. 2013), poverty rates and exclusion of large sections of the population (Benfield 2010). When conventional actors and systems fail, they may be complemented with or replaced by unconventional actors, as well as subcultural norms and an accompanying system for their enforcement that subverts the dominant and more social normative order.

The community institutions, such as its basic school, various aspects of daily social life and indeed its identity, are intertwined with the Spanglers. Many of the young men in the community make no distinction between gang and community. Prior to 2005, "all" were regarded as Spanglers and, it is reported, would self-identify with the Spanglers.[12] Any recognized identity-based boundaries between the group and the community were erased. The recruitment pool of the group therefore approximated the youth population of the community, and group renewal and longevity were thus guaranteed.

The politics of the community and the distribution of state-allocated resources are also bound up with the Spanglers. The community has had a long history of gangster leadership and administration. The Spanglers "ran" the community, that is, had rule-making and rule-enforcing power over the community. This is another case of the garrison phenomenon which, it must be emphasized, is not the typical community of the urban poor or even the typical urban gang-occupied or gang-dominated community.

Until recently, the leader of the Spanglers was Donald Phipps, who was often referred to as "Father". In the community context, this is a title that is loaded with meanings. It describes the relationship between Phipps as the leader of the group and other members of the community. He was "father" in a functional sense – he was provider and protector. His position as leader of a successful criminal group allowed him to play this role. The Spanglers group replicates the paternalism and patron-client relationships that are typically observed in the political domain. Therefore, these types of negative relationships with the people are mutually reinforced. To the extent that it depicts the content of the relationships (provider-protector), "father" as an honorific title legitimizes the don. If he successfully fulfils this role, then he becomes an authority figure. In the particular community of Matthews Lane, the myth that the community is a "family" serves to promote and validate the role of the don as "father".[13] This representation supplies cohesion at the community level and the gang level and creates an interconnection between the two.

The provider role involves securing jobs from state agencies via party networks – from state-hired contractors through a combination of political influence and coercion and from other private-sector firms mainly by coercion. The provision of welfare support and other materially significant services for residents is a standard feature of the Spanglers' method. These activities have several effects that are internal to the group. They increase group attractiveness, pride and cohesion, and give some credibility to the group's social justice narratives. These activities thus enhance its authority in the community and make it more resilient to purely suppressive responses from the state (indeed, badly implemented suppression risks increasing group cohesion).

Fathers are also expected to play a disciplinary role. They tend to exercise a violent-punitive style of informal social control of their "children". Gang and organized crime rules may thus become community rules and the paternal (violent-punitive or penal) style of discipline and control is imposed on the community. In these conditions, conventional informal social control may be expected to atrophy, and formal (state-administered) control is supplanted. Disciplinary power is passed to the monopolistic power-seeking crime boss and is structured as a self and gang-protective "jungle court".[14]

In 2006, Phipps was convicted in a Jamaican court and is now serving a life sentence in a Jamaican prison. This development presented an opportunity to break the Spanglers' hold on the community. The conviction of Phipps marked a new phase in the efforts of the state to weaken and perhaps dismantle this group. Such actions may be expected to increase the level of public confidence in the police, especially if these actions are systematically followed up with efforts to create a better relationship between the community and the police.[15]

This new phase was characterized by a greater reliance on social interventions but in concert with law enforcement. There is a lesson in this: Social interventions work best in coordinated action with the police. In contexts of gang domination, social interventions are unlikely to alter the power relations in the community by themselves. They may create better conditions for social control, but do not automatically result in improved social control. The same is true of police action. In the absence of any effort to alter the material conditions of the people, police action risks greater gang and community cohesion, thereby weakening the chance of yielding any sustained control outcomes. Social interventions and police action together are more likely to yield success than either tactic alone. What follows is an account of these efforts following the removal of Phipps and the initiation of coordinated programmatic action.

The Community Development Approach (In Practice)

The approach that was and is still being taken toward the "development" and "transformation" of gang-dominated communities and neighbourhoods involves the following elements: (1) the mobilization of the communities and the development of their governance structures, (2) the "normalization" of state services to these communities, (3) a re-engineered relationship between citizens and the police, (4) improved access to opportunities and (5) peace-making. This process is developmental in the political sense because it opens and improves channels of participation for all community members, improves the capabilities of the community leadership and residents, and extends their freedoms and broadens their choices (Sen 1989; 1999). It is transformative in terms of community governance and community-state relations, including the relationship to law enforcement. In the most general terms, the approach seeks to be integrative by working to resolve issues of marginality and differential treatment of these communities by the state.

With the exception of "normalization", the elements of the Community Based Gang Reduction Strategy (CBGR) as it was implemented in Matthews Lane are to be found in the Comprehensive Community Model that is described in Howell (2010). However, the Jamaica community development model lacks evaluation, evaluation design or published assessment. The CBGR seeks to strengthen formal control but does not intentionally seek to improve informal social control within the community, even as a means of strengthening formal control or policing; consequently, any strengthening of informal control that does occur is an unintended outcome. Here (as the case of the Presidential Click was primarily a discussion of suppression) we may simply note that the Spanglers organization was weakened by law enforcement and that this triggered a full engagement with the community that began with its mobilization that is discussed below.

Community Mobilization and Shifting (Political) Power

The methodical mobilization of the Matthews Lane community began in the wake of the Spanglers' decapitation. Mobilization should be pursued in order to build collective efficacy by encouraging citizen participation and self-managed organizations and, in the process, build trust and confidence in one another.

Maintaining a high level of interpersonal trust is an important problem-solving asset. The significance of interpersonal trust as a precondition for collective action may nevertheless be overrated (St Jean 2007, 48–49). The Jamaican experience suggests that high participation in community organizations and high levels of confidence in them may accompany low levels of interpersonal trust. Jamaica is a low-trust society (see Powell 2007; Powell, Lewis and Seligson 2011, 202–8). This conclusion must be qualified in the light of more recent findings that are derived from the HDR 2012 dataset. Although Jamaicans may believe that unknown strangers are untrustworthy, they regard most members of their own communities to be trustworthy.[16] Findings from the HDR 2012 suggest that there is a willingness to act at the community level and that there are high participation rates in community organizations. Interpersonal distrust was not a hindrance to mobilization in Matthews Lane. Moreover, any prior distrust existing within the community could have been overcome by open methods of work and rule-governed decision-making, or in other words, by confidence-building.[17]

Prior to 2005, in the community of Matthews Lane the form of local political administration was decidedly authoritarian characterized by gang administrative co-rule with the monopoly party. In these types of settings, the process of transformation is best begun by erecting new structures of administration that shift power to the more pro-social forces within the community. The development of participatory structures legitimizes the new power centre and contributes to community efficacy. Through these structures, community members learn to accept and value self-authored rules of conduct (beginning with rules for the conduct of their meetings) and also learn to accept the authority of their elected leaders. This process is, however, not without some contestation between the democratically grounded legitimacy of the new organization and the traditionally grounded authority claims of the Spanglers, who now must make their claims to community leadership in the absence of "Father Zeeks" or a comparable leader. It is not clear that the purposes of mobilizing the community were as they are stated here. Rather, what is suggested is that if properly designed and implemented, the new community structures would be expected to have these effects.

In the Jamaican context, where there are two powerful political parties, there is always the danger that state-led mobilizations may result in submissiveness to the state or the entrenchment of party power and influence on the communities. We may call this latter process *channelization*. Some of the more positive effects of mobilization, noted above, were also observable and indeed were more pronounced than the effects of channelization. In any event, in the context of garrison communities, even channelization that shifts power from co-administration of gang and party to party would represent an advance.[18]

Unlike the situation elsewhere where crime is not perceived to be as closely associated with social injustice, the challenge for community mobilization is not primarily to build approval for interventions that are supportive of programmes that allocate resources to gang members who may wish to exit the gang and youth at risk. In Jamaica, such community support exists prior to any programme.[19] The purpose of mobilization is rather to make the community less facilitative of criminality, less dependent on crime, and indeed to improve its capacity for informal social control while contributing to the broader development of the community. For this to occur, a shift in local power is necessary.

The process of mobilization in Matthews Lane began in late 2005 with the establishment of a participatory structure with elected representation from each street. The community's interest and motivation were sparked when another state agency promised a community clean-up programme on the condition that such a governance structure should be established. The Matthews Lane Development Council (MLDC) was thus formed.[20] This structure was critical for creating the vertical and horizontal linkages that enhance collective efficacy – that is, "vertical linkages" with institutions that are external to the community and may make resources available to the community and "horizontal linkages" between organizations within the community (Sampson 2011, 216). During the period under review, strong vertical linkages were formed, and these were crucial for the advancement of the project. State and non-state agencies, including the security forces, subsequently worked with the MLDC.

The community's women became the first interface between the state's response agencies and the community. This is typical. It is most often the women who help to blunt the efforts of law enforcement, and it is the women who may help to open the possibilities for community transformation. The men are typically more suspicious and distrustful of outsiders. They are considered to be more disreputable and are consequently more vulnerable in open, confrontational and involuntary contact with law enforcement or connected agencies. Thus, approximately two hundred women attended the initial MLDC organizational meeting while the men were absent. With the exception of the police, women predominantly staff the associated response agencies of the state. This facilitated the initial encounters and provided an environment for developing the confidence that would be useful and perhaps necessary for the further progress of the programmes.

The fact that the community's women were first to be mobilized, however, gave them an exclusive voice and allowed them to shape the programmes of the intervening agencies. Thus, the early interventions and opportunities were largely feminized. Consequently, the men continued to be excluded or perhaps elected to stay away because of the project offerings. If males, and particularly young males, are not engaged in community mobilization decisions and actions, then little direct impact on crime, and particularly violent crime, may be expected. We will return to this issue.

Gang members, despite the loss of their leader and the distancing of some people from the remnants of the gang, sought to maintain the gang's dominance in the community by intimidating the emerging community leadership. They attempted to label selected MLDC members as police collaborators. Their attempts largely failed as the power resources of the gang diminished, and its influence declined. A critical factor in this decline of the gang's influence was its loss of control over the distribution of state resources. A change of government in December 2011 may have assisted this process. The political process is dynamic, and advances are easily followed by reversals, especially when state institutions are weak and political parties are powerful.

Re-Routing State Resources (via the MLDC)

Prior to community mobilization, the Spanglers' ability to extract and allocate state resources was a source of the group's power and authority in the community. Such access demonstrated its ties to political power in the state, and it enabled the Spanglers' provisioning role in the community. Importantly, it validated the signature methods of organized crime. These methods include the voluntary and often uninvited (but welcomed) supply of violence in the party's interest so that the party incurs a debt-obligation. This method is bolstered by the use of threats of violence and extortionist negotiation strategies to secure resource transfers. In a moral universe, where the outcomes validate the methods used, the visible success of those methods leads to diffusion and increased generalized use by others. A common technique is to demand that if one's needs are not met (by government, a firm or an individual), then there will be a consequence – the persons making the demand will turn to violent crime. Using violence as a method of manipulation becomes a lever or bargaining chip for access to resources. Where this technique is successful, as was the case for the Spanglers, violence is thereby valorized, validated and reinforced. By these means, electoral politics and public policy help to manufacture the gang and organized crime problem.

During the period of this study, there was considerable success in re-routing state and other resources that were intended to support the prevention projects and programmes through the MLDC. This meant that the gate-keeping role of the criminal leadership was interrupted. In these garrison communities, gate-keeping and controlling access to the community directly connects the dons and gang leaders vertically. They exploit these linkages to external agencies, including state agencies that deliver or wish to deliver services and implement projects in the community. Any community connection to resources is done via the criminal leadership, which further amplifies their status and power as the gatekeepers.[21] This even allows them to leverage the political power and voting resources of the community. Ending this role, which is so critical to the survival of organized crime groupings such as the Spanglers, weakens their hold on the people and makes those groups less valuable to the political parties. By connecting directly with external resources and legitimate organizations, the community's collective efficacy is potentially enhanced. There is, however, a danger that accompanies the development of a negative pattern – a rupturing of the old relationships and mechanisms during crisis moments, but a later return to old ways. This reversion eliminates the potential for progress, instead of consolidating the advances that may truly and positively transform aspects of community life. With consistency, public policy may become an important part of solving this problem and may do so by helping to consolidate the shifts in power and control.

The role of social hierarchies and status relationships in social control is generally understood. There are some well-established patterns – for example, the old are able to control the young. In communities that lack social differentiation, and where age-related authority (and authority more generally) has been weakened, there is great difficulty with social control. The gang creates its own status hierarchies and demands that these be "respected" by the community.

The anti-gang and development-oriented programmes that were introduced in the Matthews Lane community, however, created new status hierarchies and power relationships. The MLDC leaders now make decisions and influence the allocation of resources. They become authoritative voices. This outcome marks a turn toward becoming a normal community.

Normalization of the Community

Mobilization and the emergence of participatory structures opened a process for normalizing the community. There are two senses in which the word normalization is used. It may be taken as a process of accepting specific types of crime and ending the negative social sanctions that were applied to those types of behaviour. This process is evident where there is a pattern of collective resistance to efforts by law enforcement to deal with these types of behaviour as crimes. This resistance takes various forms and has been a feature of police–citizen encounters in garrison communities such as Matthews Lane. A second meaning that is given to the word "normalization" is the process of de-garrisoning the community or bringing it into the normative order. At the level of ideas, this involves acceptance that the garrison phenomenon is not normal, that it is outside the boundary of what is considered to be the normal crime landscape, and that it is not acceptable as a form of political organization or local regime type. Both uses of the word reflect these two conflicting processes.

Normalization as moral acceptance of the garrison aligns with the view that law enforcement should "leave its dons alone". Demonstrations protesting the arrest or anticipated arrest of gang leaders Phipps and Coke have demanded that the police "leave Zeeks (Phipps) alone" and "leave Dudus (Coke) alone".[22] This idea may be transposed as "leave the garrison as a safe haven for hyper-violent criminality". Therefore, de-garrisoning must entail putting the garrison outside the boundary of the normal and consequently targeting it as an unacceptable criminal cum political phenomenon. In so doing, the first challenge is to get the population of the country and of these communities to reject it as normal. The second is for the latter to become actors in the transformation of the garrison and partners with law enforcement toward this end. The general idea being presented here is that a retreat from extraordinarily high levels of violence should involve boundary marking and maintenance as a principle in dealing with high-violence (generating) communities as concentrated expressions of the problem.

Normalization, in the sense of de-garrisoning the community, was double-edged for Matthews Lane. As was the case with Tivoli Gardens, it meant losing some of the benefits of crime but, unlike Tivoli Gardens, it also meant access to a wider range of services that would allow fuller integration into the society. The lure and the promise was that the community would gain greater access to legitimate opportunities and to more reliable provision of state services.

Improved service provisioning by state agencies meant an opportunity to get the relationship between state and community right. This involved replacing the services which were traditionally funded and delivered by the gang, such as early childhood education, welfare support for the aged and "justice", and re-routing the state-funded services and opportunities, such as temporary jobs, that previously had been delivered via the gang. New structures, including Community Development Committees (of which the MLDC is one), have served to better connect the state with this and other marginalized communities and may help to better channel state resources, reduce conflict associated with their distribution and provide a measure of accountability of the state agencies.

Very early in the process, the immediate needs of the community were identified and quickly met by the project-animated state agencies. One of these immediate needs was a broken sewage system that the community was exposed to. It was particularly threatening to the young children at the neighbourhood basic school (which was funded by the former don and named in honour of an earlier don). This problem represented, in an attention-getting way, the neglect of the community by the state. This negative symbol associated with the state sharply contrasted with the functional, well-appointed basic school that served as the gang leaders' positive contribution. The sewage problem was promptly fixed by the responsible state agency.

Fixing this problem, as an outcome of community participation in what was expected to be a permanently established channel of communication with the state authorities, symbolized an emerging or at least a promised new relationship with the state agencies. It became an emblem of their improved responsiveness and a change in how services and resources would be allocated to the community, that is, a shift in the channels of influence from party to state structures and in more open and transparent ways. Meeting the immediate needs of the community, especially those that were related to its public and collective poverty, underlined the importance of ensuring that the changes and efforts to de-garrison the community brought benefits and alleviated the pain from losses.

Normalization of the community, however, also meant decriminalizing aspects of everyday life by removing some of the benefits of gang dominance and the reputation for violence.[23] One of the more valued benefits offered by organized crime had been "free" electricity for home and commercial purposes. This benefit was curtailed late in the normalization process, after some state resources had been deployed to the benefit of the community. In fact, free electricity service did not come to an end until five years into the process. In Matthews Lane, unlike Tivoli Gardens, the gains and benefits from normalization were delivered *before* the material losses related to gang dominance were experienced. This may not have been due to a deliberate strategy, but it was the outcome.

Immediately following the operation of the security forces in the neighbouring community of Tivoli Gardens in May–June 2010, the Jamaica Public Service Company (JPS) took the initiative to end illegal connections to its power lines in this and other communities and to "regularize" the supply of electricity to the community. Regularization was a cost associated with becoming a free and normal community. It was just not possible for the community to retain all of the benefits of illegality while demanding the removal of the stigmata that were associated with criminality.

The existence of the MLDC made these changes and the inevitable losses that were associated with the process of normalization more acceptable to the community. The MLDC was able to mediate between the utility company and the members of the community, and in doing so, avoid conflicts between the parties. This mediation led the utility company to offer support for community programmes, which helped to cushion the negative effects of the loss of free electricity on the poorest members of the community.

Without the community structures, the loss of benefits would perhaps have led to conflict with the service providers, community support for a return to the old ways, and the community making common cause with the Spanglers. There may have been a call to revitalize the gang as protector and benefactor. Instead, such voices were and have remained muted. The pain associated with losing the benefits of crime was alleviated somewhat by increased access to opportunities.

Improving Access to Opportunities

Improving access to opportunities is the material element in rule conformity. It is regarded as an imperative of social justice and, therefore, it is related to the legitimacy of the main state institutions (including the law) and feelings of belonging to the society. As integrative action, it weakens the crime as an excusable response to the social injustice narrative, which effectively influences greater convergence of the definitions of problem behaviours such that they elicit more robust informal social control responses. More positively, it improves identification with the society as a whole, not just with the community, which engenders an expected greater conformity with mainstream conduct norms. The effort to increase access to legitimate opportunities for residents of Matthews Lane had the following elements: training in social skills, remedial education and training, job placement, preparation for employment/self-employment and job-holding support services or "aftercare".

Training in Social Skills

Early in the initiation of the intervention programmes in this community, it was discovered that many persons who were interested in accessing new opportunities for work and business-related means of gaining a livelihood were unprepared to grasp these opportunities.

Chronic unemployment and survival strategies that are utilized to make a living in the informal economy lead to adaptive behaviour sets that make it difficult to fit into the world of employment. The patterns of behaviour that were well suited for hustling were not always useful in more conventional work settings, where greater interdependence and more cooperative social interactions are essential for productive activity. These behaviour patterns reinforce the exclusion and marginalization that gave rise to them in the first instance. There were problems of reliability, of incivility in interactions, of job-status-related sensitivities that led to frequent false attributions of insults to job-superior others, and of not taking responsibility for one's actions, among other issues.

The requirements of integration were therefore not unidirectional, that is, it was not all about public policy resolving inequalities and social injustices. It also required transforming mentalities and behaviour patterns that may be observed among the community members. This change agenda called for taking greater responsibility for self and community and making changes in the expectations and pressures from below that helped to create "big men" in the form of dons and politicians. In other words, some self-transformation is required. Participation in a behavioural change programme was thus made a condition for access to work and business opportunities. The curriculum of this programme included behaviour modification with modules on conflict resolution and the value of taking responsibility for one's actions.

In gang-dominated communities, promoting responsibility for one's actions and choices is a useful and necessary aspect of any violence and gang reduction programme. Gang-involved young people tend to avoid responsibility for their actions and in so doing, they deny themselves agency. The youth effectively shift responsibility for gang-involved illegal activity to an external agent. Such an agent may be a "big man" manipulator who is considered to be outside the gang and community, such as a political party official. Political alignment may be expected to empower and, in the case of the Presidential Click and other organized crime groupings, it does, and yet self-efficacy and responsibility for one's actions may be denied. Externalizing responsibility may involve transferring it to an otherworldly manipulator or even to a more remote otherworldly initial programmer of individual human actions. These brands of fatalism may be observed among the general population. They are supported in Christian authoritarian religions as well as the folk religions that still thrive in Western Kingston (Harriott 2002). Erich Fromm makes a distinction between authoritarian and humanistic religions. Authoritarian religions are marked by an external, controlling God that is "entitled to obedience, reverence and worship". Moreover, "the reason for worship, obedience and reverence *lies not in the moral qualities of the deity* [my emphasis] but in the fact that it has control, that is, has power over man" (Fromm 1978, 34–35). This authoritarianism, when coupled with multiple deprivations and exclusion, partially explains the messianic politics found in the garrison constituencies. In effect, these institutions tend to deify don-like political leaders and illuminate the near deification of dons like Phipps and Coke – as was evident in the slogan "Next to God is Dudus"[24] (see, for example, "Willing to Die for 'Dudus'", *Jamaica Observer,* 21 May 2010). Gang members may draw from this source of ideas because it would find appeal among the residents of the home communities of the gangs.[25] If, however, the group is sufficiently powerful, perhaps the gang leader is cited as the locus of responsibility for the actions of the group. It is well established that within gangs, responsibility either tends to be diffused, or it resides solely in the gang leaders. Support programmes may show the liberating effects of taking responsibility and its relationship to self-efficacy, self-correcting and self-directed behaviour and improved relationships with others. On this basis, both communities and individual lives may see real transformation. Taking self-responsibility encourages national support programmes to invest in such individuals.

Many programme participants exhibited a pattern of conflict-prone behaviour. Conflict resolution skills were transmitted to them and were to be applied at the interpersonal level. Application at the inter-group (gang) level is discussed more fully below. The objective was to provide participants with a language and a set of skills that would allow them greater self-control, and consequently, both a greater sense of choice and a newfound responsibility for their actions. Once these ideas are internalized, then, even when conflicts are poorly handled, participants are able to accept responsibility for their actions and potentially repair any damage that their prior actions may have done to a social relationship. The expected outcome would be a more (internally) peaceful community and a population better prepared to function in a socially healthy society. Given the deep attitudinal and behavioural problems, a challenge of programme design is to determine how much treatment is required in order to sufficiently correct this problem set. This is a matter for programme evaluation.

The social skills programme was used as a filter for access to the other work-preparation programmes. This presented problems for the males who had more deeply internalized the norms of the subculture (Harriott 2008, 42–43), and whose childhood socialization (unlike that of females) oriented them more to self-reliance (and innovative solutions to problems – in the Mertonian use of the word) and less to responsibility (Chevannes 2001, 25). Interestingly, male participation in the behaviour-modification programmes was much higher than that of women. Approximately 64 per cent (428) of all participants in this programme were male, but due to the high male failure rate, only 31 per cent (58) of males were able to participate in the skills-training programmes.[26] These males were either filtered out or opted out of the available opportunities. They were, however, allowed to participate in the education programmes.

Education

Several education programmes were launched in the community with the help of different non-state actors. These offerings ranged from basic literacy and numeracy to remedial work aimed at the completion of the high school examinations that are set by the Caribbean Examinations Council. Churches and universities became involved in this programme. Such cooperation multiplied the possibilities and made human and material resources for human development available to the community that were traditionally not made available to them even by an attendant and responsive state.

These educational programmes were highly valued by the community because they provided second-chance opportunities that reconnected the young people to the education system and to training and work opportunities later in life. To them, there was also a deeper meaning that was attached to this effort. Many members of the community saw this programme as an affirmation of their self-worth and also as a way to illuminate the potential of the people in the community. It represented unbiased access to opportunity and the virtues of achievement.[27] The success of this programme was thus a great source of pride for the community leadership. It also fostered feelings of greater connection to the society. The involvement of such a wide range of organizations and the opportunities, albeit limited, that they offered led to an outcome characterized by connectedness to the mainstream of society.

Work-Specific Skills Training

For most people, a basic education was not sufficient to access work opportunities – practical work-related skills were needed. During the five-year period ending in 2010, a Skills Training Programme was implemented. It was intended to deliver training in vocational and technical skills through established national institutions such as the HEART Trust/NTA.[28] These programmes were identified by matching the training needs of the residents with areas of need in the labour market. Training was offered in a wide range of disciplines or fields of competence. Measures were implemented to support the participants and enable their participation in the programme. These measures included the provision of transportation, tuition costs, books and a stipend. Moreover, flexible training times were negotiated with the training institutions.

Despite these incentives, many participants did not complete the training. Others persisted and enjoyed the benefits of participation, but did not acquire the necessary competences. There are at least two aspects to this problem. The first was the unrealistic expectations of the participants. In communities where state benefits were historically accessible via party-gang channels, state provisioning is hardly ever seen as assisting transformation of the existing arrangements. They are instead perceived as efforts to maintain the existing political relationships and old patron-client dependencies, and thus are hardly ever accompanied by sufficient responsibility for self-transformation including self-transformation via employment and conventional non-state sector, albeit low-wage, work. The involvement of non-state actors and the new ways of accessing and administering state benefits may have helped to change or moderate these attitudes, but not sufficiently. Thus, for example, to take the most extreme cases, after being provided with training and job-placement opportunities, some programme participants requested bus fares and lunch money for a job interview. Some abandoned the jobs that were secured for them and requested better jobs. The participants who exhibited this behaviour pattern and mentality believed that everything was up for negotiation and always demanded more.

The second aspect of the explanation for the behaviour pattern described above is that the participants were not socially prepared to compete for jobs. This experience emphasizes the importance of training in social skills and of self-change. These are requirements for stable employment and even self-employment.

Employment Readiness and Job-Placement Programme

The training in social and job-specific skills was not enough. In order to ensure successful job placement, another level of preparation was required. It was necessary to invest in preparing participants to enter the work force.

Under an Employment Readiness Programme (ERP), participants were screened, counselled, given additional training and assisted with the documentation that is required for formal and informal economic activity. Screening and counselling also helped to better align the expectations that the participants had regarding the likely levels of remuneration with their levels of education, training and work experience.

Participants were placed with employers in the public and private sectors. Employers are generally regarded as being reluctant to employ young males who reside in these communities, and thus there are claims of victimization caused by "area stigma" (Levy 1996, 2012). This victimization is, however, not without some rationality. The prospective employer may feel that a young male from a gang-dominated community may present the firm with an elevated risk of criminal victimization. As is typically the case with highly emotive issues such as this one, if its rational core is dismissed, then it is never resolved. In an effort to overcome these difficulties, the programme assured employers by monitoring or tracking participants and providing the latter with a support network. Experience suggests that as crime rates are reduced, employers become more supportive of the programme.

The monitoring and support efforts ensured that the programme-assisted participants were able to adjust to the new level of discipline that was necessary to function on the job. Problems were systematically identified and corrected, including behavioural problems as well as job competences. High-intensity support efforts were required in order to achieve limited success with placement in conventional employment. Self-employment and micro-businesses were other options for participants.

Entrepreneurship Development

Programme participants who wished to start new businesses were trained in how to do so. At the end of the training, the state agencies assisted them in starting businesses.

All training courses included "entrepreneurship". Participants were trained in how to establish and manage businesses and to differentiate between business finances and personal finances. In the Jamaican experience, state-assisted business ventures that are intended to help the poor typically fail because too little is accumulated to maintain the operations of the business. Cash inflows are typically spent on personal needs, or allocated to dependents and other assertive proximate people. Yet there is a long tradition of self-employment and micro-enterprise that is based on self-help forms of financing (Kirton 1996). Programmes need not be totally dependent on state-assisted financing and may tap into this latter tradition and know-how.

Skills acquisition was able to effectively stimulate self-employment. Groups of participants started their own micro-businesses. These efforts have been successful thus far largely because many of those who enlisted in the programme had a positive work attitude, prior work experience, a desire to be certified, and/or had ideas about how to make the best of the opportunity. The success cases are not those who were the poorest, but rather those with some prior social assets.

The experience indicates that intensive effort is required for early-stage progress. This level of effort was made possible by NGO support and volunteers who operated in concert with the other efforts of the state agencies. However, significant sums of cash were needed as well.[29] This level of effort is not possible for larger-scale programmes that include a much higher number of communities. Indeed, the level of effort exhibited in Matthews Lane was not made possible for Tivoli Gardens (at a time when it was politically represented by the prime minister). However, even if the financial resources were available, the state institutions do not appear to have the capacity to effectively implement these programmes in high-violence and gang-occupied communities. Extending these programmes and projects will likely reduce the effectiveness of each program because they will most likely lack the proper funding and implementation. Although concentrating the efforts means privileging some communities, thinning out programmes will likely increase the risk of failure and reversals or worse – co-option by the gangs.

Gender Filters

The gang- and violence-prevention outcomes are also likely to be less effective if there is insufficient participation by gang-affiliated young males, because they account for the vast majority of gang members and operatives in organized crime groups and networks. As noted earlier, sex initially served as a filter to opportunities via the social skills programme. Some 674 persons participated in the social skills or "behaviour modification programme". Of these, 63.5 per cent (428) were male and 36.5 per cent (246) were female. This programme acted as a planned funnel to skills training which, in turn, allowed them jobs and self-employment opportunities. Thus, of the 442 persons who participated in (work) skills training, 29.4 per cent (130) were male and 70.6 per cent (312) were female.[30] Both steps in the programmes determined access to the available opportunities and excluded males but selected females.

There were a number of reasons for this outcome, some of which have already been noted but are perhaps worthy of repetition with elaboration. Males were more likely to exhibit problematic behaviours that made them well suited for gang life and "hustling", but left them unfit for conventional work. They were therefore more likely to be filtered out at the first stage of the programme. Second, fewer males self-selected for the second-stage skills-training programmes because the offerings were determined by the females and thus favoured skills that were regarded as feminine.

Initially, therefore, these programmes did not offer much in terms of alternate livelihoods to the more troubled Spanglers-affiliated males. This latter problem was later corrected. Male participation in the work-skills training programmes was improved by crafting some of these programmes for the traditionally male occupations while making them open to females or treating them as gender-neutral occupations. This is one disadvantage of a community-development programme that attends to the gang problem versus a gang-intervention pro-gramme that is situated in the community or neighbourhood. With the former, the gang members who wish to end their gang careers and those young people who are at risk of becoming gang involved are not directly targeted for attention or intervention.

Interventions: Targeting Gang Members

Gang members are targeted by law enforcement as gang members, not as mem-bers of the community.[31] Conversely, social intervention programmes target gang members as members of the community rather than as gang members. As such, they have access to the opportunities that are generated in Matthews Lane, but not as gang members. Thus, as was already noted, these programmes are unable to address specific needs that are associated with their gang mem-bership, such as security. Moreover, the absence of this element means that there is insufficient counselling and individualized support for those who may wish to leave gangs and organized crime networks. These programmes are also unable to target the gang as a group. While the absence of the former type of programming (targeting gang members as individuals) may have led to less effective results, the absence of this latter type of programming (targeting the gang for social intervention as a group) may have allowed for the successes that have occurred. Interventionists elsewhere rightly caution that group work with gangs may elevate the levels of gang cohesion, increase membership and lead to heightened criminal productivity (Curry 2010, 119; Klein 1995, 144).

Similarly, there are no re-entry programmes for ex-convicts. The numbers of ex-convicts are few, but their return to this and other communities may animate the gang(s), thereby triggering leadership contests within gangs and/or attempts to politically realign a gang and reinvigorating old unsettled blood debts with rival gangs. Left unattended, this problem increases the risk of programme set-backs. This is thus a gap to be filled in future iterations of these programmes. Such effort requires a national framework that provides for a community re-entry programme that communities may tap into for support. A national re-entry programme for ex-convicts from national and foreign jurisdictions could be made more efficacious by coordinating with organized communities.

Peace-making may be considered a type of intervention because it involves direct work with gang members aimed at stopping specific episodes of gang violence and preventing future violence. Peace-making was also conducted at the level of communities. Great effort was put towards assisting groups of neighbouring communities that have a history of gang violence and political conflict. In the case of Matthews Lane, efforts were made to build peace bridges with old rival Tivoli Gardens. Both were brought together in the same remedial education programme and leadership training courses.

This is a promising feature of the work of the Ministry of National Security via the then-CSI, but it is double-edged. As group-level work, it risks aiding group cohesion because it takes place in conditions of intense rivalry and "wars". It may bring about peace, but it could also backfire and create new gang alliances. In the case of the peace-making work with the Spanglers and the Presidential Click, Matthews Lane and Tivoli Gardens, it has risked reinforcing an unholy alliance between old enemies.[32] Thus, during the armed confrontation between the security forces and the Presidential Click of May 2010, there was an attempt to mobilize the Spanglers-affiliated young men in support of the Presidential Click.[33] The leaders of the MLDC were, however, able to dissuade most of them from joining forces with the Presidential Click in defence of Coke. A few members of the Spanglers did participate in the armed action supporting the Presidential Click, and two were killed. The rest of the community viewed their participation as individual adventures, not as an organized gang effort with community support.[34] This event occurred after seven years of anti-gang social intervention programmes. It marks significant progress in informal social control, as the community was able to influence this particular type of gang behaviour *by using a persuasive-conciliatory style of control*. This style of control best approximates what Black (1998) calls conciliatory as it implies that the behaviour in question (joining the Presidential Click's "war" against law enforcement) would strain relationships with the community. This development may signify programme effectiveness and the potential for programme sustainability.

If it is done properly, peace-making may lay a foundation for successful gang exits and community re-entry programmes. Peace, however, requires forgiveness, reconciliation and the restoration of healthy social relationships, and this is difficult in communities with a violent subculture with an unforgiving, revenge-seeking orientation (Harriott 2008, 41). It is difficult but necessary and useful work.

Two national state-supported institutions exist for the purposes of conflict resolution and peace-making. These are the Peace Management Initiative (PMI) and the Dispute Resolution Foundation (DRF). The PMI works with gangs in community contexts, and the DRF has a much broader mandate but supports community efforts. Together, they promote the restoration of relationships within and between communities.

In Matthews Lane, peace-making and mediation work were not left to the external agencies. Attempts were made to develop these capabilities within the community. The Dispute Resolution Foundation trained members of the CDC in restorative justice, conflict resolution and mediation. The community leaders were thus able to function as mediators, and they were able to prevent day-to-day conflicts in the community from escalating to physical violence. Elsewhere, that is, in other communities where the conditions were more favourable, an additional step was taken to train the local police in a similar manner. This allowed the community mediators and those in the police force to speak a similar language and to make common purpose.

To conclude the discussion of this case, it should be noted that there was considerable responsiveness of the people as a community to the efforts at community transformation. Yet there are still deeply held mentalities that are tied to old patterns of crime dependence. The experience shows that the gang problem may be controlled and perhaps the community transformed but only with great effort, considerable patience and consistency of effort.

Good community governance appears to be vital to the success of all other activity. Investing in the development of the community leadership, training in how to infuse community democracy via the local structures/democratic decision-making, willingness to compromise, consensus-building, and thus greater community unity have borne some success. The process of community mobilization actually shifted power in favour of the pro-social elements in the community.

There are indications that the community is better integrated as a result of these programmes. Its governance structures and their accomplishments are real advances that have shifted power from the resident criminal group to these structures and more in favour of the state control agencies. This shift is, however, yet to be consolidated.

Conclusion

The experience that has been documented in this chapter highlights both the successes and the potential for developing the collective efficacy of gang-dominated communities. It further demonstrates that reviving informal social control ensures sustainable gang and crime prevention and control in those settings. The Jamaican state and society have an opportunity to reverse the high rates of violent crime and to remove the garrison phenomenon, even in difficult economic times.

The case discussed here instantiates strategies that were observable prior to elaboration of the Anti-Gang Strategy and Plan (AGSP) of the JCF, which was discussed in chapter 7. There are gaps between the practised strategies and those that are presented in the AGSP (Amiot and Foster 2011). The practices described here provide a basis to further refine strategy and suggest that evaluating prior actions may be worthwhile as a means to perfect practice. There has been some muddling through, but the advances that have been made reflect genuine advances in thinking, in institutional configuration and capabilities, in building partnerships, in programme design and perhaps even in the implementation of these programmes. Future successes will depend on additional learning and better implementation. There is much experience here that may be further distilled for its valuable lessons.

Aspects of the anti-gang strategy appear to have achieved violence-reduction outcomes. Targeted gang suppression has yielded positive results, but the integrated strategy that incorporated social prevention has accomplished more than suppression alone might account for. In addition, the integrated approach is likely to yield a more sustainable reduction in the rates of violent crimes, as long as the programmes are not too ambitious and do not require excessive financial resources and commitments that would overextend the implementing institutions. There have been considerable advances in developing institutions that are able to design and implement social interventions. Several such organizations now exist within and beyond the state. If properly coordinated, programme implementation may become more effective.

Improved community integration has presented opportunities for de-garrisoning the gang-dominated communities. For these extreme but high-impact cases, breaking crime dependency, improving access to legitimate opportunities, and increasing attachment to the helping and opportunity-creating institutions that operate in the mainstream of the society appear to result in greater commitment to conventional norms and means of achieving one's life goals.

If the processes described in this chapter are to be consolidated, change is demanded of both the state and the people. In all of the communities, significant sections of their populations and an emergent leadership were willing to work for change in concert with external actors, particularly the state agencies. In the wake of power shifts away from the gangs and towards the pro-social elements in the community, greater participation of the people via democratic participatory channels is likely to stimulate a more robust informal social control that will be directed against delinquent and gang-affiliated youth.

The cases of the Spanglers and Matthews Lane, and the Presidential Click and Tivoli Gardens encapsulate the advances, the difficulties and the further possibilities for violence reduction and gang prevention and control in Jamaica. If the programmes are to truly go beyond controlling organized crime and gang activity and become preventive, then these programmes must be better informed by the Jamaica-specific sets of risk factors for violence and gang joining at both the individual and community levels and must also be better designed for evaluation and learning. The advances in strategy to date have already yielded lower rates of violence and a decline in the power and influence of the gangs. Gang suppression has had immediate and significant impact and, in concert with social prevention programmes, these results have been sustained (nationally) for approximately nine years. The prevention programmes are yet to be evaluated, but their independent impact is expected to be more medium-term as they help to consolidate and stabilize the gains of the suppression strategies. The Jamaican authorities have a promising opportunity now to further refine their anti-gang strategy, as well as to look beyond it.

Notes

1. Communities and neighbourhoods are not equally vulnerable and receptive to gangs. Structural differences may matter. Subjectivities that may be considered to be dimensions of social cohesion also matter. The effects of these latter variables are discussed in UNDP 2012.
2. These are aggregate data for the Caribbean 7. When disaggregated by country, these data reveal that for Jamaica the social-justice orientation is even more prevalent (than the mean for the Caribbean 7).
3. This protection need not always be actively or directly negotiated with law enforcement. It may at times be the outcome of a self-imposed restraint by the police that is induced by knowledge of the relationship between gang and party.
4. For example, the obya, vagrancy, cannabis (ganja) and gambling laws. These are activities that should be regulated, not criminalized and responded to in a penal style. For a further discussion of this issue see, for example, McCree (1996).
5. For a discussion of normative change in Jamaica, see Stone (1992), and for evidence of the emergence of a subculture of violence, see Harriott (2003, 2008).
6. Although here we focus on the positive effects of social cohesion on social control, it is well established that social cohesion may also enable negative behaviour.

7. It is well understood that in some contexts social cohesion as expressed in integration at the level of values may be criminogenic. This is this Mertonian strain.
8. Computed using the Human Development Report (UNDP 2012) dataset.
9. Much of the fieldwork and the processing of the experiences with the gang prevention programmes in this community were done with the help of Patricia Ball, then head of the Citizen Security Initiative (CSI), and other members of the CSI staff. I was invited by that agency to assist with an assessment of its work. My efforts had the benefit of access to the documents and experiences of the CSI. I have relied heavily on this prior effort.
10. Amanda Sives (2010) gives an account of the activities of Group 44 which provided political muscle for the PNP and from which the Spanglers later emerged. There is a line of continuity between Group 44 and the Spanglers, but it has not yet been carefully mapped and may still be contested.
11. In 2001, its population was less than 2,131, which was the census count for the Central Downtown Kingston area. The community of Matthews Lane is a part of the Central Downtown Kingston area.
12. From field notes taken during repeated visits to the community and interviews and group discussions with older former gang members and younger males who still self-identify with the gang.
13. When stripped of the idea of the community as a "family", the don is still a special (criminal) type of "big man" who "runs" the community, typically as an actor who operates within the political system.
14. For a discussion of these "jungle courts", see Charles and Beckford (2012). Earlier, Phipps was arrested for the attempted murder of one of the victims of disciplinary action by his jungle court. In response to the action of the police, the people of his community rioted and marched to the police station where he was held to demand his release.
15. These efforts were made but the outcomes have not been measured.
16. Some 82 per cent of the respondents felt that "people in their community are generally trustworthy".
17. High levels of confidence in organizations may conceivably co-exist with low levels of interpersonal trust.
18. In chapter 7, it is suggested that there was such an early-stage outcome in Tivoli Gardens. This development occurred after the operation of 2010 that was directed against the Presidential Click.
19. See the findings on support for social intervention in the UNDP 2012.
20. Many communities have Community Development Councils that enjoy linkages to state agencies and which participate in community governance.
21. A graphic example of how gate-keeping elevates status and tightens the grip on power was the distribution of United Nations food aid in Cite Solei, Haiti, by local

gangsters. This process was observed by the author. A similar routing of state and other resources via Jamaican gang leaders has had similar power effects.

22. This message was to be found on the placards that were held aloft by the demonstrators during the marches of May 2010 in support of Coke and a similar one in 1998 in support of Phipps. This slogan has also been presented in other demonstrations in support of some other dons and gang leaders elsewhere in the country.

23. Reputation for violence matters materially. It reduces the risks associated with the actual use of violence but brings many of the benefits that are associated with demonstrated capabilities and will to deliver violence. Thus, even when the actual levels of violence are reduced, the benefits may remain so long as the capabilities and the reputations remain.

24. Placards with this message were hoisted during the pro-Coke demonstration of 2010 that is discussed in chapter 7.

25. Some Jamaican gang leaders, including Christopher Coke, have been noted for their religiosity.

26. From data provided by the CSI. These data are for Matthews Lane only. Here I give the frequency counts so that these calculations may be checked.

27. These sentiments were not associated with the state-run programme or rather were not expressed in relation to it. The more negative manifestations were associated with the state-led activities. The point here is not to discount the role of the state, but rather to suggest that for the state-sponsored programmes, perhaps some intermediary organizations may best run them or be involved with their administration.

28. For additional information, see http://www.heart-nta.org.

29. For the most problematic communities, the programme costs are crudely underestimated at some US$1,500 per person per year. This estimate includes the expenditure of the CSI and the CSJP, but excludes MNS budgetary expenditures on special projects in the community and the cost of the services that were/are provided by other state agencies.

30. These data were provided by the CSI. There were more females in the jobs-skills programme than the number that were filtered from the social-skills programme. Many were exempt from the filtration process as they were regarded as being free of problem behaviour.

31. This is stated as a general truth. Violation of this generality may no doubt occur.

32. Peace-making between these two gangs preceded the work of the CSI and was gang initiated. The CSI reinforced the process.

33. There was this fear that the Presidential Click would mobilize other powerful gangs and present the country with a nation-wide episode of armed violent conflict with the security forces.

34. This bit of information was given by leaders of the community and was confirmed by cross-checking it with a list of the dead that was provided by the JCF.

References

Amiot, M., and R. Foster. 2011. *Jamaica Constabulary Force: Three Year Anti-Gang Strategic Plan* (AGSP), 11 April. Commissioned by the European Commission in consultation with the MNS and JCF.

Benfield, W. 2010. *Poverty and Perception in Jamaica: A Comparative Analysis of Jamaican Households.* Kingston: University of the West Indies Press.

Black, D. 1998. *The Social Structure of Right and Wrong.* San Diego: Academic.

Charles, C., and O. Beckford. 2012. "The Informal Justice System in Garrison Communities". *Social and Economic Studies* 61: 51–72.

Chevannes, B. 2001. *Learning to be a Man: Culture, Socialization and Gender Identity in Five Caribbean Communities.* Kingston: University of the West Indies Press.

Curry, G.D. 2010. "From Knowledge to Response and Back Again: Theory and Evaluation in Responding to Gangs". In *Youth Gangs and Community Intervention: Research, Practice, and Evidence,* edited by R.J. Chaskin, 109–28. New York: Columbia University Press.

Francis, S. 1969. "The Evolution of Community Development in Jamaica (1937–1962)". *Caribbean Quarterly* 15(2–3): 40–58.

Fromm, E. 1978. *Psychoanalysis and Religion.* New Haven: Yale University Press.

Girvan, D.T.M. 1962. "The History of the Jamaica Social Welfare Commission, 1937–1962". In *Working Together for Development: D.T.M. Girvan on Cooperatives and Community Development 1939–1968,* edited by N. Girvan, 1993, 221–35. Kingston: Institute of Jamaica Publications.

Girvan, N. ed. 1993. *Working Together for Development: D.T.M Girvan on Cooperatives and Community Development, 1939–1968.* Kingston: Institute of Jamaica Publications.

Harriott, A. 2002. "Captured Shadows, Tongue-Tied Witnesses, Compellants and the Courts: Obya and Social Control". In *Jamaica in Slavery and Freedom: History Heritage and Culture,* edited by K. Monteith and G. Richards, 115–43. Kingston: University of the West Indies Press.

———. 2003. "Social Identities and the Escalation of Homicidal Violence in Jamaica". In *Understanding Crime in Jamaica: New Challenges for Public Policy,* edited by A. Harriott. Kingston: University of the West Indies Press.

———. 2008 *Bending the Trend Line: The Challenge of Controlling Violence in Jamaica and the High Violence Societies of the Caribbean.* Kingston: Arawak.

Harriott, A., B. Lewis, K. Nelson, and M. Seligson. 2013. *The Political Culture of Democracy in Jamaica and in the Americas, 2012: Towards Equality of Opportunity.* LAPOP/Vanderbilt University.

Hirschfield, A., and K.J. Bowers. 1997. "The Effects of Social Cohesion on Levels of Recorded Crime in Disadvantaged Areas". *Urban Studies* 34 (July): 1275–95.

Horwitz, A.V. 1990. *The Logic of Social Control.* New York: Plenum.

Howell, J. 2010. "Lessons Learned from Gang Program Evaluation: Prevention, Intervention, Suppression, and Comprehensive Community Approaches". In *Youth Gangs and Community Intervention: Research, Practice, and Evidence*, edited by R. Chaskin. New York: Columbia University Press.

Kirton, C. 1996. "Rotating Savings and Credit Associations in Jamaica: Some Empirical Findings on 'Partner'". *Social and Economic Studies* 45(2–3): 195–224.

Klein, M. 1995. *The American Street Gang*. New York: Oxford University Press.

Knight, P. 2008. *Inequality and Stratification in Jamaica during Economic Adjustment (1991–2000)*. Kingston: Sir Arthur Lewis Institute of Social and Economic Studies, University of the West Indies.

Levy, H. 1996. *They Cry "Respect!" Urban Violence and Poverty in Jamaica*. Kingston: Centre of Population, Community and Social Change, University of the West Indies.

———. Forthcoming. "Community in Jamaica Nation". *Journal of Social Work*.

McCree, R. 1996. " The Chinese Game of Whe Whe In Trinidad: From Criminalization to Criminalisation". *Caribbean Quarterly* 42(2–3): 1–29.

Munroe, T. 1999. *Renewing Democracy into the Millennium: The Jamaican Experience in Perspective*. Kingston: University of the West Indies Press.

Powell, L. 2004. "Mapping Jamaican Perceptions of Distributive Justice: An Equity-Based Heuristic". *Social and Economic Studies* 53(4): 63–88.

———. 2007. *Probing Jamaica's Political Culture*, Volume 1. Kingston: Centre for Leadership and Governance, Department of Government, University of the West Indies, Mona.

Powell, L., B.A. Lewis, and M.A. Seligson. 2011. *The Political Culture of Democracy in Jamaica, 2010: Democratic Consolidation in the Americas in Hard Times*. LAPOP 2010. http://www.vanderbilt.edu/lapop/ab2010.php#Jamaica.

Putnam, R. 2000. *Bowling Alone: The Collapse and Revival of American Community*. New York: Simon and Schuster.

Robinson, C. 2013. "Dancehall Pushing Crime – Bunting". *Sunday Observer*, 13 January.

Sampson, R.J. 2011. "The Community". In *Crime and Public Policy*, edited by J. Q. Wison and J. Petersilia, 210–36. New York: Oxford University Press.

Sampson, R.J., and S. Raudenbush. 2001. *Disorder in Urban Neighborhoods: Does It Lead to Crime?* Research brief. Washington, DC: National Institute of Justice.

Sampson, R.J., S. Raudenbush, and F. Earls. 1997. "Neighborhoods and Violent Crime: A Multilevel Study of Collective Efficacy". *Science* 277: 918–24.

Sen, A. 1989. "Development as Capability Expansion". In *Readings in Human Development*, edited by S. Fukuda-Parr and A.K. Shiva Kumar, 3–16. New York: Oxford University Press, 2003.

———. 1999. *Development as Freedom*. Oxford: Oxford University Press.

Short, J.F., and L.A. Hughes. 2010. "Promoting Research Integrity in Community-Based Intervention Research". In *Youth Gangs and Community Intervention: Research,*

Practice and Evidence, edited by R.J. Chaskin, 127–54. New York: Columbia University Press.

Silver, E., and L. Miller. 2004. "Sources of Informal Social Control in Chicago Neighborhoods". *Criminology* 42(3): 551–83.

Sives, A. 2010. *Elections Violence and the Democratic Process in Jamaica 1944–2007*. Kingston: IRP.

St Jean, P. 2007. *Pockets of Crime: Broken Windows, Collective Efficacy and the Criminal Point of View*. Chicago: University of Chicago Press.

Stone, C. 1992. "Values, Norms and Personality Development in Jamaica". Mimeo.

UNDP (United Nations Development Programme). 2012. *Human Development and the Shift to Better Citizen Security: Caribbean Human Development Report 2012*. New York: UNDP.

9 | Faith-Based Interventions for Reducing Gang Violence in the Caribbean

Reflections from a Professor and a Priest

EDWARD R. MAGUIRE AND C. JASON GORDON

Gang violence is a complex phenomenon that requires comprehensive solutions. While many people instinctively view gang violence as solely a police or a criminal-justice problem, it is best conceptualized as a *community* problem. This perspective widens the range of potential strategies and tools that might be used to prevent or reduce gang violence. In designing comprehensive strategies to address gang violence, a basic principle is to leverage resources from different sectors, whether governmental or nongovernmental, that might be able to play an important role. Thus, a preliminary step in diagnosing a gang violence problem (see chapter 6 for information about diagnosing gang violence) is to conduct a detailed inventory of community resources that are currently being used and that might be mobilized to address the problem. The faith community constitutes a vital resource with potential to contribute in unique ways to preventing or reducing gang violence.

This chapter discusses a set of faith-based initiatives that were launched in 2005 and 2006 in and around Gonzales, a distressed community located in East Port of Spain in Trinidad. Gonzales was experiencing serious problems with gangs and gang violence, and community leaders placed significant pressure on the police and other government officials to address these problems. We present a unique perspective from two people whose backgrounds and vantage points for thinking about gang violence differ. Edward Maguire is a criminologist and university professor from the United States who was hired by the Government of Trinidad and Tobago to serve as an advisor on issues related to policing, gangs and violence. Jason Gordon is the bishop of Bridgetown (Barbados) and Kingstown (St Vincent and the Grenadines). Previously, Father Jason (as he was then known) served as the parish priest at a Catholic church in Gonzales.[1] Together, we examine the gang violence problem in Gonzales, reflect on its nature and sources, and discuss the role of the faith community in addressing that problem.

Gang violence strategies are often placed into three categories: prevention, intervention and suppression (Klein and Maxson 2006). Prevention efforts are designed to keep youth from joining gangs in the first place. Intervention efforts focus on those who are already in gangs and encourage them to leave the gang, provide them with new skills or opportunities that can provide alternatives to gang life, or encourage them to mitigate the severity of their behaviour if they decide to remain in the gang (for instance, encouraging them to choose options other than violence for resolving disputes). Suppression involves the use of the criminal justice system to monitor, arrest, prosecute and punish gangs. Though all three of these components are necessary for a comprehensive approach to gangs and gang violence, here we focus primarily on the intervention component. The faith community often plays a vital role in prevention efforts as well – and we applaud those vital efforts – but our primary purpose in this chapter is to reflect on the role of the faith community in gang violence *intervention* strategies.

The Role of the Faith Community

There are many reasons to anticipate that the faith community can play an important role in addressing gang violence in the Caribbean. First, at the most general level, research shows that religion exerts a moderate negative effect[2] on crime (Baier and Wright 2001; Evans et al. 1995). This effect is thought to operate through various causal pathways. For instance, at the individual level, studies show that religion enhances self-control and self-regulation as well as the selection and pursuit of more pro-social goals (McCullough and Willoughby 2009). At the community level, studies show that religious participation and religiosity serve as sources of informal social control, mainstream values, civic engagement and social capital (Johnson and Jang 2012). Though research evidence on the relationship between religion and crime is not unanimous, the majority of studies find an inverse relationship (more religion, less crime) at both the individual and community levels (Baier and Wright 2001; Evans et al. 1995; Johnson and Jang 2012; McGarrell, Brinker and Etindi 1999; McCullough and Willoughby 2009).

Second, Caribbean communities typically hold the faith community in high regard. For instance, a survey of more than ten thousand residents in seven Caribbean nations found that 88.4 per cent of respondents said that religion is "very important" or "rather important" in their lives. This compares with 67.4 per cent of respondents in the United States and only 43.9 per cent in Canada.[3] This same survey shows that the trust and confidence with which faith leaders are viewed in the Caribbean is equally prominent in communities without gang problems and those with serious gang problems.[4] This trust and confidence serves as a potentially solid foundation from which to launch intervention strategies aimed at reducing gang violence.

Third, throughout the world, the faith community plays a vital role in distressed, impoverished and socially disorganized communities where public services and infrastructure are often weak and gangs and crime tend to thrive. For instance, Foley, McCarthy and Chaves (2001, 215) note that "religiously based social service efforts carry an important part of the burden of providing for the needs of poor communities". Similarly, McGarrell, Brinker and Etindi (1999, 7) note that the faith community has "a centuries-old tradition of caring for the poor, the disadvantaged, and the troubled sectors of our society", and doing so in a proficient and committed way. Faith-based organizations care for the disadvantaged through a variety of programmes, including food banks, clothing drives, tutoring classes, after-school programmes, healthcare programmes, substance abuse counselling and more (Dilulio 1998). Because the faith community has such a long record of experience in addressing a wide range of social issues, McGarrell, Brinker and Etindi (1999, 6) argue that it can serve as "a key mediating institution" for addressing crime problems.

Fourth, although working with violent offenders is inherently risky, faith leaders are usually considered off-limits for violent victimization. This is an important consideration in communities where outsiders are often unwelcome and may place themselves at great risk for violent victimization when trying to work in certain neighbourhoods, particularly with gangs. For instance, an outreach worker who works with gangs in and around Gonzales told us that gang members sometimes shoot at workers from the power company when they come to make repairs. The gang members will then complain when the lights do not work. So he asks them: "If you're shooting people when they put the ladder up, how they going to fix the light? Why are you shooting?" In Trinidad, several people have been shot while attempting to work within gang communities (such as utility company employees, contractors, taxi drivers) because gang members perceive them as encroaching on their territory, working in their area without prior authorization from the gang leader (in some cases, without paying a "tax" or a "security fee" to the gang leader) or threatening their economic interests. Similarly, numerous "peacemakers" who attempted to mediate gang disputes have also been killed. In the face of such risks, faith leaders are often unique in their ability to navigate the community in ways most people simply cannot. They often hold a special place in the hearts of community residents by virtue of their important role as spiritual advisors and their key role in the community's most intimate rituals and events including childhood rites of passage, weddings, funerals and religious holidays.

Faith leaders around the world are actively addressing serious social problems including economic injustice, homelessness, human trafficking and prostitution, hunger, illegal immigration, teen pregnancy and other issues. The faith community also has an important role to play in reducing violence in all of its various manifestations, including child abuse, elder abuse, sexual violence and intimate partner violence (Horton and Williamson 1988; Peters 2010; Rotunda, Williamson and Penfold 2004; Wolff et al. 2001). This chapter is particularly concerned with the role of faith leaders in addressing *gang* violence.

Two Examples of Gangs, Violence and the Faith Community

To begin our discussion of faith-based interventions for reducing gang violence in the Caribbean, we draw on two of the most well-known examples from the United States. Both initiatives have served as an inspiration for similar efforts elsewhere, including the Caribbean. The first involves the long-standing efforts of Father Gregory Boyle, whose work with the gangs of East Los Angeles has been chronicled in two books and a movie (Boyle 2010; Fremon 2004; Mock 2012). The second involves the work of Reverend Eugene Rivers and his colleagues in Boston's TenPoint Coalition. Although we highlight these two examples, we acknowledge that many other faith leaders around the world have also intervened with gangs to reduce gang violence.

Homeboy Industries (East Los Angeles)

Father Gregory Boyle, a Jesuit priest, was appointed as pastor of the Dolores Mission Church in the gang-ridden Boyle Heights community in East Los Angeles in 1986. In 1988, Father Boyle started Jobs for a Future (JFF), a job-training programme intended to provide high-risk youth in the area with an alternative to gang life. Through JFF, Boyle was able to find jobs for "recovering" gang members. In 1992, just after the riots that consumed Los Angeles, Father Boyle launched Homeboy Bakery in order to provide additional job opportunities for recovering gang members. In 2001, Father Boyle launched Homeboy Industries as a non-profit organization. In 2007, Homeboy Industries moved into an impressive $8.5 million building in downtown Los Angeles. Homeboy Industries now provides a variety of services, including case management, legal services, tattoo removal, job training, mental health and substance abuse counselling, and life skills classes, among others. It is also home to enterprises that employ former gang members and help fund the organization's outreach activities, including farmer's markets, a bakery, a diner, a catering operation, and a silk-screening and embroidery shop. Some have called Homeboy Industries "the largest gang intervention program in the nation" with an annual operating budget of nearly $15 million that allows them to employ hundreds of former gang members.[5] Two mottos summarize the approach of Homeboy Industries: "nothing stops a bullet like a job" and "jobs, not jails".

Father Boyle, known as G-Dog by his "homies", reflects on his efforts in his autobiography, *Tattoos on the Heart* (Boyle 2010). The book is a gut-wrenching testament to the difficulties faced by kids growing up in the projects in East Los Angeles and those like Father Boyle who try, often against the odds, to help keep them on a positive path. Father Boyle shares the stories of many anonymous young men and women he has worked with who lost their lives to gang violence. He established Homeboy Industries to create "a community of unconditional love" because "community will always trump gang" (p. 94). He reminds us that gang members come from broken communities and broken families where few services and opportunities are available to the children growing up there. The passage below summarizes his views on the role of the faith community:

> We imagine, with God, this circle of compassion. Then we imagine no one standing outside of that circle, moving ourselves closer to the margins so that the margins themselves will be erased. We stand there with those whose dignity has been

denied. We locate ourselves with the poor and the powerless and the voiceless. At the edges, we join the easily despised and the readily left out. We stand with the demonized so that the demonizing will stop. We situate ourselves right next to the disposable so that the day will come when we stop throwing people away. (p. 190)

For Father Boyle, gang intervention means investing in young people, providing them with services and jobs, and constantly reminding them that their lives matter – that they are "exactly what God had in mind when God made them" (p. 192).

TenPoint Coalition (Boston)

Boston's African American community has historically had a negative, conflict-filled relationship with the police. Boston's African American ministers, acting in their roles as advocates for their communities, also had historically strained relationships with police. As Berrien and Winship (1999) note, "individuals within Boston's religious community were some of the most vocal and publicized critics of the Police Department's aggressive tactics during the late 1980s and early 1990s." Reverend Eugene Rivers in particular earned a reputation for his harsh criticism of police. Also, Boston's faith community struggled to work well together. This all changed due to one tragic and unexpected event in May 1992, when violence erupted among gang members attending a funeral at the Morning Star Baptist Church for a young man who had been shot to death in a drive-by shooting. A church is considered off-limits for violence, even in troubled communities, and the shootings and stabbings that occurred during this incident were shocking to the collective conscience.

As Berrien and Winship (1999) noted, "the brazenness of this attack, taking place within a church sanctuary, inspired many of Boston's black clergy to take action. They realized that they could no longer effectively serve their community by remaining within the four walls of their churches. Instead, youth and others in the surrounding troubled neighbourhoods needed to become extensions of the church congregations." Thus began Boston's TenPoint Coalition, a group of approximately forty churches working together to address issues affecting Boston's youth, particularly those at risk for serious social problems like violence, drug abuse and other forms of delinquent or destructive behaviour. The TenPoint Coalition allowed clergy to step outside of their churches and engage more fully with youth using a street-based ministry approach (1999).

Boston's dramatic drop in violence in the 1990s, particularly youth homicide, is now well storied. Multiple explanations have surfaced to account for this drop in violence. Some credit the police, while others credit the faith community, police-probation partnerships, a public health initiative intended to reduce violence, or a combination of these factors (for example, Berrien and Winship 1999; Braga et al. 2001; Braga, Hureau and Winship 2008; Corbett 2002; Prothrow-Stith and Spivak 1996). Berrien and Winship (1999) argue that the faith community played an important role in reducing violence, but their explanation suggests a more complex causal process than might ordinarily be expected. They argue that the "key contribution of TenPoint and efforts by other church based groups does not lie in their outreach and programmatic work with at-risk youth" because there were simply too few of those activities to have produced such a dramatic effect. Instead, the TenPoint Coalition served as an intermediary institution between the police and the community.

The faith leaders acknowledged that some gang members were so violent and intractable that the formal criminal justice system was necessary to prevent them from offending. Thus, the TenPoint Coalition provided police with "an umbrella of legitimacy" that enabled police to work on reducing the violence. The faith community contributed an extra layer of surveillance for police by providing information based on their extensive network of contacts on the streets. At the same time, the faith leaders made it clear to police that they would not tolerate unnecessarily aggressive policing tactics and would go to the media if necessary to prevent such behaviours. Boston's faith community had manoeuvred themselves into a unique position in which both the police and the community viewed them as partners. Berrien and Winship (1999) argue that these multi-way partnerships between the clergy, the police and communities generated a stock of legitimacy and cooperation that contributed to the drop in Boston's youth homicides in the 1990s.

Background

Nothing in seminary trained me for this.
– Father Jason.

On 6 January 2003, Father Jason was appointed parish priest of two inner-city parishes: Holy Rosary, a Gothic church on the corner of Henry and Park Streets in Port of Spain, and St Martin de Porres in the community of Gonzales. By

Good Friday of that year (18 April 2003), there had already been five murders in or around Gonzales. The community was thrown into deep crisis. The war was ostensibly between gangs in Upper and Lower Gonzales, but the presence of other very active and violent gangs in immediate proximity complicated the network of alliances and conflicts between gangs in the area. A gang led by two brothers (Pig and Bumbles) in St Barb's, a community located just above Gonzales, had a long record of violence and an avowed dislike for Muslims. Next to St Barb's was Snake Valley, with a small gang led by Prophet. Located just below Gonzales on Charford Court was the G-Unit gang, led by Fresh. Nearby, there was also a small gang on Quarry Street. Its leader was reputed to be wild and irrational and was suspected in a number of killings. Father Jason viewed him as the greatest challenge. There were many gangs in the Port of Spain metropolitan area, but these six gangs located in and around Gonzales were the ones of greatest relevance in the areas where Father Jason was assigned. So he began working with them.[6]

Professor Maguire was hired by the Government of Trinidad and Tobago in late 2004 to begin teaching a course on strategic crime control for police managers. His responsibilities were later expanded to include advising the government on police reform, gangs and violence issues more generally. Very quickly, Maguire began looking for additional resources within the communities where gang violence was most problematic. After decades of criminological research in the United States, researchers have clearly established that gang violence issues are more than just a policing problem; they are a community problem. Many of the communities in Trinidad with the highest levels of gang violence have little or no resources to draw upon in mounting prevention and intervention efforts. Maguire was brought on to build improved capacity in the police service, but he reasoned that concentrating only on the police would constitute an incomplete solution. A truly comprehensive approach to gang violence would also focus on building capacity in troubled communities.

In many of Trinidad and Tobago's most distressed areas, the faith community – the churches, mosques, temples and other places of worship – is highly active and provides an obvious vantage point for launching interventions. Thus, at Professor Maguire's request, an assistant police commissioner arranged an interview with the leader of one of the major religious organizations in the nation's diverse faith community. In this meeting, Professor Maguire explored what role the faith community might play in a partnership with police to focus on Trinidad's gang violence issues. The faith leader kept insisting that gang violence was a police problem. It was a long and frustrating conversation, and it went nowhere. Back to the drawing board.

Professor Maguire continued to search for faith leaders who would be willing to work with the police to address gang violence issues. Eventually he heard about Father Jason Gordon's work in Gonzales. Professor Maguire and Father Jason met for the first time in early 2005. By that time, Father Jason was fully ensconced in his position in Gonzales, and Professor Maguire was searching for someone in the faith community who was willing to take a leadership role on the gang issue. In April 2005, Maguire and Gordon met with officials from the Trinidad and Tobago Police Service (TTPS) and the Ministry of National Security to design a plan for an ambitious community-policing programme for Gonzales that would augment the ongoing Pride in Gonzales initiative. This community-policing programme was launched in February 2006. Very quickly it won a community-policing award from the Association of Caribbean Commissioners of Police but, due to a lack of sustained support from the TTPS, it never fully took shape in the way it was originally envisioned. Although the community-policing initiative hatched by the initial meeting participants was unable to focus on gangs and violence in the ways we had hoped it would, Father Jason and Professor Maguire continued to work together to address the gang violence issue that plagued Gonzales.

The Intervention

Gonzales is like an old medieval town, located on a hill with five ways in and out. Its population is only about fifty-six hundred, but it generates a substantial amount of violence despite its small size.[7] Gangs control all of the access points. A three-hundred-acre community with six gangs located in and around it means a lot of egos and guns in a very tight space.

In response to the crisis, the parish hosted a meeting for all leaders in the community to begin a conversation about possible paths to peace. Out of this initiative grew the Community Intervention for Empowerment (CIT+E) Programme. CIT+E featured homework clinics, an Internet cafe, sports programmes, a photography and video club, and a drama programme. By 2005, CIT+E had partnered with the City of Port of Spain and the Canadian Institute of Planners to bring participatory governance to Gonzales.

At the time, Father Jason believed that there is a simple dynamic to move a community forward – get participation, make it real and make it revolve around the real issues of the community. Most importantly, make sure you deliver on whatever you promise. In 2005, Father Jason started by asking the community what its main concerns were and recorded the community responses onto a flip chart. The answers started rolling out, and twelve were listed. Father Jason and his team grouped them and then started a voting process to put the list into hierarchical order:

- crime, indiscipline of youth,[8] and lack of community integration
- unemployment
- disposal of garbage
- reconstruction of roads and infrastructure
- community centre
- inadequate social activities
- water

The stark reality of a visible list provided a sense of priority and a place to start. The process involved the collective participation of community residents; this process was unique because it gave them a voice without the usual litany of woes that go nowhere. All participants worked together to gel the group into a community with a purpose and a mission.

Naming the issues proved to be fairly simple, but moving the group toward solving them was significantly more challenging. Father Jason and his team went through the list item by item and asked the community for solutions. They began with crime, indiscipline of youth and lack of community integration. The solution was to hire a social worker to work with the youth, both one-on-one on the streets and in groups. The aim was to improve community integration and socialization of youth. Community members who attended the meeting discussed the solution and then voted unanimously that this was a good way forward. The intervention was deepening, and the community was beginning to trust and move from despair to hope.

The year 2006 began with underlying tensions between the gangs in Upper and Lower Gonzales. The long history of conflict was reaching a fever pitch, and on 9 January, war finally broke out. Two of the "lieutenants" from Snake Eye's gang, Tim[*9] and Brian*, came together to encircle Upper Gonzales. One Sunday night the guns rang out, and the young men scattered. There was one casualty – an eight-year-old girl hit by a splinter launched by a bullet. Father Jason met with both leaders, trying to understand the issues and bring some resolution. It did not work. Father Jason went to visit Snake Eye one morning in early January. It was Eid al-Adha, and the mufti, a local Muslim faith leader, brought a bull to sacrifice and cook. Snake Eye said he would call off the war, but Father Jason looked into his eyes and knew he did not mean it. The guns spoke instead. Lower

Gonzales went on the offensive as a result of some robberies in Jubilee Crescent. Then the rapes came, and gang warfare seemed inevitable.

Father Jason made night-time visits to Upper Gonzales a few times and called the lieutenants to hold them to the cease fire; it did not work. In the last week in January, when an automatic weapon rang off, Father Jason called a meeting between the leaders of the two main gangs. They brought the leaders of two other gangs into the meeting as well. The location was secret and transportation was provided. The gang leaders present at the meeting included Tommy Gun* from Upper Gonzales, Snake Eye from Lower Gonzales and Belmont, Prophet from Snake Valley (located just above Gonzales near St Barb's) and Fresh from Charford Court (located just below Gonzales). Two other gang members were present: Kevin* (a member of Tommy Gun's gang) and Tim (a lieutenant in Snake Eye's gang). Absent from the meeting were the leaders of the gangs in St Barb's (located just above Gonzales) and Quarry Street, neither of whom were invited to participate.

Also present at the meeting were Professor Maguire, a mid-level police official with close ties to the Gonzales community, a female police official who was selected to lead the community-policing project in Gonzales, and a police sergeant with extensive knowledge of gangs and gang violence in the area. The sergeant assigned a complement of officers to stand guard outside the meeting to prevent any acts of violence. Later, Professor Maguire learned from contacts in the police service that a rival gang had planned to shoot up the meeting, but when they drove by and saw the sergeant's heavily armed team outside they called off their plans. Luckily, disaster was averted.

The discussions held during the truce meeting revealed that one of Tommy Gun's young gang members, together with another young member of the St Barb's gang, was behaving in ways inconsistent with "the order" – the informal set of values and expectations among the gangs for what constitutes acceptable behaviour. Others described them as "loose cannons" who did whatever they wanted without appropriate approval from their leaders. The other gang leaders told Tommy Gun that he was no longer able to control his people. The police sergeant told him that he "lose his belly", a euphemism meant to suggest that he was no longer as courageous or as effective a leader as he had once been. The truce focused on this problem by encouraging Tommy Gun to control his youngest members. As young men began to assert their independence and failed to heed "the order", they reinforced a theme that emerged prominently not only in our study of Gonzales, but also in our study of gangs and violence in Trinidad more generally. There is a steady and unrelenting supply of young men coming of age, ready to challenge the status quo not only about *what* is acceptable, but also about *who* is in charge.

According to Father Jason, the meeting seemed to work "like magic". Fresh intervened at a pivotal time when Tommy Gun and Snake Eye were at each other. Professor Maguire remembers being awestruck by the fact that Fresh – a notorious gang leader who had committed or ordered numerous acts of violence – was able to calm Tommy Gun with his reassuring words and by patting Tommy Gun's leg in a gentle way. Fresh also took on Prophet, resolving their differences and providing a way forward. Tommy Gun and Snake Eye followed and a four-way resolution happened. All four leaders committed to a ceasefire. It worked. The objective was achieved.

As the meeting ended, and participants began to disperse, Father Jason arranged for people to be driven home. Father Jason took Snake Eye and Fresh in his car. When they pulled up to Charford Court, Fresh invited Snake Eye to lime[10] with him. Father Jason thought, "Great! They are now trusting and bonding." That night, on 26 January 2006, a young man was killed around the corner from where they were, just below Gonzales. The dead young man was the brother of the gang leader from Quarry Street who had not been invited to the meeting. A new dynamic had emerged – Fresh and Snake Eye against the leader of the gang on Quarry Street. Just two days later on 28 January, another young man, the Quarry Street gang leader's eighteen-year-old stepson, was killed at his home in Gonzales. He was an innocent victim unrelated to the war. When gangs cannot locate their intended targets, they sometimes choose to victimize the families or friends of the target instead.

Father Jason notified Professor Maguire of the second murder just after it occurred, and they both went to the home. The young man's bullet-ridden body was still lying in the bedroom where he had been shot. The room was eerily still. Children milled about on the covered porch just outside of the bedroom, with a clear view of the body. Professor Maguire observed this phenomenon at several homicide scenes, where parents would allow children to remain in the area near a homicide victim. He worried that allowing children to grow up around this kind of violence might desensitize them. Exposure to violence as a child is one of the risk factors for violence as an adult (O'Keefe 1997; Song, Singer and Anglin 1998). Gang members will often say that they expect to die early because that is the life they have chosen. That is not to say that they don't fear death, because most do. But this young man was a casualty of a war that he was not involved in. And the suspected shooters were from a gang that just days before had agreed to a truce in our presence. But, very importantly, they had agreed to a truce *with each other*, not with gangs who were absent from the truce meeting. While this decision calculus may appear senseless through the lens of conventional logic, it makes perfect sense through the lens of gang logic. Father Jason reflects:

> Once more, Indi, like Rachel, lamented. Two years before, on Good Friday morning, another young man from that house was killed in the same way. It was Jamal's death which started CIT+E and the whole Gonzales initiative for me. To this day, I hold responsibility for these two deaths. I did not pull the trigger, but I set in motion the dynamic that produced the logic. Gang intervention is a messy business. These two deaths were the direct result of the meeting. The gangs did not violate the Assumption Accord – the agreement forged at that church where Father Garfield gave us hospitality. But they violated the spirit of the meeting. That was a subtlety lost on the gang leaders. I was hurt, shattered and betrayed. But it was not about me; it was about peace.

The Sunday after the meeting in Upper Gonzales, a young man named Fonzie* said to Father Jason: "Fada, why you leave we out?" Fonzie was a member of the St Barb's gang, located just above Gonzales, and they had not been invited to participate in the truce meeting. Father Jason had been warned by Snake Eye and Tommy Gun never to go to St Barb's. "Fada, dey dread and evilous," they'd said. The mythology surrounding the St Barb's gang was legend. They were reputed to have killed Chen, the powerful Muslim boss who controlled the Unemployment Relief Programme, a government-sponsored work programme that had been infiltrated extensively by criminal gangs. The St Barb's gang, led by brothers Pig and Bumbles, had a reputation for being fiercely independent and violent.

Father Jason went to St Barb's at 3:00 p.m. the next day and found a warm welcome. At 8:00 p.m. as he was making his way down the hill, he experienced something that felt stirring and powerful. He returned on Wednesday and met with Roger*, a government-based gang outreach worker who did a lot of work with the gangs. Together Father Jason and Roger used the Gonzales methodology to find out what the gangs really wanted. Thirty young men came out – lean, mean and curious. The real gang members were the target audience. They wanted to organize themselves for business in a new way. Father Jason promised to return with a facilitator to take the next stage of the journey.

Father Jason called Ravi*, who was at that time involved in founding a tertiary level organization in Trinidad. Ravi agreed to facilitate the process and mentor the young men in business. He had started a home for socially displaced young men many years before and was accustomed to the "rough and tumble". At the same time, Martin*, a local businessman who had called Father Jason about a personal matter, ended up offering to lend a hand in working with the gangs. Martin, Ravi and Father Jason came together and went up the hill.

That Wednesday was the most hopeful that Father Jason had ever been. Martin and Ravi facilitated and mentored, while Roger was present and supportive. More young men turned out, and they were enthused about the programme; they wanted to start business, to make legitimate money. They had ideas and passion. Ravi told them, "If you are serious, we need a day of training." Sunday at Club Dominoes was the decided location. They organized to borrow chairs and cook lunch. It was impressive.

"That Sunday," according to Father Jason, "we arrived heart in hand." Everything was in place. The meeting began half an hour late, as is customary, but a full house turned out, and Brothers United for Peace (BUP) was formed. They established a mission and vision statement, as well as a list of priority projects: feeding the community, distributing goods wholesale on the hill, creating a recreation club with a large-screen TV, infrastructural contracts and a sports day. They were on a roll. Euphoria came to the hill. The group comprised St Barb's led by Stretch*,[11] Upper Gonzales led by Tommy Gun, and Snake Valley led by Prophet. The future seemed secure. Integral development through participation was taking root. They were the architects of their own destiny. Father Jason recalls, "It seemed to me that day, peace broke out."

The euphoria lasted, built further with a football match in March. Ravi lent them TT$4,500 (US$750) to fund the event. In part it was a test of the ability of these young men to organize and to be accountable and honest. It was a success for the most part. The event was well organized and managed. The money was repaid, and expectation grew. However, the tide of hope turned that day. After the success of the football match, Josh, the economic leader of the Sandy gang in St Barb's, was killed Sunday evening [the night after the match]. Stretch was the acting leader of St Barb's because his brothers, Pig and Bumbles, were both in prison. Josh had wider acceptance by Prophet (from Snake Valley) and Tommy Gun (from Upper Gonzales) because he controlled the marijuana trade and thus the money. The brothers were not included in the peace process, which turned out to be a costly omission. They controlled things from jail with a cell phone. Josh was a casualty of war, the war for control. It was an inside job, and everyone knew it. Father Jason recalls, "On the Saturday before the sports, Josh had told me he wanted to talk 'personal'. We never did. A bullet came between us."

This death broke the alliance. Once again, Tommy Gun and Prophet couldn't trust St Barb's, which changed things dramatically. Ravi had a group of fifteen people attending a computer-literacy course in a facility at his institution. This continued for a long time with great success. Martin and Father Jason visited the three gangs on a regular basis to keep lines of communication open. Then in May, Prophet, the leader of the gang in Snake Valley, was killed. Everyone knew it was St Barb's. In fact, Prophet knew they were coming for him at some point. Father Jason reflects:

> The deaths of Josh and Prophet were directly connected to the alliance that we created. For the second time in the year, our best intentions did not keep people alive. To live with this is not easy. Welcome to the real world of the 'hood where the coming of the Christ has a high price – murder. Have you ever seen this dynamic at work in your life; the unexpected appearance of the God experience followed by mayhem? That year, I touched the powerlessness of God. Imagine what it must have been like for the Father to sit and watch the slaughter of the innocents and do nothing. That is God, His signature in transformation. Living with it is living the Christ mystery.

While things in St Barb's heated up from March onwards, Gonzales cooled down. In March, Mack* (from Upper Gonzales) and Brian (from Lower Gonzales) had a few face-offs in Jubilee Crescent. Brian was running a job there at the foot of the steps, and Father Jason recalls that "Mack would jumbie him just for so".[12] One day, Brian could not take it and went and shot up the Upper Gonzales community. Father Jason intervened and asked him why he broke the peace.

Brian:	Fada I had to send a message to dem, I had to tell dem we ain't taking it no more.
Father Jason:	You went to Upper Gonzales and fired shots to send a message!
Brian:	Is de only ting dey understand!
Father Jason:	You fired off bullets to send a message?
Brian:	YES!

Father Jason recalls thinking, "Wow! My lesson of the year! The gun is a tool of communication!"

Together, they explored the way Brian's message was probably received and brainstormed alternative and more effective ways of sending his message. They agreed that Brian would call Father Jason next time to help convey the message in a more peaceful way. This was a significant step forward. One week later,

Father Jason received a call from Brian. Father Jason called Mack and then called Brian back. It worked like a dream, and Brian was amazed. A week later a call came again and Father Jason went out at night and found Mack. He then called Brian on his phone and had the two of them speak. It went well until an all-out "cuss-out" took place – what a disaster!

Four days later, Brian stopped Father Jason: "Fada, sorry about the other night, no disrespect was meant. Anyway, me and Mack sort out we business."

"What, how?"

"Well I was working by the step and I saw Mack above and called out to him and said, 'We is big men and we can't have de Fada carrying messages between us like dis.' Mack said, 'I agree, but I have my piece on me.'"

Brian said, "Me too," and handed his gun over to one of his friends. Mack did the same. They met, they spoke and they found new ways to send messages. Father Jason reflects:

> Peace has a literacy of its own. It requires communication and this requires skill and imagination. Brian and Mack had never imagined a different way. So, even in a time of ceasefire, they did not see alternatives to their conflict. This, too, is the Christ story. Peace has been given to us and we keep going with the same old ways of living; the ways that continue to perpetuate the mess that we have. There is a literacy for peace that we must learn and teach. Yes, it is about communication and imagination but, fundamentally, it is about believing that peace is given, believing that our role in salvation history is finding alternative ways to send messages. We might not pick up a gun but a tantrum, a fit of anger, shaming someone, resentment, bad talking, are all the same destructive path. On that day when Brian and Mack spoke, the war and all of its logic and machinery were dismantled. They soon began meeting in each other's part of the community. The Community could not believe what it saw, yes, a miracle! Through all of the pain and disappointment, peace was born.

In the new circumstances, the community wanted to do an Easter extravaganza. Three community leaders from different faiths came together to do this: a Muslim, a Rasta and a Seventh-Day Adventist. Together with all of the other events, they wanted to do a walk through the community to demonstrate the newly found goodness and peace. Father Jason listened deeply, and together they decided it would be a Holy Saturday event. A mixture of parishioners and some residents gathered at the church, and interestingly, nobody found it strange. One of the community leaders had prepared signs; each had one word – goodness, peace, blessings, love, unity. They had jerseys printed with the new logo of Pride in Gonzales, each with one of those uplifting words. At 5:30 p.m., they departed, travelling up Indian Hill by the temple, through the dreaded walkway where the war was launched, into Upper Gonzales. Tim, one of the lieutenants from the gang in Lower Gonzales, met them on the hill, greeting them with smiles. He had heard about the walk and was joining. When they reached Upper Gonzales, Father Jason asked him if he would come. He said, "Fada, if you going, I going with you." Father Jason reflects:

> We went, and elation in the group of pilgrims mounted slowly. Tim had not walked in Upper Gonzales for five years. Brian and Mack had agreed to a peace two weeks before. The community had heard but did not really believe. We met Spider*, one of the "lieutenants" from Upper Gonzales. Tim was on one side of me and Spider on the other. Holy Saturday! This was Resurrection!
>
> We reached the playfield around 6:30 p.m. The sun had set and the acolytes had already lit the Easter fire. I spoke to the young men sweating on the court and they fell into the assembly. Tim said: "De Fada have to pray. Let's form a circle." A circle emerged around the fire as the last light faded. I invited each person to say something positive about Gonzales, then light a candle from the fire. It was the most profoundly moving Easter experience that I have had. The positives and the candles being lit, the two gangs present with the church and the community. When the candles were lit, I prayed, the community rejoiced and we continued the pilgrimage towards the church through other parts of the community, bring-ing blessings. We did not need feet to walk. God carried us that night.
>
> Roger Turton has an architectural concept that the inner space of a building is in conversation with the outer space of the community, and vice versa. Well, that is good pastoral theology and good liturgy. We brought the inner space of the church into the outer space of the community for Easter. This "conversation" continued within the inner space of the church for a long while. And this is what Pride in Gonzales is about: a conversation among the different constituents, building the logic for peace. Dialogue and Solidarity are the twin foundations. Pope Benedict XVI, in his message for World Day of Peace 2007, says: "Likewise, peace is both gift and task. If it is true that peace between individuals and peoples – the ability to live together and to build relationships of justice and solidarity – calls for unfailing commitment on our part, it is also true, and indeed more so, that peace is a gift from God."

In July, war broke out between Upper Gonzales and St Barb's. Bumbles and Pig from St Barb's had been released from prison in June. It was the second time they had been released after murder charges against them were dropped. Pig resumed leadership of the gang, which brought things to an impasse; Martin and Father Jason went up the hill that Sunday to mediate. Pig's army had already been assembled and after some negotiation he said, "Fada, I just make up my mind we have to have war. I want you to leave and don't come back. In war, anyone moving between the sides can be seen as the enemy."

Father Jason recalls, "That was as direct a threat as I have ever received. I tried to negotiate but he had passed that point. I told him to call me if he changed his mind. Pig said, 'Fada, when you leave, I will delete your number.' It was final." That Sunday, the Fatima devotions began with a pilgrimage in Gonzales walking to the Shrine to pray for peace. It involved passing through the troubled area. Father Jason reflects:

I left St Barb's and went to the St Martin Church to begin the pilgrimage. We walked, we prayed, we believed. That afternoon, St Barb's came down and shot up the community. It was mayhem. Whenever we do not know what to do, the golden rule is to sit and wait and watch, because God is doing something and we need to be in tune with it. In grief and disbelief, we waited and watched and, that Thursday, I received a call that I never expected – Pig. He wanted to re-open negotiations.

A week and a half later, Martin and I were driving back up to St Barb's at 7 p.m. with an offer from Tommy Gun for a ceasefire and a commitment to step back from the war. Pig was shocked that we came up at night and elated that negotiations had reached that far. While there, Tommy Gun called to see if we had a deal. Pig guessed it was Tommy on the phone and asked to speak to him. We hesitated, but handed him the phone. In the midst of the conversation Pig said, "Tommy, we sleep in the same bed as children, we grow up together, we went to war together, plenty people try to put me against you. What hurting is that you believe I am against you. Well, let me tell you, I will never, never, never, never, never, never, never, never, never, never raise my hand to kill you." With tears in his voice, Pig poured out his heart. The war was because he could not reach Tommy, because of hurt, because a friend misunderstood his intentions. About communications! Literacy and peace go together. Two weeks later, in St Barb's, there was a meeting of all the gangs. They all signed for peace.[13] It was fragile and tenuous, but it was clearly the thing that God was doing. The thing we have to work hard to maintain.

Pig was killed in late November 2006, shot while sleeping in bed with his girlfriend; an inside job, it would seem, a disgruntled inner faction of his own gang. Later we learned that part of it was that he had proposed to kidnap Martin and Father Jason. His men would have no part of it and lost faith in him. According to Father Jason, "We managed to build relationships that kept us safe."

Pig kept the peace between St Barb's and Gonzales, and he kept the peace in the wider Laventille community. He was buried at the Shrine in a magnificent liturgy, a service of remembrance led by his father, then the funeral. It brought healing to the hill and changed the role of the church in the peace process. On 3 December 2006, Father Jason was reassigned to the Social Justice Commission of the Catholic Church, and Father Clyde Harvey became parish priest at St Martin de Porres. Father Jason reflects:

> On that Good Friday morning in 2003, when I led the Stations of the Cross from Rosary and got the news about Jamal being killed that morning, I had no idea what God was doing. The passion of Gonzales and the Passion of Christ inter-mingled. In my conversations with Leela Ramdeen, then head of the Social Justice Commission of the Catholic Church, about a Catholic response to the violence on the hill, we did not know what we were beginning. When the archbishop asked that we start a project to address the crime and violence in Laventille, he could not have known what he was asking.
>
> This has been a season of Grace. Let me be more specific: God has been build-ing peace in East Port of Spain; block by block it is happening. The work is beyond anything we have done collectively. Like the Christ story, it is God's appointed time. The birthing of peace is what the Kingdom is most deeply about, what Christ is most deeply about. It is what God has been about in Gonzales.
>
> There are many parts of this story that I cannot tell, these remain in my heart; like Mary I ponder them and see the magnificence of God every day. We built a team in three and a half years that made a significant impact upon Gonzales, East Port of Spain, Trinidad and Tobago and the Caribbean. In 2006 we won a prize from the Association of Caribbean Commissioners of Police for community policing. Little Gonzales! The prime minister, in his 2007 budget speech hailed Pride in Gonzales as the leading community initiative in the country. He pledged support for any community using this approach or method to bring peace and build the community.
>
> Gang intervention is a messy business. To do good, evil follows. Responsibility is a difficult thing to work through. Does the lowering of the murder rate and drop in murders justify the four lives lost directly? No! Every life is sacred! Every one is precious. It is only relationships that are deep and true that can keep you safe in this fluid environment. I was threatened directly more than once. I made peace with God going to a meeting more than once. I walked into a serious threat and plan to kill me for bringing the police into Gonzales and because I faced the leader squarely and spoke directly, he did not use the 9mm when it arrived. Why did I do it, why put my life in danger? Well I did a thirty-day retreat and during it God said if he would ask me to do something, would I say yes? One week after the retreat

I was introduced to the gang leader in Upper Gonzales. I knew that walking the street and intervening the best that I could was the thing God asked me to do. Any other reason would be either suicide or madness.

Reflecting on the Effectiveness of the Intervention

A comprehensive impact evaluation of the gang intervention carried out by Father Jason and his partners in and around Gonzales is beyond the scope of this chapter. Evaluating these types of initiatives is difficult for many reasons. First, crime data compiled by the Trinidad and Tobago Police Service do not match up with the boundaries of Gonzales. The majority of Gonzales is situated within the Belmont police station district, but the police service did not have the capacity at the time to disaggregate crime records to account for crime at anything less than the district level. Moreover, although the boundaries of Gonzales are contested, a small portion of the community is actually situated in the Besson Street police station district, further complicating our ability to gather crime records for Gonzales specifically.

Second, even if we were able to compile the crime data for the community of Gonzales, it would be very difficult to determine the most appropriate geographic boundaries for the evaluation. Gangs typically have their own geographical boundaries, which do not coincide with police districts or census tracts (known as "enumeration districts" in Trinidad and Tobago). For instance, Snake Eye's territory was distributed; he lived in Belmont and controlled portions of Belmont outside of Gonzales, yet he also controlled Lower Gonzales at the time of the intervention. Moreover, gangs often commit acts of violence in locations separate from territories that they or their rivals control. It is very complex to determine what geographic boundaries to use in evaluating the effectiveness of a gang intervention. We discussed six gangs in this chapter – two in Gonzales, Snake Eye in Lower Gonzales and Tommy Gun in Upper Gonzales, and four located on the outskirts of Gonzales: the G-Unit run by Fresh on Charford Court, Prophet in Snake Valley, the St Barb's gang, and a small gang on Quarry Street. Yet, the Port of Spain metropolitan area was home to at least twenty-eight street gangs with many connections to those included in the intervention described in this chapter. Those gangs had their own collection of conflicts and alliances, and other interventions occurred among some of those gangs at around the same time as the intervention described here.

Third, the fact that the intervention described here was distributed over time and included a variety of different elements means evaluating its effectiveness is very difficult. Most quasi-experimental methods used to evaluate the impact of interventions rely on the idea that it takes place at a specific point in time (the "interruption" in interrupted time series analysis, for example). As a result, it is possible to determine whether that intervention affected the outcomes of interest. Here, the intervention unfolded over time and included multiple components. There are statistical methods for evaluating temporally distributed interventions like this, but they are nearly impossible to apply with the types of data available to us here.

Finally, another much larger truce was launched throughout the Port of Spain area in September 2006, and it involved several of the gangs in and around Gonzales. It would be very difficult to separate the effects of the ongoing intervention taking place in Gonzales from the effects of this larger truce.

Although we cannot carry out a formal impact evaluation of the intervention described in this chapter, the limited data available to us allow for some crude inferences. First, we examine the relationships between the six gangs in and around Gonzales before and after the truce, which was just one component of the intervention. Our knowledge of these conflicts and alliances is based on Father Jason's street work with the gangs and Professor Maguire's access to police intelligence on these issues. Figure 9.1 contains a sociogram illustrating conflicts and alliances before the truce, figure 9.2 illustrates the same phenomena one week after the truce, and figure 9.3 illustrates the same phenomena six months after the truce. It is impossible to construct a meaningful sociogram for the end of the intervention period (which occurred in December 2006 when Father Jason was reassigned). By then, the larger gang truce negotiated in September 2006 had occurred, thus complicating our ability to draw inferences about the effects of the truce organized by Father Jason. Furthermore, the leader of the Quarry Street gang had gone into hiding from his rivals and the police by that point. Pig and Prophet had also both been murdered, along with numerous other members of the six gangs discussed in this chapter. In addition, new gangs were emerging in the area as young men came of age and sought to make their mark on the streets. These sociograms demonstrate that the truce was successful in transforming conflict relationships into alliances, though a number of violent incidents continued to occur between the gangs in an around Gonzales.

Second, the Crime and Problem Analysis (CAPA) Branch in the Trinidad and Tobago Police Service provided us with data on violent incidents in

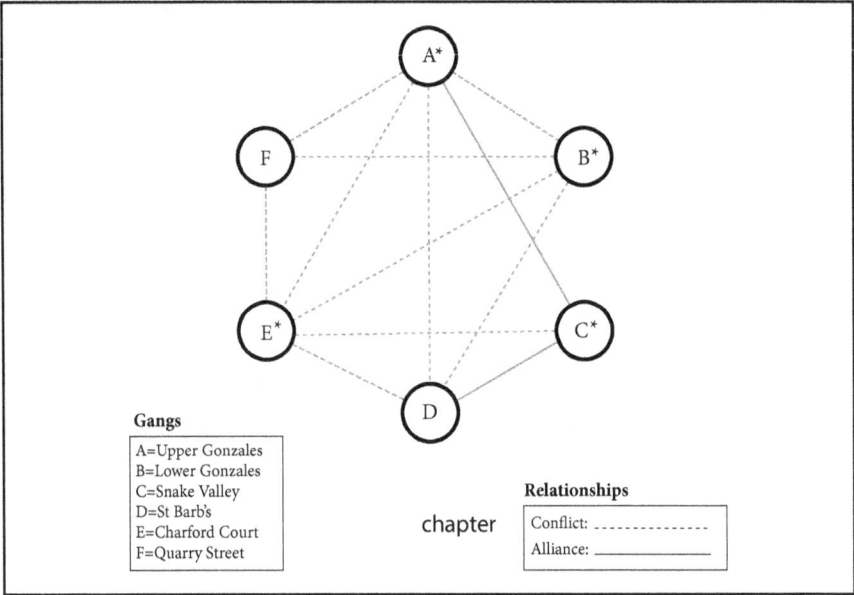

Figure 9.1. Conflicts and alliances between six gangs before truce

Note: * = Truce participants.

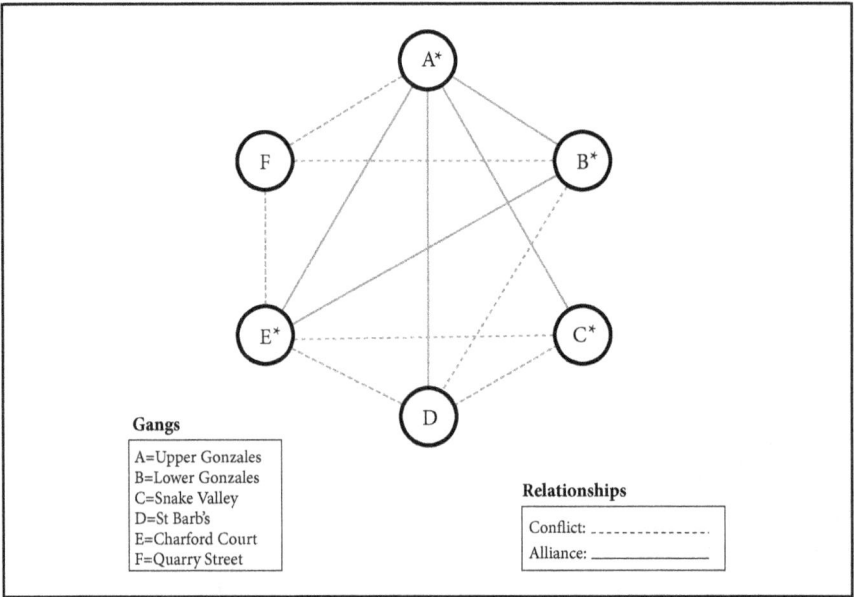

Figure 9.2. Conflicts and alliances between six gangs one week after truce

Note: * = Truce participants.

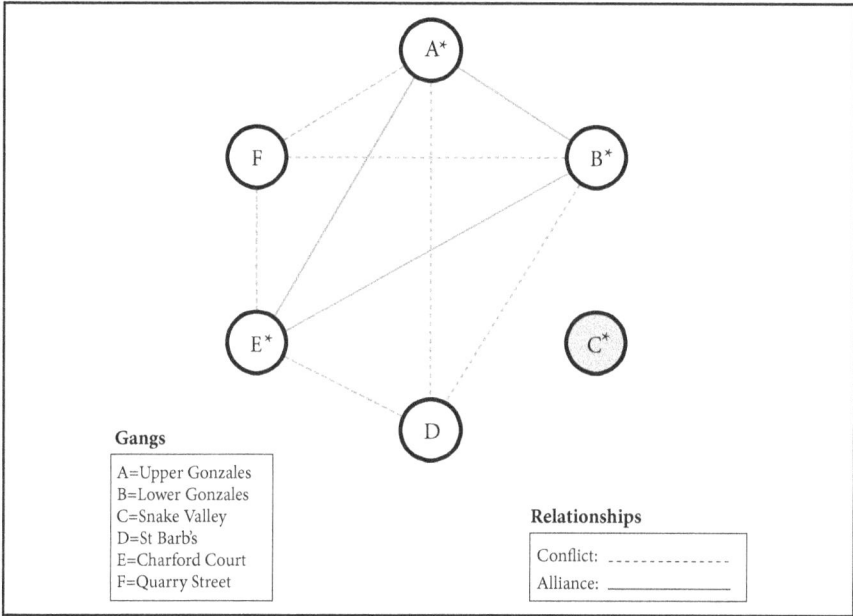

Figure 9.3. Conflicts and alliances between six gangs six months after truce

Note: * = Truce participants.

Gonzales from 2000 to 2010.[14] We selected three incident types most characteristic of the types of violent incidents that gangs participated in: murder, wounding with intent to do grievous bodily harm and shooting with intent to do grievous bodily harm. These data represent our best effort to characterize crime trends in Gonzales over time, although we acknowledge the limitations of these data (as described earlier). Figure 9.4 provides a graphic depiction of crime in Gonzales from 2000 to 2010. Within this tiny community, ten people were murdered, shot, and wounded in 2006, and only one in 2007. These data suggest that *something* happened in Gonzales to reduce violent crime. The intervention described in this chapter is a likely candidate for explaining the reductions in violent crime in Gonzales, but we cannot definitively rule out competing explanations. Interestingly, violent crime began to escalate again starting in 2008.

Discussion and Conclusion

Father Jason delivered a well-publicized sermon in September 2007 that was highly critical of the Trinidad and Tobago Police Service. Father Jason's

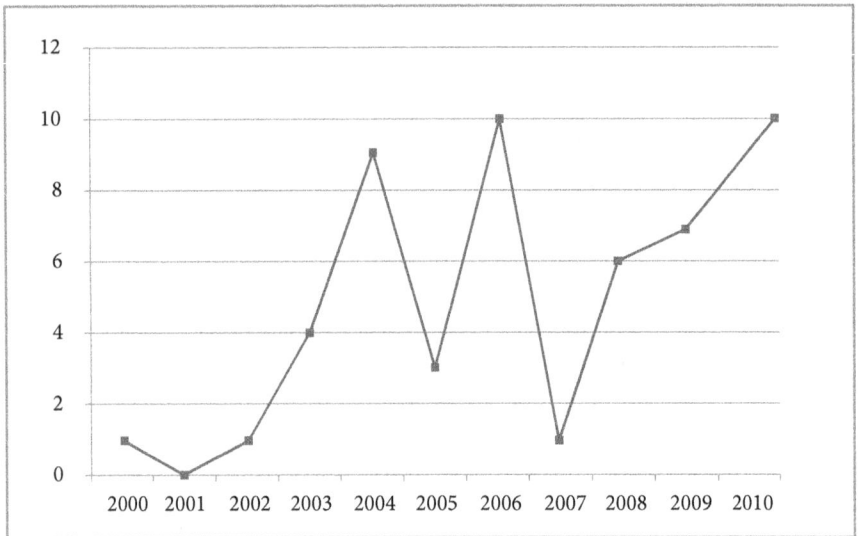

Figure 9.4. Violent incidents per year in Gonzales, 2000–2010

Note: Includes three offence types: murder, wounding with intent to do grievous bodily harm, and shooting with intent to do grievous bodily harm.

comments, which noted that a recently deceased gang leader did a lot more to control crime in his community than the police, were not well received by the police. Father Jason's sermon, coupled with the strong reactions to it from some of the nation's government officials, illustrates the tension faced by faith leaders when involved in interventions meant to reduce gang violence. On the one hand, they are advocates for the community and must be viewed in this role in order to maintain their legitimacy with the community. For instance, when they see police behaving in ways that are not ethical, legal or sufficiently protective, they must stand up for their communities. At the same time, they must be advocates for peace, which will necessarily sometimes place them against those gang members who choose to victimize others. In that role, faith leaders are likely to be on the side of the police. Walking this fragile line is very difficult. Berrien and Winship (2009) argue that the capacity of participants in Boston's TenPoint Coalition to walk this line was part of their success: They were advocates for the community, but they also cooperated with police, sharing information when necessary to keep the peace. Father Gregory Boyle also found it difficult to walk this line. Professor Maguire was visiting a police department in the Los Angeles area recently and decided to pay a visit to Homeboy Industries.

(Father Boyle was away at the time.) A police officer that Maguire was interviewing had previously served as a member of the LAPD's gang unit. He told Maguire that he had had an encounter with Father Boyle and his homies one night that left a bad taste in his mouth because it seemed like Father Boyle was on the side of the gangs rather than the police. When Father Jason's editorial was published, police officials told Professor Maguire that any hope of a partnership between the police and Father Jason was no longer possible.

Professor Maguire and Father Jason also collaborated in an effort to form a working group involving people at the community level who were already working with gangs or who were interested in doing so. The Ministry of Social Development had three outreach workers who were already working with gangs. Father Jason invited several members of the faith community, including a Muslim (the mufti) and a Catholic priest from St Barb's. The group met several times. Professor Maguire brought reading assignments that discussed the potential unintended consequences of community-based interventions with gangs. In particular, he was concerned about the possibility that community-based interventions would increase gang cohesion and further cement the gang as a social grouping. This working group fizzled out. It seemed like everybody had their own theories on how to perform this kind of work, and coming together was simply not in the cards. Creating sustainable working relationships between police, the faith community, the gang outreach community, and other entities is painstakingly difficult work. Even once these fledgling relationships are formed, they are difficult to sustain.

There is a large potential for community interventions to have unintended consequences in these kinds of projects. The most common unintended consequence is increasing the level of gang cohesion by validating the gang's sense of itself as a legitimate social unit. Malcolm Klein, a prolific gang researcher in the United States, has been writing for many years about the tendency for well-meaning people to increase gang cohesion inadvertently. Consider Klein's comments on Father Gregory Boyle in East Los Angeles:

> Greg Boyle is the most emotionally dedicated gang intervener I've come across in many years. He is streetwise, empathic, energetic, and unflappable in the face of abject failure. He mothers and fathers his gang members. He is the ultimate street worker, a one-man agency with his own schooling and jobs programme for "his" gangs. His one-to-one relationship with individual gang members is genuine, warm, and supportive. Greg Boyle epitomizes the very best in individual,

caring gang intervention. He also epitomizes the kind of ill-conceptualized reinforcement of gang life and cohesiveness that I have found to exist in almost every
traditional gang city . . . I have trouble seeing the translation of his heavy and
loving involvement into the reduction of gang violence. There are so many ways
to feed gang cohesiveness and so few to reduce it. (Klein 1995, 158)

Approximately fifteen years after the publication of Malcolm Klein's critique, Father Boyle published a book about his work (Boyle 2010) in which he
notes that he began to stay away from direct intervention with gangs to reduce
violence:

I promoted any number of truces, cease-fires, and peace treaties. I spent a great
deal of time in a kind of shuttle diplomacy, riding my bike between neighbourhoods . . . securing signed agreements from the warring factions. Some were
Pyrrhic victories such as an agreement not to shoot into houses. I learned early
on that all sides would speak so positively about the peace process when first
approached . . . but once you brought them together, they couldn't resist posturing
in high gear in front of one another. I eventually ceased having these meetings, and
like the Soviet Union and the USA, I worked out all the details of the peace before-
hand and just had the principals sign the agreements. That was then; this is now.
Though I don't regret having orchestrated these truces and treaties, I'd never do it
again. The unintended consequence of it all was that it legitimized the gangs and fed
them oxygen. I eventually came to see that this kind of work keeps gangs alive. (p. 5)

By the summer of 2010 when Maguire's work in Trinidad ended, only two of
the six gang leaders in place in early 2006 were still alive; the leaders of four of
the gangs had been murdered, and in one case, the replacement to a murdered
leader was also murdered.[15] In another one of the gangs, after the leader was
murdered, several family members of his replacement were also murdered. In
the two gangs whose leaders were still alive four years later, only one was still
running a gang, although at a significantly reduced capacity. Informants told
us he lived like a prisoner in a fortress and largely avoided outside contact. The
other one was on the run from the police. Such is the nature of life and death in
street gangs.

Direct intervention with street gangs is messy business. As Malcolm Klein
and Father Boyle note, it is easy for well-meaning people to do more harm than
good. For anyone thinking of engaging in direct intervention approaches, it is
vital to keep in mind the perils of gang cohesion. To be fair, the major complaint
of the working group that Father Jason and Professor Maguire attempted to
mobilize was that Klein tells us what we *should not* do, but he does not tell us

what we *should* do. The collective wisdom among gang researchers seems to be that when intervening directly in the lives of gang members, it is best to treat them as individuals and not as members of a gang. This means avoiding any activity that expressly or inadvertently treats the gang as a legitimate social unit. To paraphrase Father Boyle, acknowledging the legitimacy of a gang as a social unit may inadvertently "feed it oxygen".

Avoiding unintended consequences requires those who engage in direct intervention to have a deep knowledge of gangs and the communities where they thrive. Gang members often have a vastly different worldview than those who live outside of gangs. For instance, gang members in Trinidad will describe themselves as "old heads" by the time they reach thirty because so many of their peers die young. In gang logic, it makes sense to shoot at a peacemaker, a contractor working in their community without authorization, or an unknown taxi driver. Father Boyle tells the humorous story of driving with a young gang member whose car was low on fuel. When Father Boyle pointed out that the needle on the fuel gauge was pointing toward "E", the young man told Father Boyle that he thought "E" stood for Enough and "F" stood for Finished. A gang outreach worker in Trinidad had to tell a gang member to hold a party for his daughter's birthday. Afterwards, the gang member proudly informed the outreach worker that he had held the party as instructed. When the outreach worker asked him how old his daughter was, the gang member responded that he was not aware that he should have asked his daughter how old she was.

Gang members often lack perspective, spending much of their time in an environment that has a radically different code of behaviour. Gangs are like fragile ecosystems, where it is easy for well-meaning people who don't understand the environment to make things worse inadvertently. However, the faith community represents a vital social resource for improving the quality of life and the sense of connectedness to something larger in communities beset with gang violence. Thus, we hope our cautions will be regarded as food for thought, and not as an excuse for inaction.

Notes

1. For the remainder of the chapter we will refer to ourselves as Professor Maguire and Father Jason, which is how people referred to us at the time.
2. When social scientists refer to a negative effect, they are referring to the direction of a statistical effect, not a value judgment. In this instance, the finding that religion exerts a negative effect suggests that *more* religion is associated with *less* crime.

3. These findings are based on 2010 survey data from the Latin American Public Opinion Project (LAPOP 2010). They are based on the survey responses of 10,644 participants from seven nations: Belize, the Dominican Republic, Guyana, Haiti, Jamaica, Suriname, and Trinidad and Tobago.
4. Of respondents who said that the effect of gangs on their neighbourhood was "none", 88.2 per cent rated religion as "very important" or "rather important" in their lives; the percentages were 88.2 per cent for those who said "little", 88 per cent for those who said "somewhat" and 88.6 per cent for those who said "a lot". The differences were not statistically significant (F=.062; p=0.98).
5. For more information, see http://www.homeboyindustries.org; also see Flores (2012, 5).
6. Many of the names and gang affiliations discussed in this chapter are (or were at the time) well known in Trinidad. Much of this information is already publicly available in newspaper articles and other sources. Father Jason has already released much of this information in sermons and Christmas greetings, some of which were widely distributed and are available online. Nonetheless, although much of this information is already public, we adopted the following decision rules around the use of names in this chapter. For those gang members who are known to be deceased, we refer to them by their "street names" (nicknames used widely by gang members). In those instances where deceased gang members did not have a street name, we use their first names. For those gang members who are still alive or whose current status was unknown as this chapter went to press, we use generic descriptions ("member of gang A") or pseudonyms. We do not use any surnames. Moreover, gangs in Trinidad are sometimes referred to using the name of their leader. In those instances where a gang took on the name of a leader who is not known to be deceased, we refer to the gang using the geographic area where it was based.
7. The "official" population of Gonzales from the Central Statistical Office (CSO) is 2,811, but the enumeration district boundaries used by the CSO ignore the community-defined boundaries about what areas constitute Gonzales. Using these community-defined boundaries increases the population estimate to approximately 5,650.
8. The word "indiscipline" means a lack of discipline. However, it is used very commonly in Trinidad and Tobago as a synonym for the word "delinquency". Thus, the phrase "indiscipline of youth" in Trinidad and Tobago is similar to the phrase "juvenile delinquency" which is common elsewhere.
9. As noted earlier, we use pseudonyms for gang members who are not deceased or whose current status is unknown. We use an asterisk to denote the first instance of each pseudonym.
10. In Trinidad and Tobago, the term "liming" refers to "the art of doing nothing". Put differently, it refers to "any leisure activity entailing the sharing of food and drink, the exchange of tall stories, jokes and anecdotes, etc., provided the activity has no explicit purpose beyond itself" (Eriksen 1990).
11. Stretch served as acting leader in St Barbs because at the time Bumbles and Pig were being held in prison on murder charges.

12. To "jumbie" someone is to agitate or annoy them deliberately.
13. The truce meeting that Father Jason references here is different than the one he arranged in January 2006. A much larger and more publicized gang truce meeting took place at the Crowne Plaza hotel on 3 September 2006. That meeting was attended by senior government officials and the media.
14. We are grateful to the CAPA Branch for compiling these data for us.
15. Snake Eye, leader of the gang in Lower Gonzales (and in parts of Belmont) was murdered in July 2010.

References

Baier, C.J., and B.R.E. Wright. 2001. "If You Love Me, Keep My Commandments: A Meta-Analysis of the Effect of Religion on Crime". *Journal of Research in Crime and Delinquency* 38(1): 3–21.

Berrien, J., and C. Winship. 1999. "Lessons Learned from Boston's Police Community Collaboration". *Federal Probation* 58(2): 25–32.

Boyle, G. 2010. *Tattoos on the Heart: The Power of Boundless Compassion*. New York: Free Press.

Braga, A.A., D. Hureau, and C. Winship. 2008. "Losing Faith? Police, Black Churches, and the Resurgence of Youth Violence in Boston". *Ohio State Journal of Criminal Law* 6(1): 141–72.

Braga, A.A., D.M. Kennedy, E.J. Waring, and A.M. Piehl. 2001. "Problem-Oriented Policing, Deterrence, and Youth Violence: An Evaluation of Boston's Operation Ceasefire". *Journal of Research in Crime and Delinquency* 38(3): 195–225.

Corbett, R.P. Jr. 2002. "Reinventing Probation and Reducing Youth Violence: Boston's Operation Night Light". In *What Is Community Justice? Case Studies of Restorative Justice and Community Supervision*, edited by D.R. Karp and T.R. Clear, 111–34. Thousand Oaks, CA: Sage.

Dilulio, J.J. 1998. *Living Faith: The Black Church Outreach Tradition*. Jeremiah Project Report No. 3. New York: Manhattan Institute.

Eriksen, T.H. 1990. "Liming in Trinidad: The Art of Doing Nothing". *Folk* 32: 23–43.

Evans, T. D., F.T. Cullen, R.G. Dunaway, and V.S. Burton Jr. 1995. "Religion and Crime Re-Examined: The Impact of Religion, Secular Controls, and Social Ecology on Adult Criminality". *Criminology* 33(2): 195–224.

Flores, E. 2012. "Latinos and Faith-Based Recovery from Gangs". In *Sustaining Faith Traditions: Race, Ethnicity and Religion among the Latino and Asian American Second Generation*, edited by C. Chen and R. Jeung, 113–32. New York: New York University Press.

Foley, M.W., J.D. McCarthy, and M. Chaves. 2001. "Social Capital, Religious Institutions, and Poor Communities". In *Social Capital in Poor Communities*, edited by S. Saegert, J.P. Thompson and M.R. Warren, 215–45. New York: Russell Sage Foundation.

Fremon, C. 2004. *G-Dog and the Homeboys: Father Greg Boyle and the Gangs of East Los Angeles*. Albuquerque: University of New Mexico Press.

Horton, A.L., and J.A. Williamson. 1988. *Abuse and Religion: When Praying Isn't Enough*. Lexington, MA: D.C. Heath and Company.

Johnson, B.R., and S.J. Jang. 2012. "Crime and Religion: Assessing the Impact of the Faith Factor". In *Contemporary Issues in Criminological Theory and Research: The Role of Social Institutions (Papers from the American Society of Criminology 2010 Conference)*, edited by R. Rosenfeld, K. Quinet, and C. Garcia, 117–50. Belmont, CA: Wadsworth.

Klein, M.W. 1995. *The American Street Gang: Its Nature, Prevalence, and Control*. New York: Oxford University Press.

Klein, M.W., and C.L. Maxson. 2006. *Street Gang Patterns and Policies*. New York: Oxford University Press.

LAPOP. 2010. "Latin American Public Opinion Project". Public opinion survey data. Nashville: Vanderbilt University. http://www.vanderbilt.edu/lapop/.

McCullough, M.E., and B.L.B. Willoughby. 2009. "Religion, Self-Control, and Self-Regulation: Associations, Explanations, and Implications". *Psychological Bulletin* 135(1): 69–93.

McGarrell, E.F., G. Brinker, and D. Etindi. 1999. *The Role of Faith-Based Organizations in Crime Prevention and Justice*. Washington, DC: Hudson Institute.

Mock, F.L. 2012. *G-Dog* (documentary film). http://gdogthemovie.com.

O'Keefe, M. 1997. "Adolescents' Exposure to Community and School Violence: Prevalence and Behavioral Correlates". *Journal of Adolescent Health* 20: 368–76.

Peters, K. 2010. "Faith-Based Programmes as a Means to Combat the Revolving-Door Syndrome in Trinidad and Tobago". *Caribbean Journal of Criminology and Public Safety* 15(1, 2): 399–409.

Prothrow-Stith, D., and H. Spivak. 1996. "Turning the Tide on Violence (Op-Ed)". *Boston Globe*, 24 November, D7.

Rotunda, R.J., G. Williamson, and M. Penfold. 2004. "Clergy Response to Domestic Violence: A Preliminary Survey of Clergy Members, Victims, and Batterers". *Pastoral Psychology* 52(4): 353–65.

Song, L.Y., M.I. Singer, and T.M. Anglin. 1998. "Violence Exposure and Emotional Trauma as Contributors to Adolescents' Violent Behaviors". *Archives of Pediatric Adolescent Medicine* 152(8): 531–36.

Wolff, D.A., D. Burleigh, M. Tripp, and A. Gadomski. 2001. "Training Clergy: The Role of the Faith Community in Domestic Violence Prevention". *Journal of Religion and Abuse* 2(4): 47–62.

10 | Moving Forward
Responding to Gangs and Organized Crime in the Caribbean

ANTHONY HARRIOTT

The contributions in this book focus on responses to the gang and organized crime problem in selected countries of the Caribbean. As others before us have noted, designating something as a "problem" is suggestive of its complexity and of the difficulty in finding appropriate solutions to it.[1] If solutions are suggested and perhaps even tried, contending alternatives remain. Considerable intellectual effort is therefore required to better understand this problem set and to generate evidence-based solutions. In this volume, we find that the gang problem is just that – a problem that requires focused attention from a large number of persons.

We have advanced the level of understanding of the problem by probing the dynamics of gang violence, its spatial features, the structural features of society and the local community conditions that facilitate gang formation, the risk factors that are associated with joining gangs, and the sources of gang persistence and resilience. Further, we have done so by viewing the problem in terms of both its "root" and proximate causes, but with emphasis on the latter, as these are more amenable to measures that may alleviate the problem in the short term.

In the introduction, some of the issues noted above were discussed. In this concluding note, we comment on some of the cross-cutting themes and selected issues, some of which are not particularly dedicated to understanding gangs but which are illuminated by the study of gangs and organized crime. These are the gang-related issues that help to advance our understanding of state and society and indeed to explain the responses (or lack thereof) of the political administration and state institutions. As a concluding note is not the place to further extend the analyses of these or any other issues, we simply highlight the issues for further attention and focus for academics and policymakers. There are four such issues.

First, the severity of the gang and organized crime problem in the Caribbean warrants concern with short-term results, that is, with bringing this problem under control and providing the population immediate relief from violence and with checking the power and corrosive influence of criminal groupings and their leaders. Short-term measures involve suppression. Reliance on suppression enhances the policy influence of the experts on the use of force and the institutions that administer suppression, that is, the security forces and their intelligence organizations. This reality, however, should not mean a reliance on excessive and lawless suppression. Referring to larger socio-political processes, Errol Miller in his Grace Kennedy Lecture of 2001 warns of the danger of repeating the errors of the past – and thereby exacerbating the problems of the present. With regard to the use of force by the Jamaican state he describes the following pattern: "Amelioration and change is implemented in the medium term. While massive and brutal repression is the short-term response, the medium-term response, usually after commissions of inquiry, is amelioration of the conditions of the marginal majority" (Miller 2001, 47). Coercion, and especially the use of state violence, must have justifiable cause, be right-regarding, and thus lawful, measured and accountable.

Suppression need not be limited to the use of violent methods. There are other elements of suppression and control. At the time of writing, in Jamaica, for example, some J$26 billion in criminally acquired assets were identified (by the responsible state agency) for seizure.[2] We do not have comparable data for the Dominican Republic and Trinidad and Tobago, but we expect that these countries experience problems on a similar scale. It is reasonable to assume that the sum that is stated above represents a fraction of such funds and wealth that is held within Jamaica. It may also be assumed that these assets were not acquired by individual acts of criminality; they represent group effort and network capabilities. These funds exemplify criminal influence, power and impunity, and the state's incapacity and ineffectiveness. The magnitude of this problem renders it unresponsive to short-term solutions.

Academics ought to better contribute to this level of "solution", and they should be permitted to do so without having to explain at every turn why more is not being written about "root" causes. These different levels of solution should not be set in opposition to each other. Root cause analyses are usually accompanied by calls for programmes of social prevention. The problems, however, also have to be managed and controlled. This is especially true for countries with very high rates of violent crimes. Thus, a shared concern among most of the authors in this volume is to shift the analysis closer to the problem in order to better contribute to measures that may have short-term impact. Our discussion attempts to move beyond the traditional approach that highlights deep structural factors and calls for attention to "root" causes and instead, focus on alternative policy responses. In making this shift, we have tried to spur advances in understanding the proximate sources of the problem and to generate information and analyses that are supportive of gang- and crime-control strategies and prevention programmes. The concern with law-enforcement approaches and capacities, with truce and peace making and with targeted community-level interventions as projects and programmes, is a concern with short-term effects and a respite from the high levels of violence. Policy, strategy and gang prevention, control and intervention practices have advanced and now have more available evidence that may inform their development.

Approaches that are intended to yield short-term results at their best do just that; they yield short-term results. In order to sustain these results, it is usually necessary to link these efforts with long-term programming. Such programmes cannot be effective if they simply continue short-term projects over a long duration. (The designation "long-term" is a matter of programme design, not simply duration). The extension of short-term projects as long-term programmes is a formula for marking time.

The deep structural problems will not disappear and thus should not be made to disappear from the narratives about violence and crime in the region. These "root" problems include the growth of informal urban settlements, inequality of opportunity and, in conditions of protracted economic stagnation, an outright lack of opportunities or even blocked opportunities via poor-quality education, high rates of youth unemployment, underemployment and other forms of exclusion. The community-level adaptations to exclusion have become more complex as is evidenced by what is described in chapter 2 by Lilian Bobea as transgressive ecosystems and what is known in Jamaica as garrison communities. Poor governance and party-serving rather than country-serving politics compound these problems. If, for example, local politics is territorial monopoly seeking, it is also likely to protect territorial gangs that serve narrow party electoral interests. Root cause responses involve increasing capabilities, opportunities and thus choices for all, but particularly for the marginalized. This ought to be an ongoing aspect of the general developmental process. This approach is, however, quite different from deliberate and more immediate gang-reduction and -prevention policy and programmes for gang reduction and prevention.

An agenda for further research on gangs and related issues should include continued systematic investigation of the proximate causes of gang formation and gang-related violence. More generally, it should also include efforts to better understand the factors and processes that are linked to short-term changes in the rates of gang-related crimes.

Second, it is understood that solutions to social problems tend to be most coherent and cogently argued when they are theoretically informed. As noted by Mears (2010), effective policies and practices, however, require both applicable theory and context-specific knowledge. This balance is not often achieved. Theories carry generalizations, but policy and programmes demand context-specific thinking. Solutions to social problems are crafted for specific problems and places. They are implemented in specific contexts where there are known opportunities and constraints. Advances in the knowledge of Caribbean peculiarities are vital steps toward more effective policies and programmes for gang prevention and control. However, this discussion is not an attempt to revisit the old debate regarding the development of a Caribbean criminology. Readers who are interested in this issue may access the literature on this matter (Pryce 1976; Bennett and Lynch 1996; Birkbeck 1999). This debate aside, a general and perfectly valid concern among Caribbean scholars is to develop a better understanding of the region. The rather modest aim has been to develop a body of knowledge about ourselves, and on this basis, to better craft solutions to the region's problems.[3] Through this effort, we may also contribute to the development of various disciplines and fields of study.

This volume has modestly contributed to this project, though more effort in this regard is needed in order to better discern and estimate these peculiarities (for example, the risk factors that are associated with gang joining). These advances in basic research are critical for informing policy. The real contribution of the essays in this volume, however, is in the approaches that are taken to the problem and in encouraging critical reflection on what is being done.

Given what is now known from the basic research on gangs in the region, there should be an abundance of caution in uncritically transferring anti-gang programmes from elsewhere to the region. The example of (Chicago) Ceasefire is cited in the introduction to this book. The better programmes are iterative but (as noted in the introduction) the evaluations of Ceasefire in its country of origin have returned what at best may be regarded as mixed results (Boyle et al. 2010; Fox et al. 2012). Indeed as a general observation, this point is true for gang prevention and control programmes (Esbensen 2013). Ceasefire and other programmes that claim portability (even in their most recent iteration) may be bedevilled by conceptual problems as well as implementation issues.[4] Regardless of the nature of the issues, recipients of such programmes should be alert to their likely sensitivity to context. Alertness to context sensitivity will increase as the body of knowledge about the countries of the region is increased. Regional knowledge permits better judgement of the portability of programmes that are developed here and elsewhere. The argument then is that much more basic work needs to be done to build evidence-based programmes for the countries of the region. As these advances in knowledge are made, this would allow for greater innovation as well as better-informed borrowing and adaptation of best practices from elsewhere.

In advancing this research agenda, Charles Katz has initiated the study of risk and resilience factors for gang joining in the region. More work needs to be done to isolate these risk factors and excavate the pathways to gang joining and to test the findings in different national settings within the region. This kind of comparative work is a good way to better understand the criminogenic processes in the region. Caribbean street gangs and organized crime tend to be territorial. Community- and neighbourhood-level of gang formation and gang joining would advance our understanding of the community contexts and their effects on gang activity. Lilian Bobea's chapter should stimulate some further work in this direction, including multi-country comparative studies. Similarly, gang adaptations to police strategies and tactics, and community-level gang-prevention interventions – and how these are influenced by the various types of relationships between gangs and community – are useful lines of research.

The third issue is the relationship between state and gangs and organized crime groups. Students of the crime problem are typically interested in what this relationship means for the character of criminality and crime. The objects of study are some form of crime. For example, in chapter 1, an attempt is made to highlight the political inducements or the opportunities and capabilities that are associated with the rise of organized crime. This is standard criminological inquiry. It is, however, not just crime that is affected or even transformed by the relationship between gangs and political actors. The state (and political parties) may also be changed by this relationship, or the changes in that relationship may be the outcome of deep changes in the political realm including changes in the character of the political parties (becoming self-interested organizations). What these processes mean for the character of the state is thus of considerable consequence for people's quality of life. Concern with this latter set of issues may take the direction of inquiry into specific institutions of the state as enablers of crime and how degenerative changes in this regard affect the functioning of the state and its relationship to the citizenry.

The process that is associated with the gang-state relationship and gang-organized crime influences in the state is characterized as statetropism (Bobea, see chapter 2), a hybrid state (Jaffe 2012), and a parasitic state (Gray 2001). All of these characterizations suggest a problem of weak Caribbean states that adapt in somewhat similar ways to the gang and organized crime phenomena. Gangs are co-opted as political actors and are able to negotiate access to state resources. Party representatives and political administrators collude with state bureaucrats and criminal organizations to raid the resources of the state via the award of contracts to the latter for the supply of goods and services. This pattern is very evident in the case of the Shower–Presidential Click, which is discussed in chapter 7, and there are other similar relationships that may be found in Jamaica. Here, at the national level but not necessarily in every locality, the co-opting party is the main power holder, and the disciplinary power of the albeit weak state may be used to maintain the power balance locally. In some localities, power shifts may favour criminal groups and alliances that develop their own systems of control. In the case of the Dominican Republic, Bobea suggests that at the local level, "alternative social orders" have been created. In these settings, the study of gangs and organized crime may become the study of alternative social orders. Comparative work within the region ought to further deepen and enrich the debate.

Despite the state degenerative processes that led to and are deepened by the gang/organized crime-politics nexus, the state still has some capacity to be responsive to the security needs of its citizens. This responsiveness is expressed as an ability to even momentarily initiate and advance gang-control programmes that are not just symbolic rituals of state functioning, but truly meaningful efforts. This is true for the two countries in the English-speaking Caribbean where the state degenerative process is most advanced, that is, Jamaica and Trinidad and Tobago.[5] Some states' responsiveness is retained. These states are more or less responsive to the gang and organized crime problem depending on the power configurations in the political administrations and states, as well as within parties. Thus for example, with changes of political administrations new and meaningful gang and organized crime control and prevention measures

may be taken. These changes tend to occur in the early stages of a new administration as was the case of Trinidad and Tobago (2010–2011). A change of
political administration in the Bahamas in 1992 led to measures that improved
the responsiveness of the police service and a reversal of the trends in drug
trafficking and related violence. The degenerative processes, regardless of how
they are named, have not totally permeated the political system nor completely
incapacitated the state.

Even where the process is most advanced – Jamaica and the Dominican
Republic – there are still pressures for change from within the political system. While external pressures may hasten change, the process of change for
greater responsiveness is not completely dependent on external shocks and
pressures.[6] Where the gang problem is chronic, and the gang-party nexus is
strong, events that reveal the character of the problem and shock the political
system may mobilize the populations for effective gang and crime control. In
these conditions, civic pressures for good governance and the power shifts and
structural changes that they help to bring about contribute to improved state
responsiveness.[7]

Caribbean states have also exhibited some degree of policy responsiveness.
Much of the recent anti-gang legislation that has been passed – St Kitts and
Nevis, Trinidad and Tobago, and that which is still in the drafting process in
Jamaica – is in the main legal symbolism.[8] As some of the provisions are needed,
these laws may placate publics that want "something to be done". They however mask ineffectiveness and state weakness more generally, and they increase
police powers without the police and state having the capability to enforce the
laws in procedurally just ways. Without correspondingly strong systems of
police accountability that give expression to a countervailing civic power, these
legal instruments are likely to lead to abuses of power and few gang-reduction
results. Nevertheless, Caribbean states have demonstrated policy responsiveness
as evidenced by the shifts in crime-control policies to include greater emphasis
on social crime prevention including gang prevention – although these efforts
are still very limited and underresourced. The state degenerative processes have
not led to policy stasis. Statetropism is a characterization that entails statements
about state unresponsiveness to the crimes of the powerful and to policy inflex-
ibility. Greater specification of this process is required, as well as further work
to advance the theoretical understanding to the state in the region. A related
issue is how to arrest the state degenerative processes and to advance a governance agenda for the countries in the region that will make these states and the
policy process more responsive. (In general terms, this is understood to mean

the design of stronger systems of accountability and greater transparency of the institutions of the criminal justice systems and their existing oversight bodies that are appointed by governments).

The relationship between gangs, organized crime on one hand and the state and political parties on the other, may be better understood by an approach that probes the state and systems of governance and the circuits of power and influence in law enforcement and crime control more closely. More deliberate studies of the policy processes in the field of crime control and security are needed. These studies may yield further insights into how political protection for gang immunity from law enforcement works and the correctives that are related to this problem, such as gang and crime prevention as well as structural arrangements for improved state responsiveness and accountability.

There is always a demand for research in support of evidence-based policies. Generating such research, however, does not automatically result in sound policies. Good policies and programmes will not occur simply because of their rational appeal. People must be mobilized in support of them and civic participation in the policy-making process must be encouraged. In some countries of the region, civic groups have already been invited by governments to participate in consultative process with regard to the drafting of gang-control laws. People are already actively involved in community structures that engage in crime prevention. These developments are positive although not without risks such as politicization, and in some places racialization, of the problems.

The fourth, and related, issue is the evolution of the response-set of the state. The old impulses remain, but there have been advances and attempts to break with the old pattern of neglect followed by an overreliance on suppression. As a result, some countries now have more comprehensive policies and programmes (relative to their recent past). This is most evident in Jamaica and to a lesser extent in Trinidad and Tobago. It is, however, not a well-planned theoretically informed comprehensiveness. Instead, the state agencies initially threw all the available policing and suppression tools at the problem in the hope that something would work; then as the problems deepened further (as gang-related and other types of violence) there was an effort to throw everything, including localized social prevention measures, at the problem. More lately, there have been attempts to systematize these efforts. There is an intellectual challenge here. The systematization of comprehensive and integrated approaches to the gang and organized crime problems requires a deeper understanding of the criminogenic processes and some innovative application of these understandings to the particular national and local settings.

Evaluation studies and even simply lesson-drawing from the existing efforts and particularly the most promising practices within the region would be very useful. If from these efforts the programme design issues are perfected, there would still be difficulties associated with institutional responsiveness. The agility of the institutions and their sensitivity to the environment are critical elements of success.

State institutions are central to solutions, which is a recurring topic in this book. Some chapters highlight the limited response capacity of Caribbean law enforcement and social crime-prevention agencies. They problematize the capability to make evidence-based gang and violence prevention and control policies and programmes (in contrast with influence-based politically driven policies and programmes) and the institutional capacity to effectively implement such policies. They explore the directions of change that are required within law enforcement and the security establishments and the importance of partnerships with non-state actors as compensating for some of the limitations of the state. The roles of civic actors in getting these outcomes and in enabling alternative options ought to be further probed. Mobilizations that shift power open opportunities that may make the political environments more difficult for gangs and organized crime. Jamaica's crisis of 2010 is a case in point. Where such shifts cannot be achieved nationally, they may be done locally.

Thus, despite the weaknesses in the state systems, there have been recent advances in developing greater state capabilities in law enforcement and crime prevention, some of which are documented here. These have been occasioned by crisis moments that disrupt the routines and practised ways of thinking about solutions to the problems.

The experiences show the possibilities for success at the national level and, where the conditions may not favour a national turn, progress is still possible at the neighbourhood level. The scale of the problem in the region is manageable, especially when it is assessed in terms of its spatial concentrations. The vulnerabilities that are associated with smallness are well known. In small states with limited state capacity, a few gangs may have considerable national impact as has repeatedly occurred in the region (Guyana, St Kitts and Nevis, and Jamaica). If, however, smallness is the source of the vulnerabilities, then in relation to the problems of gang and crime control and prevention, smallness is not just a measure of the vulnerability of the state and society; it fixes the scale of the gang problem. Community-level intervention should not be overrated, because they can highly impact small countries with high crime concentrations. Smallness is generally viewed as a disadvantage. However, in the Caribbean, with respect to crime prevention and control, smallness has some advantages. For example, the number of high-crime, gang-dominated communities is low, and therefore, resources may be concentrated on these few with great national impact. Attention to community-level structures and community resilience would add much of value to the stocks of knowledge on gang prevention and control.

In this concluding chapter, we have made certain suggestions for further lines of research. Problem solving motivates research, but academic research outputs are not usually presented as user-ready programme ideas. This lessens their appeal to policymakers. The impact of research on problem solving is related to the proximity of research to programmes. This distance usually measures the relevance of academic research in the conditions of the region where the crime problem is acute. Knowing the risk factors for gang joining, for example, is a long way off from developing programmes that will reduce gang crimes. From this perspective, knowing the proximate causes of gang crimes is better, but is still inadequate. Evaluation research may solve some of these problems as they more directly and closely show how to develop more effective iterations of existing programmes.

Much more research is required. We may deepen our understanding of gangs in the region by means of dedicated studies of each gang type and examining their development processes and group dynamics comparatively within the Caribbean and across cultures. Our knowledge lacks studies of Caribbean-based transnational organized crime networks. This is difficult but necessary work. Related to this phenomenon is transnational law enforcement cooperation in responding to gangs and organized crime. Ben Bowling (2010) has already initiated this line of research. There is indeed much to be done, and much of it is best done collaboratively.

Notes

1. Erich Fromm (1978), in his *Psychoanalysis and Religion*, for example, makes this point.
2. This is according to a senior representative of the Financial Investigations Division, Government of Jamaica, at a July 2013 presentation at Runaway Bay.
3. The aim of self-knowledge has little or nothing to do with island insularities. It is more related to not having a self-authored set of histories.
4. For example, it is argued that the problem of project impact on gang cohesion has not really been solved. See Spergel (2010) for a discussion of this issue.
5. Guyana could arguably be included in this group.

6. The Jamaica experience of 2010 with the Coke extradition raises this issue.
7. Examples of this include the INDECOM in Jamaica that may force new ways of policing.
8. See the Gang Prohibition and Prevention Act (2011) of St Kitts and Nevis, the Anti-Gang Act (2011) of Trinidad and Tobago, and the Criminal Justice (Suppression of Criminal Organizations) Act Jamaica (draft 2013).

References

Bennett, R., and J. Lynch. 1996. "Toward a Caribbean Criminology". *Caribbean Journal of Criminology and Social Psychology* 1(1): 8–48.

Birkbeck, C. 1999. "By Your Theories You Shall Be Known: Some Reflections on Caribbean Criminology". *Caribbean Journal of Criminology and Social Psychology* 4(1–2): 1–31.

Bowling, B. 2010. *Policing the Caribbean: Transnational Security Cooperation in Practice.* Oxford: Oxford University Press.

Boyle, D.J., J.L. Lanterman, J.E. Pascarella, and C.C. Cheng. 2010. "The Impact of Newark's Operation Ceasefire on Trauma Center Gunshot Wound Admissions". *Justice Research and Policy* 12(2): 105–123.

Esbensen, F.A. 2013. "Civil Gang Injunctions". *Criminology and Public Policy* 12(1): 1–4.

Fox, A., C.M. Katz, D.E. Choate, and E.C. Hedberg. 2012. "Evaluation of the Phoenix TRUCE Project: A Replication of Chicago CeaseFire". Phoenix: Center for Violence Prevention and Community Safety, Arizona State University.

Fromm, E. 1978. *Psychology and Religion.* New Haven: Yale University Press.

Gray, O. 2001. "Rethinking Power: Political Subordination in Jamaica". In *New Caribbean Thought*, edited by B. Meeks and F. Lindahl, 210–31. Kingston: University of the West Indies Press.

Jaffe, R. 2012. "The Hybrid State: Crime and Citizenship in Urban Jamaica". Typescript.

Mears, D. 2010. *American Criminal Justice Policy: An Evaluation Approach to Increasing Accountability and Effectiveness.* New York: Cambridge University Press.

Miller, E. 2001. *Jamaica in the Twenty-First Century: Contending Choices.* Kingston: GraceKennedy Foundation.

Pryce, K. 1976. "Toward a Caribbean Criminology". *Caribbean Issues* 2(2): 3–21.

Spergel, I. 2010. "Community Gang Programs: Theory, Models, and Effectiveness". In *Youth Gangs and Community Intervention: Research, Practice and Evidence*, edited by R. Chaskin, 222–48. New York: Columbia University Press.

Contributors

Anthony Harriott is Professor of Political Sociology and Director of the Institute of Criminal Justice and Security, University of the West Indies, Mona, Jamaica. His many publications include *Police and Crime Control in Jamaica: Problems of Reforming Ex-Colonial Constabularies, Organized Crime and Politics in Jamaica: Breaking the Nexus,* and *Understanding Crime in Jamaica: New Challenges for Public Policy.*

Charles M. Katz is the Watts Family Director of the Center for Violence Prevention and Community Safety and Professor in the School of Criminology and Criminal Justice, Arizona State University, Phoenix. His many publications include *Policing Gangs in America* and *The Police in America.*

Lilian Bobea is Adjunct Assistant Professor of Sociology, Bentley University, Massachusetts. Her areas of specialization include security and defence issues, civil-military relations, violence and citizen security in Latin America and the Caribbean.

Christopher A.D. Charles is Senior Lecturer, Department of Government, University of the West Indies, Mona, Jamaica. His research interests are crime, gangs and violence, criminological psychology, the psychology of political behaviour, and black identity, skin bleaching, popular culture, and sexuality.

Andrew M. Fox is Assistant Professor, Department of Criminal Justice and Criminology, University of Missouri–Kansas City. His research interests include social network analysis, gangs, crime prevention, mental health and communities.

C. Jason Gordon is Bishop of Bridgetown (Barbados) and Kingstown (St Vincent and the Grenadines) in the Roman Catholic Church.

Edward R. Maguire is Professor of Justice, Law and Criminology, American University, Washington, DC. His many publications include *Criminal Justice Theory: Explaining the Nature and Behavior of Criminal Justice* and *Organizational Structure in American Police Agencies: Context, Complexity, and Control.*

Randy Seepersad is Criminologist, Department of Behavioural Sciences, University of the West Indies, St Augustine, Trinidad and Tobago. His research interests include economic deprivation and crime, gang violence, youth crime and justice, and penology.

Basil Wilson is Executive Director, Research Institute, King Graduate School at Monroe College, Bronx, New York. His research interests include urban violence, globalization, poverty in urban communities, and understanding homicide rates from a comparative perspective.